UNDERACHIEVERS IN
SECONDARY SCHOOL:
EDUCATION OFF THE MARK

UNDERACHIEVERS IN SECONDARY SCHOOL:

EDUCATION OFF THE MARK

ROBERT S. GRIFFIN

LEA LAWRENCE ERLBAUM ASSOCIATES, PUBLISHERS
1988 Hillsdale, New Jersey   Hove and London

Lawrence Erlbaum Associates, Inc., Publishers
365 Broadway
Hillsdale, New Jersey 07642

Library of Congress Cataloging-in-Publication Data

Griffin, Robert S.
  Underachievers in Secondary School

  Includes index.
  1. High school students—United States. 2. Underachievers. 3. Motivation in education. I. Title.
LC4691.G76 1988   371.9   87–27530
ISBN 0-8058-0181-2

Printed in the United States of America
10 9 8 7 6 5 4 3 2 1

To the "dormant geniuses" of the world

Contents

Preface

This is a book about the phenomenon of underachievement among secondary school students and what to do about it. At present, there are large numbers of adolescents with talent who are somewhat flat, disengaged, or distracted in school. Academically they drift along at a mediocre level, if that; far below, it seems, what they could be achieving if they put their minds to it. Likewise, there are significant numbers of well-intentioned young people who, despite good potential, just do not get off the mark in their classes. I grope for a label to use in referring to students of this sort. Underachievers seems as good as any.

Even if we are not sure how to refer to these kinds of students, every school professional I encounter considers this group as representative of a significant issue that we need to confront in our work. One principal I know calls them, with a sigh, ''my 30%.'' Dealing with these adolescents is especially a problem today when there is heightened emphasis on the schools' responsibility to foster increased levels of academic excellence. Although the schools are being charged with bringing about higher levels of academic achievement, educators indicate that what they have learned about teaching, learning, and setting up schools does not work well enough with this large category of students.

To be sure, these teenagers are both challenging and frustrating to teach. At the same time, they can be overlooked amid the press of the schools' other business. They do not get the attention and accolades we grant the academic ''stars.'' At the other end of the spectrum, they do not fit into the special education category that is the rallying point for a cadre of professionals and advocates, the basis for the provision of special services, and the subject of legal mandates—all with the central purpose of serving the needs of handicapped students. The students I have chosen to focus on in this book are not the high visibility discipline problems, vandalizers, hell-raisers, or troubled young people who demand our energy. And since they probably are going to stay where they are, they do not get the same attention we reserve for dropouts and potential dropouts. No, rather than being an immediate, urgent issue, these students are more a source of a gnawing sense of "dis-ease" among educators.

What can we do about this group of students with potential who slide along, perhaps getting Cs, maybe pulling in an occasional B or even an A? They are not excited about much (or so it seems). They are not very resistant either (or are they?). What can we do for the students with ability who plug away but still do not experience academic success? Who are these students? What are they like? What accounts for their being as they are? What can we do to help them become more focused and committed and successful in school? These are admittedly very difficult questions to answer, but nevertheless, I offer some ideas and suggestions that I consider promising. I hope what I write gives us some direction in more effectively supporting this particular group of teenagers—and perhaps others as well—to become happier and more productive in school.

This book is the result of many years of life and work. I owe so much to so many who will go unacknowledged here. I can list, however, some people whose contribution has been especially valuable in recent years. Of special mention are Anastas Harris, Joel Kirsch, Russell Ellis, Judy Carr, Russell Agne, Charles Tesconi, Linda Nielson, Herbert Walberg, Marjorie Lipson, Charles Letteri, John and Helene Krause, and Robert Nash. Stephanie Gross provided generous secretarial support and personal encouragement. Sandra McLaughlin, Barbara Matthews, Marjorie Cavanaugh, and Joan Carrassi contributed superb typing assistance. Also, I extend my appreciation to the University of Vermont—Martha Fitzgerald, Charles Rathbone, and Joseph Abruscato in particular—for providing financial support to this project. All the people at Lawrence Erlbaum Associates, Lori Baronian and Judith Suben among them, were fine to work with. Especially I value editor Karen Kinney's perceptive and sensitive contributions to the manuscript in progress. And finally, though I have chosen not to acknowledge individuals from the more distant past who mattered, I do want to make three exceptions. Three people who are no longer alive continue to live inside of me and through me: my mother and father, Helen and Walter Griffin, and my sister Marilyn.

Acknowledgments

Excerpts from "3:16 and One Half . . . " by Charles Bukowski, 1972, from *Unmuzzled Ox*, which appeared in Field, Edward, *A Geography of Poets* (pp. 116), New York: Bantam Books, 1981, reprinted by permission of copyright owner.

Excerpts from "A Soft Answer" by Terry Dobson, which appeared in slightly different form in *Reader's Digest* (Vol. 119, pp. 187–188), 1981, reprinted by permission of the author.

Material drawn from "Knowing, Teaching, and Supervising," by Madeline Hunter, 1984, *Using What We Know About Teaching* (pp. 174–176), P. Hasford (Ed.), Alexandria, VA: Association for Supervision and Curriculum Development. Used with permission of ASCD and the author.

Material drawn from *In Pursuit of Excellence* (pp. 21, 118–120) by Terry Orlick, 1980, Champaign, IL: Human Kinetics Publishers. Used with permission of publisher.

Material drawn from *The Unfolding Self* (p. 26) by Molly Brown, 1983, Los Angeles: Psychosynthesis Press. Used with permission of the author.

1 Introduction

If I were to mark a beginning for the creation of this book, I would place it at the time, some years ago now, when I learned of the work of Samuel Woodard. At a conference in the late 1970s as I remember, a colleague approached me and said, "I understand you are working with teenage kids who are having big trouble in school. Have you heard what somebody named Woodard is doing?"

As a matter of fact, the teenagers I was working with were having more than just trouble in *school*. I was teaching in a secondary school set up for adolescents locked up in a juvenile correctional facility—a jail, if you will.

My friend said he did not know too much about it, but he had heard that Woodard was getting results with kids who had not been doing well in school, or had good insight into the issue of difficult students; or something like that. "Anyway," he said, "I'll mail you some stuff if I can find it around the office."

A week or so later some material arrived in the mail. Included was a newspaper story or editorial (no indication of what newspaper or the date) and an article from an issue of *Woman's Day* magazine.[1]

I found the material fascinating. Instead of doing what we usually do in education, try to figure out why children do not succeed, Woodard, a professor at Howard University in Washington, DC, turned the coin over. He was studying children who *were* achieving academically despite what would seem to be overwhelming adversity. Woodard was seeking to understand why children manage to excel in school despite shattered homes, bad schools, tough neighborhoods, and—these were black children — racial prejudice. He had spent a year studying junior high school students who did not succumb to deprivation, poverty, or difficult home situations. The students in his study did well in school in spite of it all. Woodard used four criteria to determine whom he would investigate: at least one parent missing; income at the poverty level; housing below standard;

and, despite the other factors, solid achievement in school. What were the qualities in these children, or in their upbringing, that made them want to work hard and do their best? What accounted for the academic results they were getting? Woodard hoped that answers to these questions might help raise academic achievement for all students.

What did he learn? At that time he was still writing his report, but I found his preliminary conclusions extremely provocative. For one thing, he noted that children who do well academically under adverse conditions tended to score well above the median on self-acceptance and self-respect measures. Woodard concluded that a child who thinks little of herself or himself is likely to turn the frustration, anger, and sadness he feels into vengeful behavior, or just give up. In either case these children waste the opportunity to use these feelings to propel them toward actions that could have brought satisfaction and achievement. In addition, despite their deprivation these students saw their families as worthwhile and valuable. Though it would have been understandable if they had blamed or put down their family, they did not do so. Instead they understood that poverty and the other difficulties they had to live with were but a circumstance and not an indication of their family's inherent inadequacy.

Nor did these students see their difficult personal situation as a determinant of what they could become. Though these successful students were as victimized by poverty and racism as their neighbors, they did not dwell on their victimization. Instead, they believed that they—not their situations—were in charge of their lives. These students had the attitude that whatever good or bad happened to them depended on their own behavior. They did not wait for fate or miracles to improve their lot in life.

Woodard found that from their earliest years these children had been expected to meet high standards and had been rewarded for doing so within their families. To illustrate this point Woodard pointed to his own experience, crediting his successes in school and later to the heavy demands that his sister, who cared for him after his mother died, put on him: "She would not allow us to accept mediocrity. I had only one shirt, but she wanted it kept clean. When it was my turn to scrub the floor, she'd make me do it right. She'd tell me that instead of complaining about racism I should just do the best possible job."[2] It is Woodard's view that, as in his own situation, high expectations and rewards for meeting them lead these achieving students to set high standards for themselves. The last factor Woodard cited as characteristic of these successful students was described in a one sentence paragraph in the newspaper article: "And they were loved."

Particularly heartening to me in reading about Woodard's study was that it was so positive and held out so much hope. Kids from difficult situations can indeed be successful in school. More, their success can be understood. And with this understanding, I concluded, there is the possibility of teaching what it takes to achieve academically to students who do not possess these qualities. It was especially important for me to come to this conclusion because so much of what I was reading in those days was in the form of large-scale, statistics-based, social-science analyses that were leaving me with the feeling that the problems in schools were bigger than anything school people—like me—could take on.[3] The conclusion I drew from these studies was that schools and teachers were not what made the difference in the academic attainments of children. What did matter were the social and economic circumstances in which the children lived. Very impressive statistical data were marshaled to demonstrate that children from disadvantaged social situations do not do as well in school as others, regardless of the quality of the school, the nature of the teaching—any of the school-related factors.

At the level of generalization I suppose this is so. If you compare a group of disadvantaged children and advantaged children, on the average, as a group, you can predict the poor kids will not succeed as well in school. But the point is that this is a generalization. If you break from looking at the entire group and look instead at specific individuals within the disadvantaged group, it becomes obvious that despite what is generally the case, some disadvantaged children *do* succeed.

What was happening in the 1960s and 1970s, however, was that generalization was becoming all-inclusive fact: These kids are not going to make it and it does not matter what schools do, period. Hear me, I am not saying these studies said that exactly. What I am saying is that is the message that those who read these studies tended to receive. Well, actually most people did not read the studies themselves, which tended to be somewhat less than a James Michener novel in style and interest level. It was more likely that they heard about them from journalists, or from somebody who had been told about them by someone else who had read a summary of them, if you get the point. Anyway, based on these kinds of analyses, in those years it seemed that only vast social engineering, a political and economic overhaul if you will, would make a dent in the problem. Busing children to achieve a particular social and racial mix in schools is an example of a strategy that came out of this perspective. Another example, Christopher Jencks, one of the major investigators and theorists during that time, called for socialistic political and economic changes as a way to get at the social context factors that were seen as truly at the heart of success and failure in America. For certain, it was a bigger issue than schooling per se.[4]

That was all well and good, accurate and advisable and all that, as far as I knew. But at the same time it left me not knowing what I could do. I cared about the students who came out of difficult situations and those who were not making it in school. But it was being painted as such an overwhelming, multifaceted issue that I did not know where to begin. I was an educator and not an activist, social worker, or psychologist. I knew something about teaching and curriculum and schools. But knowing about those things did not seem to count for much because, as it went, school-centered reforms for whatever reason never seem to get put in place in ways that give them a chance to work; and even if they do get implemented, so what, because curriculum change is not where the action is in any case.

So there I would be. It would be a Tuesday, and while deep down I still had a faith in the power of teachers and schools to make a difference, I did not have a way forward that I could see that would make a dent in the problem.

Parenthetically, this focus on individual "success cases" a la Woodard became a cornerstone of what came to be called the "effective schools" movement in the late 1970s and early 1980s.[5] These researchers did not focus their investigations on a sample of all schools, good and bad, with the likely result that the successful and unsuccessful schools would balance each other out, leaving the impression that they all are inconsequential in the lives of students. Instead, they singled out individual schools that *did* work as measured by tests of academic achievement and other objective criteria and sought to understand just what it was about these schools that made them successful. As it turned out there *were* discernable characteristics that successful schools had in common. The challenge then became, as the effective schools advocates saw it, for other schools to approximate these characteristics as a way to become successful themselves.

Of course a key question to ask yourself as you review the effective schools research—or Woodard's or any other—is what is their definition of success? Success is a very subjective term, meaning different things to different people. You will only want to work toward creating schools of the sort they advocate if you agree with their concept of success. In the case of this book, consider carefully my definition of success. Whether or not you should take any action coming out of what you read here will depend greatly on whether you agree with my concept of what it means for a student to be successful in school.

Even though Woodard's study, like the others at that time, stresses factors outside the school—the family in this case—nevertheless his material was an "aha" experience for me. Of course! As, really, I had known all along, some kids *do* make it despite all the odds. America has always been that way. *People* have always been that way; some you just cannot keep down. A behavioral science generalization that "your kind" do not go anywhere does not mean *you* are not going anywhere. And yes, we can learn a great deal by studying successful students. Though it is important to find out why things do not work in students' lives, at the same time it is vitally important to discern what is happening when it *does* work. If we can see what successful students have going for them, perhaps we can teach less successful students the insights, attitudes, and skills that are instrumental to transcending the limitations they must overcome to achieve in school.

It hit me as I read the Woodard material that although I had studied education intensely I had read or heard little about what successful students do to be effective. In contrast, I had read and heard much detailed talk of what successful teachers did to bring about learning and growth in their students. Put another way, we knew—or thought we knew—about good teaching (whether or not, given the perspective of the time, it made any difference that we knew it). But we as educators did not have anywhere near the level of understanding of what comprises good, to coin a term, *studenting*. (Nor do we now for that matter.) What *does* characterize achieving students? It seems self-evident that it will go better in school if both parties, students as well as teachers, are good at what they do. Would not a better understanding of, call it, effective studenting make schools and the students themselves more powerful?

Reading Woodard prompted me to ask of myself: "What *are* achieving students like? What *do* they do?" I was struck by the realization that I did not really know. All I could do was call up, "Well, they work *very* hard," or "They are *highly* motivated," or "They put in a *whole lot of time* at their schoolwork," that kind of thing. But the simple fact was that I had given over virtually all of my time trying to figure out how to design a curriculum that made sense and teach well; and putting out any "fires," discipline problems, and so forth, that got in my way. The point came home to me that I needed to complement the attention I gave to instruction and curriculum and school organization by taking on a more systematic analysis of how achieving students get things done. With adolescents being my particular area of interest, I decided I wanted to know more about a special creature: the capable and motivated secondary school student.

And it was the student himself or herself that I wanted to focus upon. Clearly Woodard sees the family as the unit of concern in all of this. To Woodard, it is the way the child is treated in the family which fosters the qualities in the child that allow him or her to transcend the serious obstacles to school success that get in the way. From the material I read it seemed clear that Woodard is encouraging us to explore ways to produce the sort of families whose children turn out well. Although I saw that as a promising tack, my style and position as an educator prompted me to look more at the young people themselves to try to see better the difference, in this case, their family experience had on their capabilities as students. So my focus was not so much on where things, good and bad, came from—though I cared about that. Rather, it was on what these students were like, regardless of where it came from.

Is this point clear? It is important, because this orientation is a major operating premise of this book. I am not downplaying the value of efforts to improve the contexts in which students live, whether it is the home, the community, or the school itself. Absolutely, keep those efforts going; they are necessary, vital, activities. My argument is that in addition to these environment-altering activities, it would be helpful to work directly with the students themselves, to begin to assist them in the development of the qualities they need to have in order to achieve in school. My assumption is that the best chance for improving the level of school success for students who are not doing well comes from a combined, integrated effort involving both environment enrichment—better curriculum, teaching, school organization, and so forth—and what can be called "student effectiveness education.'' Beyond all of that, very practically and very personally, this perspective of working directly with students to improve their school-going skills has provided me, not a psychologist or a social worker, a way to proceed forward with an issue, the fate of these kinds of students, that I care deeply about.

From the perspective of the students themselves it was striking how the factors Woodard cited as responsible for school success were not the typical academic skills we usually think of—reading and writing skills and the like. Rather they were personality characteristics, attitudes, and beliefs these children had about themselves. Notice what he wrote about: self-acceptance and self-respect, the absence of self-pity, setting high standards for yourself; believing that you and not circumstances are in charge of your fate; seeing your family, despite its difficulties, as worthwhile; and the experience of being loved.

This last characteristic, the one about love, can be used to illustrate how important a difference it makes what perspective you take on an issue. If you focus on the family, your prime concern is likely to be that the family *gives* love. In contrast, if you focus on the child your prime concern is likely to be that the student be able to *receive* the love that comes from others; or learn to create it or give it to himself when it is not there. Ultimately, what made it work for these successful students in the Woodard study is that they *possessed* these characteristics, attitudes, capabilities, and beliefs. Certainly what their parents or teachers were like is important, as perhaps these children ''caught'' these qualities from these central people in their lives. But when it comes right down to it, it was not enough that these good things—high standards, and so forth—were ''out there.'' It was only when ''out there'' resulted in changes ''in there,'' inside the student himself, that it mattered.

This ''out there/in there'' distinction is a crucial one for me. Because the fact of the matter, as I see it, is that for many students the family, school, and community are not promoting, and likely will not promote, the qualities that result in school success, whether it be feelings of personal responsibility or high standards for oneself, or any others we may discover to be significant. (By the way, self-confidence may be one of these school-success factors. A very intriguing finding from longitudinal study that has monitored the fate of a group of socially disadvantaged children since 1969 from an early age to adulthood, shows that self-confidence is the most crucial ingredient in school and career success.[6]) The point is that for many students there is no use looking out into their world for these good things; because they are simply not there. Furthermore, my experience and study leads me to conclude that as a practical matter for many, many young people, despite the good intentions and hard efforts by school and social service professionals and others, they are not going to be there in the future either. And if these conditions in which students live are in many instances not amenable to change, then what? Does that mean these students must resign themselves to failure? From our perspective, the educators and other ''caretakers'' of society, the answer may be yes or no. For us, as much as we care about a student, the student is one of many; and even more fundamentally, the student is not us. So we can afford to debate the question. But from the perspective of an individual student, from the place inside him or her that looks out into the world, there can be only one answer: "No, I will not resign myself to failure!" Unless that student is going to give up on the only life he or she has, he or she is going to have to put a satisfying life together despite the negative, limiting circumstance of that life. Of course it is wonderful, empowering, to be loved. But what if you are not? And what if your efforts and those charged by the society to care for you cannot create it in your situation? Well, the reality is that unless you want to compound a lack of love with the penalties that come with school failure, even if you are just 15 you are going to have to take up the challenge of doing well in school anyway. From where you are, you have no choice. You must believe that you do not *have* to be loved, and that you can proceed in a positive way in school in its absence; or that you can learn to find or give yourself the love you need. If you are not self-respecting, or you do not feel in charge of your life, you must believe you can learn these things. You must if you are the student, because even though others can live with the *explanation* of why life is not going well for you, you have to live with the *experience* and the *consequences* of life not going well. And that is all the difference in the world.

Similarly, focusing on the school, it is glorious when the teachers, the curriculum, and the materials are excellent. But the fact is they will not always be excellent. Oh, perhaps they will be next year or the next upon the implementation of the new curricular program being contemplated. But for the student it is *this* year, and the reality for this young person (I am not claiming students necessarily see it this way; most undoubtedly do not) is that whatever the school and its teachers are like—good, bad, or indifferent—he or she must learn anyway or pay the price in ignorance and limited opportunity.

A major focus of this book is to share with you my search to find what needs to be learned by students in order to be successful in school and how it can be taught. The book is about a lot of other things as well; but do look for that.

For the rest of this chapter I continue to work to get us, you and me, on the same track so that you can get the most out of the time you put into reading this book and I get the best possible return for the time I put into writing it. I describe in some detail just what group of adolescents are the focus of these writings. Also, I tell you more about who I am, share something of my experiences and beliefs and my reasons for putting this book together. I give you an overview of the organization of the book, the chapters and topics and all. And last, I make some suggestions as to how I would like you to read the book.

This is an "I – you" book, from me to you. I assume that you are a school professional, a teacher, administrator, or counselor—or you are in training to become one. Perhaps you work in a college or university. In addition, I know you may be a parent, school board member, journalist, or politician. It would be wonderful for me if secondary age students read this book, but I suppose few if any will. This book is written in the spirit of a direct one-to-one message, and though I will not be able to see and hear your response, I hope that you will be doing just that, responding with your best judgments and ideas.

This is a book about the way we educate a particular group of students. It is going to take more than a few words to describe who they are because I do not have a single term to describe them that completely satisfies me. Though I will say at the outset if I had to choose one word it would be *underachievers*, even though others have pointed out to me problems associated with the use of that label. The students of focus here are secondary-school students—junior and senior high. These students, in grades 7 through 12 roughly, have academic talent but for whatever reason just do not get off the mark in school to the extent that we (people like you and me) would like them to. These are the kinds of kids who are in the "middle" and "lower" classes in the ability grouping arrangement. Perhaps they are in the vocational, business, or general track, whatever it is called, even if it is not a formal program. Though at the same time I do not want to imply that I am speaking only to the issues of the non-college-bound student. In this day and age many of the not-really-getting-on-with-it students *do* go on to college (where, I suspect many keep drifting along). The picture of these students I have in my mind includes the ones who are a bit flat emotionally (in school, at least), not very involved in class, and at the same time probably not giving anybody a major problem. This may sound as if I am talking about the average students or, as they are sometimes called, the "vast middle." Although I hope what I say applies to these students, I come back to the term underachiever—the student who has talent, but for some reason, does not use it. Though even as I write this I vacillate, because so-called average students fit this got-it-aren't-using-it description. *They* could do so much more in school if only they would.

In any case, something is getting in the way of these students taking better advantage of the opportunities in school to learn and grow. It could have to do with their social or cultural circumstance. Perhaps there is a family or personal or health problem. It could be a lack of academic skill. Or it might have something to do with a deficiency in the school program.

Are you getting a sense of the students I am talking about? The "level two" kids who could be and should be "level ones." I hope this is not stereotyping and unfair, but I have this image of students in classes, somewhat emotionally flat and distracted; listening (sort of) to lectures; speaking in short phrases, if at all, in question-and-answer recitation sessions; reading (sort of) texts; mechanically doing worksheets; watching (sort of) movies and slides; and writing (sort of) book reports from dust covers and encyclopedias. The students with a short blurb in the school yearbook. You know? Though at the same time I do not mean to imply that I am only concerned about students who go to school "by the numbers" as we used to say when I was in the army fixing tanks, just mechanically and thoughtlessly doing the minimum. I want to include in our concern students who are more connected to school and giving more "oomph" than this sketch I have just drawn. Although, as gloomy as it might seem, I will not back off from the negative picture that led off this paragraph. There are many students who are going to school in just this way. They are not really students in the sense that they are *studying* anything. They are *going to school*; that is by and large all they are doing.

A term for these kids, suggested to me by a colleague, that I have used as a shorthand term, even though it does not fit all of them, is *diners*. Do you recall those kids in the movie *Diner* a few years ago? They were nice, bright, and some of them anyway, unsophisticated working-class adolescents. They were the sort of young people toward which armed forces recruitment ads seem pitched. Kind of Bruce Springsteen people, if you know what I mean. Using "diner" as a way to talk about the kids in this book appeals to me because I have a strong interest in how social class affects aspiration, school-going style, and achievement. Plus these are the types of kids I feel most able to talk about, the ones who do not drop out or shake up the place or get in anybody's way too much.

But at the same time, as a label *diner* does not completely work for me. I want to attend to rural and middle class kids too. That pushes me back to underachiever again. Though, I think back to the time a colleague admonished me with: "Un-derachiever? *Under*achiever?! Oh, Bob. Such a negative label." I can see myself replying: "But it does focus on academic achievement, and that *is* what I care about, even though I know staying in school and self-esteem and all that are important. And the term does call up the idea that there is untapped potential in these kids, and I like that." To which she just replied, "Oh, Bob!" So what can I do.

Shifting focus, another way to clarify who these kids are is to list those I am *not* referring to in this book; or at least not emphasizing or focusing on directly. I am not really dealing with the extremely difficult and complex problems of the dropouts, vandalizers, hell-raisers, lawbreakers, and major league, hard-core "get out of my life and stay out" types. I have had experience working with these adolescents; but frankly their problems are bigger than I am. Though I do applaud those who can speak usefully to the issues confronted by educators who try to work with them. I am also not a special education person and can not speak to the issues confronting students with serious mental handicaps. In any case, there are many good books centering on the needs of these kinds of students. Nor am I dealing with just the issues of underachieving gifted students, as many of the students I care about are not referred to by that label as it is generally applied. And I do not go into how much natural talent, genetics, IQ, and so forth, has to do with school success. It may be a lot; but I just do not know much about that. I do not know how much native endowment, whatever that means, accounts for a young person rising above limitations in himself and in his world and doing well in school. One thing I am certain of, however: Intelligence is not everything. You and I can think of so many exceptionally bright kids who are also stuck in an academic rut. Also, I am not focusing per se on minority or handicapped students, or race—though all of these factors come up in the course of the book. No, the student of reference in these pages could very well be a white male from rural Wisconsin, Tennessee, or Vermont.

And last, as indicated in passing earlier, I am not speaking strictly of the average or, as one article I read recently referred to them, the "unspecial" student. There is too much of an emphasis in my thinking on the untapped special resource, the student who could "really do something" for that "unspecial" characterization to work. Besides, that is one label I am uncomfortable with in any case, because I believe all of us, including those considered unspecial, have something special to be and to give if we could only discover it.

One principal of a high school I know said, "Oh, that's my 30%," when I told him about the book. Once a teacher replied, "Hey, those are my drifters." Really, that was good enough for me. They and I were centered enough on the same students that we could move forward to talk about how to work with them. So I am comfortable—and I hope you are—with this admittedly somewhat fuzzy definition of who these students are. This sketch serves my purposes well enough. This book is not an empirical research study that has to neatly define who the students are by some clear objective standard. The problem is that we are unable to readily use one word to describe them, though I will probably fall back on underachievers. As far as I am concerned however, there is enough clarity on whom we are getting at to allow me to proceed with my job of writing about a group of students who seriously need some attention these days.

I say "seriously need attention these days" because so many of the students we refer to in this book are not on anybody's case load very much, if you know what I mean. If nothing else I hope that these pages will get us all thinking more about them. And we should really think about them; because, while we may differ over just what students do and do not fit into this category, every school person with whom I have spoken or worked has affirmed that, indeed, these students are in the schools in great numbers. Not only are they there, almost unanimously school people have said that working effectively with these kids is as big a challenge as they face.

A last point, concerning the age of these students. My experience and study has been primarily with older adolescents, ages 14 to 18 or so. While I hope what I write relates to early adolescence, most of the focus and examples will be on older students. So although I think the material in this book has clear implications for the middle grade years—and even earlier for that matter—I will leave it to you if you have interest in those years to give flesh to those implications.

Primarily this is a book of ideas. Though there is research data to support some of what I put forth, and though I will cite experience and examples quite often in the course of this argument, this book is primarily about a perspective, a way to look at the issue of how to educate these kinds of students. These ideas are the best I can put together. They are what I understand to be true and they reflect my values regarding what ought to happen. This book is much more of an argument I am making to you than an objective (if that is ever possible) summary or analysis of this topic. This is what I would say to you if I were with you and had the time. A major purpose of mine is that by the end of your reading you will understand my frame of reference on this topic. From this frame of reference, you, if you choose to and in ways you choose, can proceed on your own to continue to study and work in this area. I suggest as many investigation and project possibilities as I can to stimulate your thinking about where to go from here.

My primary focus is on the academic achievement of the students with which we are concerned. Whatever else is going on in their lives, in school or at home or within themselves, the academic achievement of these students is significantly lower than it ought to be, and we need to think of ways of raising it. I know there are many other outcomes that we could legitimately attend to, and indeed this book touches on them, but what I have chosen as the central focus is what I suppose could be called a common-sense notion of "doing well in school." I want these students to get better grades and more appreciation from their teachers and parents, and to learn and develop to the extent that we can reasonably hope and expect. Oh, and I will add one thing: I want these students to be happy with school and how they are doing. So I am not taking on, directly at least, the issues of social adjustment or self-esteem or what happens after high school to these students. No, the major concern is just how to get them to where a mother can tell her sister, "Susan is doing well in school."

One thing to keep in mind as you read this is that I have not set out to write a how-to-do-it manual or methods book. Although I respect this kind of book, I have concluded that a practical guide of step-by-step instructions on "what to do Monday," as they say, is not the best contribution to you I can offer. I leave the creation of that necessary form of professional literature to others more inclined in that direction and better suited to do so than I. What I do, I hope, is provide some ideas and enough direction so that you can figure out for yourself whether these concepts do apply and how to apply them in the specific situations in which you find yourself. As a matter of fact, I consider it important that I do not, even if I could, give you a "cookbook" here. There is a fundamental skill all of us need to practice: applying theory in the specific, immediate, and always unique, circumstances of our lives. Teaching is simply too much of an art and your situation is too much a one-of-a-kind that I would feel presumptuous to tell you exactly how things should be done. More than that, truth be told I simply do not know just how to do what needs to be done. What I am able to do right now is tell you how I see it, and give you a number of possible strategies—not specific techniques—that hold promise for making a positive difference with these students. I am convinced that this book will have value for you if you study, not just read, what is here.

I want to demystify the author–reader relationship. I—me, right here, in the flesh—am writing this book. You are reading it. I have a history, a particular current situation, needs and hopes, and other things going on in my life than how to teach these kinds of students. I know some things and am ignorant about some things. I have biases that color my view of reality. Because a fallible person— me—is putting words to paper, the results may be some truly insightful, useful ideas, right on the money. But just as well, these ideas may—well, undoubtedly to some extent are—contradictory to one another, incomplete, and just plain off-base. I have worked hard to see that this book is characterized more by insight-fulness than "off-baseness." But do not let the fact that these words are typeset obscure all of this.

ABOUT MYSELF

Now to who I am. I will tell you about some aspects of my background and ideas so that you will have a better sense of whom you are dealing with and how to take what is here. Also, by sharing this I can go some distance in preparing you for the forthcoming material, give you a preview of sorts; and thus provide you with a "mental set" that will allow you better to take in, organize, and work with what I have to say. (It just occurred to me that in saying this to you I am at the same time making a point about the kids we are focusing on. I want you to know what is happening. So often, though these secondary students may be going to class, they really do not know what is going on.) Also, I hope talking about myself in the next pages encourages you to think about yourself. Just who is this person reading this book? Most fundamentally, what do you believe and value about schools? What do you want to accomplish as an educator? What do you take seriously in your professional life right now (or your training if that is where you are)?

I went through teacher training at the University of Minnesota. For 5 years I was a high school social studies teacher in a working-class community in the Minneapolis-Saint Paul area. It was during these years that I developed a partic-ular concern for the way social and personal circumstances can channel and limit what young people become, both in school and later on in their lives. I continued on in my own study and now have a doctorate in education with a focus on cur-riculum and instruction. Currently I am an associate professor in education at the University of Vermont. Relevant to this book, I recently took a sabbatical year from the university and taught full-time in a Los Angeles high school serv-ing primarily Hispanic students, though there were Black and Asian students as well. This teaching experience has had a great impact on me and has strongly influenced what I write here. Also, I taught for a time in a junior high school for incarcerated adolescents. As a university faculty member I have reviewed the writings and research in this area and organized a conference focusing on these kinds of students. Last year I was a consultant to a private school that works primarily with students who have had difficulties in school. At present, I am teaching a graduate level class made up of currently practicing teachers on educating—still groping for labels—the "less successful" student. I have a background and interest in sport and psychology, which you will see reflected here. And I am interested in literature and active in theater—though they may be less noticeable in their influence on these writings.

One last but important point, I myself was an example of these kinds of kids. In school I was bounced from class to class, called "lazy" and "unmotivated" (next to my picture in the yearbook is the phrase "dormant genius"), dropped from the athletic team because of my schoolwork, and termed a discipline problem. The school counselor encouraged me to go into the army after high school (which I did) in order for it to straighten me out (which it did not—it was just a holding tank for other uneducated low income young people like me). Obviously I have progressed academically since those school days, but I sure did not get much done then—for many of the reasons I now understand and cover in this book. So for me this is a very personal book. It is an attempt to speak to the issue of educating people like I was then. I have been very lucky in my life. Now I can speak and write well and have a way to be heard. Another way to put it, I have a public persona. So many young people, and adults, are essentially only private beings, without the ability and opportunity to speak out, or the power to go beyond coping and accommodating to making things different. This book, these ideas, are what I would have told my teachers at 13 or 16 if I could have done so. Just maybe I am speaking now for some young person who is confused and frightened and bored and lost, all at the same time, as I was then.

Whether or not I say anything truly valuable here, I consider my own early experiences to have helped me write this book. My "bedroom" during my school years was first, for one year, behind a plywood partition in a downtown barber shop, and then for the remaining school years an unheated back porch; which in Minnesota winters means sleeping in a stocking cap under piles of blankets and moving very fast in and out. I know from experience what it is like to live in a home without books and without conversation being directed at you. I know what it means to go to school from an angry home and try to connect with the Monroe Doctrine, figure out what Keats meant by an ode he wrote, and what algebra is about other than a text and a series of problems to do for tomorrow. (On that last one, I still do not know to this day.) And I know what it is like just trying not to get hurt any more than you already are and having nobody seem to notice or care. Yes, in a very real and personal way writing this book, as stiff and academic as I know it will be at times, is coming back home for me.

MY BELIEFS

It is important that you as a reader understand the fundamental beliefs and values that give direction to my work in education, including the writing of this book.

I sketch out some of my key assumptions and values regarding our culture and society, schools, and students. This should clarify from just what context I write, and make what I say more understandable and meaningful to you. Also, I hope outlining my formative thoughts stimulates you to identify and explore your own. That is important to me because being an educator is much more than a series of techniques. At best it is an informed human action. It is, no less, an answer to the fundamental question, What am I going to do with my life? Teaching—or any work you do, selling insurance, farming, or working in a bank—is, when you are doing it, defining your life. More than that, it *is* your life. What do you think your life is but the cumulation of activities such as what you are doing right now, reading this book? This is it. So take it seriously and do it with a clear sense of where you come from and where you are going and how this day, this moment, fits into all that. Because one thing is certain, you have just one shot at living this moment. Oops, now it is gone . . . and now that moment is gone. And that one . . . and that one . . . and that one.

A first point: To understand schooling in this country one must see it in relation to the culture in which it functions. By culture I mean the American way of life: the values, habits, beliefs, styles, traditions, and so forth, that comprise the manner in which we live. Schooling is the formal part of a larger process of education, or it might be called socialization, which teaches young people "how we do it here." American children—well, this is true of children in any culture—need to learn what it means to be "one of us": what it means to be an individual here and what it means to be a part of the whole here. They need to learn where they fit in and what it takes to get along in this culture and the society (institutions, roles, relationships, structures) which has arisen from and in turn affects this culture. (Perhaps I should put it culture(s) to indicate that although we have enough in common to warrant speaking of an American culture, at the same time we are cultures plural, since the immigrant quality of this country has resulted in such cultural diversity—or, as it is called, "cultural pluralism.") Keep in mind, too, that whatever our cultural circumstance at any time, it did not arise out of thin air. It is continuous with a cultural history or tradition. From this perspective, schooling is at heart a cultural-social event and only makes sense if the cultural circumstance, over time, including projections into the future, is taken into account.

I say this because too often school issues stay "inside," so to speak. We debate this or that approach to teaching, say, in terms of whether it makes logical sense, or "works" (gets done what it purports it will), or feels good to school personnel, or looks more efficient compared to something else in achieving an explicit or simply understood schooling aim we agree upon. All this is to say that often what is going on in education is school people talking to one another with inadequate attention to what America is about or where America has come from. And what makes this particularly important from my point of view is that there are some trends in secondary education that make a certain internal, school-related sense but do not fit in terms of what I understand to be the overall thrust of the American experience. Three that come to mind, and I speak to them later, are the minimum competence, back-to-basics, and mastery learning approaches to teaching. My point is not that those trends are all bad; they do have their place. It is that to stress that they should be the core or predominant emphasis in the schooling endeavor runs counter to our cultural traditions.[7]

My reading of this country is that, at its core, America is an experiment in freedom.[8] This past summer I was fortunate to be granted a fellowship to study the writings and ideas of the "founding fathers" and the early history of the United States, and it is my conclusion that the most fundamental value at the heart of our cultural traditions is individual liberty.[9] This society is a test of sorts, to see what kinds of individuals and nation will result when people are as free as possible. Of course there will be the need for governmental and other controls, but those controls should be minimal. The American experiment, then, is to test the faith in a good result, both in the private and public realms of life, if individuals are trusted with the opportunity to create fulfilling and productive lives for themselves. Inherent in this conception of liberty is an understanding that the results of freedom will be differences in individual accomplishment and power and status and possession, and that is accepted. To be sure, there was a concern for equality and justice in the early years; but it was primarily a belief in equality of treatment before the law and protection against the infringement on one's liberty, not in equality of result or station in life. One has the right to *pursue* happiness, not the guarantee of *achieving* it.

I certainly understand the qualifications that have to be made in this rather simple picture. Also, I know the issues that come up, such as the limited view of just who counted in all this (White, property owning males). And yes, conditions are different now than they were in the first century of our country's existence. Those crucial matters aside, however, I want the central claim I am making understood: I am saying deep down, embedded in this culture, from way back, is the challenge of assuming the responsibility of living a free life.

It is important to stress this commitment to freedom because we have grown up in a time in which there has been both political and social concern for issues of social justice and equity of treatment and outcome. These are necessary and valuable emphases, but they could obscure what I see as the larger message to us: life in the USA is an opportunity to make it good for yourself. Although this country cares about you, and there are social service, affirmative action, civil rights, and other protections, it is not the best idea to wait around to be helped over the hurdles. This is a place where *you* jump the hurdles yourself. And, to continue the metaphor, bad leg and all you do the jumping or you will be left hanging around the starting line holding your leg and, probably, complaining about it all or putting yourself down.

What this comes down to for me is a prime challenge to all of education—not just schooling—of this society is to prepare young people to take advantage of this opportunity to be free. That means supporting the development of individuals who understand what is possible and what they want, and who can perceive the limitations, obstacles, and the injustices that can get in their way, and know how to get through them. It means creating people who can take care of themselves and provide for their own satisfaction. Education consistent with this culture, then, is an education for freedom. And no, I do not want to get into issues of whether we can ever be totally free. I am willing to accept the idea of freedom as a useful concept, and at the same time understand that as a practical matter we always live within restraints, whether it be externally imposed obstacles, limits from within ourselves—ability, energy, and so forth—or, ultimately, death itself. I view freedom on a continuum from freer to less free. It is enough for me to decide on the basis of my judgment that in any particular situation someone is freer or more entrapped than before, or than what is possible.

Freedom for me is associated with choice and power. Choice as I see it is a special thing. It means a selection, given a clear understanding of oneself and the sanctity of one's life, and insight into the options that are available and that can be created. It involves the capability to decide what is worth doing—including whether it is morally justified—in light of the consequences for the individual, his family, community, nation, and world. Also important is the ability to take powerful action alone and in collaboration with others. Without efficacy, without the ability to make things happen, an individual is not free. Freedom and power go together. Freedom is not simply living in the absence of restraint or living in a metaphorical desert without water and thus "free" to roam around until you die. It means the ability to get things done.

Also at the core of America is the republican (I am talking small "r" here) tradition of citizenship. This is the idea that one has the responsibility to the community and nation to be an informed participant in the process of representative government. Within this conception there is the ideal of service in which the public good is a paramount concern. Citizens within this view are those who are both public and private: they honor and serve the community and its needs and traditions as well as attend to their own concerns. These culturally ideal citizens, then, do not set the private and public dimensions of their lives off against each other, but rather see their potential complementarity—each can enhance and inform the other—and integrate both into their being. Again, I know all the considerations you might raise, about how few were, and are, actually called upon to act as citizens. Voting every few years is not enough, and women and minorities were for so long kept from even doing that. All I want to get across is the notion that citizenship involves being a public person: being heard, being involved, protecting one's own interests, and contributing to the interests of the larger whole. From that perspective, education in this country should prepare young people not only to be free but also to be citizens of the American republic. Which to me means more than elective politics. It also includes being a citizen, if you will, a contributing member, a vital participant, in one's work setting and church, within community organizations and the neighborhood.

Now to a third element: individualism. Individualism is a major strand of the American culture. By individualism I mean the view that individuals are important for themselves and have the right to be supported in discovering who they are and expressing themselves through their actions and creations. Individualism, in sum, encourages one to be the one-of-a-kind person he or she is. But important to remember, in this culture individualism is more a matter of extending an *invitation* and granting of an *opportunity* than providing assurance that one will *actually* live out one's uniqueness. At best, education in this country is of a kind that encourages and contributes to the development of individual persons, not walking cliches or interchangeable cogs in a social/cultural machine.

Yet another key value I see at the core of American culture is the idea of doing what you do well. There is an emphasis in America on doing the best one can, on doing something better, on creating something exemplary. Within this tradition an individual is charged with getting to the edge of his or her own personal frontier, if you will, and pushing it out. This culture says to you and me: "Let's see how far you can go." There is the expectation to be the best businessman, farmer, artist, attorney, doctor, custodian, public servant, soldier, or parent—or student—you can be. The 1960s notwithstanding, "hanging out" has never been what this country has been about. Rather, the "through-line," a term from theater, has been an emphasis on working hard and well, along with all the character traits that are inherent in that such as diligence, self-discipline, deferring rewards, and the like. America is not about adequacy, mediocrity, getting by. It is about, instead, taking initiative, and making the most of oneself and one's opportunities. It is about taking up the challenge. It is about accomplishment.

This "press to excellence" can have its negative effects, that is certain. Excellence can mean quantity instead of quality. It can mean doing something excellently that should not be done at all—for example, creating a fast food restaurant where eating out of buckets and paper bags is done as well as can be imagined. (In regard to this fast food example, it would be good if we as a culture emphasized a bit more that excellence includes doing what is natural and uplifting to human beings.) And some in our society, the poor and minorities among them, do not get the message to be everything they can be; because it is really not sent. Instead, the signal is more of the sort: "For you, get a job, pay your bills, keep your nose clean and stay out of trouble. Find happiness in your family and personal relationships, watch the news and vote regularly, and if a war comes up we'll call you." Not the worst of all possible messages to be sure, and it sounds better than Haiti or someplace. But it is not the challenge to really strive to achieve either. With all that, however, American culture has generally gotten across the value of doing whatever one does excellently. And a good education here is one that is promotive of excellence.

The impact of religious and humanistic traditions must be noted as well. To be an American is to be a good, moral human being, compassionate and decent to others. It is being trustworthy and fair. It involves a respect and reverence for life. And to grow up in America—to a greater or lesser extent to be sure—is to be brought into contact with the moral, religious, transcendent, and spiritual dimensions of human existence. Transcendent concerns, in the arts and religion and in human conduct generally, are not tangential or extraneous to American life. They are integral to it, and any process of socializing, including schooling, the young must take these concerns into account.

Does this create for you the picture I draw of the American culture and traditions? There is the emphasis on learning to live freely; on republican citizenship; on individual expression and satisfaction; on special, exemplary achievement; on living with decency, compassion, fairness toward others; and on being in connection with the most evolved, spiritual, and transcendent dimensions of human existence. This is my view of what needs to be considered in any process, formal or otherwise, which helps someone to live among us and carry on from what our ancestors have created. This is my view of America. I contend that schooling should be grounded in the cultural reality—or perhaps more accurately, in the cultural ideal, the aspects of the culture that are most admirable and worthy of continuance. I favor schooling that continues and extends the cultural elements I have just described. I want schools to help us to live out who we are.

What is your response? And most important, what is *your* view? A good activity for you would be to write out and tell others your picture of America.

Certainly a major implication of what has been said is that schooling should never be relegated to merely a discussion of techniques or strategies. The "how-to-do-it's," vital as they are, must be evaluated with clear reference to the cultural and social circumstance that gives them meaning. In summary, given the cultural circumstance as I have sketched it, these are some things I think it implies for the way we educate in schools: First and foremost it means schools that support students in becoming people who can live freely. Schooling for liberty, as I guess it can be called, goes beyond the three Rs, or acquisition of this or that understanding or skill from an academic subject at 80% "mastery" (80%, by the way, is adequacy not mastery). And it is clearly more than simply learning to be loyal or follow rules. Nor is it about being trained to fill some slot in the work force. It is about learning that you—there-will-never-be-another-like, precious you—exist. It is learning how to manifest who you are through moral and useful work, through the art you create, through service, and in other ways; and to create a rich and happy life for yourself and those you love. It is about being a public person, one who cares about the welfare of others and the nation—and the planet—and who makes the world and not just his own life better for his having lived. Schooling is about doing things care-fully (full of care) and excellently. And it is legitimately about character, about love, and about what is highest, most beautiful, most fundamentally true and natural in human conduct and creation. It is about taking responsibility for carrying on our heritage. This does not mean replicating our past, but rather understanding and honoring what has been passed on to us by those who have gone before—and being clear regarding the consequences of what we do with our lives for those who will follow.[10]

Schooling practice, especially for the "less successful," too often contradicts these aims. For many, schooling is more about completing tasks someone else has figured out than finding out who one is and pushing out one's limits. It is more about adapting to expectations and rules than about being seen and heard and participating. It is more about mass assignments and age-grading (you are 15 and therefore a sophomore) than individual expression. And it is more about adequacy than it is about being superb at what one does. It is schooling that shies away from issues of character, morality, responsibility to others, and meaning and purpose. Too much is centered on worksheets, being talked at rather than talking, completing tasks (called, euphemistically, problems), and plodding step-by-step through text chapters. Schooling that can be characterized in that way may be the best we can do. And when it comes down to it, it may be the best I can do. But nevertheless I am not going to kid myself or you by calling this brand of schooling anything other than what it is, an accommodative but not freeing education; it is not anywhere near to what is possible for students, even those not at the top of the social or schooling "mountain," or best for America.

Two theorists in education who have influenced my thinking and whom I want to recommend to you are James Macdonald and Fred Newmann.[11] Though not all that I write here is consistent with their thinking—I do differ with them in places—no two have stimulated a response from me as they have. Let me tell you about them.

Macdonald, who died within the last few years, challenged all educators to clarify what we, at the most basic level, are up to in our work: "What I am proposing is a challenge to curriculum talkers and workers to explicitly profess the basic grounding values of goodness that underlie the work they do."[12] He called upon us to do no less than base our work in education on our answers to the most fundamental questions regarding the human condition: What is the meaning of human life, and how shall we live together? I cannot claim to have gone that far, but my discussion of this country and its heritage is my attempt to deal with fundamental issues of the sort he advised us to clarify. And though I sense I am more committed to the continuity of cultural traditions than was Macdonald, I share the basic distinction he drew between an empowering versus accommodative education. Do read his work.

The concept of human dignity is a key idea that Newmann articulates that has been important to me. Newmann sees human dignity as a value that transcends all others, including civic participation and individual expression, values I have listed here. To him, human dignity is the yardstick that measures the ultimate worth of any human purpose or action. While Newmann's writings have influenced me, in turn I believe he has been influenced by Donald Oliver with whom he studied at Harvard. I mention this because it is important to see how ideas are passed down from one person to another. In this case, from Oliver to Newmann to me to you—and you can be certain Oliver himself gained inspiration from someone else. And of course you will pass them on yourself. Each time the idea passes through someone it is modified or extended, or applied to new circumstances. And though the idea and uses change with each individual, each owes much to the contributions of those who have gone before. Thus, there is both continuity and change as the good ideas of Macdonald, Newmann, and Oliver pass through me. I hope you see how this process works with ideas, and also how it is analogous to what should be happening in the culture and society generally, including schools.

Newmann proposed that the most fundamental educational goal of public education be the promotion of human dignity for all students. He defined human dignity as comprising material well-being, individuality, social attachment, and integration for each person.[13] By material well-being, Newmann meant the basic elements of food, clothing, shelter, health care, and physical security. Individuality refers to the freedom to express one's unique ideas, personality, interests, and temperament. Social attachment gets at the bonds or connections one has to other individuals and groups. And integration points toward a life where things go together, where there is connectedness and order, where things make sense and are all of a piece. So to contribute to human dignity, in schools or elsewhere, is to further the development of these four dimensions that comprise it. You will notice how my perspective as just described reflects this concept of human dignity.

One aspect of human dignity that I have not yet emphasized, but whose importance I support, is integration. I agree with Newmann that it is indeed crucial to a good life. It is best if our lives go together, that everything does not remain fragmented and disconnected. A good education helps us see interrelationships, meanings, wholes (and holes). Unfortunately, schools often make it tough for students to put things together. Everything is carved up into pieces. Schedules divide students into a multitude of 50-minute (or less) class hours, with as many as seven disparate subjects each day. Assignments often remain narrowly focused: a bit today, finish that and get a bit tomorrow; then a bit more the day after that. This reductionistic process (breaking up big things into small pieces in order to learn them) is typical of schools. The assumption is that after the student has learned each of the component understandings or skills of some area of study as sequenced by the teacher, he will then integrate the pieces and understand the whole. That makes sense logically if you do not push it too far (like into the theories of educational psychologists). The problem with it is that as a matter of fact the end result of learning this and then that and then the next thing is most often not integration and insight into the whole. Instead, unfortunately, at the end of learning a lot of little pieces the student usually winds up with a pile of little pieces. The top of the pile (the latest things he or she studied) the student can remember, but has no idea how they are connected. And the rest, everything but the top layer, is lost from view altogether. It is unfortunate that education insists on thinking in little pieces, even giving them names: daily lesson plans.

Newmann, as previously noted, included material well-being and individual expression in his concept of human dignity. I reflect these elements within an idea of *good work*. Good work, to me, means making a living in a way that expresses who one is, and that is uplifting both to the individual and to the society and culture. Work to me has the connotation of vocation or calling. It is natural to us and it is ethical. It fills our niche in the scheme of things. It is our path (in Eastern philosophies the term is *dharma*). It is something we can do with all of our being and with love.

I trust that it is possible to find ways to do good work and at the same time provide for our material well-being. I know how important working in the way I have described means to me. I do not want to promote material well-being—through what are called jobs and careers—for students unless it is sought within this ideal of good work. Some may respond to what I have just said with, "But somebody has to do the crap jobs [they use a synonym for crap] in society." My answer is, "Great, if it is so necessary then why don't you or your children take on one of the crap jobs and help us all out. We will pay you enough money to make your time payments. But of course you will be so exhausted, bored, and diminished by the job that all you will be able to do is watch your big color TV and maybe once a week shine up the Mercury Cougar."[14]

Does all this begin to paint a picture of what I hope for in education? Though I do not want to lose the layers and shadings of all that I have written so far, a simpler way to put it is to distinguish an education that is empowering to the individual from one that is adapting (another term, coopting). And there is the distinction between an education that is culturally enriching versus one that is debilitative (stagnating, corruptive, antithetical to the culture). I admit I cannot always define an empowering education, but I can feel it. I can feel when I am truly strengthened by a school experience rather just trained to fit in or know what somebody is dishing out. And though I did not have words for it, as a teenager I sensed when I was being accommodated to my place in the world as somebody saw it rather than being empowered to create a life of dignity and significance. I can feel these distinctions as a teacher too. And as I get older and have studied and thought more and am able to take a longer view of things, I can feel when something is in sync with this culture and when it is not. See if you can feel it as well.

This is a very personal, selective book. By that I mean I do not propose to be covering the subject of how to educate these underachieving secondary student. Rather I write *on* this issue, dealing with those matters that I particularly care about and think I know enough about to share something useful. I do, however, deal with enough areas so that the result will be a reasonably coherent and complete argument—more than a series of fragments.

My central focus is, and keep this in mind as you read these chapters, the students themselves. Currently there is much emphasis on what can be called technologies of teaching or instruction. We are assured that if a teacher abides by the system and does the right things in the right order, learning will result. The assumption is that good teaching will produce good learning. Also these days, many are looking at the characteristics of schools under the premise that good schools result in good learning. Effective schools are described in terms of their purposes, organization and leadership, the school climate, expectations for students, instructional and curricular patterns, and evaluation systems. I applaud those efforts; they are very helpful. But my assumption is that in order to achieve good academic results, everybody has to be able to do their jobs well, including students. Too often we have operated as if the only key actors in the schooling enterprise were the professionals. They make it happen, good or bad. The point to remember is that students shape their circumstance as well as are shaped by it. There is a reciprocal, not one-way, relationship between schools and students. The level of commitment and school-going capability of students makes a difference. An assumption I hold is that one of the reasons that not enough is accomplished academically in schools is not so much that the schools are bad or the teachers are inadequate; rather, it is because the *students* are not up to it. They do not "student" (verb form) well enough.

It takes effective schools and effective teachers *and* effective students—all three—in order to get the work done. Schools operate much better if students are collaborative, supportive, and effective at holding up their end of things. As educators we set up training programs, workshops, in-service days, read books and journals, and ponder our success and failures. And indeed we should be proud of our dedication to our work. But if you turn the perspective around, from ourselves to the students, just how much attention and energy goes into what is involved in what *they* do? They may get help on how to use the library, or maybe get instruction in some system for organizing their reading better, or go through "how to study" courses. But as useful as these aids are, nevertheless, they primarily have to learn how to be a student from observation, tips, cues, and admonishments as they go along. The result is that some catch on and learn how to go to school very nicely. And others do not have a clue as to what it takes to get their job done effectively. Simply, they do not know the skills of getting motivated and directed, or how to accomplish their work as students.

So one of the things I do is define good studenting: What comprises it? What produces it? What is its relationship to the other elements in the school (curriculum, instruction, organization, school culture)? This focus on the student supports a major contention that I elaborate in this book: If these underachieving students are going to start getting significant learning and growth accomplished, schools are going to have to become places where *their* work is what the process is about, rather than being essentially about their *response* to the work of teachers. Students are going to have to become the causal agents in the school, which now, characteristically, they are not. And if what they do, and not teaching, is the salient element in the schooling process, then it is necessary to zero in on what they do and understand it better. And what they do is engage in studenting.

We educators do not usually think along these lines because we tend to have a context-shaper mentality. This mentality encourages us to operate under the assumption that students will achieve more as soon as we improve the context by making the school and teaching better. And certainly it is enormously helpful if we are successful at doing just that. One problem with all that, however, is we often do not work as hard as we should to make the students themselves as positive an element in the context as would optimally be the case. Even more important is that we tend to talk a better context-shaping game than we deliver. We get a little better here and a little worse there, try this and then that, and when it comes right down to it things remain just about the same. Especially for the students who are not the stars (bit players might not be a bad metaphor to use), schools might be the best examples of "living history" they will encounter in their lives—a setting remarkably similar in appearance and operation to what it was 10, 20, or 30 years ago. If that is more the case then not, whether they are up to it or not the only true hope students have is to get off the sidelines and work to make schools good places for themselves.

A paradigm is a fundamental way of looking at something. Our paradigm as educators has to do with teaching and the teacher's perspective. While that perspective is reflected in this book, you are also asked to look at school from the students' perspective and consider schooling as something *students* do.

I share with you a couple of articles that came across my desk as a way of illustrating and tying together some of the things I have written in this chapter. The first is an article from *Education Week* which describes an unpublished study showing that among socially disadvantaged students, values of the sort that we associate with the traditional work ethic are linked to academic success. The research also revealed a link between academic success and religiosity among students, family emphasis on education, and students' belief in their own capability. In the article Tom Mirgen concluded: "Remediation alone does not foster high aspiration to achieve educational excellence."[15] A second article from the Wisconsin Center for Educational Research indicates that one of the problems for lower class, poorly achieving students is that they are dissatisfied with constantly being compared to other students and found wanting.[16]

These articles reflect some key themes that I have outlined so far in this chapter. The first one focuses on studenting: what the students who succeed are like. Also, there is the focus on the socially disadvantaged, family and religious influences, values, character, and psychological factors (belief in one's own capability)—all mentioned here.

The second article underscores that school—well, all of life—is not always a fair and positive place. Certainly this put-down business is a problem for school professionals, and it would help if we attended more to progress in terms of each student's own past standard of performance. But from the perspective of the students it is *their* problem. They had better learn how to respond in self-affirming and productive ways to unfavorable comparisons with others because, despite good intentions and efforts by school people, those unfavorable comparisons are going to persist. And not only in school: These young people are also likely to have to deal with unfavorable comparisons on the job and at home and with friends. Really, this situation is a gift to them if they would look at it in this way. Here is an opportunity to learn to take on a problem they are going to have. It has to be *their* issue, not just to respond to, but to act upon. Students must see that being *mad* about it and *right* about how inappropriate it is for teachers to do it is not necessarily going to stop the comparisons. In addition, griping, self-pity, petitioning, and waiting for teachers to stop doing these awful things and being unhappy and disengaged until they do is giving over a great deal of power to someone else—teachers in this instance. Teachers have control over whether the student is happy or academically productive, because these students pout, or whatever they do, until the teachers improve. Students need to see they have a choice over how to act in the face of these unfavorable comparisons. They can sulk about it and cherish their good reason for being stuck. Or they can work to understand just why that is happening to them and set up a plan (complaining is usually a reaction, not a plan) to get teachers and others to cut it out. Along with that, they can learn to make positive use of this negative energy coming their way. They can, as others have, learn to transform this negativity into a force that instead of getting them down spurs them on to greater efforts to make something of themselves. Indeed, they have choices. Do you see how this ties into the ideas in this chapter?

ORGANIZATION OF THIS BOOK

You have just about completed this first chapter.

Chapter 2 refers selectively to the research on underachievement. What is offered as an explanation for why some students achieve significantly less academically than their capability would indicate is reasonable to expect?

Chapter 3 spells out my psychological frame of reference as I look at the issues we confront with these students. I review the theories of a psychologist you may not have heard of, Roberto Assagioli. Also, I present material I derive from sport psychology; ideas on self-management from counseling psychologist Linda Nielson; analyses of the process of achievement itself grounded in the work of social psychologist David McClelland; and last, summarize some of my ideas on the issue of motivation.

Chapter 4 outlines factors I think important to consider as we look at this concept of studenting. The topics include: academic skills; learning (study) skills; learning disabilities; social and cultural influences on achievement; adolescent development and achievement; relational issues; emotional–psychological problems; and health and nutrition issues.

Chapter 5 looks at the other side of the polarity, focusing on teaching rather than studenting. What is good teaching for these kinds of students? Based on the answer to this question I analyze the current emphasis on technologies of teaching, including mastery learning, as ways to work with less than optimally successful students.

Chapter 6 deals with curriculum. What educational goals should these students pursue? What subjects should they study? I give particular attention to the place of character education in the curriculum.

Chapter 7 considers the school itself. In particular, these areas: the way the school is organized (time segments, departments, tracking); the climate or ethos of the school; and, especially, the way the school handles discipline.

Chapter 8 sets out what I am calling a student achievement construct. To me the word *construct—concept* is an alternative term—implies that it is an element in a theory. I use *construct*, even though it might not fit exactly, because I do see myself engaging in some theory-building here. I pull together all I have said in this book—about students and teaching and curriculum and schools—into a single construct that describes the elements in academic achievement from the perspective of the student. I diagram it so that you can see the components that comprise the construct and their relationship to one another. The explication of the construct should give us a way to discuss more clearly the issue of improving student achievement levels, as well as provide a basis from which to organize research and study of this issue.

Before ending this chapter, a few words about how I want you to read this book. I want you to do more than just read through it to understand what I am saying, though I do want that; any author wants to be understood. But more than reading for understanding, I hope you engage this book. This book is as much about you as it is about me and what I write here. In that regard, you should attend to me as I present myself and my ideas in the book, but you should be equally vigilant to yourself. What does reading this evoke in you? What memories, what ideas, what judgments, what projects, what issues, what hopes? The challenge is to use the book to your advantage. Go prospecting, if you will: Try to find some gold here that you can cash in to improve your effectiveness as an educator and the lives of the hidden nuggets you teach or will teach. (Sorry about the metaphors.) Think hard about the ideas I present. Extend them. Fix them where they are flawed. Figure out how they can be put into practice where you are. Come up with different or better ideas than I provide you.

You may be reading this for a course. I have not been formal about it and placed discussion questions and possible assignments at the end of chapters, but I try to raise issues and challenges as I go along which can be the basis for class discussions, papers, and projects. And please do attend to my comments and the books and other readings contained in the notes at the end of the book. The superscript numbers you find along the way—there were sixteen in this chapter—

refer you to the notes section. The notes can provide a way to enrich your study of this area. Also, if you are taking this as part of a course your instructor can point you toward some things to study. Or ask colleagues for help. Indexes to periodical literature, such as the Educational Index and the ERIC system (which has indexes to both published and unpublished materials) are also useful. A reference librarian at a college or university is helpful in getting into these. Do have a good go at this. This is an important issue. There are some students out there who need our help.

2 The Nature of Underachievement

The first chapter establishes that in order to help students excel in school we need to more clearly identify the characteristics of a successful student. That signals a major purpose of the book, to define the factors in the students themselves that account for academic achievement. At the same time, however, that should not obscure the usefulness of better understanding the reasons why things *do not* work. If we comprehend what gets in the way of students' doing well, we may be able to get whatever it is out of the way. Moreover, seeing what does not work may provide useful clues to what does work. Thus the focus of this chapter: an introduction to what educational writers are saying about underachievement.

The term *underachievement* has been an organizer for some very useful research and writing. In my academic study of the students of concern in this book, *underachievement* was the best "handle" to get me started. As a category I found achievement less useful, as it is so all-encompassing that it is difficult to zero in on my particular concerns. I invite you to investigate underachievement. Visit a university library and look under *underachievement* in the periodical indexes and the card catalog, or ask a reference librarian for help.

I have identified three articles as examples of what is written about underachievers. Reviewing these articles should do several things. These should provide some useful information about underachievement and typify how the profession looks at this issue. It should also help create a context in which you may fit the topics and arguments which are covered in this book.

I begin with the article that I found most useful. It is written by husband and wife John and Helene Krause and entitled "Toward a Multimodal Theory of Academic Underachievement."[1] The Krauses' review of the various ways researchers and practitioners have worked with underachievement provided me an excellent way to get some background and orientation regarding this issue. Also, their basic thesis has proven to be the most stimulating and useful idea I have encountered over the past several years. The Krauses conclude that although those who have studied underachievement have focused on specific factors or causes that are important to understand, at the same time they have failed to view the problem from a broad enough perspective.

The Krauses point suggests we need to remember that just because we have a single name for a phenomenon—in this case *underachievement*—this does not mean it is a single phenomenon; it might be several phenomena. For example, I understand cancer is not one thing but many things, different from one another in significant ways. Furthermore, because we have a single label does not mean we can agree on its meaning. In the next pages, it becomes obvious we do not agree in the case of underachievement. Certainly too, having a single label does not necessarily mean that there is a single cause accounting for its occurrence. Even if underachievement is a single thing and we can agree about what it is, we cannot assume that there is only one factor creating it. In any individual case there may be one cause, or many. From the argument the Krauses marshal, it is clear to me that underachievement is a function of different factors in different students. That is, if we look at two students, both underachievers, we may well find that one reason for the lack of success applies to one student, and an entirely different reason to the other. As obvious as this point may appear, it is important to emphasize, because so often educators have a "pet" cause that, as they see it, accounts for most every manifestation of a particular problem. Self-esteem is a favorite these days. Name a problem a student is having in school and somebody will authoritatively put forth, "This is a self-esteem problem." This book attempts to look more closely at what is really going on. Even if, staying with this example, self-esteem is involved, the student may have other problems as well. Another possibility is that self-esteem may be one of several factors which *combine* to produce underachievement, none strong enough to produce the circumstance by itself, but sufficient when accompanied by these other factors.

A *multimodal theory*, as the Krauses term it, needs to be developed to explain academic underachievement. This multimodal theory would take into account various factors, and their interrelationships, which are associated with underachievement. In chapter 8 of this book I respond to their challenge by putting together what I call a "student achievement construct." My aim is that this construct—I am not ready to call it a theory—will provide a frame of reference from which we can make sense of this very large issue of student achievement (or, the other side, underachievement). Beyond the creation of the construct, my approach of looking at student achievement in a broad, multidimensional, integrated way has been greatly influenced by the Krauses' work. More personally, I very much appreciate their generous and helpful response and the discussion of our work during my visit to Harvard.

Another article I review is a summary of research on underachieving gifted students by Cynthia Dowdall and Nicholas Colangelo.[2] The third is "What to

Do When They Can But They Won't'' by Robert McCall, which is typical of articles on this issue and directed at a more general readership.[3] Considered together, these writings provide a good sense of the current investigation regarding underachievement.

WHAT DEFINES AN UNDERACHIEVER?

How do we know one when we encounter one? It is clear that there is no clear-cut agreement in the field of education about who is or is not an underachiever. Most educators agree that underachievement involves a marked discrepancy (but what exactly does "marked" mean?) between predicted and actual levels of performance. Some researchers have tried to be more precise, but others have not yet decided on one hard and fast definition that would allow us to say definitively, "Yes, this student is an underachiever" and, "No, that student is not one. What it comes down to is that the criteria for determining underachievement vary. Individual investigators can decide what formal assessments or more informal judgments, of intelligence or aptitude for example, warrant the decision that a particular student ought to be doing significantly better.

The Krauses' article does not get any more exact than this "discrepancy between expected and actual performance" definition of underachievement. Dowdall and Colangelo listed no fewer than 15 different definitions of underachieving gifted students. Included in the Dowdall and Colangelo list are: "Students who demonstrate exceptionally high capacity for academic achievement and are not performing satisfactorily for their levels on daily academic tasks and achievement tests." "One who evidences a long standing pattern of academic underachieving not accounted for by learning disabilities and fittedness only appears through intellectual testing or from remarkable discrepancies in reading and math." And, "Underachieving gifted students are those for whom a gap exists between achievement test scores and intelligence test scores or between academic grades and intelligence test scores."[4]

McCall provided anecdotal descriptions of elementary age children—though they describe some secondary students I have known as well—of the sort:

> Billy has an IQ of 168, but he isn't that exceptional in class," says Ann Reynolds, his third-grade teacher. "He constantly disrupts the class. Sometimes he won't keep his mouth shut and tries to be the class clown. Other times, when he gets in a rebellious, hostile mood, watch out! He's ready to punch someone. And he can't work in a group unless he gets his own way. "Sarah's not gifted," says her fifth-grade teacher, Bob Masters, "but she's certainly competent. Still, she's performing well below grade level. Most of the time she daydreams, fiddles with books and pencils, talks to classmates, or passes notes—does anything but schoolwork. When I assign classwork, Sarah either dawdles the time away or is the first to be finished, having dashed off almost anything and calling it done. She gives up quickly and resists explanations or help. Once in a while, though, Sarah turns in work that indicates ability. It shows she can achieve, but just won't.[5]

McCall went on to point out that while most attention has been paid to gifted underachievers, young people at various levels of ability perform significantly below their potential. This inclusion of those capable but not necessarily gifted—at least in our, probably limited, perspective of what it means to be gifted—is consistent with the orientation I have adopted in this book. I do not want to limit us to the concerns of the gifted, even if we could agree upon a definition for giftedness. I worry that any definition of giftedness right now would reflect an overly narrow definition of what it means to be gifted or talented. For example, some people are remarkably sensitive to other people. This is a gift that is extremely beneficial in this world but is less acknowledged than other gifts—intellectual in particular—that we typically focus upon. (For some good writing on this subject of the multidimensional nature of intelligence, refer to the books of Howard Gardner.[6])

McCall noted that some underachievers go virtually unnoticed whereas others call such attention to themselves they are hard to miss. Some are shy and some are outgoing to an obnoxious degree. McCall provided more formal definition. An underachiever is a student whose grades are substantially below what might be expected on the basis of IQ, aptitude, or achievement test scores. He points out that boys outnumber girls in this dubious distinction. McCall also listed what he calls "telltale signs": these students do not try, they appear lazy, they seem immature (for example, getting upset if they do not get their way), act up, appear very shy, blame others for their failure, dismiss the whole enterprise as "stupid" or "boring", or lack self-confidence, or are rebellious (lose assignments, etc.)—or, I would add, some combination of the above.[7]

There is a basic definition available (significant discrepancy between capability and accomplishment) that gives us direction, and in using it we can, by and large, agree what students we are talking about. But at the same time it is quite open: How big a gap between capability and achievement does there have to be for it to warrant being called significant? Just what areas do we count as crucial—intelligence? reading scores? aptitude measures?—when determining that a student is not succeeding in his schoolwork? What this means, depending on your purpose, is that you can be very loose or exact in how you define underachievement. If you want to do some quantitative, statistical research, you must be objective and decide, for example, that students qualify as underachieving if they have a score on a particular standardized test of ability or aptitude of some specified number, and also have a grade average in class below some particular level. For my purposes in this book I am comfortable with the definition Barry Goldwater, I think it was, gave to pornography. He said he did not think he could define it, but he knew pornography when he saw it. A clumsy analogy I will admit, but the basic point is made, especially if we agree that underachievement, while it implies unrealized potential, is not reserved to only those students deemed *gifted* as we conventionally define the term.

In fact, I have faith that we are all gifted at doing what we are naturally meant or suited to do. The trick is for human beings to discover what it is in their nature to do. But that speculation aside, I also assume it is usually a good idea to become proficient at doing whatever the school assigns as the academic work for students. I recognize that some of the academic work in school is not much worth doing. Still, my goal here is just to get students to do better in school in ways that the school itself values. As a practical matter I do not think a 16-year-old, though perhaps right in our eyes, can live his life suffering the consequences for his rebellion: low grades, bad recommendations, being "worksheeted" into a stupor, remaining in ignorance, being personally disconfirmed, ignored, or heaped with scorn, and so forth.

WHAT ACCOUNTS FOR UNDERACHIEVEMENT?

In their historical review of work with underachievers the Krauses identified three major "camps" or theories. One group sees underachievement as a result of a weakness in academic skills in areas such as reading, note-taking, mathematics, exam-taking, or in neurologically-based perceptual and motor skills. This is quite a disparate, mixed bag of concerns; do not conclude that all the investigators whom the Krauses clustered in this camp know or identify with one another. Rather, the Krauses looked at a number of individual studies and decided that they all identified academic skill deficits as the prime factor in underachievement. A second group the Krauses identified views underachievement as a result of deficiencies in behavioral self-control skills. Examples include problems with self-monitoring, self-reinforcement, stimulus control, and the ability to schedule time properly. A third group emphasizes what the Krauses called "interfering affective factors": over-dependence, poor motivation, and lack of self-confidence (they term these kinds of things "personality dysfunctions"), and test-taking and other anxieties. The causes grant credence to each of these three perspectives, but also deemed each incomplete in its view of the problem. Instead, the Krauses proposed that underachievement results from the interplay of all three of these areas:

> Academic underachievement can best be viewed, therefore, as a complex interaction between deficits in academic skills, such as reading and mathematics, deficient self-control skills, and interfering affective factors. Since the personality dysfunction and anxiety models described above are similar in that they interfere with academic function, they can be grouped together as affective factors in underachievement. The multimodal theory, therefore, considers an interactive, three-pronged model to describe academic dysfunction. As a complex interaction, underachievement cannot be simply understood or conceptualized as resulting from any one of these three components alone; to attempt such an explanation misses the mark through naivety and oversimplification.[8]

The Krauses then provided an example of how this interplay can occur:

> Students who do poorly in reading develop negative self-concepts and low self-esteem

based on their performance. These personality factors can cause the students to avoid studying and seek distractions or diversions. The self-control problems thus created then act to bring about further decrements in the student's academic performance, and the cyclical pattern continues. The multimodal theory proposed here attempts to understand the relative contributions of each factor on a case-by-case basis, as well as offers suggestions for better assessment, treatment, and research in academic underachievement.[9]

The implications of the Krauses' speculations are profound. First, they challenge us to consider the "big picture," as it were, and identify the multiplicity of factors which may be involved in underachievement, including some we may not normally think of (confidence and self-monitoring capability are two examples). In addition, they challenge us to discern the ways these factors interact with one another, influencing and being influenced, bringing into being and joining other elements, complementing and contradicting each other. At the same time, however, they invite us to find the one or two or three "levers" in all of what is going on that we can push to start the ball rolling or initiate a chain reaction—whatever the (mixed) metaphor—to help a student turn things around and move in a positive direction. It is all very multidimensional and complicated, so where can educators start in taking on the issue? Lastly, given that all these elements are at least potentially involved in underachievement, and that no single professional can deal with all of these factors, the Krauses' writing clearly implies the need for teams—teachers, parents, administrators, counselors, and social service professionals, among them—to work together to confront the complexity of the problem of underachievement.

In the chapters that follow I examine many of the factors that the Krauses identified and address many of the challenges they posed either explicitly or that I infer from their writings. I try to assemble it all in a way that increases our understanding of this issue as well as gives us a way forward to deal with these students who are not progressing academically. I pointed out earlier that all of us who study this or any issue owing a great debt to those who have gone before. The Krauses' work proved to be an enlightening experience for me, and I thank them for it.

Dowdall and Colangelo concurred that underachievement is a complex matter, with many factors contributing to the development of this syndrome. They reviewed the existing literature and cited a number of explanations. Some theorists point out that in more than a few cases underachievement is due to an error of measurement or assessment. Simply, we have misjudged the young person. In fact, he is not as far from doing what is reasonable to expect as we think he is. Other theorists—Woodard fits here—see underachievement as a product of family interaction patterns or attitudes toward education. Still others see it in terms of a choice a student is making, a form of social self-defense in light of strong cultural or peer identification. Other studies center on gender issues, noting that some girls and boys are responding to perceived sex-role expectations (for girls, do not look too smart or beat a boy at tennis; for boys, school is not a man's work like tilling the fields or hunting geese). There are also those who contend that the problem lies with teachers' and counselors' attitudes (though Dowdall and Colangelo did not spell out what attitudes they are referring to here). Some studies suggest that a student's underachievement is due to a lack of skill or creativity necessary to get school tasks accomplished. Furthermore, other theories compare underachievers and achievers and find that underachievers exhibit more instances of social immaturity, emotional problems, antisocial behavior, and low self-concept. Then there is research that indicates that underachievement occurs more frequently in males than females. And last, according to Dowdall and Colangelo, in terms of family circumstances, underachievers are more likely to come from unstable, lower income, single-parent homes, and have fewer social-educational opportunities.[10]

The challenge is to see what generalizations or conclusions can be reached about underachievement amid this diversity of perspectives. One thing is clear, the kinds of answers you get depend on what you look at and what questions you ask. If you focus on families you will likely draw conclusions that make what the family does seem central to understanding and remedying the problem. The same applies with teacher and counselor attitudes, peer group identifications and the rest. Pay attention to what you find, but first look hard at what you decide to explore.

In his article McCall did not explore causes of underachievement beyond the descriptions of underachieving students listed earlier. Considering only material from the Krauses and Dowdall and Colangelo, it is striking how many different factors seem to relate to underachievement. My forecast, however, is that in the future we will probably discover that a smaller number of underlying factors account for the great many we observe now. Also, we will most likely find a few elements or processes that are especially crucial as keys or triggers to turning students around. Nevertheless it is clear to me that no matter how far we take it, underachievement is still going to be about different things for different students. At this point the job is to explore the major factors that appear to be most often involved and understand them better. And then, with individual students, informed with insight regarding what may be the issue, we can find out exactly what the issue is and go from there. Though at the same time, this emphasis on working with individuals should not preclude creating programs and approaches that can be employed with groups of students. Exploring group methods is important because it is very expensive in time and professional resources to work only with individuals. In addition, based on my work with this issue I surmise that if we explore group approaches we will indeed find strategies that work despite differences in students' individual situations. The final result will probably turn out to be some effective combination of group- and individual-based intervention strategies. The chapters ahead explore, at least in a beginning way, all of this.

REMEDIES FOR UNDERACHIEVEMENT

Predictably, the diversity of explanations has led to a diversity of remediation strategies. Among those the Krauses listed are:

- Efforts to improve academic skill deficits. Especially in the area of reading, but also in what are called study skills (note-taking, effective use of study time, etc.). As expected, given their theoretical orientation, the Krauses caution those committed to academic skill improvement that academic skills may not be the root problem for particular individuals. And even for students with academic skill problems, these efforts may not be enough because the students have other problems in addition that need attention. (This point of the Krauses—that the strategy may not be appropriate or enough—applies to the rest of this list, though I will not take the space to reiterate it. Do keep this criticism in mind with each of these, however.)
- Programs geared to deal with personality and attitudinal variables (level of student satisfaction, motivation, self-confidence, self-esteem, dependence, etc.).
- Self-control programs, focusing typically on three components: self-monitoring, self-reinforcement, and stimulus control.
- Anxiety reduction techniques (to reduce test-taking fears, for example).
- Rational problem-solving strategies. John Krause has successfully taught problem-solving to underachievers as part of a program also including academic skill and behavioral self-control training.[11]

The Krauses talk about formal efforts to deal with the problem. Actually, they failed to mention the three most commonly employed approaches in my experience. The first is the "You could do so much better, Johnny" approach. These are the conferences and quick exchanges in which the student is informed that he's not performing up to his potential. Though we persist in employing this tactic, the results are usually not positive. For one thing, we are often unintentionally paying off or reinforcing the student. After all, we are telling him he has ability, and ability is a prime value in schools. Also, we may, without realizing it, be threatening to a student with our "Oh, you can do it" messages. School is hard work and the student worries that just maybe he or she *cannot* do it; or at least not as easily as the teacher imagines. So from the student's point of view, perhaps it is better to stay where he or she is and maintain this high estimate—as the student sees it, it is probably overly high, because you seem to think he or she could achieve so readily—than to take on the challenge and fail, thus revealing that he really is not as bright as his teacher assumes. In this regard I think the best way to conduct these conferences is to acknowledge that to do well in school is tough work and that there will be failures as well as successes along the way; but that you believe in the student, care that he does well, will help any way you can, and encourage him to work hard. The key is to focus on a hope for the future. Do not dwell on the failures and disappointments. These students know they have a problem. What they need is a hope; and the support and encouragement to pursue it.

A second commonly used tactic employed by school people not mentioned in the Krauses material is the "kicking ass" approach, if you will pardon the expression: threats, admonishments, punishments, scare tactics, all of that; and the displays of disappointment, disapproval, disconfirmation, perhaps even resentment (because, after all, these students are causing us to fail as educators). Again, these are not noted for their effectiveness in turning these kids around. Why? Because although it seems to make abundant sense to believe that disapproval and punishment motivates students to try harder, psychological research has not been very supportive of that assumption. True, to some extent you can get students to do something out of fear of the negative consequences that will result if they do not do it. But for the most part, negating students just results in their discouragement, resentment, sense of defeat, self-recrimination, anger, self- pity, and the like—not enthusiastic efforts to improve and turn things around. Being called a loser tends to make one feel like a loser, and then do what losers do, rather than make one want to win and work to win. Moreover, some underachievers actually try to rig negation—not that they are consciously aware that they are doing this—because somewhere in their history they have come to believe that it is their lot in life to be put down. For some underachievers to be unsuccessful in school is a way of confirming what they are already convinced they are: a misfit. Calling these students a name will not, as we intend, propel them toward academic success, but only lead them to do more of the same that got them the "victory" of getting the rebuke that deep down they think they deserve. We must stop looking only at what things mean to us and look as well at what things mean to students. And even more important, if we try something and it does not work, we need to try something else. So often we try punishment and it does not work. So we punish again, figuring I guess that we just did not do it right or do enough of it the first time around.

A third, and this is probably the most prevalent strategy, is to do nothing at all. There is really no absolutely compelling reason to attend to the needs of the majority of underachievers. Most of them do not out-and-out flunk. And although underachievers are well represented among the hard core discipline problems in school, most are not creating any major disruptions. Schools are big places with many problems to resolve, and the presence of a student wasting his potential may well not seem very important.

Dowdall and Colangelo pointed out that interventions, as they call them, fall into two categories: The first category addresses the problems of self-image and feelings of inferiority. These often involve counseling-type sessions, though for some years teachers have been taking on these issues as well.[12] Dowdall and Colangelo concluded that counseling interventions have not been shown to be consistent or effective—at least with gifted underachievers, the particular concern of these authors. The second category they identify centers on altering the classroom environment. Examples of this approach include smaller class size, grouping similar students together (homogeneous grouping, as it is called) and—the authors do not explain this one—greater classroom flexibility. Unfortunately, Dowdall and Colangelo reported these classroom environment change approaches have not worked too well either. They conjectured that while the classroom environment may change, the core of what goes on in the classroom, what is studied, and how teachers teach, quite persistently remains the same. I would also add that the "Krause dictum" applies here too (possibly not appropriate; probably not enough).

When I read about teaching and content (the subjects or areas studied) which persistently remain constant, the information confirms my suspicion that in these areas schools are readily observable time capsules. By that I mean that if you want to know what was going on 10 years ago in classrooms, just go in and observe one today. Teachers and students essentially do the same things in response to the same things, and deal with others in the same ways, year after year. That leads me to conclude—I hope I am wrong—that we will likely be disappointed if we assume that we can help underachievers by bringing about changes in instructional strategies or areas of study. These elements are the most deeply ingrained in the minds and hearts of school professionals and highly resistant to change. Even though we in education think we are doing things differently, often we only adopt a new terminology or add a few new wrinkles. The basic way we conduct business remains fundamentally the same. This implies a strategy of working directly with the student to help him or her learn how to successfully deal with the current teaching and curricular arrangements. Because as a matter of fact what is *is*, and the student might as well learn how to deal with reality. More importantly than that, despite our best efforts at instructional and curricular reform what *is* likely also *will be*. So if the student is going to become happy, it may have to come from what he or she *does* rather than from changes in what happens in his world. Extrapolating from what we have covered so far, one promising approach to working with the underachieving students themselves is to compare them with a profile of achieving students, and then work on those areas where there is the greatest or most significant discrepancy. To adopt this tactic we must be very clear about what achieving students have going for them. Thus this is the importance of the Woodard-type research.

WHERE DO WE GO FROM HERE?

The Krauses list some questions to resolve, either through formal research activities or through what they call "naturalistic observation." One area they consider fruitful for future research is the investigation of the interaction between student aptitudes and instructional methods. There is evidence that students differ in their abilities to profit from various educational techniques. The Krauses also encouraged the study of the characteristics of overachievers:

> What factors cause students with only modest test scores to perform at a superior level in school? With what means are these individuals able to achieve consistently more highly than would be predicted from their test score? Might it be that their actual performance is raised by their strengths in precisely those areas in which underachievers are weak? The multimodal theory proposed here would predict such to be the case. Just as deficits in self-control and interfering affective factors can cause a decrement in actual level of performance among underachievers, good ability to monitor and regulate one's own behavior and the presence of psychological characteristics such as self-confidence, high motivation, and emotional stability may contribute to optimal student performance. The implication of such an hypothesis is that areas in which the greatest discrepancy between over- and underachievers is noted would be the most appropriate for specific intervention and remediation. Research is needed to confirm the accuracy and utility of this hypothesis.[13]

In addition, the Krauses pointed to the family and home environment, specifically at such factors as the value placed on education in the home, parental expectations for academic success, sibling rivalry, and birth order. Moreover, they noted the need to know more about the effect of the death of a parent, divorce, and chronic illness on achievement. In addition, they encourage the creation of more accurate and complete measures of academic achievement, motivation, and study attitudes. The Krauses specifically recommended a longitudinal study to examine the phenomenon of underachievement in students from the time they begin school on through their academic careers and into young adulthood. The study could investigate the age when the pattern of underachievement begins, and such things as the level of cognitive (thinking, processing of information) and psychosocial development (see chapter 4 for treatment of this) at the time of onset. This research could also monitor the school's response to underachievement: How do the school professionals treat underachievers? How do they teach them? What classes, programs, do they offer them? How do they advise them? Another dimension, what is the nature of underachievers' vocational, social, and psychological adjustment after they leave school? In regard to this, I mentioned in chapter 1 the longitudinal study of 1,000 rural, low income children begun in 1969 (I made the point that educational and career attainment was linked to self-confidence). Reading over this study, as useful as it is, I am left with much regret that the kinds of issues that the Krauses listed were not built into the research.

Dowdall and Colangelo urged a comprehensive and long term commitment to dealing with the problem of underachievement. They advise early identification and family involvement as the best way to proceed with this issue. Specifically, they note that interventions must begin in the elementary school years and not, as is the case presently, in later years when the pattern of underachievement is already established.

McCall did not provide specific recommendations, but he did underscore the importance of concern for this issue, quoting a parent who affirms: "I know budgets are tight and teachers are overburdened and dumped on and everything, but this is not a frill—this is basic education for the capable."[14]

WHAT IT ALL MEANS

First, I hope the discussions in this chapter have provided you with some useful information. Even more important, I hope it has created a context and set an agenda for a closer look at the variety of factors that may be involved in contributing to, or inhibiting, a student's commitment and ability to achieve. Certainly this chapter underscores that underachievement, and its other side, achievement, are multidimensional phenomena and that we need to take a broad, inclusive look at the many factors that may be involved with any particular student. The Krauses in particular offered many fine suggestions for possible areas of study. I am especially taken with their idea of developing a profile of overachievers (those who achieve more than we might reasonably expect) as a means of better understanding and working with underachievers. Included in our explorations too, though, should be areas that the writers reviewed in this chapter did not consider as well as the ones they did review. For example, I noticed that the Krauses and Dowdall and Colangelo did not have much to say about teaching and curricular approaches that have been tried with underachieving students. And not much was said about developmental circumstance (physical, mental, psychosocial) and its effect on achievement.

The next chapter sets out the psychological frame of reference that is foundational to the way I perceive and work with this issue of promoting increased levels of academic achievement. Following that, the rest of the book analyzes many of the topics that surfaced in this chapter, along with, as I indicated, some that did not. Some things you can do: This chapter has provided some ideas and areas to study. What you probably need is some direct experience with underachieving students. Why not pick out two or three underachieving students and observe them in classes? See what you can learn about them from their teachers or school records. Spend some time talking to them. Try to get them to tell you what school is like from their side, what they are trying to get done, and how they assess their own situation. As I pointed out in the first chapter, the best thing for you is to engage in study concurrently on a number of levels. There is this book. There is introspection into yourself, when and how you succeed and fall below your potential. And there is direct observation and analysis of underachieving students in their school environments. Perhaps you can also set up a research study of your own. The important thing is to move from just reading a book to reaching out to inform and empower yourself in this area of concern.

3 A Perspective on Achievement

In this chapter I will outline my perspective on how students function and change as human beings. This is important to do because ultimately that is what we are talking about when we discuss improving school achievement from the adolescent's perspective: helping a human being change how he or she lives, in school in this case. In order to support that human being in becoming different, a more successful student, we have to be insightful about who that individual is, what comprises that person, and how he or she gets things done (or fails to). Obviously, to speak to all of that is a tall order, a book in itself. What I can do here, however, is say enough so that you will understand the fundamental—I guess the best word for it is psychological—frame of reference I bring to the issue of how to promote positive school-going thinking and behavior among underachieving students.

ORGANIZATION OF THE CHAPTER

The first part analyzes the concepts educators do and potentially could use to refer to individual students. When we attend to a particular student, to just what aspects or elements of that young person are we considering? Also, there is so much talk in education about self: self-esteem, self-concept, self-awareness. I want to make clear how I see all of that.

The second section deals with the theoretical formulations of psychologist Roberto Assagioli. His ideas have strongly influenced my view of how human beings tick, so to speak; more so than other theorists such as B. F. Skinner, David Ausubel, or Jean Piaget who are more familiar to educators. However, do not read this as saying that I do not value the work of Piaget and the others. Indeed I do incorporate their ideas into my own perspective. It is just that you may not have heard of Assagioli and I want to introduce you to his work. Also, without an understanding of the ideas that I have drawn from Assagioli and his followers, you cannot fully comprehend the way I approach the educational issues we are confronting in this book.

The third section explores concepts and practices I have derived from the field of sport psychology. Athletes have to achieve, and coaches help them achieve. While there is not an exact parallel between the athletic and classroom contexts, I find enough similarity to warrant looking at what sport people do and to see what we can learn from them. Also in this section I make the point that we need to look for insights in areas outside the field of education. The challenge is to be able to spot ideas and practices in these other contexts that might help us in the classroom, and then creatively adapt them to serve our purposes and fit our circumstances.

The fourth section is a summary of the ideas of counseling psychologist Linda Nielson on promoting self-management skills among students. One of the problems underachievers often have is an inability to organize and control their lives enough to get things accomplished. Nielson's work suggests ways to help students who confront this problem deal with it effectively.

The fifth section explores achievement itself. What accounts for achievement? What do people who achieve do? What do they think? What makes it all work for them? I focus on the work of Eric Johnson, who in turn has been greatly influenced by the research and theories of social psychologist David McClelland. Several times thus far I have alluded to the need to look at ''success cases'' to understand just what defines an achiever. This section begins to provide an answer to that challenge.

The last section reviews my ideas on motivation. What can a teacher or other educator do to maximize the chance that a student will be committed to getting on with the work of doing better in school? I tell you how I personally answer that question.

What I want you to do is put all of the material in the six sections together and see if you can discern an integrated, overall perspective or frame of reference on this issue of promoting academic achievement. Do not just leave it with six distinct sections. In addition, add what you already know to all this. You probably have taken educational psychology courses or have read or experienced things that fit into this discussion. Insert your own ideas as you go along.

ELEMENTS OF THE INDIVIDUAL
AND CONCEPTS OF SELF

This book makes much of focusing directly on the student in contrast or school.

But if we are going to do that we need to be clear about just what we are focusing upon. When we talk about a student, to precisely what aspects or characteristics are we referring? To what dimensions of that individual are we not referring? When we use the term *self*, what do we mean? No matter how new you may be to the field of education, or how remotely connected to it, you cannot have missed all the talk about self. There is self-concept this and self-esteem that. It is a pervasive concern among school people. As well, as we all know, adolescence is a time for attention to self. So it is extremely important that we clarify just what we mean by this term. Is self the same in every context; or do we mean different things at different times when we use the concept? And when a student says "I must get better in school," literally—apart from the word "I"—to what is he referring? If *I* must change, what exactly must be different? And if *I* must improve myself, who or what is the entity that is improving the rest of me? We use words like "I" and "me" and "my" all the time without stopping to figure out just exactly what those terms mean. For example, when you say "I am happy," does that mean your foot is in on the happiness? Is your eye happy? Just your brain? All of your brain? Who exactly is the "I," or what is it, that is happy? And when you talk about self-esteem, does that mean the same thing as self-concept? The same thing as self- acceptance? If not, how are these ideas different? We are not very precise about the way we think about individual students and employ all the self-related terms. And yet the claim is made all the time in education that, for example, self-esteem (or self-value, or self-awareness, or self-concept, the terms vary) is a key factor in academic success and failure. Certainly if we are going to focus on the student himself we are going to be drawn to employ such concepts; and it is crucial that we do, they are important. I outline here how I analyze and define terms that refer to the student himself. Think critically about what I say. Correct me where I need it. Extend my thinking where you can.

Who Are You?

Assume someone asks you to talk about yourself or to assess yourself. When you answer, just what are you referring to when you talk about you? If you think about it, it could be any number of things. You might talk about what you do for work, or your marriage or relationships, or your religious affiliations. In all of these instances you are talking about your place in the world or, the social science term, your *roles* in life. Also, you might list your activities: what you are creating, the projects you are taking on these days or what you have done in the past. That gets you into your *plans* and *actions* and *creations*. Or, another possibility, you might refer to your *characteristics* or *qualities* as an individual or your *personality*—whether you are outgoing or retiring, funny, reliable, a mess-up, and so forth. Another alternative, you may relay your *feelings*—that you are mad, glad, sad, or afraid. You might get into the *physical dimensions* of you, how you look (your big nose, your blue eyes), the pain in your foot, or your new haircut. You might discuss your *abilities* (or lack of them); how you write well, that you are good at volleyball, or that you cannot do math. You might discuss *thoughts* you have or had: your ideas about politics, marriage, art, school, your memories, or perhaps whatever is in your mind at this moment. Your thoughts include your *assessments*, *rankings*, *opinions*, and *conclusions* on all the rest of you: "My ears are too big." "I should be more assertive." "That was a good job I did fixing the carburetor on the car."

Another aspect of you is your *impulses* or *desires*. As people we feel ourselves being pushed toward the satisfaction of goals that arise from within us. Examples certainly include the basic desires for sex and food, and also, though open to debate, such things as power, status, social exchange, and territorial control.

According to many, yet another dimension of you, though very tough to be articulate about, is that part of you that is "beneath the surface" of your conscious thoughts, feelings, and sensations. We call this "inner world" the *subconscious* or *preconscious* (the latter term indicating more that it is potentially available to conscious awareness). It is made up, according to the theory, of our most basic drives and repressed memories and events which can be, without our realizing it, the root cause of much that we want, think, and do in our lives. This submerged part of us shows itself in our dreams and our fantasies, and reveals itself, though in a transformed way, in our conscious thoughts, wants, and actions. Though it tends to remain hidden from our awareness, the content of this inner world of the subconscious can be raised, at least in part, to our explicit understanding. That is what psychoanalysis is about in large part. ("Inner world" makes it sound like an it, a thing that exists some place inside us, but where? Perhaps the term *subconscious* is a name for a process, not a thing. But if it is a process, where is it going on, and among what?)

In any case, this submerged dimension of our being can manifest itself in our mind and behavior; often indirectly in what are called "sublimations" and "projections" and other such phenomena described by psychologists of a Freudian nature. Jungians (followers of psychologist Carl Jung) go so far as to speak of a "collective unconscious" that we share with others of the human species, including those who lived long ago. Before you dismiss that idea, consider that we are a biological organism with a genetic inheritance passed down through millions of years of evolution. It could be that we inherit more than height, eye color, sex drive, and the rest of the things we usually can agree are passed on from our forebears. In addition, perhaps we inherit memories and images from hundreds or thousands or even millions of years ago that persist beyond the grasp of our immediate comprehension, and it could be they make up an important part of who we are.

Frankly, I am most unsure of what is going on "down there," "up there," "in there"; wherever it is, or if it even makes sense to talk about it as if it were anywhere in particular. If I had to vote, however, I would vote yes to the idea that there are things that I do not know about pushing me to do what I do and affecting what I think and feel and want. I would also vote yes to the idea that a lot of what students do in school can be explained by factors not readily available to their conscious minds. In any case, we have a category to use: the subconscious.

In addition to all the rest of the ways of referring to yourself, you are also a *physical, biological* entity. You are, I am, an animal with a specific genetic inheritance and representative of a particular point in the evolutionary process. We are comprised of cells. We are a biochemical organism, with a particular brain chemistry, with hormones, organs, and predilections that stem from our inheritance as animals. And like every other animal, we die. Simply, we are a physical entity. Some would say that is all we are, with the rest—thoughts, feelings, desires, and so forth—a kind of fiction, just a lot of names for things; but I do not find that a useful way to view the human being. In any case, one way you can talk about yourself is to speak literally about your brain, about synapses and neuroreceptors and the rest. Consequently, one way to look at underachievement is to take into account physical and biological factors: disease one example, perceptual difficulties another.

Do you see all the possibilities? There is yet one more, and it is an important one. Sometimes when we talk about "me" or "I" we are not referring to any of the things listed in the previous paragraphs. We are not getting at activities, thoughts, roles, or emotions, but at something more basic: the fundamental core of our being, our sense of aliveness, me, I, at this moment. We are referring to our *conscious self*. Let me try to explain what I mean by the conscious self. Right now, look at something: a lamp, a tree, or a painting, anything. Do not think about or judge whatever it is you have chosen to consider. Just look at it. Next, break from attending to whatever it is and gently ask yourself, "Who is looking?" Refer back to yourself and connect with that part of you that is doing the looking. Do not refer to your thoughts or feelings, or to your eyes themselves—they were not doing the looking. It is what you might call a "buzz of aliveness"—*you*. It is the you that has always existed. It is the same you who was in the fifth grade. Remember when you were in the fifth grade? Close your eyes and in your imagination, from inside you as you were then, look around the room. See the desk? See the teacher and the blackboard and the other kids? Look down at your own hands. . . . Now who was looking? It is the same person who is looking now, right? Certainly everything about you is different from what it was in the fifth grade. Your clothes are different and your thoughts are different and you are not doing the same things. Science tells us—I think this is so, anyway—that all of your cells are different. So not only were you small then and bigger now, the physical "stuff" of you is not the same as it was then. But nevertheless it is the same you now and then. Try it some more: Remember the high school football game? Put yourself there. Who was there experiencing the game? *You* were. The same person who was in the fifth grade and is alive right now. Do you see what I mean? Just for a moment be with what I am calling the "conscious self." Be with *you*.

The conscious self is so obvious. All of us live with it literally every moment of our lives. But at the same time it is very elusive because it exists within the jumble of thoughts, feelings, bodily sensations, and perceptions of external phenomena that are also present at all times. As I see it, this element of me, what I am calling the "conscious self," is the central aspect of my being. When the conscious self dies, as far as I am concerned I die. I might lose a leg, change my work, eliminate some idea I have, forget something, or turn from elated to sad, but *I* have not died. If that constant goes, if the conscious self goes, if the Bobby and then Bob and then Robert who was 5- and 25-years-old and who exists this moment goes, then *I* go.

I hope the discussion so far has given us some categories to work with. Of course this leaves all kinds of questions unanswered. Even if we do have words for all these things, do they exist as more than just words, and if they do exist what are they? For example, *is* there such a thing as a subconscious? And, apart from the word, what *is* a thought? A sentence we say to ourselves? A picture? A physical sensation? Are these concepts actually separate, or are they duplicative and/or overlapping in some way? How do they relate to one another? Can you have a feeling without a thought? How *does* genetics affect who I am? Let us leave it with this: self, myself, I, individual, person, those kinds of terms, as far as I am concerned refer to any or all of these dimensions of a human being that I have mentioned in these last pages. Self-analysis, then, is the process of figuring out how any or all of these dimensions operate and what they mean. This suggests that if someone is referring to a student or the student is referring to himself, we need to discern exactly what is most salient in the discussion. Are school professionals talking about a student's personality? About appearance? Roles? Strengths and weaknesses? Accomplishments? When students are self-referring, what aspects of themselves do they most identify with who they are? Their mind? Their body? Opinions? Relationships? What meaning or significance do teachers or students give to what they are discussing (important, unimportant, good, bad, related to something else)? How do they put things together? What conclusions do they reach? For example: "His personality gets him in trouble with teachers." "I'm not too smart, so I don't get anything done in school." Notice these things as you go along in your day-to-day life. Notice how you deal with yourself in these regards.

Concepts of Self

Using all that has been said as a foundation, I will some terms that are used extensively throughout education and central to the concerns in this book. I am not contending, incidentally, that others see these concepts as I do. I am contending, though, that the definitions I will outline make sense and are the most useful way to distinguish among ideas that now tend to get mushed together inappropriately and dysfunctionally in education.

Self-Concept

Self-concept is a *conclusion* one draws about oneself that is derived from observations of the various elements of one's being. We all take in the "facts" (in quotes because we may or may not be objective in our perceptions) about our physical appearance, roles, personality, accomplishments, and so forth. From these "facts" we derive generalizations that summarize our views and perceptions. One's self-concept, then, is a collection of thoughts and associated feelings and images that answer the question, "What am I like?" Of course in deciding on a self-concept—and to me it is ultimately a decision, a conclusion someone reaches about himself—nobody equally weighs all the factors that could possibly be taken into account. In every case, some elements are more influential or important than others in determining one's final conclusion. My sport prowess, for example, may overweigh my intellectual skill or personality (style or way of acting), while in someone else it might be the reverse. There is also the idea of a good or bad self-concept. As I see it, one has a good or bad self-concept depending on (this is a judgment call) the positive or negative nature of the qualities one attributes to himself. If I think I am dumb, clumsy, and socially inept, it is probably reasonable to say I have a bad, or negative, self-concept. This is especially the case if it can be seen or inferred that this view of myself is, or likely will be, in the way of my happiness or success.

A last point, self-concept can be broadly or narrowly defined. I can, on the one hand, talk about my overall self-concept, the package of generalizations I derive from my perception of "all of me." On the other hand, I can talk about my self-concept in a narrow way: my self-concept as a student, as a member of my family, as a citizen or musician, and so on. Looking at it this way, I have self-concepts plural, not a single self-concept. It is important to remember that we have these, call them, sub-self-concepts. A student, for example, may have a negative self-concept ("dodo bird") in math class and a positive self-concept ("loyal parishioner") as a member of his church. At the same time, though, since human beings are "all of a piece," one sub-self-concept affects others to a lesser or greater degree (if I have a poor self-concept as a son, it might affect my self-concept as a student), and all together these ideas affect and go into determining one's overall self-concept.

Self-Esteem

Self-esteem has to do with the *regard* that one assigns to the attributes that comprise the self-concept. Self-esteem has to do with prizing oneself, and valuing (in the sense of worthiness) oneself. Self-esteem can be high or low: one can have a high or low opinion of himself. *High* and *low* self-esteem relates closely to good and bad self-concept. A bad self-concept means that I see myself as a "low life good-for-nothing." Low self-esteem means that I have little regard for the low life that I am. Following this, I could have a bad self-concept ("I am ugly as sin") and it could get in the way of a full life (I hide out with the television set instead of going out). But my self-esteem might still be OK if I maintain a high opinion of myself. It just might be that I think my lot in life is to watch TV. This is a negative self-concept with high self-esteem.

I am still trying to think this through. I am clear that my self-concept(s) has to do with the attributes I ascribe to myself. And that self-esteem has to do with the regard I have for myself, whether I like or dislike who I am, and my sense of worthiness. It seems clear that self-concept and self-esteem can be primarily derived from an acceptance of how others see me rather than from my own independent assessments. I am perplexed by the differentiations between good and bad self-concept and high and low self-esteem. I think I have these concepts straight, though. What do you think? How do you define self-concept and self-esteem? Also, where do perceptions of personal effectiveness fit into this? Is a high or low sense of efficacy as an individual part of self-concept? An aspect of self-esteem? Both?

Self-Awareness

Self-awareness refers to one's insight into the various dimensions of self. It has to do with being sensitive to one's thoughts, feelings, roles, actions, values, physical state, and so forth; including what I am calling the "conscious self." Self-awareness involves knowing and understanding one's self. Self-awareness is not an all-or-nothing, I am aware/I am not aware, phenomenon. Instead, self-awareness exists as a continuum: On one end, I have the most rudimentary or inaccurate notion of who I am. On the other end, I really know myself. And of course I can be at some point between those two opposites. It is a matter of judgment whether I deserve to be spoken of as having high or low self-awareness. I suppose there are ways to make these judgements quite objective. By that I mean self-awareness could be defined in terms of a number of clearly distinct categories or some other system lending itself to quantification, thereby allowing for a method of determining somebody's level of self-awareness in a way that we can agree makes sense and gets precise and consistent results. For my purposes, however, I am comfortable with fallible human beings who just observe others and themselves and decide, yes, this person (or I) has a high (fairly high, low) level of self-awareness, and then provide justification for that determination to others who are able to respond critically. However, I tend to be quite easy on these matters. Researchers doing quantitative, statistical studies need to be more precise. How a term is defined depends on the method of procedure.

Critical Self-Awareness

When the word *critical* is added to self-awareness, it means *self-awareness* as defined above and three other things in addition: First, not only does the person have insight into himself, he also has insight into his world external to himself. By this I mean the people, events, and situations in which he is living at this moment. By using the term *his* world rather than *the* world I am emphasizing a concern for those things outside this particular individual that directly connect to him. (Read him *and her* into all these examples.) The individual is the referent in this: The focus is on the thing that he interacts with, and not on all that is going on in the world as the evening news defines it. (On this point, much of what is called the news, when I reflect on it, is interesting and provocative; but only in the remotest way does it relate to anything that touches my life or anything that I can do something about. The evening news is becoming more and more an experience in alienation. It is just something else to watch—like the academy awards—rather than do.) By *his* world I mean such things as his family, school, work context, peers, cultural and social (including political and economic) circumstance where it can be demonstrated to have a significant impact on him, love relationships, religious involvements, and the like; *his* world. Another way to put it, world in this sense, and I will use the term a great deal, refers to those aspects of reality outside the individual that provide the context within which he lives his life. Think about *your* world for a few moments. What comprises your world?

The second added element over simple self-awareness allows the critically aware individual to clearly understand (do not ask me to define exactly what I mean by clearly, it is another judgment) both what is "out there"—his world—and "in here"—inside himself—and gives him insight into how these two worlds *interrelate*. The critically aware individual is "on to" how the external environment influences him, as well as how his existence and activities have an impact on this outer context. Each of us has a reciprocal relationship with our world; we shape it, and it shapes us. To be critically aware, therefore, is to know how that process of exchange operates in our lives.

The third added element is the factor of *time*. From conception to the present, you and I have been in a situation characterized by the interaction of the inner and outer realities I have just described. Critical awareness involves having a clear understanding of how that interrelationship functions. It involves having insight into our own history. And that means not only knowing *what* happened, but also the *meaning* or *significance* of what happened. In other words, we know the difference the events in our lives have made to us. Even more, critical awareness involves the ability to *project into the future*. If I am this way now, and if my world is as it is now, critical awareness is being able to say where things are likely to go contingent on the particular goals and actions I can choose to adopt.

What critical awareness comes down to is an understanding of one's life from a broad perspective, considering one's past, present, and future. If you remember or read about the 1960s, this notion of critical self-awareness, although certainly different, is not antithetical to "living in the now," as we used to talk about it. The idea of living in the now was to live in the moment. This did lead to some fresh perceptions, new experiences, and a sense of greater freedom from social convention. But it also resulted in people in the 1970s and 1980s rather unhappily "hanging out," smoking a joint, and listening to Grateful Dead records. There *is* life after high school (or college, or 30 or 50; or 84 for that matter), and the critically aware person appreciates this reality. One can experience the present, now, fully, and at the same time realize that life is a process and that tomorrow and next year and the next decade will indeed arrive, and that what happens now affects how it will be later.

Self-Consciousness

Self-consciousness can have one of two meanings as I use the term. I guess you will have to decide from the context which meaning to use. First, there is self-consciousness as a kind of awakeness. This means being sensitive to what is going on with you at the moment; the whirl and interplay of thoughts, feelings, felt sensations, perceptions, and what I termed earlier the *conscious self.* I might say "He is self-conscious right now" to get at a student's attentiveness to what is going on with him or her at the present moment. Another, and narrower, use of self-consciousness—though still a vitally important usage—refers to living with a connection to that fundamental, ongoing, experience of aliveness. To be self-conscious is the experience of *I am.* It is important to emphasize the word *experience* in this last sentence. Self-consciousness is more than an understanding that this core of me exists, this core that has always been and that is right now . . . and now . . . and now. Self-consciousness is *living* from this buzz of aliveness. This is the part of me that can witness all that is in my inner and outer worlds. And it is the part of me that chooses, right now, to uncross my legs as they were getting a bit sore. It is the part of me that wills that I finish writing the pages I set out to write today rather than walk by the lake near where I live on this sunny April day. (Later on I use the term *personal self* to underscore the close connection between the willing and awareness dimensions of consciousness.) It is *me.* Right now, again connect with the you who is reading these pages. If you did that, you were for that moment self-conscious. And if it is characteristic of you to connect with that part of you, your conscious self, then it is fair as I see it to call you a self-conscious person.

A last point, note that for me *self-consciousness* is a positive thing and contrasts with the use of the term to mean somebody falling all over himself. As you might expect, I am going to contend that self-consciousness among students, in both meanings of the term as just described is a positive step for them toward greater academic achievement.

Self-Acceptance

Self-acceptance is difficult to define. As it is typically used, it refers to viewing oneself favorably (which I would call "self-esteem," "self-value," or "self-regard") or to believing in oneself (which I would call self-confidence, or just confidence). I think of self-acceptance more in terms of an acknowledgement that, yes, this is as it is and I am as I am and I can accept that. Indeed I may decide that it would be better if I changed how I am. And I may not give high approval to all that I am. But at the same time I am gentle with myself. I refrain from self-condemnation. I agree—accept—that things are as they are with me. I do not fight off or deny the reality of who I am or waste time in self-denigration. I am always valuable, always worthy of my own kindest and most supportive treatment. I grant myself that, no matter what I have done or have not done, even if I do not approve of my actions, I accept me. I accept the way it is. I simply assess the realities and possibilities, make whatever judgments and choices are appropriate, and get on with life, changing what needs to be changed and doing what needs to be done. Self-acceptance involves all of these things.

Clearly, one thing I am saying with all this is that if we are going to focus on students with the goal of empowering them, let us be clear on just what we are focusing. This is important because my reading of education demonstrates that too often we are not precise enough concerning what it is we care about. We talk about self-esteem and self-concept, self this and self that, and talk about a student—which part(s)?—and it all remains quite fuzzy and diffuse much of the time. I have put forth some concepts that, as I see it, "define the territory," and give us more precise ways to center our attention on what is important. Think critically about these concepts. Do they make sense? Are they helpful distinctions? What is off about them? What is incomplete? Do they conform to the way these terms are used in other materials you have studied? Can you improve upon them?

Defining things this way allows us to raise some important educational questions: In all of this going on with the student, where should we put our energies? With academic skills? Thinking? Personality? Self-awareness? Self-esteem? Self-esteem is one I hear very often with regard to the kids who are not succeeding academically, as in "These kids have low self-esteem, that's their problem." My answer is to focus on self-consciousness, critical self-awareness, and academic skill-building as crucial aids in helping a student become more powerful and productive in school. In any case, I hope I have succeeded in providing a useful definition of the individual student and the self. I use these terms throughout the book, including in this next section on the ideas of Roberto Assagioli.

THE THEORIES OF ROBERTO ASSAGIOLI

I have studied educational psychology, and psychology in general, quite intensely, and no theorist has been as informative as Roberto Assagioli. More than any other theory, Assagioli's perspective on the way human beings develop and change is foundational to the way I approach improving the manner in which underachieving students go to school. I do not attempt to provide a summary of Assagioli's work here. However, I do outline some of his ideas that particularly relate to the issues of concern in this book and my response to these ideas. This discussion draws upon both Assagioli's and his follower's writings, my workshop experiences with strategies derived from those writings, discussions with those who have studied and employed his approaches, and my own use of these ideas in school settings. I invite you to continue on your own from the base I provide here to study Assagioli's orientation. Reference notes in the back of the book should be helpful in this regard.

Assagioli's work establishes that things do not have to be new to be good. Assagioli, an Italian psychiatrist, a colleague of Jung and Freud, died over a decade ago after a long and distinguished career. Drawing inspiration from a number of sources, including both Eastern and Western psychologies and philosophies, he developed a comprehensive psychology known as *psychosynthesis*. *Psychosynthesis* emphasizes the tendency of individuals when healthy and unimpeded to move naturally toward *harmony*—other terms are integration and synthesis—within themselves, and with their world. Assagioli's writings have been translated from the Italian. Two of his books I recommend are *Psychosynthesis* and *The Act of Will*.[1] In places he is difficult to understand, and I suspect the translations are a bit rough. You may find these books by his followers easier going or good supplements to Assagioli's writings: *The Unfolding Self* by Molly Brown and *What We May Be* by Piero Ferrucci.[2] In addition, check periodical literature under Assagioli's name or under *psychosynthesis*. Study of his work may provide you with an alternative or complement to the humanistic, behavioral, and/or cognitive psychological perspective(s) to which you now may ascribe.

I use Assagioli's book *The Act of Will* as the primary organizer for what I have to say in the following pages, with less frequent references to the other sources. See if the next pages create a coherent and useful way to look at less-than-productive students; and whether a *work agenda*, to use that term, to guide efforts with these students arises from this discussion, along with some direction for ways forward to implement this agenda.

Early on in *The Act of Will* Assagioli pointed out that in order to live effectively one needs to simplify one's "outer life."[3] This point reminds me that it is a particularly pressing issue for adolescents to resolve the question of what their priorities in life should be. What is worth doing? What will make me happy? What is appropriate for me to do? Where am I needed? What can I do well? Where do I fit? If a school is to be responsive to developmental needs of adolescents—and I think it should be—it must provide a context which supports the successful resolution of the fundamental issues of priority and direction adolescents face. Of course, that still leaves the question of *how* a school can set up a curriculum and a way of life in the school that gets that accomplished. In the next pages and chapters I intend to take up the challenge of speaking to that question.

Assagioli's emphasis on a simple outer life recalls the time I spent reading a number of biographies of successful individuals. Beyond the pleasure of reading about these people, I wanted to see if I could find similarities in the lives of people who were all successful but in very different fields. The list included Bob Dylan, the anthropologist Margaret Mead, Babe Ruth, and Supreme Court Justice William Douglas. I found some fascinating similarities among what would seem on the face of it a most disparate group. In relation to this discussion, it occurred to me how simple their lives were. They did a very few things well, had a few friends and people they loved, and, for the most part followed a simple routine. This simplicity is in such marked contrast with the here-there-and-everywhere life of the secondary school student: five or six classes differing greatly from each other in content and probably in pace, expectations, and ways of doing business; athletics or clubs; perhaps a job; and a number of relationships with family and peers. Practically, there may be little that can be done about this life of bits-and-pieces for young people. But I do worry that the way we organize schools unintentionally promotes (among teachers, too, as well as students) a kind of dilettantism, people who touch down lightly on this and that. Contrast that to Picasso painting his pictures or Hemingway writing his books (two more biographies that I reviewed). In my own mind I have come to call this simplicity the "Woody Allen phenomenon" (another biography). The biography of Allen I read painted a picture of Woody writing all day (when he is not filming), having dinner with Mia and his friend Tony Roberts, and once a week playing the clarinet with a band. Simple.

The conclusion I reach is that it is not just that these successful individuals have chosen to live this way; it is *natural* to the human being to live simply. I think we were meant to get up early, till the fields or throw a spear into something, tend to the children, have dinner with the family, sing a few songs, and go to bed early. Yet here is "modern" man—including modern student—with schedules, multiplicity, and disparateness. We can handle it, the human being is a flexible creature. But there is a cost: anxiety, frustration, a growing sense of incompleteness, alienation, and the list goes on. One thing underachieving students may be responding to, not that they necessarily are articulate about it, is living in a situation that is quite literally anti-human. For that matter, teachers live this way too.

I am not sitting here with any profound solutions other than to make a point, one I elaborate on some later, and say that we ought to see if we can find ways to simplify schools. It may mean blocks of time instead of 50-minute hours, the integration of subjects, the chance to spend a few weeks on just one or two things instead of the usual five or six at a time. For the most part, I am just raising an issue for us to think about: we carve people up into little pieces. And it starts early. In elementary school, for example, art may be Thursdays only for 45 minutes. What if somebody told me I had to write this book trying to pick it up where I left off after a week's absence, and then only allotted me 45 minutes to do it! For so many years (including college), we are carved up into so many pieces, some of which we are not good at or do not care about, and then we are expected to find or define a core to our lives that makes sense. Some major contradictions are built into this process. This is not to say, however, that I am in favor of students specializing in just one or two things in high school. It is good at this age for students to explore a number of areas. But we need to understand that if we, as educators, do not help students see the meaning of all that, and explain how it all goes together, we may have to deal with student disaffection, frustration, and the rest—the problems we confront in underachievers. And even more than helping students make some coherent sense of their work, we should help them begin to define the core of their lives: what to do and with whom to do it in order to serve what purposes.

Assagioli also emphasized the development of what he calls the individual's "inner powers."[4] His writings remind me of how the school curriculum is almost exclusively "outer" focused. School is predominantly about what happened there and then and how things are connected. It is about Abraham Lincoln, math theorems, and chemistry. It is about everybody and everything but the student. The student gets to learn it and respond to it, whatever it is, but it is about it, the subject, and not him. What is not studied much at all is *his* world as I defined it earlier. And certainly little is done with what might be called the "inner" curriculum—how we function as human beings, how our minds work, how we get things done, what is happening inside us. For those of you who remember it, I am not talking here about values clarification. I am not referring to just what "I believe" or "I value," or about interpersonal relationships, though I am not denigrating those concerns either. Rather, what I mean here is a focus on understanding and developing those elements I referred to as comprising the individual and self. It is particularly important for us to think about what Assagioli called "inner powers" with these less successful students. We may well need to set up more appropriate curricula for these kids, teach better, organize the school better, and create a more encouraging school climate—all the school context factors. But in addition, these students need to somehow become more powerful. They must develop their inner powers in order to get their schoolwork done more effectively. It has always been our job as educators to motivate these students. But this leaves the students reactive. We have to try to redefine school to be ultimately *their* job and see how that changes the approaches we adopt and the way students view their own involvement.

Next, I investigate what Assagioli focused upon when he dealt with the development of inner powers. Some areas that he explored may be potentially useful as a means of improving levels of academic achievement among students. The inner power that is the central concern of Assagioli is the *will*. This is the power to be volitional and to stay with something through to the end—often a failing among students who do not achieve academically. Many times the problem is not so much that the students do not mean well. They set out to do the assignment. They are not unmotivated or negative. They have some positive goals and they have the academic skills well enough in hand. They embark on the road to academic success. The problem is they just are not willful enough to hang in there and see things through. They start up the road; but they wind up sitting on the curb. Assagioli put it this way:

> Fundamental among these inner powers, and the one to which priority should be given, is the tremendous, unrealized potency of man's own *will*. Its training and use constitute the foundation of all endeavors. There are two reasons for this: the first is the will's central position in man's personality and its intimate connection with the core of his being—his very self. The second lies in the will's function in deciding what is to be done, in applying all the necessary means for its realization and in persisting in the task in the face of all obstacles and difficulties.[5]

Notice first of all that he is pointing toward something we do not normally attend to in any systematic way in schools—the will; that is, beyond admonishments to students to "get to it." How little we deal with exactly what the will is—or if it exists. We do not analyze how the will functions, how it develops, or why it is strong or weak. Yet we know in our own lives that our problems are not so much from being confused about what to do or being ill-intended. No, more frequently our problem is that we know what we need to do—we just do not do it. We have a problem of will. We only refer to it in passing in schools, and yet Assagioli is saying that it is the foundation of all human endeavors. It is at the core of what it is to be human. To be human is to have the capacity to be willful. The problem with some of these underachieving students is that they are not willful enough. Although in saying that, I am not absolving the school or teachers of responsibility. It is but to recognize that, at times, the students themselves are part of the problem. As educators, we have taken on the blame when things do not go right. That is laudable of us, but it can work against what we want to accomplish if it results in a preoccupation with improving ourselves and precludes our ability to attend to some other areas—like a student's inner powers—that need some work.

In this last quote Assagioli spoke of "unrealized potency" and its training. He said that the will can be developed. This opens up the possibility—and I realize this is all very speculative—of programs to educate the will. Perhaps we and our students can become more powerful in maintaining our efforts to realize our goals. The first step on the road to doing that is to have a concept to organize our thinking. We have one: will. Think for a moment about yourself: How willful are you? When are you resolute and accomplish what you set out to do? What happens when you do not? Why is it that sometimes you take responsibility for getting the job done and do it, and other times have every good intention but quit along the way? It is important to look at all these questions because I think whatever is going on with you in this regard is also going on with students. I can think of so many students who start out in September to turn over a new leaf: get good grades, stay out of trouble, all that. And they mean it. They clearly know the payoffs for attaining school success. And within reason they know how to do it. But nevertheless, within 2 weeks or a month they are right back into their pattern of failure. Ask them what went on to cause them to fall back into their academic rut and they will, after some moments of silence, talk about it for a while, and then finally say something like, "I just don't know." Or they blame themselves, their teachers, or parents, or somebody. But do they understand it? Do they know how to be more willful? No. They probably say the kinds of things we all say when we go off our diet: "This time I've learned my lesson. I'll *really* work hard and get it done"; only to fail in exactly the same way again. Or worse as I see it, they label themselves a failure or declare the task impossible and give up.

I say a few things about willfulness here, and I do recommend *The Act of Will* as a starting point. I know I cannot take this very far, but it is an area that intrigues me. I work at times with adults who have personal difficulties. It fascinates me how they somehow suddenly, after months and years of failure, invoke their will and do what they need to get done in their lives to resolve the issues they confront. One of the reasons that I wanted to study Assagioli is because he gives the will a central place in his theoretical analyses of the human psyche and the process of change.

Although Assagioli underscored the crucial nature of will to human beings, he also notes resistance to this concept due to misunderstandings about its function and nature:

> The Victorian conception of the will still prevails, a conception of something stern and forbidding, which condemns and represses most of the other aspects of human nature. But such a misconception might be called a caricature of the will. The true function of the will is not to act against the personality drives to *force* the accomplishment of one's purposes. The will has a *directive* and *regulatory* function; it balances and constructively utilizes all the other activities and energies of the human being without repressing any of them.[6]

This is potentially relevant This concept of will gives us a good way to think about underachieving students. The hypothesis is that part of the problem, for some students anyway, is that they have not sufficiently developed this inner power of will. As yet, they are not capable of staying with what has to be done amid the obstacles and distractions that get in the way. One job we may need to tackle is that of helping students develop this power of willfulness and then give them practice using it. Of course this is going to be difficult. Right now most of us do not know enough about willfulness to do much more than cheer on students or pass on advice to "*really* get to work" or "apply yourself"—or threaten them with dire consequences if they do not work harder. What do we say to the student who replies: "But as far as I am concerned I *am* really getting to work. Or I think I am. Something happens though, and I just don't stick with it. What can I do?"

Schools do not challenge students to be willful in anything approximating its full measure. Rather, there are assignments of tasks calling for short-term responses from students: "Watch this film." "Read chapter 3 and we'll discuss it." "You had better write this down because it'll probably be on the test." This is especially important to consider because Assagioli is saying that willfulness is essential to being fully human, and that we live in a culture and society which places particular emphasis on individual initiative, self-directedness, and diligence.

Assagioli discussed goodness and love and their relationship to will. He says this about the good will:

> We are constantly influencing others, whether we are conscious of doing so or not, whether we desire to do so or not. And the more we are aware of this, the more we can see to it that our influence is beneficient and constructive. . . . The good will is a *will* to do good; it is a will that chooses and wants the good. It may be said to be an expression of love and this raises the great problem of the relationship between love and will.[7]

Assagioli pointed out the problem of the lack of goodness and love among those who have will and, the reverse, the lack of will in those who are good and loving. The challenge for students, for all of us, is to integrate goodness, love, and will.

Classes in schools deal with how things get done, what works, what happened, what is so, and what is preferable. That is predominantly what science, math, English, foreign language and social studies are about. But they should also be about, and they are not very often, challenging students to consider what is right and good and loving. What is good science? Not just effective science, but good science. What is moral in the arts?[8] What is decent in politics?[9] In making a choice of career, beyond what is available and what you are good at doing and what you find interesting, beyond money and status, what is good work for you? What is fair and just work? What work can you do in a loving way, as an act of your love for others and yourself? I am reminded that when Freud was asked what the primary issues of an individual's life were he simply replied, "Work and love." It is ironic that schools have not dealt with either vocation—good work, expressive of one's essence—or love in its many forms. Certainly these matters are important in our private life. But they are equally important in our public life as citizens and workers. What place do morality, decency and love have in the way we conduct our public business? Beyond what works, what is right?

To Assagioli the complete willful act consists of six phases:

1. The purpose, aim or goal, based on evaluation, motivation and intention.

2. Deliberation.
3. Choice and decision.
4. Affirmation: the command, or "fiat" of the will.
5. Planning and working out a program.
6. Direction of the execution.[10]

In many ways this list looks consistent with problem-solving and decision-making strategies that are typically employed in education. However, there are some interesting twists in this concept of the volitional act that are worth mentioning. For one thing, having a clear aim or goal is not enough in this Assagiolian framework. Its appropriateness and moral rightness needs to be assessed. To be a goal in this conception, it must be a *fitting* thing to strive to accomplish. Also, a goal means more than simply a good idea or something possible to do. It is something I am *motivated* to do. I want to do it. And even more than want to do it, I actually *intend* to do it. I will accept responsibility for achieving this goal. One last feature to note, step 4 underscores that I must find ways to affirm the choices I have made, say yes to them.

This concept of the willful act raises some questions of teaching strategy that I do not see resolved in the professional literature in education. Through exactly what process can students decide on a goal's meaning, goodness, and appropriateness? How can students explore and understand their own motivation? How can motivation be activated? What creates the intention to achieve one's goals? How can goals and actions be affirmed in ways that help us on the road to actually doing what we set out to do? Clearly, as educators, these are aspects of goal attainment we need to think about more than we do. (Well, that may be a generous way to put it. I am sure we do not deal with these issues at all now.) And just as important, if students are going to be more self-directed and successful, these are questions *they* also need to resolve. But unfortunately students do not get much chance to resolve them. Schools are not known as places for students to practice *willing*. In fact, it is strange to even use the term, despite its centrality to what we are as human beings. Most often schools are places for doing tasks at the bidding of the teacher. And even when students are engaged in what is called "inquiry" or "problem solving" it usually does not approximate what I am calling an act of will. The math teacher assigns the math problems, the science teacher designates the experiment to run, and the coach puts together the plays. Outside of school, McDonald's shows you how to smile, tells you what to cook, and how to cook it. This is not to say that schools—or McDonald's—can ever be any different than they are. All this is an enormous issue, certainly bigger than I can resolve. But at least I can note how ironic it is that a country that values autonomy and choice and individualism makes people wait until they are about 27-years-old before they get a chance to assert these values, if then.

In his discussion of inner powers Assagioli lists traits such as determination, firmness, persistence, clear-sightedness, and wisdom. There is a term for those kinds of qualities: *character*. It has not been fashionable, during the past 2 decades at least, the course of my career in education, to talk about the promotion of character in schools. It has seemed too much a matter of "imposing our values on students" to deal with things such as persistence, determination, and self-control. However, I recently read Plato's *The Republic* and it was all about character. The author Somerset Maugham once said the most significant achievement of the human being is to learn to manage himself; and self-management is a central element of character. Some of these students need to work on their character. And I do not mean that there is anything morally inferior or inherently inadequate about them; the connotations of "lacking in character." (That, by the way, is why I like the term *inner powers*. This makes it a matter of developing the skills and does not carry all the moral baggage connected with the idea of character.)

If you think about it, the children who are exposed to a great amount of character education are those from socially advantaged backgrounds. Directly and indirectly—from their parents, friends, from the private schools to which they are often sent—these children are taught such qualities as diligence, patience, self-discipline, control of impulses, and the deferring of rewards. I have always felt that we can learn much from parents who educate their children to maintain the power and influence to which they were born. Notice what qualities these parents instill in their children. Notice the elements of style and manner they encourage. Notice the kinds of schools they send their children to and the curriculum of those schools. These parents are not fools. They know how things work in America. We could enrich our knowledge base as educators if we analyzed the ways those who know how to attain status and power raise their own children. My conclusion is that they know what is up, what really counts in attaining success, more than many of us professional educators. Short of that, we have nothing to lose by studying them as examples of how to socialize children to be successful. We may not choose to emulate them in every instance. Though, frankly, in this willfulness/self-management/character area I think we should take up many of their methods.

In this regard, a good book on the children of the advantaged is *Children of Privilege* by Robert Coles.[11] I especially remember from his book how sensitive these children are to the importance of style and bearing in getting what they want. It also struck me how savvy they are to the way schools work and how to deal with teachers to their own advantage. Talking about students who work teachers to get what they want may all sound rather cynical and manipulative to you, but try to keep an open-mind. Think about it. Think of how some unsuccessful students get teachers to reprove them. Read Coles' book, and think about how you yourself have been educated to develop your inner powers.

This is especially important to me because I worry that among children from less advantaged backgrounds what I am calling the education of inner powers is not strong enough. Moreover, the schools for the children of the poor—think of how they contrast from schools for the very advantaged—do not compensate for the absence of these "inner power-building" influences in the other areas of children's lives. That is why I welcome what can be called a character education movement that has become especially prominent in the last several years.[12] Surely, I do not want indoctrination of children into mindless acceptance of some "cardinal virtues." As a matter of fact, I think that is what the "have-nots" get a lot of right now. But, back to the example of advantaged children, indoctrination is not what they are receiving. No, they are getting an education for inner power to a far greater extent than many realize.

Assagioli also refered to *wisdom*.[13] It is ironic that the term wisdom—in contrast to facts, knowledge, and understanding—is used so seldom in education. Wisdom implies more than just knowing or being capable. It denotes penetrating insight, discretion, sound judgment, perspective, and goodness. In *The Republic*, Plato, through Socrates, includes wisdom in his definition of character.[14] In many cultures it is the responsibility of the teacher to pass on wisdom to the young. Do we as teachers pass on wisdom? Should we? Can we, really? Is there such a thing as wisdom? And if there is, what wisdom is worth teaching? I ask of you: What is your wisdom? Among all that you have learned in your life, what do you know that you would call wisdom? If nothing else, answering these questions stimulates us to reflect on the nature of our own education. Have we been educated to be wise, or just effective? Also, it invites us to think about what is truly worth teaching to young people. Schooling should be more than teaching certain subjects because, reminiscent of what Hillary said when asked why he climbed Everest, they are there. Schooling should be about the most profound and most empowering features that the culture has to share with its children. It should be nothing less than that. What is the wisdom of this culture? How can it—can it at all?—be taught in schools? All of this raises the question of whether we are schooled but not enlightened by our 12 and 13 years of preuniversity education. The psychologies that have been predominant in education have not seen the need to deal with wisdom. Assagioli, to his credit, did.

Assagioli placed great emphasis on what I defined as the conscious self some pages earlier. He thinks it crucial that individuals conduct their life from this center of their being. Assagioli refers to this aspect of each of us as:

> the existential experience of pure self-consciousness, the direct awareness of the self, the discovery of the "I." In reality, this experience is implicit in our human consciousness. It is that which distinguishes it from that of animals, which are conscious but not self-conscious. Human beings go beyond mere animal awareness and *know that they are aware*. But generally this self-consciousness is indeed implicit rather than explicit. It is experienced in a rather nebulous and distorted way because it is usually mixed with, and veiled by, the contents of consciousness (sensations, drives, emotions, thoughts, etc.). Their constant impact veils the clarity of consciousness and produces spurious identification of the self with these changing

and transient contents. Thus, if we are to make self-consciousness explicit, clear, and vivid, we must disidentify ourselves from all these contents and *identify with the self.*[15]

Assagioli urged us to learn to be able to identify with the conscious self, thus disidentifying with the other aspects of ourselves. Brown's book contains an exercise that gets at this awareness of being aware. Try it yourself.

Take a few moments to observe your body. What position is it in?. How is it moving?... Where is it comfortable and uncomfortable?. Check out the further reaches of your body: Your big toe, the top of your head, the small of your back. Feel your breathing in your throat and chest. Sense your heartbeat, your digestive processes... As you continue this scan, ask yourself gently: Who is aware?

Now inquire as to your emotional state. What are you feeling?... What are the feelings attached to various sensations in your body? . . . Open yourself to the subtle nameless feelings as well as the obvious emotions. . . . If it is helpful, recall your feelings during earlier events of the day or week, feelings you may still have traces of within you. . . . Now, once again, ask yourself gently: Who is aware? Who is aware of my feelings?

For the next few minutes, notice what you are thinking. Watch or listen to your thoughts go by. . . . Notice how your thoughts follow one another, how your mind focuses or wanders... When you realize you have gone on a mental trip, notice where you went and what brought you back. . . . Ask: Who is aware? Who is aware of my thinking?...

Turn your attention now to the room you are in. Notice the temperature of the air, the smells, the sounds, the texture and feel of your chair. . . . What is the quality of the light?... What colors do you see?... Allow your awareness to expand beyond the room to the whole building and beyond. . . . Continue to expand your sense of what is there, into the neighborhood, the community, the countryside. . . . Pay attention to the sky. . . . and to the earth beneath you. . . . Can you sense the distance to the stars?... Notice yourself in the midst of all this. . . . Who is aware?... Who is aware of the stars and the space and of you in the midst?... Who is aware?...[16]

Why should we identify with this core of awareness, the conscious self? Because Assagioli finds a close connection between the conscious self and will. One becomes more willful by learning to conduct his or her life from the I, the conscious self. The individual who lives from an awareness of being *experiences* the truth of "In that I am, I can will." This may all sound very exotic, but the point for educators is quite clear. If we want students to be more autonomous, more in charge of their lives, better able to get it done—willful—they need to learn to make contact with their conscious self. Another way to say it, they need to be more self-conscious. Adolescents tend to be very self-referring, but I do not believe they are very self-conscious. Nor, truth be told, are we. We make decisions, respond to things, and get things accomplished, but not necessarily from an experienced reality of "I am aware and I am willing."

If I read Assagioli correctly, another reason for attention to the conscious self, beyond its relationship to the will, is—this could be more me talking than Assagioli—that the conscious self is also intimately linked to a kind of personal wisdom that each of us has inside us. Connection to the conscious self greatly increases our chance of making the wise choice and selecting the most skillful, harmonious, just and decent way forward in any situation. Connection with this wise part of us provides the best possibility for breaking from decisions and conduct based on impulse, habit, conditioning, immediate reward, selfishness, and expediency. Connection with the core self also helps us transcend the limits of rational analysis. Reason has operated to justify some of the most harmful, self-defeating, immoral, and even atrocious human actions. This is an idea that can be tested in practice. The next time you are in a dilemma, instead of only thinking about it—and, indeed, do that—just quiet down, be with what we have been calling your conscious self, consult your wisdom, and wait for an answer. Do not impose an answer; that is your rational mind in operation. The rational mind is a useful part of us but sometimes not very wise. Let the answer come in whatever form it comes, words or pictures or feelings. See what that is. In any case, if nothing else this will slow you down and give you a chance to get some perspective on what is going on for you. What may be in the case of secondary students, is that they are doing things in school and outside that are both fun at times and make sense—or at least they are consistent, all of a piece—but just not very wise.

It is important to emphasize that all this refers suggestively and metaphorically to the way we work as humans. I do not mean to imply that the human psyche includes an actual cluster made up of awareness, wisdom, and will—for definitional purposes let us call this cluster the *personal self*—sitting in the middle surrounded by thoughts, impulses, feelings, and the rest; any more than Freudians think there is a tangible superego, or than Piagetians think we can pull schemata out and examine them with a microscope. Rather, these are ideas that provide us a useful way to look at things. As far as I am concerned, it is their usefulness that makes them valuable, more so than whether they exist in concrete form in nature; or even whether they describe actual processes or give us an accurate perspective on human beings at all. For instance, the Freudian ideas about ids, egos, superegos, and childhood complexes may all be ridiculous. But even if they are nonsense, Freud's concepts have given us a way to pause a bit, look within ourselves, and deal with what we find. These ideas have resulted in many people living in happier, more productive ways. They have provided the basis for newer, probably more accurate, discoveries about the way we function that would not have otherwise occurred. The same is true of Assagioli. My experience tells me we operate *as if* what he describes were true. His ideas do result in positive outcomes. And he does encourage us to investigate some crucial dimensions of human beings, ask some fundamentally important questions, and try some new things that we ought to be testing out. That is a contribution of significance to our field. It expands our perspective; or it has mine, anyway.

It is important to weigh this crucial idea of self-as-pure-awareness-and-will (and wisdom?) and to explore its nature and importance. In her book Molly Brown quoted author Sam Keen as describing it this way:

> At the heart of the self there is both an active and a passive element, an agent and a spectator. Self-consciousness involves our being a witness—a pure, objective, loving witness—to what is happening within and without. In this sense the self is not a dynamic in itself but is a point of witness, a spectator, an observer who watches the flow. But there is another part of the inner self—the will-er or the directing agent—that actively intervenes to orchestrate the various functions and energies of the personality, to make commitments and to instigate action in the external world. So, at the center of the self, there is a unity of masculine and feminine, will and love, action and observation.[17]

As I mentioned earlier, for definitional purposes I refer to this "heart of the self" as the *personal self*. It contains our consciousness (the conscious self) and the active, directing agent (the will). And I hypothesize a third element: personal wisdom. I find it useful to view individuals as if they possess a wise part inside them to which they can always refer. What is centrally important about this theoretical discussion is that the personal self is the one constant in our being. All the rest are changeable, which is especially valuable and encouraging to realize if you have been unproductive in your life and you need to change. And the element that directs and regulates personal change, at least potentially, is this core self.

Brown got at this distinction between the self in this sense and the rest of the elements of our being this way:

> I have a body, but I am not my body. My body may find itself in different conditions of health or sickness, it may be rested or tired, but that has nothing to do with my self, my real "I." I value my body as my precious instrument of experience and action in the world, but it is only an instrument. I treat it well, I seek to keep it in good health, but it is not my self. I have a body, but I am not my body. . . .
>
> I have emotions, but I am not my emotions. My emotions are many different feelings, always changing, sometimes in confusion. They may swing from love to hatred, from calm to anger, from joy to sorrow, and yet my essence, my true nature, does not change. *I* remain. Though I may be temporarily washed by a wave of emotion, I know it will pass in time; therefore, I am not this emotion. Since I can observe and understand my emotions, and learn to direct, utilize, and integrate them harmoniously, it is clear that they are not my self. I have emotions, but I am not my emotions. . . .
>
> I have a mind, but I am not my mind. My mind is a valuable tool of discovery and expression, but it is not the essence of my being. My thoughts are constantly changing with new ideas, knowledge, and experience. Often my mind refuses to obey me. Therefore it cannot be me, my self. It is an organ of knowledge of both the inner and the outer worlds, but it is not my self. I have a mind, but I am not my mind. . . .[18]

According to Brown, who am I? I am a center of pure awareness and will that is capable of observing all of these other elements. I am the one who is aware. I am the one who chooses.

Though, as much as I am taken with this idea, I am at the same time somewhat uncomfortable with Brown's formulations. To say I have a body but am not my body tends to set me off against my body. This view could lead to an inappropriate dichotomization of me from the-rest-of-me. It could promote a dualistic this *or* that, or even this *against* that, perspective on human beings. And that is not good. As I see it, indeed I *am* my body. That is me, or a part of me at least. At the same time I *have* a body in that I—the personal self—can monitor and, to some extent, change *my* body (through nutrition and exercise, and so forth). So my body is and is not me, both at the same time. Actuality is often made up of apparently contradictory realities (that I both am and am not my body, for example). I have been told that we are very Aristotelian (the Greek philosopher, Aristotle) in our culture and have difficulty moving out of the Western tradition of seeing something as either one thing or the other. It is difficult for us to conceive of something being one thing *and* its opposite at the same time. But I believe I need to try in this case, because I want my body to be me, and at the same time I want it to be not-me. Similarly, my mind, emotions, and drives are both me and not-me. I can see them both ways. And I can see the complementarity of these seemingly contradictory perspectives. And I can choose to look at myself in the way that best serves my purposes at any particular time.

How might these concepts apply to what we do in education? Assume one of our less-than-successful secondary students has the personality of a "wise guy" or "screw-up." We can all think of a few of these kinds of students. They can be particularly difficult for us to manage. If this student thinks that this personality is who he is, then the cause (namely, becoming a responsible, contributing member of the class) is lost. If he identifies with his persona, then what else is he going to do in a class situation but be who he is—the screw-up or the wise guy or the dumb guy, whatever it is.

Many unsuccessful students are confusing themselves with their act. A good beginning for a student is for him to realize that *he* is not a wise guy. "Wise guy" is in Assagioli's terms a *sub*personality. The concept of *subpersonality* emphasizes that wise guy is likely not a total personality. The student probably is not a wise guy in every context: not when having dinner with his grandmother, for example. In addition, the "wise-guy-in-school" may not always have been this way. For instance, he was not that way in the second grade. Yet that was still *him* in the second grade. It is more that he *has* a personality. Or better, that he *chooses* a personality. There is an aspect of himself (the personal self) that can observe his personality and regulate it to better serve the purpose of getting along in class. From this perspective, what we call *personality* is actually a pattern of self-perceptions and behaviors that we have reified, made into a thing, an it. It can become who you think you are. But as a practical matter it is much easier to change something you have than something you are. Because if you are that way, from where can come the impetus to be different?

Someone who brought this distinction between self and personality home to me was the late comedian Andy Kaufman. Kaufman said he drew great inspiration from professional wrestlers who would adopt a persona and then—this is what he loved—never "come off it. " At no point do wrestlers do a "Don Rickles," stop and say, "Hey gang, I was only kidding." Wrestlers are not hanging on so strongly to their *real* personality that they have to, even for a moment, be themselves just to show us who they truly are. In his work Kaufman played with the distinction between himself (what we are calling the conscious self) and his persona. For instance, he took on the identity of Tony Clifton, a seedy Las Vegas lounge singer, and developed all but a separate career for Clifton. Never once did he peek out at the world and say, "This is really me, Andy." Because, here is the catch, he *was* Tony Clifton. If personality is a series of choices and a pattern of actions and not a thing, and "really me" is the conscious self, then he *was* Tony Clifton when he was *doing* Tony Clifton (as much as personality ever is who we are) and was not when he stopped doing it. In the same light, for one night a month Kaufman *was* a busboy in a Los Angeles restaurant. Another example, I had a friend who worked on the old television show "Fridays," an ABC rip-off of "Saturday Night Live." She listened in on a meeting between Kaufman and the producer as they discussed what Kaufman was going to do on an upcoming show. It was decided that Kaufman, a Jew, should come on as a born-again Christian. To my friend's amazement, not only did Kaufman play a born-again Christian on the show, but he kept it going at the cast party and for some time afterward.

I hope this has gotten you to think more closely about what things like personality really are, and what it means to change personality. This is crucial here, because some of these kids we are talking about have a personality that gets them into trouble. At least I hope this discussion has served to place a check on some of the "I gotta be the real me," authenticity talk of humanistic psychological and educational perspectives. In addition, I hope it increases our sense of freedom and hope. A student can be different! Depending on how it has gone for him, or what is needed, or where he wants to go, he can put on different hats, if you will, he can try it different ways. The student doesn't have to play out the same act all of his life and pay the same negative costs all the way through.

This point also occurred to me during my work in theater. I have done a lot of acting, and I find that no matter how different the ways of the character are from the ways I normally think and behave, when I am on stage it is still *me* doing it. I find that the role I play is just as much me as the roles I play in "real life." It is more that I have come to identify certain styles, mannerisms, preferences, and all, with who I am. And I, for whatever reason, take on the task of keeping the act I call me going: "No, I wouldn't do *that*." "That isn't me."

I certainly would not quit this whole thing and go become a waiter in the Bahamas.

At the same time however, I do not want to go too far with this, because during a theater performance there is also a strand of "this is not me" there too. I do not deny the genetic, inherited element in personality. Many parents, I am included, would tell you how they could spot the personality of their children as small babies. There may be a "real me"—and at the same time it may be arbitrary, at least within a certain range. This may be another instance of something being both a thing and its opposite. In this case, personality is a manifestation of our nature and at the same time a choice of how to be. Or, perhaps a better way of looking at it, personality is an interplay of nature and choice and, another thing, social conditioning. We are to some degree, back to the theater analogy, "directed" by our world from infancy on. Add one more influence: Our physical state affects personality. Drink four or five cups of coffee in a couple of hours if you want to experience what I mean.

The challenge for you is to look at something we talk about all the time, personality, and ask, "What really is it?" "Where does it come from?" "How much, if any, can it be changed?" If your personality is inconsistent with getting you what you want or need, what can you do? We all know that style counts for so much in life. Some students' style is grating on others and self-defeating in terms of attaining school success. The question becomes: Is there anything they can or should do about it? I know that assuming the role of someone else who would appear to be completely different from who I think I am and having an "I'm this too" reaction has broadened my sense of what is possible in my life. The humanistic psychologies of the 1970s seemed to be telling me that I was supposed to be "authentic" and "congruent" and "who I really am" As high sounding as that comes across, doing it that way can get you in trouble. You may go through with your "real" personality and have it result in very real unhappiness, as is the case with some of these underachieving students. What I am finding in my own life is that it is simplistic to assume I have a real personality, when it is, to such a large degree, a matter of social conditioning, thoughts in my head about what is called for, my state of health, and so on. As far as I am concerned the one constant "real me" is the personal self. To some extent the rest is arbitrary. I can choose and I can change. At least within limits, for at the same time I am a biological, finite being and I am shaped by forces in my environment. I am dying as much as I am living.

Think about all this and discuss it with others. The same analysis of personality applies to the other dimensions of myself: what I think, what I do, what I am capable of, my physical state, even my feelings. All these things are changeable. Frankly, I do not know whether my subconscious is malleable. Perhaps ways of surfacing subconscious material (psychoanalysis, imagery, dream analysis) alter its contents or impact. But then again, it could be only I hold the ultimate power (suicide) to end its existence, and that I can learn only to manage or cope with the subconscious forces within me, not change them.

Consequently, as human beings we are able to monitor and alter most all of what we are. Though again, I do not mean this in any absolute sense. There are the physical limitations that I referred to earlier, as well as limitations of time, energy, and resources. I am only sketching out the beginnings of a perspective on human functioning. If we are going to begin to change or help others to change, we need to work to understand what we are. Ironically, in this regard our schooling does not help us very much. We are essentially left to our own resources to figure out what goes on inside our skin.

Assagioli's work proposes an ideal of human functioning as a model. The picture is one of the development and harmonious integration of the various aspects of the human being directed and regulated by the center of awareness, wisdom, and will—the personal self. Here, I deal with this idea in greater detail. Understand that in what follows there is probably a lot more of me than Assagioli. My foremost concern is to talk about human beings in a way that provides educators with a useful perspective. The first part refers to a human being in a qualitative way. The elements of a human being—all those aspects of one's person I mentioned in the first section—can exist in a relatively developed or undeveloped state. To be fully and completely human, the human being over the course of his or her life should (there is an "ought" here) enhance, grow, and expand each of the elements that comprise him. That means there is an assumption that we should develop ourselves physically, emotionally, morally, and intellectually, in character, personality, and capability. Moreover, that we should "put it all together," synthesize these elements into a graceful, positive, satisfying and productive whole (the harmonious part). The last part, at the center of it all, is the personal self: the witness, the chooser, the wise, the always-me. There may yet be more—a soul, a transcendent nature, God. I leave you to think about that. What makes up you? What makes up those students you teach?

This conception of the human being is very close to the Jungian principle of *enatiodromia*, a tongue twister that refers to the development of the individual through the clash and integration of opposites around a self. In his autobiography *Half the House*—which I highly recommend to you, by the way—the educator Herbert Kohl described it this way:

> C. G. Jung uses an interesting word: enantiodromia. It means the drama of the opposites, the battle of love and hate, pacifism and violence, sanity and madness, honesty and corruption, joy and misery, trust and suspicion, separateness and togetherness, individuality and community, creativity and destructiveness. For Jung, life develops through the interplay of these and many other oppositions and comes to its fullest integration when they all hold together about a center he calls the Self. There is no moment of completion in the development of the Self, but rather an open-ended process of continually integrating internal and external experience about the center. Neither one nor the other of the terms of the oppositions described above is denied; instead, they both serve other, humane purposes.[19]

In this quote Kohl emphasized what are more accurately called qualities or experiences than the aspects or elements as I referred to them. But the concepts overlap: my spin-off from Assagioli and this Jungian reference. In both cases there is an emphasis on valuing and developing all that I am and on living from a center, a self. Thinking is not more important than or set off against feeling. The development of my mind is not of higher priority than or antithetical to the development of my body. Opposites are valued; the development of each is seen as complementary to the other. Contrasting elements are to be integrated into a harmonious relationship with one another and with the rest of one's being. Practical and spiritual or transcendent concerns are not conflicting opposites. Rather, they—and all of the various aspects and qualities and experiences that make up me—are polarities that balance and complete one another. Note the stress on development and the evolution of the human being. Notice the emphases on centeredness, selfness, personal harmony, and the maximization of all the diverse dimensions of the individual. This picture of the developed human being becomes a criterion to direct and assess programs of education.

In contrast to this orientation, humanistic education in the 1970s tended to be a dichotomizing, in contrast to this integrating, perspective. Opposites were set off against one another, with one more valued than the other. Feelings tended to be superior to reason: "Get in touch with your feelings, and don't be on a head trip" is how it went. Similarly, spontaneity was superior to calculation and planning, self-understanding more valued than the rigorous study of external reality, and play was better than work. Now was more "where it is at" than then. Being was more valued than self-discipline and growth. Cooperation had it over competition and individual initiative. In the conception I have sketched here, there is more value on blending this *and* that than on this *or* that, pick a side. To cite some examples, what this means to me is that I want to be capable of *both* calculation and spontaneity. I want access to the private, subjective knowledge inside me *and* the public, external knowledge that is available outside me. I seek to be able to both play and work well. I work to be sensitive to this moment *and* the past *and* the future. I want to be well *and* grow well. I want to be capable of cooperation *and* competition *and* individual effort. And, also crucial, I want to manifest and guide any and all of these qualities when and where appropriate from my core, from my personal self.

Just as humanistic education, traditional education sets up its own dichotomies. Traditional education tends to focus predominantly on the outer and public realms—the world of books, events, ideas, curriculum, and teachers. It tends to emphasize less the inner world of the students who engage this material. What I have been trying to establish is a perspective that supports the belief that both the inner and outer are important, that they need concurrent and continuous attention. Simply, a student needs to be educated about who he is and how he operates somewhere. Students who face the job of turning things around in school especially need this lesson.

Schools of necessity must specialize in helping students in some areas more than others. There is just so much time and resources. Before choosing where to focus its energies, the school should have a vision in mind of what human beings become ideally, and what they need to do to get there. Operating from such a vision, the school has criteria for choosing goals and actions consistent with furthering the realization of this vision. Since the school does what it does from the perspective of all that needs to go on, it also understands what it is *not* doing as well as what it is doing. The school can then choose to do what is most needed, considering what is and is not being done in other contexts (families, churches, work settings, and so forth). If you think about it, this entire discussion has set up criteria related to a developed and functioning human being to add to other criteria we use now—citizenship, subject matter knowledge, vocational competence— in deciding upon the nature and direction of school programs.

Much else could be said. Let me just leave this for now and offer you an invitation to reflect on your own perspective on what it means to be most fully human, most fully developed, and most fully educated. What vision guides your own development and the work you do (or will do) with students?

I have thoroughly discussed the importance of personal self because I believe it to be the aspect of ourselves that can help students to take charge of their school lives and change in positive ways. As I see it, it is vital that this dimension of a student's total being be, metaphorically, ''the captain of the ship.'' It is vital, because it is my hypothesis that the other aspects—mind, feelings, impulses, personality, and the rest—cannot be trusted to steer them in the right direction. Rather, these other aspects tend to keep students floating along at the same level. Staying with this metaphor, changing direction, setting sail for new horizons, is not at the top of most students' list of favorite things to do. It is as if the crew has taken over the ship and is determined to keep it on whatever course it is on—even if it is heading into a storm. In order to change, the captain—the personal self—is going to have to take command, strengthen the crew, get them working together, and turn the ship around. And the captain must do this while in turbulent mid-ocean waters (while in the midst of conducting the business of life) and not in the calm of the port.

Have you noticed in your own life, and in the lives of those around you, how constant things are? Year after year we have just about so much money, just about so much success, just about so much happiness. Things go up a little and down a little, the details change, but things stay essentially the same. It is as if there is some kind of thermostat inside us to regulate events; if things get too different— for better or worse—they get put back to where they were. I am getting old enough to have friends who have lived a good part of their lives during our acquaintance. I am struck by the regularity of their life story. For example, I have some friends who live a distance away and whom I do not hear from frequently. When we get in touch, I am fairly certain how things stand for them. The details may well be new to me—the particular situation at work or with relationships, the particular projects, and so forth. But I am usually not surprised at their situation. It is significant to me how the overall quality, character, or tone of their life tends to stay quite constant. I remark how on a happiness–unhappiness or fulfilled–unfilled scale, they remain about the same. People "have it together," as we used to say, to about the same degree now as last year or 10 years ago. Of course there are wonderful exceptions. And maybe I am wrong on this. Perhaps life proceeds on either a slight upslope or downslope. I am not that sensitive to tell. All I can say is that the consistency of the quality of peoples' lives is striking.

This constancy of life is true of students as well as older people. An illustration, I am currently teaching a graduate level course that centers on the issues that face educators in working with underachieving students. The students in this class are practicing teachers. As part of the course they have been looking into the school histories of students they identify as having talent but who are not performing well in school. Predominantly the students in high school who are drifting, undisciplined, all the terms that are used, have cumulative files that indicate how first and second grade teachers had noted the same characteristics during those years. The patterns of school-going exhibited by these unsuccessful students are not recent phenomena. The "story" has been unfolding in a consistent manner for a long time. Though this is a generalization and there are deviations from this norm, the persistence of the negative behavior over time nevertheless is a noticeable phenomenon in many of these students' school lives. Thus there is a need to explore the tendency for sameness, for constancy in our lives, even when life has not been very satisfactory or productive.

Clearly, an issue for us to consider is the persistence of pattern and what will break it for the better. I have been systematically spending a good amount of time in what I suppose can be called meditation. What I have been doing is sitting quietly watching all the things that go on inside me. I watch my inner processes as thoughts jump in and out, as memories and images fade in and out, as impulses and desires pop up. It is fascinating. What I have concluded about one aspect in particular, my rational mind, is that it is a wonderful gift. My mind can reason things through, solve problems, develop ideas, and create things. Such an enormously empowering element of my being. At the same time it is so clear to me that my mind needs to be monitored and controlled. For one thing, it jumps all over, flitting from this to that to the other thing. If I followed it around I would be taking off in about 16 directions at once. Also, I have noticed that very often my mind provides me with wonderful reasons not to change. Whatever project I have going, my mind seems to come up with something like: "That's a really good idea, that thing you want to do. Yes sir, let's do that. But not today, OK? Today, how about a sports book and getting some sleep? We can get started tomorrow." Not yet. Not now. Later. Always reasons to do it later. I am reminded of a poem by Charles Bukowski called "3:16 and One Half":

> here I'm supposed to be a great poet
> and I'm sleepy in the afternoon

here I am aware of death like a giant bull
charging at me
and I'm sleepy in the afternoon
here I'm aware of wars and men fighting in the ring
and I'm aware of good food and wine and good women
and I'm sleepy in the afternoon . . .
some day I won't be sleepy in the afternoon
some day I'll write a poem that will bring volcanos
to the hills out there
but right now I'm sleepy in the afternoon.[20]

Similarly, other aspects of me line up along side my mind to discourage me from doing whatever-it-is—or at least postpone it awhile. My personality seems to say, "Hey, great idea, but that's not *you*." My feelings became all jangly and get across, "This is scary stuff." My body gets tired and tells me it's time for a nap. It is as if the various dimensions of me are getting together under the direction of my subconscious and it is saying something like: "Let's keep things going just about the way they are right now. Because whatever is going on, happy or unhappy, successful or unsuccessful, fun or no fun, we have been surviving this way. If we go changing, something bad could come out of it; we could *die* or something. So placate him, threaten him, distract him, talk him out of it, whatever is necessary. But get him to take on this project he's come up with later, OK? So rational mind, you give him a reason to wait until Monday. Impulse, give him a burning need for the *People* magazine cover story. Body, get real tired, got it? This guy can be moved with the time-for-a-nap stall. All right, all together now: One, two, three, WIN!''

Now I am not saying this is literally going on. But I am saying it is *as if* this were happening. I am contending that, whatever it is about, there are strong internal forces within us to keep things going just about as they are. And that is not even taking into account all the *external* forces that promote sameness. Applying this to education, the result is that the bad students will stay bad unless they (their personal selves) take control of their lives. They need to marshal all the rest of themselves, their mind, body, emotions, and so forth, and get these elements moving in the right direction. In my opinion, once you take over and get things on the right course, these other aspects will thank you for it. They want things to be better. It is just that while they can be so helpful when used to the right ends, they are just too preoccupied with survival and consistency; and, truth be told, they are not the wisest in the world. These other aspects mean well and want us happy. There is no reason to get down on them. It is just that they can never get themselves up to progressing toward needed change, but instead cling to the idea—derived from some irrational subconscious impulse?—that things have to stay the same.

I know this has all been in images and metaphors, but I hope that it provides a context for you to understand my message to students: Yes, you can change. You don't have to stay unsuccessful and unhappy (and/or bored, frustrated, unappreciated, mad, and so forth) in school. But it is not easy. The fact is most people remain the same all of their lives. The 16-year-old mess-up with potential becomes a 30-year-old mess-up with potential. In most cases, magic does not come into somebody's life and turn it around. But this doesn't have to happen to you. You don't have to stay stuck. There is hope. You can change. It is possible. But *you'll* have to do it. And to do it you are going to have to work very hard. You will have to gain control of your own life and stop doing things the same old ways and reacting to the same old signals ("This is boring so I might as well screw off," and so forth). You need to find that part of you that can catch all the things you do that keep you from being happy and successful in school. You have to develop your powers as an individual. You must learn to figure out what is going on and learn to control yourself. You need to recognize the way you are going at things is not the only way. You are going to have to dream of what it would be like and what you would be like if you did well in school. It would be really difficult to turn things around on your own, but there are people that can help. But again, you are the one who is going to have to do it. It really is up to you. Are you willing to work to be a better student in school?

Unlike other psychologies I have studied, Assagioli's work concerns itself with the issue of the meaning and purpose of an individual's life.[21] His concern is not just on *how* and *why* as is usually the case when people in the social sciences and psychology study human beings. He deals as well with the issue of *what for*. In Assagioli there is an assumption that each human being has a unique essence and positive purpose to fulfill in his or her lifetime. This purpose is to be and to give to the world what he or she uniquely is. The challenge for each human being is to create a life that is inspired by this purpose and consistent with it. And a key responsibility of education is to support students as they identify their fundamental nature or essence and learn to manifest it in productive ways.

This amounts to a kind of "niche" theory of human existence. You and I, everyone, *do* belong in the world and there *is* a place for all of us. We will be happiest and most productive in our lives if we live out our purpose during the course of our lifetime. This "niche" idea in various forms and shadings shows up a lot if you look around. For example, in Eastern religious and philosophical traditions there is the notion of finding one's dharma or life's path. In *The Republic* Plato defines virtue as doing what is natural to you. All this gets at the point that life is not all an open book. Life should not be seen as all just a matter of chance and arbitrary selections of activities to fill up one's life. Each of us needs to discover who we are and where we fit, and then live a life consistent with that discovery. At least that is what we should do if we want to be realized as the people we are. However, as human beings we can, and do, live out our lives without manifesting our essence or nature in the world. In the words of the song, you (and I) are meant to "row, row, row your boat, gently down the stream."

But so many people, instead, ride along in other's boats. Or if they do row their own, it is done harshly (not gently) up (not down) the stream. And of course, we see some lost souls dragging their boats (lives) through the thick brush along the shore. They are not even in the water.

As an educator, I consider this matter of life meaning very important. I cannot say with any certainty that a human being has a purpose to discover. Perhaps the existentialists are right when they contend that all we can do is impose meaning on an otherwise pointless world by choosing a mission or purpose, by creating a path for ourselves where none exists. For me, and I suppose this is a twist on the Platonic concept of doing what is natural, I do think there are ways to be that are simply right, just correct, for each of us. These things are what we are good at. They are needed and appreciated by others. They are morally responsible. They result in feelings of happiness and fulfillment, and they express who we are. I have not resolved all of the ultimate, metaphysical questions, but I have come to that. And I see many living lives—fairly good lives, with gold watches and a good size visitation gathering at the funeral home at the end—without ever expressing what is natural to themselves. Even though they do not have to attend to it, if they would listen, there is a knot inside them that would tell them, "No, this is not it." The point is that right now I do not see schools helping students enough to seek what "it," *their* life, is about. It is very difficult to manage schoolwork and excel to your limit when you do not have the sense that, fundamentally, it is your life that you are leading and not one someone else has designed for you, or merely an existence made up of one pointless activity after another.

So I do believe that we have an essential nature, more than the trappings of personality or the particular ideas in our head or the work we happen to be doing. We need to find and live out our nature if we are to be truly content. And I do believe there is a place in this world that will welcome and profit from our expression of what we are. In this place, where we fit, what we do will be needed and valued by others. What we do in this "niche" will matter. In this place life will characteristically—not all the time—be satisfying. There will be peace amid the hard work, and love and harmony without ourselves and between us and our world. Needless to say, many of us do not live this way. Indeed, it is possible to live our lives out of place, out of our place. But we can feel it when we are out of touch with ourselves and the things around us. There is a gnawing sense, literally felt, often very submerged but still there, that all of it is somehow not right.

This speculation aside, I have found it useful, regardless of what is actually so, to work with students *as if* they had a special mission or purpose to their lives. That perspective serves as a check on any tendency of mine to think that all school is about for students is learning the subjects and responding to my teaching methods. Students are not simply objects to be put on the track. This focus also raises for me issues of fundamental purpose regarding the whole program of schooling, as well as the aims of individual courses and parts of courses. And this perspective underscores the fact—at least it is a fact to me—that students, as all human beings, are most committed to do work that they feel to be connected to their *essence*, though I know they would not use this term. When work is connected to the core of what their lives are about, students *really*, rather than merely, engage their studies. In my view, what many students are doing, even in response to what we define as good teaching, is merely rather than really doing the work we assign. I know *merely* and *really* are subjective terms and difficult to pin down exactly. On the other hand, I think each of us knows in our own lives when we are merely or really doing something, and the enormous difference that makes. It is unfortunate that in education our foundational literature and professional orientations do not make more of such inner, personal meaning-related distinctions. School needs to be a place where students can connect the classwork with the larger process of putting a human life together, and not just completing this and that assignment. We should not be surprised to find undedicated, uncommitted students among young people who have little or no sense of where they belong, if they belong at all, in this world and see little more going on than the prospect of hanging out one more night in the Burger King parking lot.

This stress on the significance of an individual human life in Assagioli's work has profound significance for curriculum and what we ask students to do in schools. Clearly it implies that schools need to support students in confronting the fundamental question of who they are and what their life is about. These young people need to look within, analyze their talents and interests, see where they have come from and what difference that has made, review examples of what others have done with their lives, and begin to test out ways of being to see if they fit. This makes particular sense in adolescence because it is a time in which issues of personal identity and direction are central in any case. And while this is so important for all teenagers, it is especially important for the "drifters" whom we are talking about here.

In terms of school curriculum, this concern for meaning and purpose implies a need for greater emphasis on such areas as philosophy, ethics, metaphysics, religion, and theology. It means greater attention to the higher, more evolved, spiritual, transcendent—I search for the best word—dimension of being human. (As I go through this list, note the degree to which schools educate in these areas or promote these processes at present. Also remember I am emphasizing that students *study* these areas, not that schools impose particular resolutions to the crucial issues inherent in each of them.) It means the study of one's own life: reviewing one's personal history and current situation, and making projections into the future based on what is discovered. It means an assessment of one's own way of functioning, one's style, capabilities, interests, goals, and impact on the world. It means the consideration of the life examples of others in order to gain perspective on the whole of human life, and inspiration. It means learning the skill of finding a meaning in one's activities and situations instead of only finding a reason to say no to them. It means learning to take advantage of the opportunities inherent in every circumstance. And it means learning how to express *you* in the world. It is ironic to me that ideas and processes that are so crucial to living life now and as an adult with dignity, purpose, decency, and engagement are so infrequently the topic of study in schools. Rather it is about a military or political event, a science experiment, a skill in physical education, how to write a paragraph, and how to prove a theorem. Those things are important to study, but that is not the point. This is meant to offer that the ideas people hold, what they consider just and fair, and how they organize and give meaning to their lives are important too—especially for some of the lost kids in our schools.

Theodore Roszak has written beautifully on this subject of personal essence in his book *Person/Planet*. Roszak told of his daughter in high school who has a deep commitment to dance.

She has the gift, she is a dancer, the ballet is her calling. I have no idea (for who can be sure of anything in so mad and fickle a world as that of the ballet) if it will also become her career. Even if it does not, it will still have been the true school of her early life, the tough and lovely discipline from which she learned the music of her body, the meaning of art, the wealth of the imagination.

From the day I first realized the seriousness of Kathryn's ambition to dance, everything I ever believed about education has been transformed, root and branch. I have seen my daughter make an authentic personal choice of work and study. She has given herself to a fine and noble art with the intensity of inspiration; she has grown in that commitment and has found her best and worst qualities in its trials. There, she has discovered with painful vividness the meaning of excellence. The dance has brought her all the lively knowledge of high culture I have labored (largely in vain) to bring to hundreds of students over the years. I have seen the dance blossom for her into all that an authentic education should be: a commanding ideal, an illuminating vocation.

And I have seen something else. I have seen my daughter's exquisite choice of the creative life treated with indifference in every school she has attended in three countries. She has taken a rich and delicate talent into her school life—a talent which has carried her mind to the study of music, poetry, drama, history, literature—only to have that talent treated as a non-negotiable currency by her teachers. Until, at last, school became a bore and a burden for her, an agonizing irrelevancy from which she begged to be liberated at the earliest practical and legal moment.[22]

In Roszak's daughter we see a personal *mission*, something we do not talk much about in schools, despite its crucial importance in life. A dancer is now who she is (his subtitle to the chapter in which he discusses her is "But My Daughter Is a Dancer"). As a parent myself, I know I feel the challenge to encourage each of my sons to be the persons *they* are, not a junior version of me or consistent with some idea of what I think they should become. Was Roszak's daughter *born* to be a dancer? Was it a result of an interplay of her particular talents and experiences? That is for you to think through. The point is, at many levels the need to deal with mission, life meaning, vocation—choose your term—is clear.

Assagioli's theories have stimulated the creation of many strategies that have potential for usefulness in education. I refer you to his and the Brown and Ferucci books (see chapter notes 1 and 2) to see which you think apply most to your situation. In addition to that, however, I take some space here to outline some avenues I find particularly promising.

One clear implication of Assagioli's work is that it encourages us to develop what I have called an "inner curriculum." That is, a curriculum that deals with all of those aspects within the student I listed—among them, thoughts, memories, imaginings, intuition, feelings, sensations, impulses and desires, the personal self (awareness and will), personality, and physical-biological processes. Particularly with underachieving students, one or more of these aspects and the way it operates could be inhibiting their level of school success. For instance, the way they think about themselves or school may be contradictory to achievement. Or they may not have learned to control their impulses and desires and thus, for example, are not able to stay with the commitments they make to themselves to study. They may have images in their head of failure and not success. They may not be caring for their physical health (lack of sleep, drugs or alcohol, poor nutrition, and so forth). You can think of other examples.

Assagioli posited a series of "laws" of human functioning, one of which in particular underscores the importance of attention to inner processes for those who want to become more effective: "Images or mental pictures and ideas tend to produce the physical conditions and the external acts that correspond to them."[23] In other words, if you want to become something or get something done, *imagine it and think about it and feel it.* This inner reality that you create tends to result in the concrete manifestation of this inner, subjective state in the outer reality of events and situations. A simpler way to put it: what you think, you become. This implies working with unsuccessful students to get them to think correctly. They need to get some positive pictures in their heads and some sentences that describe these pictures. They need to be able to imagine success, to see it in their mind's eye, to feel it, and to put words to it. Another way to say it, they need a hope.

Assagioli wrote of "evocative words" and "affirmations" to describe one strategy of getting at this. He theorized that evocative words, as he called them, provoke internal images and feelings and, ultimately, actions. For example, a student could repeat to himself over and over and/or write a word such as "achievement," "self-confidence," or "persistence." He could also put it on a card and place it where it can be seen, say on the desk or table where he studies at home. The challenge for the student each time he says, writes, or sees the word is to experience the associated image (a picture of what it would be like if he were living that way) and feeling (how he would feel if he were that way) in order to more deeply embed this quality into his being. This quality will likely come to be incorporated into his personality, self-concept, actions, and the rest. A word—well, a made-up word—I employ as an evocative word for myself is *care-full.* That word reminds me to be full of care in what I do. It represents being attentive and engaging totally and completely whatever I do. It contrasts with doing things in a kind of throwaway, knock-it-off-and-get-it-done fashion. Some of these underachievers just do not know how rewarding it is to be care-full.

Affirmations are sentences that are used in the same way as evocative words. They describe a hoped-for personal quality or achievement as if it were a present reality. For example, "I am a good student," or "I get work done well and on time." These sentences can be written, say, ten times each morning or night. Or they can be said silently over and over. One technique is to say them to yourself repeatedly while engaging in rituals such as brushing your teeth or vacuuming the carpet. As with the evocative words, affirmations should be experienced each time they are said. To read more about affirmations, a book in education that deals with them is *Our Classroom* by Chick Moorman and his wife Dee Dishon.[24] Another element in the "inner curriculum" is to help students work with the beliefs they have about themselves and school. Though we do not need him to tell us this, Assagioli points out that actions flow out of beliefs. So if we are going to help students change what they do, we need to get them to look at what they believe (another word, assume). These ideas about oneself as a student and the school and what is possible are often inarticulate, tacit, not clearly in the student's awareness. Nevertheless these implicit, in contrast to explicit, inner meanings have great influence over how a student conducts himself in school. By beliefs I mean all the negative ideas students carry around with them such as "I can't do math," "I'm never going to get this English paper done right," "I can't find good work to do in this class," "School is boring," "I'm dumb," and so forth. The Moorman and Dishon book mentioned in the last paragraph outlines ways students can be taught the language of choice and responsibility: "I don't" and "I can't" and "I'm not" become "I choose to" and "I can" and "I will."[25]

Another source, outside the field of education this time, for helping students deal with the way their thinking holds them back is the work done by David Burns and his colleagues at the University of Pennsylvania. Burns lists 10 ways that otherwise capable people think about things that impede their getting things done:

1. *All-or-nothing thinking.* This is seeing things in black-and-white categories. If your performance falls short of perfection, you see yourself as a total failure.
2. *Overgeneralization.* Seeing a single negative event as a never-ending pattern of defeat.
3. *Mental filter.* Picking out a single negative detail and dwelling on it exclusively so that your vision of all reality becomes darkened. It is like the drop of ink that discolors the entire beaker of water.
4. *Disqualifying the positive.* Rejecting positive experiences by insisting they "don't count" for some reason or other. In this way you can maintain a negative belief that is contradicted by your everyday experiences.

5. *Jumping to conclusions*. Making a negative interpretation even though there are no definite facts that convincingly support your conclusion.
   a. *Mind Reading*. Arbitrarily concluding that someone is reacting negatively to you, and you don't bother to check this out.
   b. *The Fortune Teller Error*. Anticipating that things will turn out badly, and you feel convinced that your prediction is an already-established fact.
6. *Magnification (catastrophizing) or minimization*. Exaggerating the importance of things (such as your goof-up or someone else's achievement), or inappropriately shrinking things until they appear tiny (your own desirable qualities or the other fellow's imperfections). This is also called the "binocular trick."
7. *Emotional reasoning*. Assuming that your negative emotions necessarily reflect the ways things really are: "I feel it, therefore it must be true."
8. *Should statements*. Trying to motivate yourself with shoulds and should nots as if you had to be whipped and punished before you could be expected to do anything. "Musts" and "oughts" are also offenders. The emotional consequence is guilt. When you direct should statements toward others, you feel anger, frustration, and resentment.
9. *Labeling and mislabeling*. Extreme form of overgeneralization. Instead of describing your error, you attach a negative label to yourself: "I'm a *loser*." When someone else's behavior rubs you the wrong way, you attach a negative label to him: "He's a jerk." Mislabeling involves describing an event with language that is highly colored and emotionally loaded.
10. *Personalization*. Seeing yourself as the cause of some negative external event which in fact you were not primarily responsible for.[26]

This is all very speculative, but it seems to be a promising venture to explore ways of assisting students to analyze the "cognitive distortions," as Burns calls them, that impede their achievement in school. The following are examples of such distortions I have noticed in less successful students: "I flunked this math test, so I'll never be any good at math and might as well quit." (Overgeneralization.) "The teacher didn't call on me when I had my hand up, so he must not like me." (Jumping to conclusions.) "I really feel dumb; I must be stupid." (Emotional reasoning.) You can think of other examples.

It is the assumption of Burns and his colleagues that feelings and emotions grow out of thinking. Particularly, negative feelings—such as defeat, hopelessness, resentment, and anger—stem from the illogical thought patterns listed above. Thus to get rid of our negative feelings we must rid ourselves of this negative and distorted thinking.

In any case, think about all of this and decide which way to go with it. I contend that if we are going to help students get better in school, we are going to have to help them to better understand how their minds both help them and keep them back. Something we might use is a simple form of meditation. Ask students to sit quietly, close their eyes, and just watch their mind. What thoughts, images, memories, urges, and feelings pop up? What, in fact, *are* these things? What is a thought? A picture? An inner, felt sensation? An internal sentence? And who is doing the watching? Of course this may be tough to do in a classroom, as it may appear overly suspicious to some who have power over you as a teacher. Students might find it embarrassing and useless (though at the same time, with a little reassurance students tend to be game to try it). Although we might not be able to do anything like this in schools, the idea has great potential.

One educator who has used meditation successfully is Beverly Gaylean. Beverly, who I am sad to report died at a young age a couple of years ago, worked as a consultant to the Los Angeles schools. She called her techniques "guided imagery," in order to avoid all the negative connotations to the term meditation. She helped inner city students reduce such negative behaviors as lateness, disruptions and put-downs, and to increase such positive behaviors as affirming communication, attentiveness, supportive actions toward the teacher, and participation in oral and written learning activities. Here is an example of an activity Gaylean used during the first 5 to 7 minutes of the class period. The teacher read this to students. (Do not write this off too quickly.)

Close your eyes for a few minutes and relax. Take a deep breath. As you breathe in, imagine yourself taking in all the most beautiful, wholesome, helpful, and good energy around you. As you breathe out, see yourself breathing forth any tension, worry, doubt, or negativity you might be feeling . . . (pause). Take another breath, breathing in the good around you. This time as you breathe out, feel yourself floating away. . . . floating gently away from this room . . . (pause). Float away now to a place where you really like to be. This is a favorite place where you feel really good. Go there now . . . gently . . . floating to your place . . . (pause). When you get there just enjoy being there . . . (pause). Now while at this place, look into the sky and see the sun . . . warm . . . brilliant. Ask the sun to descend upon you making you feel very warm . . . comfortable . . . secure. Notice how the sun warms but doesn't burn. The sun seems very friendly today . . . (pause). Now call the sun to enter your body through the top of your head. See how it lightens you . . . and makes you feel weightless. Gradually it descends through your head . . . releasing all tension from your eyes . . . jaws . . . neck . . . shoulders. Then it quietly descends through your shoulders . . . arms . . . chest . . . stomach . . . hands . . . thighs . . . legs . . . and feet. Notice how light you feel. Experience your own warmth and brilliance. Experience the good that is you . . . (pause). Now see yourself as absolutely perfect . . . capable of achieving anything you want. You have all the ability to succeed. See yourself as perfect . . . (pause). What do you look like as perfect? How are you behaving? How do others think of you? . . . (pause). See yourself as absolutely perfect. Now see yourself as perfect in this class. You have all the knowledge . . . all the ability to be a perfect student. It's up to you. What do you look like as a perfect student? What are you doing in the class? How are others responding to you? . . . (pause). Now take a moment to say some things to yourself to remind you that you are, indeed, perfect, and that you can be perfect any time you wish. Repeat to yourself: I am a perfect person . . . (pause). I am a perfect student . . . (pause). The others are here to help me continue to be perfect . . . (pause). I am here to help myself continue to be perfect . . . (pause). Say this to yourself three times. . .(pause). Now take the sun that has descended through you and slowly draw it back up through your body . . . leaving you with a feeling of lightness and brightness. Send the sun back into the sky and feel your body so light . . . so gentle . . . so cared for . . . pause). Take a slow deep breath . . . hold it at the top . . . and slowly let the air out and feel yourself floating back to us here in the room. . . .(pause). Open your eyes and enjoy the deep feeling of relaxation.[27]

If that sounds too spooky for your taste, you might try something like this: Ask students to slightly unfocus their eyes and listen to you. Say something like, "Relax, expect good feelings for yourself. Take deep breaths and fill your lungs with peace. Breath out tensions and troubles. Breath in positive thoughts, breathe out negative thoughts. You have the ability to try hard and succeed. You can do it." Or, just have students repeat silently to themselves "I can do it" for 20 seconds. However we do it, it is important to help students quiet down and "go inside." So many successful people do. I am thinking of President Truman's walk every day, President Carter's time of meditation and prayer each day, and Ghandi refraining from speaking one day a week to promote reconnection with himself. The examples are endless, the process invaluable.

Not only did Assagioli affirm that what goes on inside us affects what we accomplish, he pointed out that the reverse is true as well. What we *do* affects all of the inside: thoughts, feelings, personality, self-esteem, and the rest. As Assagioli puts it: "Actions tend to evoke corresponding images and ideas, and these in turn evoke or intensify emotions and feelings."[28] From this axiom Assagioli developed "as if" exercises. The idea is to behave as if something were possible or consistent with who you are, even if you do not think it is. For example, a student can act as if he were a good student during a class discussion even if he is sure he is not. The student's rational mind helps him figure out how he would act if he were a good student. And his personal self can choose to behave in this way even if the feelings and the messages in his head and everything else is saying "This isn't me" or "I can't do that." No matter what he thinks, no matter how big the lack of self-confidence, boredom, or negative self-concept, no matter how many aspects of him "argue" against behaving differently in school, if he just does it anyway for a long enough period of time, just acts as if he had the quality or capability associated with being able to act this new way, lo and behold he starts to see himself differently and feels different inside. The point: Changing the outside changes the inside, because we are a whole entity and changing one thing changes everything else. So if you want to be different, feel different, have a better self-concept—act differently. You can act differently in the face of all the internal negativity because there is a part of you, the personal self, that can override these elements that hold you back.

Yet another "inner" approach derived from Assagioli's writings is to use memory and recall as a way to strengthen confidence, will, or whatever else needs strengthening. Students, for example, can be asked to remember a time in which they were successful in school. They can relive it, experience it again in their mind, and then bring this feeling of how it was then, to today's work in class. Students can learn the skill of recalling those times when they were capable (I have never met a total failure as a student) and put this sense of pride and efficacy in the forefront to replace the "I'm not worth much" inner reality that may otherwise be predominant.

So much more could be said, but I end this discussion of Assagioli here. Can you think of any implications of what I have written or name some things that I have not listed? I hope this discussion of Assagioli has given you some things to explore.

THE IMPLICATIONS OF SPORT PSYCHOLOGY

Given the nature of competitive athletics, coaches and athletes are compelled to perform up to the maximum of their ability. They cannot afford mediocrity. They are measured by what they accomplish and not by the reasons they can offer for their lack of success. Researchers and practitioners in sport and physical education have explored with great intensity what it takes for an individual to achieve to the limit of his or her capability. Potentially at least, we can learn much from their work that applies to promoting greater achievement among underachieving students. But the problem is we tend to cut ourselves off from this insight because we assume sport people such as coaches are in a very different domain from the rest of us, and thus there is little cross-over to the classroom situations and student issues we confront. The key difference is that coaches work with the self-selected and motivated, while the rest of us have to take what we get, so to speak. There is no denying that this is an important distinction. At the same time, however, the lack of a complete parallel in two situations should not obscure similarities that exist. To illustrate, coaches, despite working with volunteers, still have unmotivated athletes not so very different from unmotivated students. Coaches must also deal with discipline problems and "head cases" (athletes who are eccentric, unreliable, troubled.) Coaches, like teachers, have to instill cooperation and commitment among those in their charge. They are not so very different from other educators at all.

We would do well to study sport people in order to gain greater understanding of the achieving individual and to use those examples as models or ideals when working with our students. We might also learn strategies that can be used to help students begin to approximate the same ideals in their schoolwork. In the discussion that follows see what you can learn from the analysis of athletes about the development of more capable and effective students. Does the description of the characteristics and capabilities of the successful athlete give us direction in developing a representation of the effective student? Would it be useful for students to learn some of the insights and skills of the successful athlete? Would they profit from using some of the same techniques? Obviously my answer to these questions is yes.

For the past several years I have been collaborating with a sport psychologist, Dr. Joel Kirsch. Joel worked for 2 years with the San Francisco Giants major league baseball team to increase player motivation and performance. Recently he and I produced a 45-minute video tape called "Promoting Achievement in Sport and School."[29] The program is a series of interviews with individuals who are successful in sport, and looks at how they promote maximum levels of achievement in themselves and others. Interviewees include Jim Socher, football coach at the University of California at Davis; Steve Boros, then manager of the San Diego Padres baseball team; Atlee Hammaker, pitcher for the San Francisco Giants; and George Leonard, author of *The Ultimate Athlete*, as well as writings on education. I discuss my work with Joel later in this section. In these early pages my comments are primarily in response to two books dealing with sport psychology which I have found to be particularly valuable resources: *Peak Performance* by Charles Garfield, and *In Pursuit of Excellence* by Terry Orlick.[30] In this section I outline some ways sport people see and do things that I consider to have particular relevance for us.

The Athlete Gets the Job Done

In sport the predominant perspective is that it is the athlete, not the coach, who is the prime agent in the endeavor. It is the athlete who is charged with taking on the responsibility for getting the job done. From within the athlete, playing is something *he* does. He does not just "go to football" (go to class), if you know what I mean. The coach's job is to coach. He or she supports the player in becoming the best player he or she can be; but it is the *athlete's* performance that counts. Certainly the coach, in contrast to many teachers, does not see his situation as one where he runs a stimulating practice to be judged interesting or boring by players. A practice is about what players do. The coach supports, instructs, and encourages. But at the end of the practice the issue is not so much a matter of how the coach did—though of course that is important—but rather, was the player successful? The player's orientation is much more "How did I do?" than "How did the coach do?" or "Do I like the coach?" The player is looking at it from his side, scrutinizing what is going right for him, what is going wrong, what needs to be done, and what is going to happpen. In sport terms, "his head is into it."

Compare this circumstance to what typically goes on in schools. Look into classrooms and most often the central element is the teacher, not the students. The teachers are active. They are talking, initiating, and making things happen. The students are reactive, watching, taking things in, responding to questions, doing assigned tasks. In sum, classrooms are places where teachers teach more than settings where students "student." Consider this distinction.

Human beings are quite flexible. They do what they do in accordance with how the situation is defined. In the way the sport culture defines it, the athletic context is a place where ballplayers do their best with the help of teammates, coaches, and fans. In contrast, the culture of the school makes the classroom a place where the students show up and diligently do what they are told. I know I am drawing these distinctions in rather stark terms, but I think you can see my overall point. Athletes cannot just depend on others to assess their skills and needs or to take action to improve them, which if you think about it, is what teachers usually do. The good athlete must assess himself. He must study his commitments and priorities, the way he thinks, the way he goes about things, his strengths and weaknesses, his current and hoped-for level of performance, and the limits and possibilities in his current situation for getting him where he wants to go.[31] How many students do that? How many are even called upon to do it? We, the teachers, do it for them.

Self-Understanding Is Key

Self-understanding is no less important in schools than it is on the athletic field. But while self-analysis among athletes is so integral to athletics at the highest level, it is not characteristic of students in schools. Yet it helps as much to have a self-aware and self-directed student as it does a self-aware and self-directed athlete. Students as much as athletes need to be clear on their commitments and priorities, their strengths and weaknesses, their habits, their situations, and so on.

Orlick points out self-control—a real problem in underachievers—begins by getting to know your own patterns. I contend that students are *sort of* self-aware and purposeful, and that it would be better if they *really* were. This may point to the usefulness of classes or workshops for students in which the topic is not math or science but instead their ability to come to a better understanding of themselves as students.

Athletes Have Hopes

Another characteristic of the good athlete is that he or she has a goal. Another way to put it, the athlete has a hope. While the athlete is acutely sensitive to his or her currrent situation and problems, he or she does not dwell on them as much as on creating an imagined future. He or she can visualize this future. Athletes can imagine themselves running for a touchdown in the last minute of the game to win the championship. They can feel what it will be like. In his or her imagination the athlete lives through what his thoughts will be and how others will respond. He or she can put all this into words if you ask. This athlete will tell you what it will be like if he or she is successful athletically. If you have done any sport fantasizing you know what I mean. It is also so that the athlete has a felt sense of responsibility that brings him or her to the point where these imagined good things actually occur. Athletes do not wait around for the coach to carry them across the goal line. They accept the challenge of doing it for themselves—with the help of the coach and others. This orientation is in such marked contrast to unsuccessful students who are much more prone to articulately inform you why they are stuck (bad parents, bad school, bad luck) than express a hope for things going better in school, a faith that they are capable of being in charge of their school lives, and a willingness to take responsibility for attaining academic success.

This clearly implies that a key job for a teacher is to help a student get a hope in his head. The student—not just we—must be able to picture what it would be like to score an academic touchdown (or a first step, make a first down) in math or English class. This emphasis on creating hopes in students' heads so that they can work to make them into a reality is a contrast to putting all our energy into developing and creating an effective subject-centered lesson plan. It implies sessions in which we encourage students to imagine what it would be like to be successful (including how it might be scary in some ways); how they would feel to know the subject well, to get a good grade, to get approval from their parents and teachers. Students as well as athletes need hopes; not just problems, not just the current reality. Otherwise all they have is the moment and immediate satisfaction or the lack of it. In the interview Joel did with Steve Boros, Boros emphasizes the need for athletes to do things that are, in his words, "not a whole lot of fun." He points out that what is required for athletes (and I would say, students) to do these "not a whole lot of fun" things is a clear vision of the rewards of success. Without a vision, school is, metaphorically, a television program that is in an immediate way attention-provoking or unstimulating, boring or interesting, fun or tedious.

The challenge, and admittedly this is going to be difficult to take on successfully, is to complement our efforts to capture students' attention and "make learning fun," with activities that assist students in imagining success. Certainly this is what coaches do. Yes, they talk about having fun. However, coaches also talk about meeting challenges which will fulfill and satisfy, and these are not necessarily fun each and every minute. They spend a great deal of time painting a picture of the result they seek with their players—winning the championship. Coaches hold up high, perhaps even unattainable, standards of athletic excellence and challenge their players to strive to meet them. They know that human beings, as a part of their nature, want challenge, want a mountain to climb. Coaches, unlike many of us in education, do not expect to spur excitement with statements about the minimums they will accept ("I won't take anything less than a .500 season out of you guys"). They do not pin their hopes on a pitch for mediocre or acceptable accomplishment ("If we get at it, we can be *just like* those other teams"). And yet in schools we wonder why students (and teachers, for that matter) have not gotten all charged up about meeting minimum competency standards or mastering material it is assumed that everybody can and will learn. The successful coach says: "I'm not going to define exactly what success means. I want you to be the best you can be, the sky's the limit. Go to it 110%. Let me see what you are made of." Schools, on the other hand, are prone to define things with tightly worded behavioral objectives that define exactly what accomplishment means—and at the same time kill the adventure, kill the quest into unknown territory. Perhaps these kinds of distinctions are subtle, but they are also very important. And good coaches are familiar with their importance. Unfortunately, even though the rest of us often feel superior to "jocks" we frequently miss the point.

Discovering a Mission

Garfield pointed out that the good athlete has a deeply felt—psychologicallly, personally, owned—sense of mission or overall purpose that gives meaning to the immediate goals he or she chooses to pursue. Garfield described mission as a "passionate belief in a personal philosophy that establishes the basis for setting goals."[32] If athletes need a mission, do not students need one as well? If an athlete's dedication is dependent on a commitment to a personal philosophy, why should we expect students who lack one to take off in school? To talk of this is to focus on the central issues of adolescence: Who am I? Where do I fit? What is my life worth? What is my calling? Yet, crucial as the resolution of these issues is for young people, where is the support in schools for them to work through these issues? Certainly there is not much going on in school to help a student resolve issues of this sort. Yet, what is going to bring a student *really* rather than *merely* to learn and grow is the knowledge that he needs those things to go somewhere in life; life matters, it has significance. Why learn if you do not count and your future does not mean much at all? The reality is that many students are being asked to get excited about their education when they have no excitement about their lives. They are not on the way to anywhere that is helped by schooling. They have no mission.

Obviously these are very complex and sensitive concerns. One thing I can suggest that touches on this, at least in a beginning way, is for the school curriculum to include more content directly related to issues of life meaning and purpose. This further supports drawing content from the disciplines of philosophy, ethics, and theology. It points toward students being asked to reflect on life examples, perhaps through biographies, review how others have resolved the fundamental issue of choosing or aligning with a life direction. It means students being challenged to define a personal philosophy. It means students wrestling with how one comes to beliefs strong enough so that they can serve to propel action. It means students who are challenged to affirm a personal mission and explain how being excellent in school can serve that mission.

In this regard, I am reminded of a teenage student whom I spoke to recently who is having difficulty in school. He told me, "It seems to be a bad time to be around. There is lots to do, but at the same time nothing to do. There just isn't anything for me. I don't know where I fit." This does not exactly reflect a firm sense of personal philosophy or mission. I am sure there is a great deal going on in this students' life, and in the school, that we need to understand. But from this statement alone, without knowing about the quality of his teachers or how good the textbooks are, we would guess that he is not exactly on the honor roll. We want to say, "You need some goals. One way to figure out where you fit is to get some goals to shoot for." There is a dialectical relationship between goals and mission. Finding things worth doing (goals) helps define and clarify one's mission or purpose. But also, having a personal philosophy and sense of mission gives direction to the selection of goals. Mission and goals need to be considered concurrently; they enhance and give meaning to each other and must provide the context for specific objectives and actions. So often in schools we act as though day-to-day objectives and behaviors are all that matter. No wonder so many teachers, technically proficient or not, are so exhausted, depleted, and hoarse at the end of a day after putting their charges through the paces designed to accomplish today's objectives. No wonder teachers are less than eager to face the task of teaching up a storm tomorrow, and the next day, and the next. They are pulling students along who are not going anywhere, at least not in this class.

Expectations and Commitment

Another point, coaches *expect* the athlete to be the best he or she can be.[33] It is not really anything that has to be talked about. It is just understood. This expectation is inherent in the manner, the bearing, the posture, the look in the coach's eye. And even more importantly, athletes expect themselves to be excellent and successful. Sport people know that without this self-expectation and the expectation of the coach toward him the athlete is far less likely to stick with it through the difficult practices, go through the necessary self-denial, and persevere amid the inevitable down times on the way to accomplishment. Without positive and high expectations, athletes are much more likely to quit or drift or be dependent on the coach or fans to keep cheerleading them on. And as a matter of fact, while we have some high sounding jargon to mask what we are doing, many teachers amount to cheerleaders for a desultory last place ball club. Forty years of that and a teacher deserves *two* gold watches.

Not only does the athlete expect success, he or she feels a commitment to create that success. Athletic success is something *he* or *she* is going to do. It is not something that the coach does or that falls from the sky. Athletes feel what can be called an intention to create in reality this image of success that is in their heads and that they expect of themselves. An intention is more than a goal, more than something the athlete wants or that is preferable or desirable, more than a good idea. An intention is: "I *am* going to get it done. It *will* happen. I *will* do it." As I am defining it, this posture of intentionality is very subjective; but nevertheless it is real and so important. An intention is an experienced, literally sensed, posture or way of being. It is that feeling when, this time, you really will quit smoking. Somehow you know that you are going to stay with it this time. How do you know? You just feel it.

The coach's job is to make certain that the athlete understands that without that level of commitment, without that intention, he or she cannot be truly successful. Without that, there is little of significance the coach, no matter how skilled, can do. The sport people Joel interviewed for the video production were so clear on this point. They thought that for some athletes this "drive" was "just there," in the genes or a product of family socialization, something of that sort. But at the same time they saw commitment, drive, intention, will to succeed, whatever you call it, to be a matter of choice. An athlete could *choose* to move beyond mediocrity or failure to an intention to be every ounce of what he or she can be. It is within the athlete's power to adopt this bearing, this way of being. It is under the athlete's control. Drive is not simply something you just have or do not have, like eye color. Coaches do not buy "I do not care and it is your fault because you don't coach well enough" among athletes. Teachers, in contrast, have been known to accept "I am bored because you don't teach well enough" to the point of guilt and self-flagellation. Coaches know that psychological matters of this sort are just as deserving of their time as teaching the skill of making cut-off plays in baseball. We as teachers should too.

Models to Emulate

In addition, coaches often promote the qualities they want in their athletes through the use of examples. Consider the following quote by an official of the Philadelphia Flyers hockey team about Bobby Clarke, who became a star player in the National Hockey League. Clarke later was a successful general manager of the Flyers. As reported in Orlick's book, the official noted:

> We drafted Bobby Clarke on our second round, but there was a boy we drafted on our first round who was bigger and stronger, could skate and shoot better than Clarke but Clarke made it and he didn't. He never had the heart for the game. He wasn't willing to sacrifice that little bit . . . that you need to be a professional hockey player. In practice Clarke would be there ten minutes longer and he would work harder. In a game he got himself mentally prepared to give extra . . . the other player didn't do that. Result—one went ahead, the other fell behind. Clarke did extra work on the ice, where he had to give a little more to check the man, where

he had to bear down, and where it showed more than any place is coming back.
. . .Gotta give a little more. If you lose possession of the puck, now you have to
dig down to your bootstraps, for extra adrenalin to come back and check the man.
Bobby Clarke would always show that. The other boy would put his head down
and sort of give up. That's the difference between the two.[34]

Whether we do it formally or not, we would do well to find ways to create
student "heroes" for students to emulate, individuals who embody the positive
qualities we desire in students. Baseball has had Pete Rose, who epitomized the
player who "comes to play" every day. Basketball has had Larry Bird and Julius
Erving, and football has pointed to players such as Walter Payton. In school,
on the other hand, the good student is too often viewed as a "nerd" or "drudge."
Who are the positive models for students to look to? Every culture puts forth
its models—Abraham Lincoln, Thomas Edison, Charles Lindbergh, and Harry
Truman come to mind—who represent something valued and worthy to approximate in our own lives. All religions and philosophies have the great individuals
who embody the ideal: Christ, the Buddha, Mohammed, and so forth. These individual examples take on the quality of myth and serve an educative, socializing
function. They say, "This is how to be." We have not been very good at this
in schools despite the awards days and honor rolls. It is something we should
think more about. In any case, whether we are successful or not, we should take
the issue of lack of student commitment on directly. Too often we accommodate
for the lack of commitment among students by trying to teach in such a way that
it "grabs" them; when if classes are ever going to work students are going to
have to do the grabbing. Or we hint and cue as to what we want. Generally, teaching tends to be an indirect profession. We need to be more direct. If we want
something, let us go directly and openly for it. If there has to be commitment
among students for it to work, let us confront that issue head on.

Concentration and Relaxation

Commitment is only valuable, however, if a student can concentrate on the task
at hand long enough to get the job done. In my experience working with underachieving students, I have discovered that concentration is a major problem. For
example, in my survey of 10 problem students in the school in which I was working, 4 indicated the following statement, derived from a student interview conducted on an earlier occasion, was true: "Studying is a problem. I have trouble
concentrating, staying with it, when I study. Then I wind up getting nothing done."
But if the ability to concentrate is a key "studenting" skill—and I am convinced
that it is—when do we ever teach it? And *can* it be taught? On the frontiers of
sport the answer is yes. Consider these exercises from the Orlick book that promote a relaxed concentration among archers:

Relaxation and concentration are viewed as being very inter-related by world class archers. What they are seeking is relaxed concentration. They want their bodies relaxed but ready, and their minds calm but focused. They want to get rid of tension and to focus their attention so that it encompasses a very specific target. The target may be the mental rehearsal that goes on in their head, the scan for unwanted tension in their body, or the center of the bull's eye that is sitting at the end of the field waiting to receive their arrow. Their concentration often follows a sequence, from mind (mental rehearsal), to body (scan-relaxation), to target (centering of focus). In each step in the sequence they get rid of non-esssentials so that this one focus or vision can fully absorb their conscious thought. The ability to narrow attention to a tight focus and hold it there, until the body is free to follow the visions of the mind, appears to be crucial to good performance.

Relaxed concentration is a learned art which must be practiced to be perfected. Here are some exercises involving both relaxation and concentration suggested by archers, which you can try to adapt to your situation.

- Line up several targets. Become aware of all the targets. Then begin to narrow your focus so that you become aware of only one target, then the center of that target. Let all other visions blur into the background, let all external sounds become inaudible. *Connect* with that target.
- Sit quietly and look at something, like the trees, clouds, the sky, or listen to the birds. Try to get absorbed in them.
- Practice letting your thoughts wander, then refocusing on target.
- Sit quietly and think about your shooting sequence. Visualize the perfect execution (e.g., position, form, style, technique, aim, release). Then empty your mind and let your body perform automatically.
- Repeat the thought upon which you wish to focus (e.g., 10, 10, 10; center, center, center; form, form, form).
- Seek the feel of the shot. If the feel is right the arrow will find the target.
- Slow everything down... talk slowly, move slowly, stretch slowly.
- Practice controlled breathing, slow, deep and relaxed.
- Practice not worrying by zeroing in on the one arrow you are preparing to shoot. Everything else is unimportant, unproductive, non-essential.
- After a bad arrow, practice immediately shifting concentration to proper preparation for the next arrow.
- If someone watching breaks your concentration, practice relaxed focusing with people watching (e.g., while chopping wood or shooting arrows).
- Practice taking your concentration back and forth from your body (body scan) to your sight (pin on target). Relax, then focus.
- Practice shooting each arrow one at a time, disregarding past and future shots.
- Use cue words (e.g., "relax," "let go," "focus") or thought repetition (e.g. aim, aim, aim) to keep your mind on shooting. Have a zip word or cue word that will zap you into on-line concentration.
- Will your arrows into the center of the target.
- Take pleasure in the performance.

If you experience problems with concentration, try easier. "Sitting quietly, doing nothing, Spring comes, the grass grows by itself."[35]

Is there anything we can learn from these examples? Perhaps in schools we can give students who need it time to practice exercises comparable to these archery examples. For instance, letting their mind wander from a text chapter and then refocusing "on target." You can think of many other possibilities.

Do notice the emphasis on relaxation. In schools we often tend to be wary of relaxation, seeing it as "one giant leap for mankind" on the way to lethargy. Instead, we promote a kind of "go, go, go" intensity (probably in response to all the emotional flatness and indifference we see around us). In contrast, in athletes relaxation is not set off against commitment, concentration, and achievement. Rather, sport people see the positive ways relaxation contributes to athletic achievement. It is understood that the athlete will not do his best unless he can let go of stress and tension. Sport people draw a distinction between being alert and vigilant and being tight. The good athlete has to be able to relax.

Any number of techniques can be used to relax. A simple one is to focus your attention on your breath and take four or five deep breaths. With each outbreath, let go of tensions and the thoughts that bounce around in your head. Educator Jack Canfield provided the following relaxation exercises he has used with students:

> *Breath imagery*: Imagine breathing in a beautiful white light. Imagine that with each breath you take, your whole body is beginning to fill up with this radiant white light. After several breaths, you can begin to feel your body becoming bathed in a warm (cool) glow. You can feel yourself growing very calm. This white light is dissolving any tension, anxiety, fear, doubt, worry or negativity that you may have been experiencing in your mind or your body. Just continue to imagine breathing in this wonderful, soothing, relaxing white light. You can feel yourself growing more and more relaxed with each breath.

> *Progressive relaxation*: Get into a comfortable position and relax. Start by tensing all your muscles in your feet as tight as you can. Keep them tight and notice the tension. Then relax them. Now tighten the muscles in your calves as tight as you can. Keep them tight. Now relax them. Now tighten the muscles in your hips and buttocks. Keep them tight. Then relax them...(continue this process with the lower back, stomach, chest and upper back, hands, arms, shoulders, neck, and face). This process can also be done in a wavelike fashion. Start by tightening the feet, then the calves, thighs, hips, stomach, chest, back, hands, arms, shoulders, neck and face. At this point the whole body is being held tense. Then starting with the feet again, relax each part of the body in the same order. It is like a wave of tension washing over the body and then a wave of relaxation. Once kids learn to do it, they can relax themselves very quickly with this method.[36]

A Plan

For the athlete to achieve his goals he must have a *plan of action*. He must analyze himself and his situation and devise actions that will accomplish what he hopes to achieve. Certainly the coach can help in the formulation of this plan, but wherever it comes from, the superior athlete must make it his own psychologically. He must understand it, feel that is his, and assume responsibility for its implementation. Contrast this with most school situations. The teacher is the only one with more than a fair degree of a considered and detailed plan of action—usually in the form of daily lesson plans or unit plans. At best, the students have a reasonable idea of where the teacher is going and show up each day alert and responsive. At worse, they see the class as the teacher's enterprise and only respond if something happens to catch their interest. But a true plan, no. Indeed, *both* students and teachers should be developing lesson plans. I will go even further: It is even more important that students do so than teachers.

Learning to Connect with the Task

The successful athlete must learn to engage the sport tasks fully. He or she must learn the skill of saying "YES!" to the job at hand. Not sort of, not 80%—YES!! This posture of giving "110%," as they say, is something that the sport culture values. And it is a posture athletes practice assuming. Carrying over to schooling, it is not studying, it is STUDYING! (Staying relaxed, remember.) It means being totally involved, completely engaged in doing one's schoolwork. It means total attentiveness and participation in the learning activity. In the practice of Zen it is contended that if you learn how to pour a cup of tea you will learn how to live. Just pour the tea, nothing else. Do it with all of your being, with care, with gracefulness and awareness. In sport, when you play ball, play ball. In school, go to school. Learn to say yes; learn to say no. When it is no, it is no. When it is yes, it is yes. So much of students' lives is maybe, kind of, somewhat. Life may be like a computer, a zero-sum process. That is, we are happiest and most productive when it is on or off, yes or no—not somewhere in between. Schools teach students to live life somewhere in between yes and no and this worries me. Clearly, for many students a "study skill" that is invaluable for them to learn is the ability to say "YES." At least we can begin by talking about the importance of engaging in an activity fully and positively, and through role playing give some opportunity to students to practice it. Also, we as teachers can be models of full engagement in the way we do our work for students to observe. As I think about it, it may be that being fully engaged is not so much something to learn as it is simply something to do again and again, with the result that one gets better at it.

Willfulness

The athlete must be able to count on himself to keep working. He must get to the point where he can say "I will" (or "I won't") and mean it. He cannot afford to be stuck in an "I'll try," "I need," or "If only" posture. It has to be *I will*, period. But in order to be willful, the athlete must have control of himself. He must be able to manage his thoughts and behavior. In my experience with less productive students, it is not so much that they do not want to do well in school. In fact, despite what they may first tell you about not liking school and not caring whether they do well or not, most would prefer to succeed in their studies. Talking to them for 5 minutes would leave the impression they are indifferent. After that, one begins to hear the frustratioon and anguish at failing to get as much done as they could and living with others' disapproval and disappointment, as well as their disappointment in themselves. A student's expression of "I don't care" or "I'm OK with how it's going" is often a way to try to maintain his or her sense of self-value in the face of inadequate performance.

This is not to say that some students really do not care about school. To be sure, some do not. It is to say that we tend to overestimate the numbers of such students who do not want to succeed. By its nature the human being desires accomplishment and seeks approval. This human tendency is still there despite being bored, at a loss as to how to succeed, or in a situation in which the work being assigned seems beside the point. If they were told there were strategies that would lead them to do better and be happier in school, many underachieving students would want to learn them. As it is, so many students are caught. On the one hand, they know it is not the greatest idea to drop out of school. On the other they cannot figure out how to connect with school in ways that satisfy themselves, their parents, and school professionals, and also remain on good terms with their friends. And if they do not know how to put together this intricate package of multiple and potentially conflicting interests, where are they supposed to learn?

What so often happens with students (the rest of us can relate to this, because it is characteristic of us as well) is that, at the beginning of the year in September, they set out to achieve more effectively. They mean well. But then something happens and they fall back into old patterns. A key factor is probably a failure of will and self-control. Consequently, it is not so much that we are not good teachers or that the curriculum is inappropriate or that the students are hostile or indifferent. It is that the students do not know how to be willful. Good students are willful, just as much as good athletes.

What accounts for willfulness? Can self-control and self-management and getting it done be understood and learned? This discussion is all very speculative. I can report that I have set up a series of what I call "will training" exercises for myself. I decide to do something and then *do it*, period. Small things, like washing the car. Or I might set a quota of pages to write on this book. Or even smaller things. I will look at a salt shaker and say, "I am going to count slowly to 25 and then pick it up." I do that and then witness (my conscious self) what is going on. What part of me made the choice? What part holds me for the 25? What activates me in picking it up? What allows me to say "I will" and mean it? In these little "will exercises," no matter what my feelings or body sensations offer (fear, boredom, fatigue), no matter what the external situation (the call on the phone inviting me to a movie), I do what I said I would do. Why? Because I said I would. Period. That ability to do something no matter what is an empowering skill to possess. Because there will be times when the thing that should be done is the one thing that looks least attractive at the moment (like studying for a test). Every aspect of one's self and situation lines up against keeping the personal commitment made earlier. Well, all except one; the personal self. I, the core me, can monitor and overrule all the rest if I choose to. And there are instances—no, not every time—when that is exactly what I need to be able to do.

Explore your own willfulness. When do you carry things through and when do you bail out only to regret it later? Try some will training exercises on your own. It helps for us to develop these desirable studenting traits in ourselves. First of all, possessing them ourselves will provide a good model for students. And secondly, working with these traits ourselves will teach us about how one acquires them.

Mental Rehearsal

This discussion of will underscores the overall point that a study of the frontier of sport reveals a great concern for the "inner," mental game. Sport people are increasingly exploring the workings of the athlete's mind as it contributes to athletic success or failure. Good athletes have learned that they must train their minds as well as their bodies to attain the results they seek.

Several examples: Many athletes employ mental rehearsal as a technique to increase their level of performance.[37] In mental rehearsal the athlete uses his imagination to visualize performance of the various stages of the event correctly. Another way to say it, he practices doing it right in his mind. Note the focus is on success. Success is what is lived through in imagination. The time is not spent anticipating what it might be like if things go wrong. The athlete dwells on positive and not negative images; on getting through obstacles to gratifying achievement, not on getting blocked by the things that can go wrong. In 1986 Jack Nicklaus won a sixth Masters golf championship at the ripe old athletic age of 46. I know that Nicklaus pictures every golf shot being made correctly in his mind before he swings a club. Another example I remember—sorry, I do not have exact documentation on this—is a research study that was done on two groups of basketball players who were attempting to improve their free throw shooting. I do not remember the details but I do know that practicing in their minds without actually shooting helped increase performance. For all I know, mental rehearsal provides invaluable neuromuscular practice. Or, it may be just a way to become more concentrated. Whatever is actually going on, it is clear to me that to be successful, one must stop dwelling on the problems and failure and start fantasizing success. An implication for education, we may want to simply ask students to take a few minutes to mentally rehearse doing the evening's homework completely and excellently. Or perhaps before a class discussion we should ask them to picture themselves participating in a positive way.

Positive Thinking

The good athlete needs to become a student of the way he thinks.[38] The internal messages he sends himself can either be an asset or get him in trouble. When confronted with a pressure situation some athletes think to themselves, "Oh here I go, I'll choke again" or "I'm not good enough" or "I hope they don't hit it to me." (I draw from my own experiences as a shortstop in baseball. I could field up a storm in infield practice, but an inability to relax and concentrate and a tendency to impose a negative mental barrage on myself made me mighty suspect in the bottom of the ninth.) What an athlete learns as he studies his mind is that he does not so much *have* thoughts as *create* thoughts. With practice he can learn to replace the "I'm going to botch this royally" negative self-talk with positive messages of the sort: "I'm ready. Hit the ball to me and I'll turn a double play and win us the game."

Simply, good athletes think positively. They know there will be barriers to overcome, but their thoughts center on successfully transcending obstacles, not on just bumping into them. There is often a certain amount of acting involved in all of this. Even if you do not feel all these positive things, you have to think as if you do, because if you "fake it" effectively, sort of fool yourself into actually believing what you tell yourself, I'm sure over a period of time your confidence does actually increase. (Remember Assagioli? What you think, you become.) Of course it helps enormously, too, to get to work and develop the necessary skills to get the job done, in sport or in school. Increased skill boosts one's confidence. As well, it leads to the kinds of actual outcomes that provide tangible evidence of one's competence, and this makes thoughts more positive—which in turn leads to greater real-world success, more positive thoughts, and the upward spiral continues. The trick is to get the momentum (sports term) going in the right direction. A good way to do that is to think right.

The obvious point in all of this is that many students are trying to succeed in school despite a deluge of negative thoughts: "The teacher doesn't like me." "Nothing is worth doing in this class." "This is boring." "I don't like the subject." "I'm no good at this." Now, some of this may be true. The student *does* feel this way. Things *are* like that. But that is not what I am talking about here. I am saying that, good reason for the thought or not, thinking like this is not likely to be associated with achievement and satisfaction for the student. The student must find a way to get beyond, through, or around these conclusions to find something positive to tell himself and go for in school, or indeed it is likely to be a long and hard year.

Self-Assessment of Performance

Another aspect of the "mental game" is the ability of the athlete to analyze his own performance and make necessary corrections. On the tape Joel and I produced, both Steve Boros and Atlee Hammaker emphasize the necessity for an athlete to monitor and modify what he does on the athletic field. The good athlete scrutinizes every nuance of his performance as a player. I know that Hammaker goes over video tapes following each of his pitching turns. What is crucial to note is that while it is important that coaches carefully assess what the player is doing, it is absolutely vital that the player have the desire and skill to review himself in light of his goals and make the necessary adjustments. To carry it over to education, teachers learn to evaluate students' efforts in class and modify their teaching accordingly. In fact, teachers take courses in how to do this necessary activity. But while good coaching promotes self-assessment skills in athletes, typically there is not a comparable emphasis in schools among students. Usually students receive the outcomes of teachers' evaluations rather than generate and respond to their own data. An example from my experience, I have found that at best students with reading deficiencies know they have a problem and go to reading class. But what is ideal, and seems to me attainable, is that the student be "on his own case." He knows as much about his reading difficulty and the remedial possibilities as the teacher. He has goals, a plan, and is monitoring and managing his progress even more thoroughly than the reading instructor. "Going to reading" is not enough. *Intending* to learn how to read is what is needed. Knowing what is off and working in a self-conscious way to improve it—that is better. It is, after all, the *student's* reading problem. *He* or *she* is going to be the one trying to read at 40, not us. Yet somehow the way we run the schools it is our problem. That is not the way sport people do it. They define the situation differently. It is the athlete's problem. We would do well to learn how they accomplish that.

Learning from Failure

Sport reminds us that whatever we do in life, it will involve both winning and losing. Even the most successful major league baseball team loses one-third of its games. In my lifetime only one National Football League team has won all of its games in a season. Even the most gifted athlete has to be able to deal with failure. The athlete cannot let it get him or her down. An athlete cannot let it prevent him or her from continuing on to do his or her best. I have two quotes tacked over my desk that relate to this notion. One is by Babe Ruth, the great home run slugger. The Babe said, "Never let the fear of striking out get in your way." As a matter of fact Babe struck out more than anyone in his day. But he knew that if he spent all his time staying away from strikeouts and played it safe he would not take the big swing that results in a home run. The other quote is by Pete Rose. When asked how it felt to have gone hitless in a game, Pete replied, "I learned a long time ago that you're going to get a lot of oh-for-fours [no hits in four times at bat] in your life." The next night his first hit gave him more total hits than any player who ever played the game. Both these great athletes had a philosophy and attitude that helped them deal with the inevitable failures in life.

Currently in education there is much emphasis on making sure that students are successful most every time. Lessons are structured to insure that students get things right. This is a good way to "prime the pump" in order to get students going who have had a long history of failure. As with almost every good thing we can go too far with it—because the opposite of every good thing is also a good thing in the right context and in the right relationship to that first good thing. In this case, taking a risk, failing, and then learning from it and "staying in the ballgame," is an important skill for students to learn. The nature of adolescence— all of life—is that, especially if you really *live*, you will win some and lose some. Many of our underachievers are so afraid of failing that they do not try. They overlook the fact that everybody loses in their lives. "The Cosby Show" proved to be a gigantic hit on NBC. People do not seem to remember that Bill Cosby had several prime time television shows flop in the last decade. But he did not quit, and look what he has done. In fact, failure can be a gift if students would only see it as such. It is a chance to see what went wrong and fix it.

As a teacher I certainly want my students to be successful. And indeed, creating success experiences for students is particularly important for those who have had a tough go of it and failed many times. These students may well have labeled themselves a failure and just about given up. (I say "just about" because I do not think it is possible for the human being to ever totally give up.) Or these students may, without realizing it, set up failure in order to keep their school-going "story" consistent and their negative self-label ("foul-up") accurate. People do things like that. But at the same time I do not want to contrive success to the point where the work is not challenging for students. Human beings are challenge-confronters, and eventually avoid tasks that are too easy. Or at least they do not grow as they should intellectually and in other ways, despite whatever concepts or facts they may be learning. I want school to be a struggle for students in the positive sense of that word. Any athlete will tell you that it is not fun or not really satisfying unless it stretches your ability to get it done. And when students fail, that is an opportunity to make failure itself the content of the class. What are the variety of meanings people attribute to not accomplishing a goal? Some take it as a sign of personal inadequacy, but others view it as a lesson on where it went wrong and how it can be better next time. It is all in how you look at it. In any event, students had better learn how to deal with failure, especially those who have had many "oh-for-fours" in their lives.

Applying Criticism

An athlete not only has to be self-critical, he also has to learn to take advantage of the reactions and suggestions from his coaches and others. Using criticism to one's advantage is a skill too few people, including athletes, have mastered. A key to taking advantage of criticism from others is the skill of knowing how to filter out inaccurate or harmful criticism or put it in the proper context. For example, for an athlete the kinds of carping in newspapers to hype readership or promote attendance at the games may be harmful if it is taken seriously. Unfortunately, students who have had difficulty in school are likely to have been criticized quite harshly, even to the point of ridicule. It is an invaluable skill for students to learn to welcome criticism but at the same time separate the wheat from the chaff, so to speak. The student must invite it or he might not receive what can be used constructively. But he cannot compulsively take it all to heart, as some of it will be ill-informed or ill-intended and do the student no good. Sadly, at a very young age students are exposed to reactions from the world that puts them down and holds them back: "Not you." "Who cares." "You messed up again." "You're hopeless." "Get back." The kids at the bottom have to learn how to understand and deal with such remarks and attitudes. If they are especially adept, students can use these kinds of negations to spur them on to even greater effort and achievement.

Constructive Communication

An interesting discussion in the Orlick book centers on how athletes can influence the coach.[39] He reminds his athlete audience that coaches are not mind readers and that if things are to improve, the athletes have a responsibility to communicate what they want to the coach. He suggests the athlete meet with the coach to discuss what makes him or her work best as well as what destroys the workout. Orlick suggests letting coaches know right away with a "thank you" if the coach's instruction or feedback has been constructive. Orlick also suggests asking for additional help or further clarification if you do not understand something. Moreover, he recommends, along with a whole list of other things, letting coaches know your preferences, how you want things to go.

Reading this section in Orlick I was struck by the realization of how few times in all the years I have spent in athletics I did anything that even approximates these kinds of communications with coaches. I am also struck with how few students in our schools even come close to relating to teachers in this way. This is especially an issue for the "lower" kids. An extreme example, when I taught the students, typically around 15-years-old, who were locked up in jail, I found that they were quite appreciative of me as a teacher, but it took me some time to pick that up. The students whom I had taught in regular schools were much better at letting me know if they liked what I was doing. They would look at me appreciatively, nod their head yes to what I said, and thank me for helping them. These jailed kids did not look, and did not praise. Instead, they had the strangest—to me, anyway—ways of affirming me. For instance, one student, who I had been working with quite well I thought, came up behind me one day and

punched me in the kidney. After I calmed down a bit, I saw from his manner
that this was his way to say he liked me and his attempt to get across the message, "You're included, you're one of us." I concluded that their response pattern was a problem for these kids with other teachers. So I decided to teach some
basic behaviorist (Skinnerian) techniques for these students to use with teachers.
We discussed figuring out what was a payoff, rewarding, to teachers and others,
and then how to give them that when they were helpful. One specific thing I
remember us working on: looking at teachers (respectfully) and saying "thank
you" or "that really helped" when the teacher deserved it.

Learning to Resolve Conflicts

Sport psychologist Joel Kirsch, whom I have been referring to right along, pays
special attention to *how* we do things in contrast to *what* we do. In this regard
Joel has been strongly influenced by concepts and practices derived from his study
of aikido.[40] Aikido, a relatively recently developed—this century—marshal art
originated in Japan and is now practiced quite widely in this country. Aikido is
a means of self defense, but it also provides a guide to living harmoniously, grace-
fully, positively, and powerfully in the world. For a short time I studied what
Joel and his colleague George Leonard call "energy training." Energy training—I
believe now it is being called Leonard Energy Training—is a series of physical
movement exercises which students then critique to ascertain the meanings and
lessons that can be derived from them.[41] I realized that energy training, like the
discipline of aikido from which it is derived, is wonderfully instructive on how
to deal with conflict in our lives. In fact, Joel was sent to Northern Ireland by
an agency of the United Nations to teach conflict resolution strategies to competing factions in that country and made use of the energy training exercises in that
work. Students who are not doing well in school often have conflicts with teachers,
parents, peers, and employers that hurt them academically. It would be so helpful for these students if we could help them find ways to cope with conflict other
than running, sulking, striking out at others or masochistically at themselves, or
allowing it to distract them from their schoolwork.

Perhaps energy training, or aikido itself, is a way to do this. Energy training
is a very gentle process and may be a better way to go. I practiced aikido a bit
and was sore for a week from being thrown to the mat. I know that the practitioners of the art move in a remarkably graceful and flowing manner, but I did
not get to that point. An interesting experiment would be to use energy training
or aikido with underachieving and difficult-to-manage students. Conduct, say,
8 weeks of 3 or 4 sessions per week of about an hour each. See if it has any
effect on motivation, school achievement, and the manageability of these students.
My hunch is that there will be positive outcomes. More importantly, these strategies may point the way to using physical movement as a way to teach important
concepts in any subject. This is particularly important for us because many of

the students we are talking about in this book are fed up, at least for now, with sitting and talking, and this would provide a change of pace. It may break us out of the mental set that school is just demonstrating, reading, and talking. This arrange-an-experience-then-invite-student-critique methodology, whether it involves physical movement or not, is an approach we should explore as an instructional strategy, as it is applicable in a variety of educational contexts.

Joel talks a great deal about the concepts of balance and centering. In an article by Ron Brant he contends: "Balance is going to be the key word in our society for the next twenty years. Unbalanced people do not create a balanced society."[42] Joel grounds concepts like balance and center in very specific, physical referents. For example, he gets athletes to focus on the physical center in their body, a point a couple of inches below the navel in the abdominal cavity. It is Joel's contention that being centered on this point and performing from there will allow an athlete to be more successful. Bob Brenly, a major league catcher Joel has worked with, gently presses his belt buckle when he is at bat to remind himself to breathe and move from his center.

Joel asserts that the work he does with athletes to help them improve their concentration, attitude, communication, motivation, relaxation, and performance level applies to other areas of life, including school. In any case, this gives us much to think about. It is clear that some students who are not succeeding in school are off-center, out of balance, out of control in their lives, and this plays out wherever they are, including the classroom. Sport and sport psychology may provide us with a different, and better, way to look at the problems we face in school. If you want to look further into this, a good book to read is the autobiography of the great Japanese baseball player and manager, Sadahara Oh, called *The Zen Way of Baseball*.[43] A movie, not a very good one I must report, that gets at some of these concepts is the original *The Karate Kid*. I think you can rent it from video stores.

Clearly there are things we can learn from this area of activity and research. If nothing else, I hope this encourages you to look more closely at what good coaches do and see what can be learned from them that might apply to the classroom. As a matter of fact, I wish coaches would apply the same methods in secondary school teaching as they do on the athletic field. I am often taken by how differently a coach handles, say, his social studies class from how he coaches his football team. Observing the class, I am left with: "Why don't you teach more like you coach? When you coach you give the responsibility to the players to get it done and you support their efforts, instructing and encouraging them as they go. But when you teach, *you* take the responsibility. You are what is happening. Students sit there and react, liking and disliking what you do, getting interested and fading out, learning if your lesson plan especially grabs them and goofing off when it is less than sparkling. Really, in the classroom you are doing it all, while on the field the students do the work. In the classroom they review you, deciding whether they like the class. On the field you review them, deciding whether or not they are good ballplayers. On the field you make it clear you expect their very best. Just now in class, however, you said they should learn something because it 'might be on the test.' '' Yes, even the coaches themselves sometimes miss the potentially useful insights that can be transferred from one context to another. And of course I do not just mean from sport to school. Much is going on in business, the military, and elsewhere that would inform what we do in schools if we would open ourselves to it.

At the same time I am talking about transferability, though, we do need to be highly selective in what we take from sport or any other area and apply to the school situation. Just as situations are alike, they are different. We must be able to see similarities and applicability, and at the same time appreciate uniqueness. School is *not* like anything else just as much as it *is* like everything else. So we must respect that school is a one-of-a-kind situation and attend very carefully to the exigencies of this unique circumstance. Also, do not let this discussion of sport lead you to believe that I approve of every method some successful coach uses. As a matter of fact I strongly disfavor what some coaches do. For example, there are big-time college basketball coaches so concerned with winning that they have taken the game away from the players and robbed the sport of its soul. These coaches have found they can win by calling every play for the players, avoiding mistakes (at the expense of flow and rhythm of the game and individual expression), screaming at referees, intimidating players, and enhancing their career by becoming the focal point of the games. No, I hope classrooms do not parallel so much of college basketball: a middle-aged adult letting only the best players play and reigning in young people to get *the* job done, that is, scoring more points than the other team. The hell with the *experience* of play. The point of it all to these guys is in the victories, and not the marvelously graceful, self-expressive, collective, and cooperative experience that basketball can provide.

Do look at this critically. But most of all, think creatively about what this discussion of sport means for teaching and for your work in pariicular.

THE PROCESS OF STUDENT SELF-MANAGEMENT

The last section on sport stressed the athlete's ability to manage his own performance. On the *Promoting Achievement in Sport and School* video tape Steve Boros expresses this point very clearly. He says that a major goal in coaching is to get athletes to the point where they can coach themselves. It is instructive to see that this theme and others that were outlined in this last section on sport can be found in educational literature as well. A good example is the work of Linda Nielson. Nielson has written an excellent book which, unfortunately, is now out of print, *How to Motivate Adolescents*.[44] You may be able to find it in a library. What is available in most university libraries is an article, "Teaching Adolescents Self-Management."[45] This article is based on chapter 11 of her book. Refer to either her book or the article for greater detail on what I outline in this section. Nielson provides some practical activities that can be used with students to increase their ability to manage effectively themselves as students—an ability many of these less-than-successful students need to develop. As I review some key ideas that Nielson offered on how to encourage adolescents to be more self-directed as learners, note how her approach is consistent with the discussion on sport. More generally, see what ideas this review triggers in you regarding what underachieving students may have to learn in order to become more capable students, and what sorts of strategies we may employ to help them develop these insights and skills.

To begin with, Nielson reminded us that before we begin to develop self-directedness in students we need to be clear on whether we really want self-directed students. Some educators may view the prospect of students who are able to manage themselves as disruptive of the schooling process. Self-managed students might become even tougher to get in line. I do not want to dismiss these worries completely. Certainly a legitimate responsibility of students is to cooperate with the school professionals. The adults in the school have a positive responsibility to direct and shape the experiences of students. Educators have the right to establish the curriculum, organize and operate classes, and assign and evaluate learning tasks. School professionals do represent the culture and have a responsibility to carefully select what aspects of that culture should be transmitted to the young. I am not talking about turning the schooling process over to student whim or interest. I am concerned with what happens when students learn to direct themselves. Nielson, however, makes it clear to me that, while she very much values students' ability to act autonomously, she does not set off autonomy against cooperativeness. Students can be both self-directed and defer in an appropriate way to the prerogatives of the adults in the school. In any case, it is my experience that the majority of students are not inherently opposed to the purposes and processes of the schools they attend. The conclusion I have come to is that by empowering students to achieve greater self-control, our jobs as teachers will become easier; we will be working with students who can more easily hold up their end of the teacher-student relationship. Students will be able to do things for themselves that we now feel we must do for them; and they will be able to do necessary things that will simply not get done at all if they do not do them. Most important, students will be able to manage themselves and work more effectively in order to accomplish the work we assign.

Self-management capability is particularly important for many of the students of our concern in this book. They need to learn to get on top of their own situations. So often they set out to do well in a particular class. They are going to write the book report. Then something happens and they get sidetracked and, well, it just does not get completed. In order to understand what goes awry we are going to have to move beyond general notions of low motivation and laziness, and uncover a finer understanding of what functional skills are absent or unused. Nielson's writings move us in that direction. It is Nielson's assertion that greater understanding of the process of student self-management is helpful, because the power to control oneself in a positive way can be learned. There are techniques that educators can use to significantly increase a student's chances of learning to take charge of his or her own life as a student.

I believe self-management capability is a goal we ought to adopt in schools. Beyond its value in the immediate school situation it is justified in other ways as well. Self-management is crucial if students are to be effective lifetime learners. After all, even if they go to college they are going to spend the majority of their lives away from formal school settings. They need to know how to learn without a school structure to carry them along. I am reminded of some interviews I conducted with college students. I asked them to think of their favorite course in college. I then asked them to tell me how they would go about learning more about that subject. Most were at a loss as to how they would continue on their own to delve deeper into the particular field of study. They were very dependent on formal classes and instructors. They perhaps learned a great deal in the course and respected the instructor, and certalnly they liked the course. But very few of them developed what might be called "next steps forward" capability. They had not learned how to be autonomous learners in that field. Furthermore, they had no particular predisposition to continue learning in that area. The course represented a self-contained "dose" of sorts that they took (people *take* courses). Even beyond the educational implications, I see the ability to be in charge of one's life as a vital attribute if one is to live well and contribute to American culture and society. Referring back to the discussions in the first chapter, if you are going to live in America you had better learn to take good care of yourself.

What Does It Mean to Be Capable of Self-Management?

In general, it is the ability to make wise choices and carry them out. It means knowing what is going on enough to set goals that will promote growth and learning. It means getting things done, not just spinning one's wheels or going backward. It means being able to keep the classroom "contract" with the teacher. In my opinion, classroom situations involve a contract of sorts between the students and the teacher. I teach with all I have got and you "student" with all you have got. I owe it to you to be as good at teaching as I can be. And you owe it to me to be as good at studenting as you can be. Self-management involves watching what you do so that you can profit from both your successes and your mistakes. It means going about the work of learning and growing and at the same time supporting the work of other students and the teacher. Good students do these things, and the other students should learn them too.

Nielson listed some specific skills she deemed vital to a student becoming more capable of self-management. One is the ability to set *realistic* goals. The word *realistic* is important in this last sentence. Nothing sets-up a student for failure more than unattainable goals. (Though, nothing is more un-American than to play it safe.) Referring back to the last section, the student needs a goal just as much as the athlete needs to know what he is shooting for. Nielson emphasizes that a student needs to be able to express his goals *behaviorally*. That is, in terms of what he will be *doing* if he is successful in accomplishing his objectives. Too often it is only the teacher who has clearly expressed goals. There is one unfortunate outcome of the way we tend to plan our daily, and longer term, lessons. Although we as teachers are clear on our goals and objectives, there is nothing built-in that makes students do the same. Similarly, although lesson, unit, and yearly plans make us arriculate what we will do and have others do, they do not compel students to make a similar plan. Without reflecting on it very much, we have operated under the assumption that the necessary work gets done in classes if only we, the teachers, get clear about where we are going. Indeed it is shortsighted to think we can accomplish significant learning and growth when students do not have a clear purpose. If students do have goals they are often vague or actually contrary to those of the teacher. And when students do not really know what is up, or work at cross-purposes from those of the teacher, what happens? The teacher often tries to cover for the situation by attempting to put on a good enough show to capture students' attention for the hour. This is an exhausting and ultimately futile endeavor if learning that makes a difference is the criterion for judgment.

A second element of self-management Nielson listed is the ability, as she put it, to "observe the self." By this she meant the process of self-analysis the sport people talk about. It means the students must resolve the following questions: What am I doing and where is this getting me? What do I need to change in how I am going about things? Nielson stressed the ability of a student to monitor his own progress toward a goal. What am I getting done? Am I sticking with it? What am I allowing to pull me off course? Do I have to change either my goals or the strategies I am using to achieve my goals? One technique Nielson recommended to get at this is for students to record their progress toward their goals in their notebooks. What this means, then, is not a notebook about math or English, but rather a notebook about being a good student. She also mentioned the use of audio or video tapes of students in class so that they can actually hear or see how they conduct themselves as students. This is akin to athletes going over tapes of their performance on the field. In support of this approach, Nielson quoted a study that shows that disruptive students have trouble identifying their inappropriate conduct. Also, it has been my experience that underachieving students are not clear about what circumstances trigger or set off their self-defeating actions. Through the use of technology perhaps they can come to discover these things for themselves. The point is that we excessively observe students, and that is good. They have to learn the skill of self-observation to complement what we are doing. In fact, it would be more beneficial if students could discover what is lacking in their academic performance than if we tell them.

Nielson also talked about self-reinforcement, drawing on the ideas of psychologist B. F. Skinner. Students need to learn how to reward themselves for staying on track. Nielson gave the example of a student who rewards herself for doing her math with a telephone call to her boyfriend. Another example I can think of is a student reinforcing himself with a movie for finishing the English paper. Another good reinforcer is self-praise. Give yourself a brief talk about how special you are for doing the best you could possibly do on some piece of work. Of course the challenge is to find something that is rewarding as well as constructive. A 2-lb box of bonbons for reading the history chapter can lead to its own problems. Anyway, once these reinforcers are identified, the idea is to give these things to yourself contingent on your keeping your agreement with yourself to get something done.

Biblioeducation

This approach uses individual life examples to provide insights and inspiration for students. I discussed sport people doing this a great deal to provide direction to athletes. The Bobby Clarke and Pete Rose examples are means of cultural transmission. They are ways for the sport culture to pass on its customs to new people. I support Nielson in her contention that we might be able to find non-threatening and nonembarassing ways of holding up positive examples of effective studenting in much the same way. Also, I have thought for some time that the study of biographies of successful people would be a useful class in itself. Or perhaps it could be integrated into English or social studies classes. Let students look for "rules of living" in their study of the way these individuals manage their lives. Let them look for alternative ways to conduct one's life, and think about themselves in terms of these alternatives. A student can resolve the question, "Which of the ways is appropriate to me?" It is especially important that students get to review the lives of others over the entirety of the life span in order to get a beginning sense of the whole of life. They may start to see that life is continuous, and that their life now is part of the seamless whole of their life. They are not *wanting* to live; they *are* living. What they are doing now is life. Moreover, what they do now affects the rest of their life. (The British film *28 Up* illustrates this point well.) My contention is that many students are not so much indifferent to school as they are unconnected to their own life. Why should school make sense if their life has little meaning? School is a place they happen to be, so they play out their posture, whatever it happens to be, in school. Many students would probably do the same thing wherever they were. Being able to give of yourself maturely to school involves having a sense of what this engagement means to you now and in the future. Without a sense of what your life is about now and what you dream it will be about in the future and how now is connected to then, there is not much else to do but try to have a good time.

You know of some good biographies. I mentioned the ones about Margaret Mead, Bob Dylan, Justice William Douglas, and Babe Ruth (by Robert Creamer). *The Autobiography of Malcolm X* by Alex Haley provided a very important life example to me personally years ago. Here was the example of somebody figuring out what had been going on and turning his life around. Another possibility, in its December issue *Esquire* magazine has had theme issues entitled *Best of the New Generation*. These contain pictures, articles, and brief biographies of individuals from business and industry, arts and letters, science and technology, education and social service, politics and law, entertainment, sports, and what *Esquire* calls "style" who have an impact on this society. It could be a matter of asking students: Which of these people do you most admire? What can you learn from them? What are *you* going to become? Who are you *now*? Of course, biographies can be used in science and math and other such classes where we do not usually expect to encounter them. Biographies of scientists or mathematicians could prove most valuable. We need to learn what ABC sports found out long ago. People are interested in other people. It helps to get "up close and personal." And last of course, good fiction can be excellent "biblioeducation." A wonderful book I read recently that might prove useful is *Easter Parade* by Richard Yates.[46] It is the story of two sisters from about the ages of 5 to 50. It's not the happiest of stories, and there are the problems of alcohol and physical abuse in marriage and a floundering career, but the book is beautifully written and so true of what can happen in life.

Self-Talk

Again similar to the sport examples in the last section, Nielson discussed what she terms *self-talk* as an aspect of self-management. Nielson underscored the importance of a student learning to control the thoughts that run through his head. Nielson affirmed that the way we think has great consequences for what we feel and how we act. She cited the example of a student who fails a test and sends himself the message, "I'm too stupid to even try to pass this course, so there's no use studying anymore." In contrast, in exactly the same situation another student might say to himself, "Wow, I flunked the exam. I better go to bed earlier and study harder for the next one. I deserve better than I gave myself last time." It is obvious that the first student in particular would be empowered by paying more attention to how his mind works.

A method Nielson proposed for combatting the negative messages students send to themselves is for them to write "counter-thought" cards. Through this technique students learn to observe what they are thinking and to replace negative, self-defeating thinking with more positive, productive thoughts. For example, a student can watch himself thinking something like, "There's no use trying to do these math problems" and substitute, "As a matter of fact by working harder last week my score, though not so hot, was 5 points better than the last time—so work does pay off." Nielson suggests that students practice these counter-messages by saying them silently to themselves or writing them repeatedly, say for 5 minutes. Perhaps students could take 10 minutes a day and write down all their negative thoughts about themselves as students and then systematically respond to each with a counter-thought. Another approach she recommends is a formula for testing thoughts which goes: "My interpretation of this situation is true if . . . and false if. . . ." To illustrate, a student might decide that his belief that homework is a waste of time is true if most people who do their homework fail and most who do not pass.

Another technique of self-talk is the use of affirmations of the sort I outlined earlier in the Assagioli section. There are several interpretations of the idea of affirmations but the one I prefer is as follows: An affirmation is a sentence that describes a future circumstance in which one's goal is realized as if it were being experienced at this moment. For instance, a student may have a math test coming up. He might decide to use the affirmation, "It feels so good to get a 92 on my math test." As he says it over and over silently (say while he gets dressed in the morning) or writes it repeatedly (say 5 or 10 times before he goes to bed) he tries to experience it as if it is actually happening. Why affirmations work— and so many people swear by them—is open for debate. It could be that they simply serve as reminders of what we are aiming to accomplish. Maybe they help us focus our energies and get clearer on our priorities. For all I know, they may be a way to get a reluctant subconscious to feel that this particular achievement is "us" enough and safe enough for it to give its permission for it to happen. Whatever the case, the use of such self-talk appears to hold promise. Let us see what happens if students simply wrote 5 times each day, "I am proud to be a good student."[47]

Another good source of direction in helping students deal with the way they think is the work on cognition by David Burns and his associates at the University of Pennsylvania. I reviewed this work in the section on Assagioli and refer you to those pages.

Nielson ended her article in the following way. I think this sums up our present position:

> The research demonstrates that most adolescents can, indeed, learn the skills of self-management. But whether adults will elect to teach youngsters these techniques is another matter. Some adults undoubtedly feel threatened and uncomfortable when youngsters become independent enough to manage certain aspects of their own lives without outside assistance. We adults may even occasionally punish independent, self-managed adolescents, and applaud submissive youngsters for their "maturity". It is hoped grownups will become increasingly relaxed with adolescents' self-management skills as they realize that their own lives are enhanced, not undermined, by youths' independence.[48]

THE NATURE OF ACHIEVEMENT

You and I both know people who are achievers. I am not just referring to athletes or students here. These achievers find good things to do, decide to accomplish something, and they get it done. In addition, we both know people who mean well, but for whatever reason things just do not work out for them. We know we could have predicted this result in the first place, despite their expressions of good intention. In this section I explore the nature of achievement. Not achievement in some particular area such as school or business or politics, but rather achievement across the board. Can we say anything about achievement and achievers in a general way? Can we look at achievement as a concept in itself? What accounts for achievement? What are achievers like? What do they do? If we are going to work to promote higher levels of school achievement among students, it would be helpful if we spent some time figuring out what accounts for it among human beings. I ask you right now at the start: Why do some people get it done and other people just give it a try? What do you know about achievement? You know a lot and you should reflect on it some.

Some assumptions of mine to start: Achievement is probably related to intellectual ability, but that is not all there is to it. There are just too many bright people around, adults and young people, who do not get nearly as much accomplished as others who we would agree have less native intelligence. In addition, achievement is not just a matter of being motivated, or wanting to do well. In schools we often operate as if motivation is everything. Motivation is undoubtedly part of it, but there are just too many committed and unsuccessful people around for it to be simply a matter of motivation. Academic achievement is not just a matter of proficiency in the basic skills necessary to do schoolwork: reading, writing, speaking, listening, and clear thinking capability. Although it obviously helps to have those requisite skills, and certainly problems in these areas can retard achievement, we can both think of students who have the academic skills and still do not achieve. The same is true with students who are orderly, show up every day to class, listen attentively, take notes religiously, and study every evening. Indeed this helps, but it can still be just a ticket to mediocrity or less.

We need to look at school achievement on several levels. At one level there are the specific school-going skills. These are being able to read and write and study effectively, and the like. However, we must also concern ourselves with achievement on a more generic level. We need to look at overall goal attainment capability. We need to identify the understandings, attitudes, and capabilities related to doing a good job in whatever the area, whether in school or somewhere else. It is crucial to look at achievement in a general way because, as I see it, it is an overall orientation and capability that is needed to make good things happen. This provides a proper context for a student to acquire and use the academic achievement skills—reading, computation, writing, and so forth—we usually identify as important. That is, the general predilection to achieve versus fail provides a frame of reference which gives meaning to these more basic skills, and makes it possible to integrate and employ them effectively.

What I am saying is we try to teach good, potentially useful basic academic skills to some students who fundamentally are just not achievers. These students do not know what do to with the opportunity to learn the things we present. They are, to coin a term, *opportunity-missers*, not only with us but in other areas of their life as well. Consequently, what we are doing much of the time with under-achievers is attempting to get things across to people who do not know how to make sense of the ideas and how to use them to their advantage. For example, a school might have a good remedial reading program. Or it might set up an ex-cellent study skills program that teaches students how to listen better in class, manage their study time more effectively and so on. The problem is that the stu-dents who are not achievers waste the opportunity to profit from these learning opportunities. And it is not even that these students skip the sessions and are off gallivanting someplace. That might be shortsighted, but at least they would be having a good time. No, mostly they show up, sit there feeling trapped and bored, go through the motions, meet with the teacher's disapproval, and do not learn a thing. Now I know it is a laborious task for us to have to teach these kinds of kids. But do not forget that the kids have a problem. They just passed by yet another chance to take advantage of an opportunity to learn something valuable.

I am reminded of an encounter with one of my students in a low-level second-ary English class. He was very bright but did not read well at all. There was a special program in the school to help students who were behind in reading. I asked him whether he was attending the program and he said he wasn't. As it turns out, he did not attend the class because he thought the teacher did not like him and gave him a hard time. I asked him what else he was doing to work on the reading problem since he was not attending the remediation sessions. He said he was not really doing anything. I asked the student if he wanted to learn to read better. He answered that he would, and that it was really embarrassing to be 17 years old and barely able to read. He indicated that he knew it was going to be difficult for him to go out into the work world with such poor reading skills.

My response, and I told him this, was that what he was doing was understand-able, but I still thought his actions were self-defeating. I explained that I under-stood it was easy for me to preach, not being in the situation, but nevertheless if it were me I would get myself to those reading classes no matter what. If I wanted to learn to read, I would learn to read. Whether or not I liked the teacher or he liked me, somehow I would get in that class and learn. I would learn to get along with the teacher, get around him, ignore him, anything it took. If I want something I go get it, and I wanted this student to go get it. I did not want this student to be standing in an unemployment line someday with a story about how he did not learn to read because he had a lousy teacher. I told him I would much rather he learned to read now than have a good reason why he did not learn. More than likely, 10 years from now that teacher will not remember his name. But this student will still be coping with a reading deficit. Employers are not go-ing to say, "Oh, sure you're hired. At first I was worried you couldn't do the work. But now I know *why* you can't, that incompetent teacher. So it's OK." The USA does not work that way. Our system pays off for what you can do, not for the excuse you have for not being able to do it. The test of this student, the challenge, the thing that is going to take guts and determination, is to take advantage of this reading opportunity, despite the barriers, whether it be this teacher or anything else.

As I look at it, this is a student who did not have the generic achievement capability I have been talking about. I know there are students who have no more going for them than he does—who are no brighter, have no better homelife, no better past experience in school—who would have made use of this chance to do something about their reading. Our challenge as educators is to gain greater insight into the distinctions between achievers and nonachievers in this general sense. Perhaps if we understand what achievers are like we can help students who are not developing the attributes that result in an increased capability to effectively use the learning and growth possibilities present in the school. This is so important because my conclusion is that despite the criticisms schools often receive, there is nevertheless rich learning and growth to be found if students know how to look for it and know what to do with it once they come upon it.

Is all this clear? What I am hypothesizing is that we would do well if we could assist students to become more achiever-like than they are. We may be trying to get academic skills to students who are just not achievement-oriented enough to take them in and make use of them effectively. Though, at the same time I do not want to make an either-or, this-before-that argument. Perhaps the best way to say it is that we have to give concurrent attention to both achievement skills and the other academic skills. Or we must develop a way to look at school success capability that incorporates this idea of a general result-getting ability.

What Accounts for Achievement?

One writer I find particularly useful in this regard is Eric Johnson. Johnson has written a great deal, but the book I most recommend is *Raising Children to Achieve*.[49] Johnson and David McClelland of Harvard University have also authored a student workbook, *Learning to Achieve*, that can be used in secondary schools.[50] These workbooks can be employed in special school achievement classes or workshops, or as supplementary materials in most any regular class. McClelland's theoretical work on achievement motivation undergirds Johnson's work. To a great extent Johnson's writings are an application of McClelland's ideas to family and school settings.

In Raising Children to Achieve, Johnson began by describing achievers:

The have initiative. They are motivated to do a good job in whatever they undertake. They set goals and work hard to attain them. They keep trying to find better ways to do things. They are self-starters and self-reliant. Yes, they sometimes relax; they know how to enjoy themselves. But one of their main joys is accomplishment. Also, they have a strong sense of self-respect. This self-respect is the basis for a genuine respect for others. It's true that they do not always do exactly what they're told to do, but that's because they have a sense of independence. They want to achieve their own goals, short-range and long-range.[51]

It is Johnson's contention that achievement is a natural drive in children but that families and schools often squelch this tendency. Families place too much emphasis on simple obedience. Parents believe that only they know what the child should do and how, and that the key to child-raising is to get their children to do what they are told promptly. Johnson sees parents spending far too much time attending to what children do wrong than in praising and encouraging their actions when they do something right. He contends that children are owned rather than owning themselves, with the result that only the exceptional learn to be achievers. Instead, they develop the habits of obedience, self-destructive rebellion, blaming others as a consequence of feeling powerless to control their own life, or take on the pattern of avoiding issues by doing nothing. The challenge is, as Johnson put it, "for all societies to provide opportunities for all individuals and families to achieve on their own, to make it on their own, often against odds not of their own making, to become independent, responsible, productive achievers."[52]

Johnson listed characteristics of parents who raise achievers. They set high but appropriate standards for their children, aware of what the child is capable of at his or her age, and expect them to meet them. They let their children set many of their own goals and give plenty of realistic response and support as the children work to achieve the goals. They are generous with positive feedback ("That's great," "Good job"). They make help available when it is really needed but they do not over-interfere in the achievement process. They express realistic, honest, and enthusiastic enjoyment of progress and jobs well done by their children and praise taking on a challenge. Parents of achievers also deal well with failures: "Of course you feel discouraged." "You worked hard and intelligently." "There will be a next time." "What did you learn from what happened that you can use next time?" Parents of achievers *let go*. They allow the child to set goals and make mistakes. But at the same time they attend closely to what the child is doing. And parents of achievers are patient with the child; becoming an achiever takes time.[53] Although Johnson is referring to parents and families in this writing, it seems obvious to me that school people would do well to take note of his insights.

Johnson referred to the distinction Richard de Charms draws between children who are "pawns" and "origins." Johnson cited de Charms belief that the "origins" are the ones who become achievers.

An Origin is a person who feels that he is in control of his fate; he feels that the cause for his behavior is within himself. A Pawn feels that he is pushed around, that someone else pulls the strings and he is the puppet. He feels the locus of causality for the behavior is external to himself. The motivational effects of these two personal states are extremely important. The Origin is positively motivated, optimistic, confident, accepting of challenge. The Pawn is negatively motivated, defensive, irresolute, avoidant of challenge. The Origin feels potent; the Pawn feels powerless.[54]

It is Johnson's contention that whatever good things schools may be teaching children, they are also keeping them pawnlike. Students learn to be quiet, follow instructions, do routine tasks whether or not they see any purpose in them, and are rewarded for doing work exactly the way the teacher wants it done. If students do any thinking it had better be on the teacher's terms. "Consequently," Johnson offered, "after a few years, too many children come to feel inadequate, or bored, or docilely obedient, or rebellious, or like dropping out—out of school and into life."[55] Remember what he means by achievement from the quote a few paragraphs back—achievers do more than get along. Most people get along; few achieve.

At the same time, Johnson did not argue that parents or schools say to students: "Be free. Just express yourself. Do what you want. Everything's OK." Unfortunately, many of the "free schools" that were particularly prominent 15 years ago tended to send that message. He sees that approach as another way to obstruct the natural development of achievement motivation in young people. Johnson quotes the poet T. S. Eliot as saying, "Too many of us think we are free when in reality we are merely unbuttoned."[56]

Johnson identified television as a major impediment to achievement motivation. He saw television as lively, vivid, jumpy, and absorbing, a great attention-grabber. But at the same time it detracts from some key elements of achievement such as the processes of thinking, asking questions, setting goals, planning, doing, and asserting one's independence. His advice: Control the amount of time children sit in front of the tube. I would add that we have to be very careful of the seductiveness of television. We cannot let the apparently good things on television obscure the fact that no matter what is *on* it, we are always *doing* the same thing: watching television. And it is the watching of television, the medium itself, that results in the outcomes that detract from achievement. I believe all of us who are either parents or educators owe it to ourselves and the children we care about to study the nature of television and its effect on this culture and on viewers. I have found Neil Postman's books to be especially helpful. Two I recommend, both dealing with television, are *Teaching as a Conserving Activity* and, more recently, *Amusing Ourselves to Death*.[57]

Johnson dealt briefly with the effect of religion on achievement, noting that religious influences can cut both ways. On the one hand religion can promote, as Johnson puts it, "unquestioning, unthinking, strictly obedient, ritual-bound church-goers who are detached from the world and expect supernatural powers to determine all that they do. . . ."[58] I recently read Friedrich Nietzsche's essay, *The Genealogy of Morals*, which is supportive of a negative view of the influence of religion. In this work, Nietzsche accused religion of "aesthetic idealism," a perspective that makes a virtue of being meek, lowly, self-negating, obedient, and inactive. It is a kind of "isn't life a bed of thorns" and "woe is me" posture. As Nietzsche pointed out there is resentment of those who live adventurously and with elan.[59] On the other side, Johnson pointed out the element in some religions that promotes the responsibility to work actively and to improve one's own circumstance and that of others in order to make a better world. Remember from the first chapter that religiosity was linked to school achievement in that research study I quoted. So it is a mixed picture.

Johnson listed the characteristics of high achievers:

1. Achievers are self-reliant and reasonably self-confident.
2. Achievers are realistic about their strengths and weaknesses.
3. Achievers feel responsible for their own actions.
4. Achievers set challenging but possible goals.
5. Achievers plan carefully and intelligently.
6. Achievers take obstacles into account as they plan and work toward their goals.
7. Achievers know how to find and use help.
8. Achievers are good at keeping working toward their goals—good at striving.
9. Achievers check their progress.
10. Achievers enjoy achieving and dislike not achieving. They keep themselves at work by imagining how good it will feel to succeed and how much they will dislike not succeeding.
11. Achievers want to do a better and better job, or to do jobs in better and better ways.[60]

The question becomes, of course, if these are the characteristics of achievers, can we and should we teach students to be that way? Johnson (and I) say yes, it is worth a try. Both the *Raising Children to Achieve* book and the *Learning to Achieve* workbooks (there are two levels, one for younger and one for older students) provide many activities that can be used with students to increase achievement capability. I refer you to these sources. To give you an idea of what they contain, the workbook has exercises in which students analyze short biographies of successful individuals. Included are I.M. Pei, the architect; Mildred Dressehaus, an engineer at the Massachusetts Institute of Technology; and Sadee Magee, a basketball coach. There are also activities that deal with setting standards for yourself; goal setting, planning, and self-monitoring; overcoming obstacles and setbacks; dealing with competition; and staying with work to completion. The workbook, at the end of the readings, checksheets and exercises, lists 28 possible projects. Two examples cited by Johnson and McClelland:

Think of a time you needed more than one source of help to achieve a goal. Write a brief report telling what the goal was and what kinds of help you needed. Then explain whether the help strengthened or weakened you and how. If it weakened you, explain what you could have changed to make it help that strengthened. If the help strengthened you, explain how, and explain why you didn't let the help weaken you.

Some people have nothing to look back on with pride and nothing to look forward to with hope and confidence. Imagine that someone has said this about you. Write as convincing an account as you can to prove that you do have achievements you look back on with pride and future goals that you have confidence you will achieve. Before you start writing, jot down all your ideas about achievements and future goals. You might talk to people who know you to see if they have more ideas.[61]

Do check into the Johnson material. Or find other sources that get at the same thing.

Another source I have found useful is the book *Developing Talent in Young People*, edited by Benjamin Bloom.[62] The book reports the results of a study of 120 highly achieving young men and women to determine how and why they were able to attain such an exceptional level of accomplishment. The study focused on individuals in music and art, athletics, mathematics and science. These fields fall into three talent areas: athletic or psychomotor; aesthetic, musical, and artistic; and cognitive and intellectual. Bloom and his colleagues planned to investigate fields that emphasize interpersonal relations such as school teachers, social workers, psychiatrists, administrators, and supervisors. However, a problem in deciding on selection criteria (just who is most talented in these fields, and how do we know that?) led to the decision not to include this talent area in their study. So keep in mind that they were selective in whom they studied.

Bloom wrote a concluding chapter in the book in which he included the following generalizations about talent development in the exceptional individuals they studied:

- Initially the child looked upon talent development as play and recreation. This was followed by a long sequence of activities that involved high standards, much time, and a great deal of hard work.
- The home environment developed the work ethic and the importance of doing one's best at all times and was itself a model of the work ethic. Parents placed great stress on achievement. To excel and to spend one's time constructively were emphasized over and over again.
- Their teachers liked children and rewarded them with signs of approval when they did things right. They were extremely encouraging. They also promoted the child's discovery of underlying ideas and processes. Their expectations for their students were high. As the child got older, their teachers gave them a perspective on the field, including the meaning and purpose of the field in its largest dimension. They provided many public events where the chil-

dren could "show their wares." More and more as years went on, teachers demanded precision and accuracy and excellence.

- As the children grew older they developed their own long-term goals to develop their skill. These aspirations provided the internal motivation to do the work necessary to achieve. They saw the endeavor as their work, with the teacher providing support and encouragement. These children developed the ability to analyze their own performance to determine needed changes. They developed in themselves commitment and endurance and strength of will and character. Much of what they learned was by doing. They sought to express their own particular uniqueness and style.[63]

I hope this discussion has gotten you thinking about achievement, and that you will join me in the study of this phenomenon. One place to begin is to read the Johnson and Bloom books. Also, study the life examples of successful people you know personally or those you have read about in books. I am interested in film and for the past couple of weeks I have read everything I could get my hands on concerning the film director Alfred Hitchcock. I have also viewed about 15 of his films on my VCR. Beyond having an enjoyable time and learning a great deal about technique and art in film, I have learned much about the way this man achieved what he did in his life. You could do something similar in an area of your own interest.

Another thing you can do is carefully study the students with whom you work. Among students of comparable ability, what distinguishes the achievers from the nonachievers? What is it the achievers have going for them? Perhaps you could do something akin to what Woodard did: Study some students who conventional wisdom would lead us to predict are not going to achieve—but they do anyway. These kids may be from a bad home situation, poverty, and may not be the geniuses of all time. But nevertheless they excel in school. Wood focused on what went on in the family of "success cases," and looked at what these students do in school: What do they think? What do they do that separates them from the others? How does the school treat them? Another potentially useful area of investigation would be to look into the situation of what can be called "transition cases." These are students who turned their situation around in school. They changed from being unsuccessful to successful academically. What accounted for the transformation? What was their circumstance? And most important, what inside them allowed them to achieve success in school when they had failed before? An idea I have is to set up self-help groups in schools made up of students who want to do better in school. The leaders of the groups could be these "transition cases." A student who used to be unsuccessful and is now achieving academically may be just the person to help peers who are trying to do the same thing. They could meet once or twice a week to share their experiences and get support, encouragement, and advice from the others in the group. It might be worth a try.

A last point, one of the ways to study achievement is to study yourself. What is it, fundamentally, that contributes to your ability to achieve? What impedes accomplishment for you? What do you need to learn in order to be more capable of achievement in your life? What can you learn from your study of yourself that applies to your work with adolescents? Consider this or any of these things discussed in the book; you always have a rich laboratory close at hand that holds valuable information and direction: yourself. So at the same time you look into the world for guidance, reading books or observing classrooms or talking to colleagues, do not forget to also look into yourself and your own life.

THE WAY I VIEW MOTIVATION

We have to face facts. The reality of our lives as teachers is that we are trying much of the time to get students to do something they would just as soon not do. And that is especially true when working with underachieving students. The experience of trying to get people, who see no compelling reason to do so, to cooperate and put out good effort can wear down even the most resilient of human beings. I can think of no more compelling issue in education than that of what to do about student motivation. Every individual either contemplating teaching or already in the field is faced with resolving this issue. I take some space to share how I have resolved it personally. See what you think.

The motivation I am centering on here is the incentive that a student has to do well in school. It may be in terms of a particular assignment or subject. Or perhaps there is a general commitment to achieve academically in one's classes. There are a number of perspectives from which you can choose to explain where that incentive comes from. Some see it as the result of inner drives and needs; some think it is a response to external conditions; and some feel it is a choice the student makes or a skill he or she possesses. Whatever its source, and I tend to see motivation as resulting from an interplay of at least the factors listed in the last sentence, the important thing is that motivation is something the *student* has; it comes from within. He or she has it or does not have it. The student possesses it, not me. And because I do not have it, I cannot give it to him or her. Another way to put it, I do not believe I can motivate anybody. They motivate themselves. What I can do, and this is a lot, is to invite a student to choose to be motivated. And I can create conditions in his or her world that tend to stimulate a greater desire to learn and grow. And I can be persistent in making the invitation to be motivated. But that is it. Beyond that, the student must make the choice to care about getting things done in school. It is up to him.

Another way to say it, I will be responsible to a student, but I cannot and will not be responsible *for* him or her. I say this because, however well-intended, I think many educators send the message to students that motivation is our affair. As I have said before, we are in a very self-referenced business. Whatever goes on with student motivation, teachers feel they are the cause of it, for better or worse. In reality, motivation levels are affected by many things other than what teachers do. Other significant influences include school policies, leadership, organization, and climate; parent attitudes; the student's past experiences and current circumstance at home and elsewhere; and social and cultural factors. We need to have a healthy measure of humility about the amount of power we have as teachers to affect motivation. Too frequently we blame ourselves for the lack of commitment among students. We try to become more interesting, more entertaining, and more of a cheerleader, with the intention of raising the level of interest among students. Things do pick up for a time but eventually drift back to where they were again. Somehow we have to learn to get it through our own heads and then pass it on to students that motivation is their business. And that it is in their interest to be motivated. They will be happier and more productive if they are motivated. It is very important that students learn to take responsibility for their state in the world and not put that on other people ("I'm turned off and it is because of you"). Ironically, the harder teachers work to hype interest, keep the pace up, and make it fun and exciting (I have actually heard teachers promise that some assignment or other will be exciting), the more difficult it becomes for students to come to grips with the reality that motivation is something *they* achieve. Beyond all that, for me my personal dignity is involved. As a teacher I always work to make something useful and I invite you to participate. But I am not going to do some kind of song and dance for you. I do not see, for example, medical doctors promising me a fun or exciting office call, or fawning over me to see if I like everything they do. The doctor is going to maturely serve a need I have, period. I think some of us in the teaching business demean ourselves with the little shows we do to entice students to be interested. I care about students, but I would rather fit shoes at Thom McCann's than compromise my dignity. That may be a strong statement, but I think you see what I mean.

In this regard, I again refer to successful athletic coaches. They communicate to athletes that it is his or her, the athlete's, job to get motivated. The coaches Joel interviewed for our videotape believed some athletes were blessed with greater levels of "internal drive," as they called it, than others due to genetic make-up or family background. These coaches saw the athlete who was not blessed with the drive to achieve as confronting a greater challenge to become motivated. Notice that the focus is on the athlete and what he or she must do—not on the coach. When faced with an unmotivated athlete the coach does not call attention to himself or herself with statements such as, "Don't you like my practices?" or "I'll make it better for you, just see." Rather, he or she turns it back on the athlete: "You aren't motivated and that's why you aren't getting it done. Can you get motivated?" Here the coach is giving feedback ("You aren't motivated") but keeping responsibility where it ought to be, with the athlete.

Furthermore, the coaches we interviewed had what I consider to be a healthy realism. Coaches understand that some athletes are never committed due to factors that are beyond their control. They do not berate themselves, as some of us do, if each and every young person in their charge does not give 100% at all times. But interestingly, this attitude that motivation is something that some athletes may never achieve actually increases the percentage of athletes who do become highly motivated. It creates a challenge: Can you do it? This contrasts with so many school classrooms where, in effect, teachers are saying: "Watch *me* do it. You won't be able to avoid getting turned on to this material." If students bothered to look up and do so, they would reply, "That's what you think."

I worry as I write this that some of you may think I am saying that all responsibility is with the student and none with the teacher. I hope it is clear from what I have said and am going to say in the following pages, that the teacher has a positive role in creating conditions that will support a student to become more motivated. The distinction I am making is between creating conditions and creating motivation. Students create motivation. Given this overall frame of reference, below are a number of ideas that may prove useful to you in helping students to become more dedicated to learn and develop.

Helping Students Develop a Vision

Good motivators, however they do it, help students develop a *vision* of positive goals. Somehow they can get students to create a picture in their heads of what it would be like to be a success in class. Students do not need problems, admonishments, pep talks, or lectures on the importance of this class as much as they need a hope. It is a hope that makes school meaningful and worthwhile and the inevitable difficulties bearable and even satisfying.

What do I mean by a hope? The word *vision* is a good one to define what I am talking about. A vision connotes being able to see something; in this case for the student to see in his or her mind's eye what it would be like to be an achiever in school. Actually this implies something more than seeing; he experiences in his imagination all of what it would be like to achieve. It means being able to fantasize about what it would be like to be a successful math student: the pride of getting an A, the praise and looks of approval from your teacher, the smile on your mother's face, the feeling of accomplishment, the sense of power and confidence that comes from really being able to do math. Note how this process of imagining success in school is similar to what the athlete does to be more self-directive. Moreover, it is empowering and motivating to have words and sentences to describe what it would be like to be successful. (Refer to the earlier discussion of affirmations.) Without a vision a student is more likely to be dependent on the class being immediately interesting and stimulating. Without a vision the student can only "like" or "dislike" a class or teacher. But school is not a TV program. A student cannot expect everything in school to be so highly attention-grabbing that he or she will be compelled to "stay tuned." While most of school can be meaningful and satisfying, it will not always be, to use

Steve Boros's phrase, "a whole lot of fun." To do well in school and in the rest of life takes self-sacrifice, deferring rewards, and hard work; and it helps greatly if you have a vision of what you can become that you value.

A good book on this subject is William Glasser's *Control Theory*.[64] He pointed out that what makes us accomplish things in any area of life is a "filing cabinet" of pictures in our heads. We call one up in our mind and work to create it in reality. In schools, what all of us need, including students, are some attractive "8 × 10 glossies" to call to mind. Too often, students and teachers have problems, analyses, and needs, but do not have a positive vision to work toward. How do we find one? How do we help students develop a vision or a hope? I do not have any specifically outlined techniques to offer. I wish I did. Somehow, in ways that present themselves to you at the moment, you can encourage students to develop a picture of what is in their future if they are successful in your class. Or it can be done in a more formal way. You can say something like, "Let's imagine what it would be like to be successful in this class. Tell me, draw me a picture. Now, carry that image around in your head and write it and think it over and over." In any case, one way or another, that is what I work to do, get a positive picture in students' heads, encourage them to create a hope.

I See You, I Notice What You Do, You Count, I Care About You, I Believe in You

I do not know how much more I have to say about this. These are attitudes in a teacher that are communicated to a student, and I consider them motivating. This is a posture a teacher assumes toward a student. There is no special technique involved. You just make it a point to do it, to be it, in any way that is natural to you. I do not think you make a speech about it. More, it is something you show or demonstrate in the way you conduct yourself. It is something you are more than anything you tell a student.

Appreciation, Encouragement, and Support

Good teaching involves observing students as they do something right and letting them know you value their effort. So often we do the opposite. We try to catch students doing something wrong so we can punish them for it. By appreciation I mean the acknowledgment of a particular accomplishment by a particular student. For example, "I really like the way you handled this image in the poem." Here you are noting the act, and you are not making a blanket statement about the student such as, "Oh, you're so wonderful." It should be an honest response, deserved, specific, and given as immediately following the action as possible. I hesitate a bit to use praise to describe this process. For one thing, praise sometimes involves fawning over someone, gushing with accolades, and raving about the accomplishment. Instead, I mean a sincere, mature, and brief statement explaining that you appreciate what a student has done. Furthermore, praise sometimes carries the connotation of patting somebody on the head for doing your bidding. With these hesitations understood, yes, praise is a motivator. I am sure behavioral psychologists would call all this reinforcement. The view they hold is that behavior followed by a positive consequence will be repeated. Thus, if you want something to happen again, reinforce it. On the other hand, do not give anybody flowers after a fight. In teaching we often do just that, swoop in with attention (often a reinforcer) for some kid messing around while ignoring another student who is working diligently.

Although we do not talk much about it in education, I like the concept of *encouragement*. This is different from praise. It is more, "Keep it going," "Hang in there," "You can do it," "Go to it." These are very motivating statements.

There's also the idea of *Support*: "I'm with you." "I'm on your side." "I'll help." Again, this is very motivating.

Success Motivates

Getting something accomplished is a stimulant to greater commitment and further achievement. We all know this, yet we sometimes act surprised if some 17-year-old who has been failing in school since he was 5 is less than eager to try things one more time. Good teachers set up success experiences for students to turn around their attitude and get them motivated. Again, I do not know what exact strategy to suggest. You use your wits. You look at what you are doing and try to figure out how you can help students succeed. This is especially important early on to prepare the student for commitment and achievement. Tying the last two points together, once you get the success going, continue to reinforce it.

High Expectations

A student is more likely to be motivated to do well if he is expected to do well. If there is a lesson I have learned in my life it is that you get what you expect, even if you are not fully aware that you expect it. In fact, one of the ways to figure out what you expect in life is to look at what you get—that, whether you consciously know it or not, is what you expect. If we have documented anything through educational research it is the power of expectations.[65] The message to send is, "I expect you to do your very best here." It is not the expectation that things come easy, because there are going to be tough times and probably some setbacks along the way. That is part of reality. The important thing is to communicate that we expect students to confront their personal frontier and expand on it. Nothing less than that.

Model Motivation

Motivation is catching. One way to become motivated is to be around motivated people. One of the problems underachieving students face is that they are often grouped by ability down to a level in which most of the students—and perhaps the teacher—are just going through the motions. That situation may be beyond my immediate control as a teacher, but at least I can work to be an example of a motivated human being for students to emulate.

Being Motivated Is Better Than Its Opposite

I have asked students if they were motivated. Their answer is something to the effect: "Are you kidding? Like I don't feel like doing anything in here." Then I ask them whether they are happy in the class and the reply is something like: "I asked you whether you were kidding. Is this a joke or something? Of course not." My comment has been, "Well, it looks like being unmotivated is not a good way to get happy, is it?" Students often do not understand the point I am making. One way to improve a situation is to attend to the quality of your experience, or your productivity, and then do something to make things more to your liking. Being unmotivated or having a reason to bail out on the class stops everything right there. To them, lack of motivation means they are not interested in doing anything constructive in the class. But at least they know *why* they are unmotivated (it's boring, irrelevant, the teacher is a jerk). The only problem with that is that they are still miserable, even if it is self-righteous misery. And I have come to the profound conclusion that I do not like being miserable.

What I have done in addition to what I described in the previous paragraph, is to try the following exercise: I have asked students to think of a time when they were unmotivated and bored. I ask them to tell me about it: Were you happy? Appreciated by others? Did you get anything done? Were you proud of yourself? Now do the same thing with a time when you were excited about something. Ask the same questions. Now compare the two experiences. The students will try to tell me *why* they were unmotivated the first time and motivated the second, which is fine. Perhaps they can learn what gets them going and what they are interested in doing and good at doing. But what I try to point out is that, in any given situation, it is better all the way around to be motivated than not to care. And if that is true, no matter what the class is like, it would be better to be motivated than to sit there bored and frustrated. Since students *are* there, they are not leaving, and it is better to be motivated than not motivated, they might as well try to get motivated. Now I know that some teachers feel these "unmotivated" students are actually motivated. They are motivated to get out of work, have a good time with their friends, torture the teacher, and so on. That is true I suppose, but I do not find students approach school that way to be happy in class or satisfied with themselves.

Motivation Is a Choice

The obvious question that comes from students: "I get it that it is not so great being unmotivated. But the fact is I *am* unmotivated. I mean I'm bored out of my mind. I *hate* this stuff I got to take. What do you mean work to get motivated?'' They see motivation as something they *have*, like brown eyes. Or *get*, like a bad cold. Or something that just is when the situation is a certain way. That is, when the textbook is like this, or the teacher is like that, or the class is at 2 o'clock, the result is lack of motivation, period. If that is so, yes, all you can do is endure or find some way to entertain yourself until the class period ends. What students do not realize is that motivation is a *choice* they make in response to the situation. It is a *skill* to become motivated. Motivation level is within their control to a far greater extent than they realize. The good news is that students can do something about the attitude they bring to class. As a matter of fact they *are* going to be in that class. One thing that students understand quite well, despite the dropout rates in some places, particularly in large urban centers, is that it is a good idea to get that diploma. And it *is* a good idea in this credentialed society to get that diploma, and then to get that college diploma too. By and large, students are not going to leave school.

One of the things I have learned from my theater experience is that if you act as if something is so it becomes so for you. I ask students to do some role playing. They pick a partner and we pick some topic to talk about. I ask them to spend a few minutes talking about it in a bored, disinterested, unmotivated way. Then I ask them to role play putting the other person down; and, last, to be interested and excited. I then ask them to discuss what it was like in each of those postures. I try to point out that they should notice that they had the power to shift gears. They had the power to act interested if they chose to. They always report that it was more enjoyable and they got more done when they were interested. I invite them in the future (a la Assagioli) to act *as if* they were motivated. The message to them is to take notice if they do not have control over the level of their motivation. Sometimes it is distinctly in their self-interest to be motivated, because they want to learn something, get good grades, get some appreciation, or feel good. The best thing I can think of then—and I hope this is understood—is to fake it. They (their personal selves) can choose to be motivated if it is best for them to do so. They do not have to be driven by every emotion (boredom), physical sensation (fatigue), and thought (''Why not get a pass and slip out for a smoke?''). They have the ability to override all of that and do what they feel is best for themselves.

Yes, it takes skill to find something in a situation that sparks motivation—and there are always such things if we look for them. Some people have the ability to find interesting and useful things to do, while others find a good reason to have a negative attitude. Because one of the tendencies of our minds is to give us many reasons to say no, it is understandable that people have a negative attitude. The mind chatters away, ''Not this,'' ''Not yet,'' ''Why bother,'' and ''Who cares.'' The challenge is to cut through the negative and find something to say yes to, to go on to accomplish something positive, and find some satisfaction.

This is not easy, because there will always be good reasons not to connect in that way. In fact, some people live out their lives being unmotivated. The message has to be: "You, the student, *can* be motivated, but you will have to do it. I will help any way I can. But when it comes down to it, you are going to have to figure out some way of being motivated and enthusiastic in this class. I hope you do."

Critical Awareness Helps

It helps students who are unmotivated to understand where their disinterest and disengagement comes from. Some students are not lucky enough to come out of family or social situations that encourage them to dedicate themselves to doing well in school. Some students' innate tendency to be positive and engaged is flattened. They are actually inverted and shaped into cynical, negative beings at home, in the community or, sadly, in school. If students study their world and gain insight into how it has operated on them, it is a good start on the way to rising above their conditioning. This is not an easy task, and many do not make it. Those who put themselves to the task may succeed. That is what is so hopeful. Despite the odds, some do take charge of their lives and transcend their circumstances.

Make It Problematic

The human being is by its nature a puzzle solver. I think it is built into our genes to be motivated, to solve problems, to put things together that do not fit, and to take on challenges. Our ancestors survived because they were able to figure out how to get out of a fix. We love to take on problems that, on the one hand, are not too easy to bring satisfaction and, on the other, not so tough that it seems hopeless or threatening to take them on. I know some views of mankind contend that we seek equilibrium. Freud talked about *thanatos*, a kind of death wish. That is not what I see. The human being I see tinkers with his car when he does not have to, works crossword puzzles, and figures out how the toaster works. He is a "busy beaver." The creative challenge of teaching is to make the lessons into a problem of some kind, where something does not make sense or go together and it is the students exercise to figure it out or provide a solution. That is in contrast to exposition, passing on information; in which case it had better be either interesting or on Friday's test. This contrasts with the "problems" that are not really problems at all but tasks to do. Make it problematic. Make them think, figure out, create, solve, judge, fix. That tends to be motivating.

Produce a Product

I also see the human being as a "show-and-tell" creature. We love to create something tangible that we can display or share with others. One of the major reasons that students in athletics or drama tend to be motivated is that their work is directed toward the creation of a product, the game or the performance. Frequently, we just learn something in school and the teacher gives us an all but secret, just-between-me-and-you reaction and goes on to the next assignment. There is no chance to say to our world, "Look what I did." Ask your students to create a product and put it on display somehow. That is motivating.

Something I Do

It is motivating for a student if he feels that the schoolwork is something *he* is doing: "I am studying math." "I am trying to understand how we got into World War II." This is in contrast to a situation in which he experiences himself in a situation in which he is essentially responding to the initiatives of the teacher, meeting requirements, jumping through hoops. Part of the art of teaching is making the class into a place where students do things rather than just show up and respond to a teacher.

Developmentally Meaningful

In each stage of our lives there are central issues we need to resolve. We tend to be motivated to deal with anything that speaks to the resolution of these issues. Adolescents are trying to figure out who they are and where they fit. They are dealing with sexual issues. They are trying to make friends and feel included. They are trying to figure out what is worth believing. And they are trying to clarify what is worth doing, in work and in leisure. They are working out a different kind of relationship with their parents. They are trying to deal with all of the physical changes that are occurring. For the first time they can really think abstractly about things, including about what is right and wrong. In short, they are concerned with what they are becoming. Anything that clearly connects to all these things tends to evoke greater motivation than something which does not. One thing I do want to make clear is I am not arguing for a curriculum of "drugs, sex, and rock and roll," content tied to the immediate interests of teenagers. Rather I am talking about fundamental human needs. Even the most traditional curriculum speaks to these issues if we and the students learn how to make the connections.

Competition and Cooperation

Human beings are both *competitive* and *cooperative* creatures. Both processes can be motivational. And, as is true of most everything I can think of, they can also turn off motivation. Competition, as we can see in sport and business, can result in the highest motivational level imaginable. But at the same time competition can be alienating, dehumanizing, instill fear and distrust, and result in retreat and withdrawal. Also, human beings, social creatures that we are, tend to become highly charged to do things when in collaboration and social exchange with others. But too, cooperation can distract us from our purpose, deaden our initiative, and generally produce the mediocrity that we know as "decision by committee." The conclusion is, however, both competition and cooperation can result in increased levels of student commitment if managed sensitively.

Grades Can Be a Motivator

My posture is to use every tool available to me as a teacher. The reality is that grades are an incentive for many students, even if nothing else about school means much to them. Grades, after all, are the way the school culture gives its verdict on a student's worth. I think we fool ourselves into thinking grades do not matter to students. For a minority, a small minority I believe, grades do not matter. My experience has been, however, that many students who claim not to care about them, if you talk to them long enough and are around them long enough, obviously do care. Most students would prefer to get good grades and would be willing to work to get them if they thought it was possible to achieve them. The challenge in working with students and using grades as a motivator is to help them discern the link between doing their work in school and achieving the good grades they want. Some tend to think good grades are a product of luck. Try to get them to imagine what it would be like to get, say, A's and B's rather than C's.

A word of caution, however: I am opposed to giving good grades to students who do not earn them. That is a violation of the grading system, a system which is meant to reflect the quality of a student's work. Furthermore, I am concerned that students getting high grades without producing excellent work are learning a false lesson: you get something for nothing. That is an inaccurate and self-defeating assumption for a young person to take with him into adult life.

IN CONCLUSION

The title of this chapter is "A Perspective on Achievement." The challenge for you is to understand the individual sections, and at the same time put all of this together. Go back though the chapter and remind yourself of what I have written and allow "all of this" to fuse into one overall perspective. Also, a good exercise for you is to add three major ideas of your own to what I have written here. Think about how what both you and I have offered applies to these underachieving students. And as you read through the rest of the book see how the material of this chapter applies to what is being considered.

4 An Exploration of Studenting

This chapter investigates the work of students—what I am calling studenting. What is it they, in contrast to teachers, have to do to get their work done well? What accounts for the level of their capability as students? What gets in their way? I have selected a number of areas to explore in order to begin to resolve these questions and they comprise the sections of this chapter. Included are academic skills, learning skill strategies and learning disabilities (the distinctions among these three will become clear); social and cultural factors; psychosocial development; relational issues; personal and psychological problems; and health and nutritional issues. As you read these sections keep in mind the questions put forth early in this paragraph. Also, look for the way the ideas in the first three chapters relate to the material in this chapter. And last, of course, add your own insights to what I offer here.

ACADEMIC SKILLS

Just as a carpenter needs to be able to pound a nail straight in order to do his job well, students must possess the requisite "tools of the trade" to allow them, if they are motivated and the school is a rich environment, to do their job well. So what are these skills? When I began looking into this, I assumed that this section would be a summary of the academic skills we—or at least I—usually list: reading, writing, speaking, listening, and basic math capabilities. I thought I would familiarize myself with each of these areas, see what researchers were up to and summarize my findings, and say these are the capabilities a student must possess to hold up his end of the schooling process.

123

Frankly, this section looked a bit forbidding because I was starting pretty much from scratch. Nowhere in my own training had I studied these basic skill areas. I have some regret about that because I know that my students have paid a price for my lack of insight into how to work, particularly, with student reading and writing problems. Ignorance is indeed bliss and I taught blithely away for years with no sense that, for example, some students could not read the textbook I was using. What is interesting to me is that this was not called to my attention during the time. But, upon reflection, it is not so mysterious. The student with the problem was not going to bring it up because it is a major sign of inability in a school culture that values ability perhaps even more than accomplishment. Given that fact, these students would rather look lazy or flunk than reveal themselves as incapable. In effect the students and I had a deal going: I did not know what I was doing but did not get called on it. Likewise, the students did not know what they were doing, and although it was brought to their attention in some quarters, at least I was not making a big public point of it. Looking back on this, I am taken with how, despite the ready availability of reading score information and such, the academic skill problem still did not register with me.

It is clear that if we are going to work with underachievers, we are going to have to know how to help students deal with their deficits in the areas of reading, speaking, listening, computation, and—I add one not usually in the list—seeing. However, you are not going to get much help from me regarding these areas. I only invite you to study them. Do take some courses or set up some workshops for yourself. A book I am reading which I am finding useful is *Language Arts: Learning Processes and Teaching Practice* by Charles Temple and Jean Wallace Gillet.[1]

What I can report are the results of my explorations in the area of academic skills. They were surprising to me. Although as I reflect on what I already know, I should have expected them. To start my investigation, I went to speak with a professor of reading with an excellent reputation, Dr. Marjorie Lipson. My question to her was, "Marge, what's up in reading? It's just not my field and I need to write something about it for an academic skills section of a book I'm doing on kids who don't get it done in school."

Marge replied that she and her colleagues were starting to see the act of reading as part of something larger and more fundamental: the ability to think and solve problems. What she was getting at in her research was not this or that reading comprehension skill. She was looking at something more inclusive, something she calls metacognition. By metacognition she means the intellectual and thinking strategies a student employs to come to grips with the specific reading task in front of him or her. Professor Lipson's concern is with answering questions of the sort: How does the learner go about the problem of making sense of print on a page? How does he think about the job in front of him? What meaning does he give it? What strategies does he employ to learn the meanings inherent in those printed words?

As time went on, this focus on how students think and how well they think seemed to show up everywhere I looked. It led me to a basic conclusion that I want to share with you early on: A most fundamental academic skill a student needs to master in order to achieve in school is the ability to engage in goal-directed thinking. Without that, he is like a painter who does not know how to hold a brush. (Yes, I know about Jackson Pollack and his drippings. But that only makes my point. A few students can get by without the ability to think effectively about their schoolwork, but it is rare. And then again, I have seen some of Pollack's conventional work, and as a matter of fact he could wield a paint brush quite well indeed.)

Professor Lipson and her colleagues have written several articles which explore this theme.[2] They write from a cognitive (thinking, information processing) and developmental (growth in overall intellectual capability) perspective. From this orientation they view reading as a specific manifestation of the "meta-skills" of planning, regulating, and self-evaluating:

> Evaluation of person, task, and strategy variables results in an assessment of the task difficulty relative to one's abilities and an assessment of the relative effectiveness of different strategies. Evaluation is a measure against a standard such as effort, ease, or certainty within a problem-solving context. Planning involves the allocation of time and effort in order to optimize task solutions. The good reader, like the good problem solver, selects reasonable goals and generates suitable means to accomplish them. Regulation refers to the ability to follow one's chosen plan and to monitor its effectiveness. Sometimes new goals and new plans must be formulated, while at other times it is better to persevere on the chosen path.[3]

Lipson and her colleagues assume that to understand why students do or do not handle reading well, one must understand the more general process of self-directed thinking. They make it a point to emphasize self-direction. Reading has to do with what a student intends, and what he or she chooses. It has to do with his or her efforts. They employ the term strategic learning to describe an ideal of student functioning that we should use as a guide. Inherent in this notion of strategic learning is that the student be purposeful and intentional. The student should do more than just go through the motions; in this case, mechanically reading whatever is put in front of him. Strategic learning involves a student with a clear idea of what needs to be done and why. And it involves the student having a felt, personal responsibility for getting it accomplished. In order for learning to be considered strategic, the learner must be self-aware; and he must behave as an agent (not a reactor), selecting attainable and positive goals and then proceeding self-consciously to achieve them.

The key to becoming a strategic learner, with reading or writing or any other academic process, is the ability to think about his own thinking. He must be able to identify the cognitive or intellectual strategies he needs to possess and somehow acquire them. He must know what affects his thinking through a task, control any negative influences, and take advantage of positive ones. He needs to learn to witness his own intellectual processes so that he will be able to be self-corrective when it is needed. All of this makes up what can be called a "meta-academic skill" (higher, beyond other skills): the capacity to effectively reflect on one's way of thinking in school. The student, then, needs to develop two levels of skills. There is this general strategic learning, thinking-about-thinking, goal-setting, planning, and self-directing ability. In addition, there are the skills which make its application possible in the various academic subjects. In reading, for example, a student must be able to skim, to use context to discern unfamiliar words, and to take notes.

Professor Lipson and her colleagues stressed that all reading is contextual. (I would add all learning, period, is contextual.) This can only be understood in light of a particular set of circumstances. The process of reading is but one element embedded in an interplay of various elements that comprise a schooling situation. The point these researchers make is that we cannot accurately label someone as a good or bad reader. One is only an effective or ineffective reader in this or that particular situation. To understand any academic skill or activity, one must comprehend the mutual effects a number of variables have on one another. That is, to get a true sense of what is happening with a student we cannot look at "pieces" of the picture—curriculum, instruction, school organization, climate, student capability or behavior—but rather perceive "all of it," student-in-context, as a dynamic, interrelative system. They list crucial aspects of the situation that must be considered, including the particular content being studied, the student's level of awareness and motivation, and the student's goals and strategic learning behaviors.

This concern for context underscores the idea that for a student to be a self-conscious, self-directive, and self-corrective learner he or she must have more than just general knowledge of how to go about things. He must have conditional knowledge: depending on what is called for in any concrete circumstance, the capability of deciding just what goals are appropriate and when and to what extent to use various strategies. Thus strategic learning ultimately depends on a student's ability to take his purposes and the immediate context into account. He must learn when and why various strategies are used to accomplish different ends. It is here that efforts to teach reading (and, to me, other subjects as well) fall short. Basal readers, for example, do assist readers in understanding the mechanics of reading and provide a good amount of practice time. However, these readers do not assist students in learning to bring background knowledge to bear on the material being studied or to develop other cognitive strategies that will empower them to read truly well.

To get at this problem, Lipson and her colleagues have designed a program they call Informed Strategies for Learning (ISL).[4] This program seeks to increase students' awareness of their own cognitive processes (metacognition) and to make use of effective reading strategies. Students are educated to be more effective self-starters, self-watchers, and self-correctors as they attempt to make sense of text. What is intriguing, and I want to broaden the concern beyond that of reading alone, is that while academic skill is involved in students' becoming effective, so is academic will and the particular learning context. The learner must understand and activate skill and will as is appropriate to the demands of a unique context. It is not enough to just teach a student some skill isolated from context and function and then give him some practice until he "gets it down"— and admonish him to "try harder" if he does not get it or know what to do with it if he does. But that is precisely what we do much of the time.

In a similar vein, Ann Brown, another reading specialist, and her colleagues provided training for students to help them increase their ability to handle text.[5] (When reading people use the word text, they did not mean a textbook; they were simply referring to any reading material.) They shared Lipson's and my own view that students need to become more informed participants in the learning enterprise. In order for students to be powerful readers, we must help them to acquire skills in self-management and self-control. They must learn to analyze for themselves the learning challenge, decide on goals, select the most appropriate learning strategies, and monitor, adjust, and evaluate their own efforts. What Brown and her colleagues provide might be called learning strategy training. They described what is involved:

Learners must themselves consider the four points and their interaction—perhaps as described in the following: (1) Learning activities: The learner should consider the available strategies, both general and specific. Specific strategies could be the rules for summarization . . . while general strategies could be variants of such general comprehension and study-monitoring activities as generating hypotheses about the text, predicting outcomes, noting and remediating confusions, and so forth . . . (2) Characteristics of the learner: The learner should also consider his/her general characteristics such as a limited immediate memory capacity for meaningless materials and a reservoir of appropriate prior knowledge. Thus the learner should not overburden his/her memory by attempting to retain large segments of text, too many pending questions, too many unresolved ambiguities, and so forth . . . The learner should attempt to tie the information content into any prior knowledge possessed, to activate appropriate schemata . . . to seek relationships or analogies to prior knowledge . . . and to see information in the light of knowledge he/she already has. (3) Nature of the materials: The learner should also examine the text itself for the logical structure of the material, its form as well as its content. Although meaning does not reside in the text alone, authors are sometimes helpful in cueing meaning. They flag important statements by such devices as headings, subsections, topic sentences, summaries, redundancies and just plain "and now for something really important" statements. Students can be made aware of the significance of these cues and induced to actively seek help from such sources. (4) Critical task: The learner should consider the aim of the learning activity, the purpose of his/her endeavors; he/she should also be aware that different desired outcomes require different learning activities and thus learn to tailor efforts accordingly.[6]

What is important for us in this book is to note the avoidance of "blind" training of students. Instead, there is a concerted attempt to create learners who can effectively design and carry out plans on their own. A program such as this makes students more aware of the active nature of learning. It helps them become better problem-solvers and trouble-shooters. It supports them in thinking more clearly and acting more effectively in pursuit of their own purposes. We should join in doing this kind of work.

The examples so far have focused on the importance of thinking in the area of reading. Educational psychologist Martin Covington has worked from a similar orientation with what he calls "strategic thinking" that applies to all subject areas. Covington defines three components of strategic thinking, which by this time should sound familiar: (a) problem (or task) formulation; (b) selection of appropriate knowledge acquisition techniques; and (c) a capacity for self-monitoring of progress toward the achievement goal.[7] To Covington, problem formulation involves a student being able to represent a problem or distant goal in the form of a set of concepts consisting of the present state, the desired end, and the steps or actions needed to transform the present state to the future condition. This requires that the student understand his own capabilities, limitations, and idiosyncrasies as a learner and as they relate to the task at hand. Furthermore, strategic learning involves the ability of a student to assess what he already knows and what is yet to be learned. While the student must be able to visualize where he wants to go, he must also be flexible and vigilant to changes in his priorities or circumstances. As the student proceeds forward he must be able to select the most appropriate learning strategies, noticing such factors as the nature of the content studied and the conditions under which the learnings will be tested and used. This is a student who knows how to go about his work.

Covington pointed out that successful students perceive school as a problem-solving event. In contrast poor learners tend to master conceptually-oriented material by rote overlearning. He notes that in secondary school, where assignments are becoming more complex, students are often quite naive regarding achievement management. At a time when they need strategic thinking skills, the only thing all too many students can say is that to do better they must try really hard. They have little sense of what "really hard" involves beyond spending more time on the lesson. More time spent doing the wrong things is going to get them nowhere. My hunch is that many unsuccessful students have tried putting in more time and gotten no payoff in terms of greater school success. If that is so, it is little wonder that they have ceased putting in long hours.

Covington has designed what he calls the Productive Thinking Program to teach these school-going skills directly to students. He reported significant success in training students who span a broad range of abilities to acquire thinking processes useful in a variety of subject areas. He did caution, however, that although the strategic thinking program can increase the capabilities and attainments of virtually all students, relative distinctions in the students' quality of thinking and achievement will persist. That is, though a less-talented student may be achieving more than previously, he or she may still not be doing as well as some others. If his self-value as a learner is based upon comparative accomplishments, the student, even though he is learning significantly more now than before, may not grow positively in academic confidence and self-esteem. Covington said the challenge for educators is to support the student in shifting his perspective. He needs to begin basing his decisions about self-worth on his own internal standards and past levels of attainment rather than on his competitive position with other students.

Continuing on with this same theme, the literature in education reveals a number of examples of very promising work aimed at equipping students with the thinking capabilities necessary to effective studenting.[8] Two important theorists in this area are Reuven Feuerstein and Martin Lipman.[9]

Feuerstein has developed the Instrumental Enrichment Program. This program improves cognitive processes crucial to accomplishing so much of what is asked of students in school: the input, elaboration, and output of information. To give you a sense of Feuerstein's approach, below is a list of cognitive deficiencies he identifies:

- Unplanned, impulsive, and unsystematic exploratory behavior. When presented with a number of cues to problem solving that must be scanned, the individual's approach is disorganized, leaving the individual unable to select those cues whose specific attributes make them relevant for a proper solution to the problem at hand.
- Lack of or impaired capacity for considering two sources of information at once, reflected in dealing with data in a piece-meal fashion rather than as a unit or organized facts.
- Inadequacy in experiencing the existence of an actual problem and subsequently in defining it.
- Lack of spontaneous comparative behavior or limitation of its appearance to a restricted field of needs.
- Lack of or impaired strategies for hypothesis testing.
- Lack of orientation toward the need for logical evidence.
- Lack of or impaired planning behavior.
- Episodic grasp of reality. The individual is unable to relate different aspects of his or her experience to one another.[10]

Feuerstein was seeking to correct these deficits and at the same time increase the student's intrinsic motivation and feeling of personal competence and self-worth. To get at this, Feuerstein devised a series of "instruments" for students to do with paper and pencil.[11] These materials are on general topics and not subject-specific. Teachers introduce the exercises and lead follow-up discussions to enhance student insight into the processes. It is not important in this context to go into the specifics of all this. The important thing is that we understand the assumption underlying this work: the ability to process information—think—is a vitally important school-going skill, useful in a wide range of content areas. Moreover, this skill can be taught directly to students.

Lipman developed the Philosophy For Children program. This program also centers on the teaching of thinking skills, conveying them through a series of stories about children in which the protagonists spend considerable time thinking about thinking. Students read and discuss the stories and engage in simulation exercises based upon them. The program is designed for upper elementary age children, but these materials, with adaptation—and certainly this general approach—should prove useful with older students. To give you an indication of the thinking skills Lipman finds important, consider the following list: concept development, cause-effect relationships, identifying underlying assumptions, working with analogies, problem formulation, and working with consistencies and contradictions.[12]

Personally, I like the concept of this Lipman program because it agrees with a couple of my biases.[13] First, it teaches students to think, and in my view there is no more empowering capability for a student to acquire. Second, it confronts students' with philosophical ideas and issues. Currently, there is not just enough of that in schools. Schooling should deal much more with fundamental questions of purpose, meaning, reality, value, and wisdom. These are crucial issues to us all, but especially to adolescents who are in a time of their lives in which they can and need to work through issues of self-definition and belief. My contention throughout has been that many students do not relate to school because nothing makes much sense to them at this time in their life.

A colleague of mine at the University of Vermont, Charles Letteri, has incorporated seven cognitive skills into a single concept he calls "cognitive control." His approach is to measure levels of functioning in each of these seven areas and create a "cognitive profile" for a student. The cognitive skill areas he focuses upon are field dependence-independence; scanning; reflectiveness vs. impulsivity; breadth of categorization; complexity vs. simplicity; sharpening vs. leveling; and tolerant vs. intolerant. An example, there are seven thinking skills and your particular profile might show that you are low on one, high on three, average on five, and so on. Thus a "picture" is formed by the pattern of scores on each of the separate skills. What Professor Letteri is able to do, and quite quickly it appears, is remediate the problem areas so that your profile matches the profile of a successful student. And then, Letteri's research shows, the student begins to perform like a successful student.[14]

Frankly, all of this is far-removed from my experience, and despite our many conversations I am not quite sure what Charlie does to modify a student's cognitive profile. But nevertheless it seems impressive to me. I have heard many accounts of his success with students. In addition, I like his basic approach of figuring out what it takes to go to school well and then teaching the student how to do it. Also, it is Charlie's assumption, which I share, that for too long we inferred a lack of motivation in students who just did not have the tools to get the academic work done. Or, alternatively, we took a lack of motivation in a student at face value, when what was really going on was a reaction to failure, a way of coping. I wonder how motivated we would be after a dozen years, the span of the elementary and secondary years if you do not count kindergarten, of trying to do schoolwork without the intellectual tools to do the job. Charlie's premise in all of this is an intriguing one: You do not necessarily start with remedial math, for example, but with getting the thinking skills to kids which equip them to be successful at remedial math. At the same time, however, I know that Charlie is making it clear he does not want to make an either-or issue out of it. Students must learn to think, and they should learn math, reading, writing, or speaking skills. He is just saying, if I read him correctly, that thinking cuts across all of them and is a contributing condition to successful learning in these content areas. Moreover, I would add, school subjects aside, thinking clearly is the best survival skill a human being can develop. If you cannot think, you are trapped and ignorant at best—and, literally, dead at worst.[15]

In the next chapter I outline some techniques I use to promote thinking among students. These ideas are only a fraction as sophisticated as the approaches just described, but though you and I are trying to make sense of these high-powered approaches it might be a place to start.

If nothing else, I hope this section has gotten you to think more about your students' thinking. A sobering statistic with which to end: research on teacher questioning strategies reveals that 20% of teacher questions required students to think as a response; and 80%, no less, did not demand thinking.[16] So not only do teachers talk all the time (research consistently shows we talk 75% of the time, while our students get to split up the remaining 25%), when we do let students talk, 4 out of 5 times we do not ask them to think about anything. And yet theorist after theorist contends that thinking is the most crucial ability for students to develop.[17]

LEARNING SKILLS STRATEGIES

One of the most promising trends these days involves efforts to improve students' ability to manage the task of going to school. When you think about it, handling all the requirements of keeping up—much less doing well—in four or five disparate classes is no easy task. From the students' side, they have to be able to listen and take notes, participate verbally in class, extract significant information out of books, conceptualize and write papers, and budget their time to meet all of the demands of their classes. That is a big job for anybody, and it is especially tough if you have only been on the earth for a decade and a half and you are trying to put a social life together, hold down a clerking job, get along with your brother, and work things out with your mom and dad.

Ironically, students are provided with little training to explain just how to do all that. For the most part a student is supposed to pick it up here and there as things go along. Teachers and administrators, faced with no tougher a job, have formal training in universities to prepare them, take graduate courses, attend conferences and workshops, and contract for days off during the school year to figure out how to do their work better (while the students, evidently, do not need any work on building up their school-going skills, because they have the time off). The result of all this, of course, is that some students figure out what studenting is all about and do it well, while others, no less inherently capable, never pick it up.

It was a major impression from my work in California that many students, bright as they are, as generally competent as they are, are just not too skilled at school-going. What seems obvious to me is that we need a dual-focused training program in schools: one designed to help teachers be good at teaching; and one designed to help students be good at studenting. Of course students may still choose not to use the capabilities they acquire. But by helping them increase their ability to do what they do well, we increase our odds that something good will result from the schooling process.

So why do we tend not to stress student training as a complement to teacher training? There are many reasons, of course, and you can think of them as well as I. But one reason I want to underscore relates to how we think about teaching and learning at the most fundamental level. Most of us, deep down, even though we do not take time to articulate it, see what happens in school as a function of what the school does and not so much what students do. There is a perception that what students become is a product of the context they are in. If the curriculum is good, the climate healthy, and we teach well, students will learn. In fact, that assumption has been put forth explicitly over the past few years. For example, school people have described effective schools, but in the list of qualities characteristic of these schools there was no mention of the level of student commitment and capability. Evidently, what the students are like or what they can do is not seen as an important factor in determining whether a school is good. As well, there is what can be called a teaching technology movement—examples include the processes of mastery learning and effective teaching. Basically, the contention underlying these strategies alleges that if teachers do certain things, learning will occur. Again, there is little or no focus on what the student wants or his capabilities or choices. Shape the context, so it goes, and you determine the learning outcome.

Most of us have grown up in a time in which there has been a basic—I think it fair use of the term—liberal assumption that the way to improve somebody is to improve the situation in which they live. In education, then, to improve the education of students, enrich their context: Put more money into their school, get better leadership and organization, provide more support services, and improve the teaching and curriculum. Obviously, these are invaluable activities. But I am coming to realize that context improvements must be augmented by efforts to strengthen the levels of capability and dedication among the users of that context in order for them to take advantage of their improved opportunity, or to create opportunities and transcend limitations when their situation is not a supportive one. It is important to discuss this because there is a ''strengthen the user'' focus throughout this book. At the same time I do not want to dichotomize things and say contexts are not important. Indeed, students need good teachers, an appropriate curriculum, and an orderly, safe, and encouraging setting in which to do their work. But students also need to know how to be purposeful, directed, and effective at the work for which they are ultimately responsible: learning and growing to the maximum level possible. What this comes down to is a need for each of us to help our students learn the skills necessary to do well in our classes. We need to figure out just what it takes to be successful and teach students those things.

There are some published materials that are directed at improving student learning strategies and I am going to mention a couple. These packages could be integrated into regular classes; or they could be the texts in special classes, workshops, or summer programs on academic skill development for students.

One example is the Harvard-Milton Study Skills Materials published by the National Association of Secondary School Principals.[18] This series is designed to teach students the procedures essential for learning and solving problems. Examples include the skills of listening, textbook reading, note taking, planning one's time, study behavior and environment, vocabulary skills, and test taking. These lessons focus on ways of solving academic problems that are useful in a variety of subjects and contexts. They aid students in understanding how they learn best, how to be better at learning, and how to take greater responsibility for their own learning. Levels 1 and 2, which include both student texts and teacher's guides, are most useful with secondary students. (There is a level 3 for college use.) Plus, math (grades 6–10) and science (grades 7–10) programs are available.

To give you a sense of these materials, one of the 12 units of the Study Skills Program, level 2, is on active listening.[19] First, active listening is defined (hearing the words being spoken and thinking about what is said). Then, ways of becoming better at the skill are listed (Ask yourself: ''What are the main points of the speaker?'' ''What is 'between the lines'?''). And last, a listening exercise is provided for the student to use during a lecture to practice the skill. The exercise includes a place to write down the main points, where you think the speaker will go next, whether ideas have been supported or proved, and what has been hinted and not said. These are very impressive materials.

Another approach is the Learning to Learn Program.[20] These techniques are based on research done some time ago at the University of Michigan. This study found that good learners:

1. "Program" their learning—identifying the component parts of complex principles/ideas and breaking down major tasks into smaller units.
2. Ask questions about new materials, engaging in a covert dialogue with author or lecturer, forming hypotheses, and reading or listening for confirmation.
3. Devise informal feedback mechanisms to assess their own progress.
4. Focus on instructional objectives, identifying and directing their study behaviors to meet course objectives.[21]

The materials stemming from this research have been used for a number of years in colleges, and more recently in secondary schools in Boston and Cincinnati. One use of the Learning to Learn materials is to integrate them into regular classrooms. A couple of examples:

Robert Stone's 10th grade chemistry class has been assigned Chapter 7, which discusses the relationship among temperature, pressure, and volume of gases. Students work in pairs, generating questions from the text and using an active method of reading to solve problems. In this regard, their chemistry texts become "dictionaries" that help them solve the sample problems presented in the text.

Albert Hart has just given a brief lecture on Greek city-states to his 9th grade social studies class. Students took notes on his lecture. Later, working in pairs, students will help each other fill in missing notes and generate questions from those notes. They will then use their questions to read-to-find-answers in the textbook chapter on Greek city-states.[22]

The Learning to Learn Program makes manuals available to teachers and students in most subject areas.

Another use, Learning to Learn has been offered as a year-long credit course directed toward helping students become independent learners in school. The course provides a chance for students to focus on the Learning to Learn skills in the special class, and then use the rest of their classes as laboratories in which to try out what they have learned. An example of a student assignment in this course:[23]

How is an Information Map Constructed?

The following pages contain a series of exercises which will show you how to put information from your courses into Information Maps. If you have any questions about how this skill applies to courses you are currently taking, talk with your Learning Skills instructor. Remember, these skills are only important if you can apply them to your academic course-work.

Exercise 1:

Take any of the following topics and build an Information Map from it: major league baseball teams; life in the city; suburbs, and country; weather conditions in different seasons (e.g., winter, etc.); and domestic and foreign-made automobiles.

For example, your map on major league baseball teams might start by looking like this:

TEAMS

Yankees Red Sox Indians

How good is the team's pitching staff?

Etc. (Other questions which can be asked in comparing baseball teams.)

The designers contend that the Learning to Learn Program brings about more active engagement by students in school, better teacher morale, improved student academic performance, and more students going on to post-secondary schools. The assumption of the program is that students can be taught higher-level learning skills that are applicable across the board in their classes (well, that are applicable throughout life, out of school as well as in).

I hope this discussion of the Harvard Study Skills and Learning to Learn programs has given you some useful things to think about. It seems to me that these kinds of approaches are especially useful if they are complemented by other efforts at student improvement. They probably are not sufficient in themselves to get us what we want. For example, these learning skill programs may improve a student's ability to handle many of the organizational problems involved in going to school, but there must still be effective remedial programs in reading and math. Furthermore, students may still need help working through personal, developmental, or health issues that get in the way of their learning. Students may also need help in getting motivated and directed enough to take advantage of the learning skills program itself, and not just toss it off as they do other things having to do with school. I see learning skills as being a piece of a larger student improvement package. You can think this through and visit schools where they are adopting this approach in order to judge for yourself.

LEARNING DISABILITIES

I don't know if you are like me, but I have always had a hard time understanding that everybody does not see the world exactly as I see it. For example, I figure that when you read you do the same thing as I do, see the words the same way, take the information in the same way, and organize and store it just as I do. And even though I know for a fact that I am red-green color blind, as ridiculous as it may sound, I still think you and I see the same colors on the Christmas tree. Another example, a few years ago I lost much of my hearing. I remember how different the world sounded (well, didn't sound) to me after that happened. But today, despite the fact I know that you, if you have normal hearing, hear the world much differently from me, I operate in life as if we hear the same things.

This tendency of mine has always affected my teaching. The minute I know something everybody must know it, including students. Or at least all I need to do is remind them for a minute or two to bring it back into their minds. The minute I can do something, I figure everybody can do it. I do not know what to make of all this. Perhaps it's indicative of some kind of arrested development involving my ability to separate out self and world. But then again, maybe it is a common problem among people to a greater and lesser degree. Since I am uncomfortable with the arrested development thesis, I will assume you share this tendency to think everybody processes the outer reality of things and events, and the inner world of thoughts and memories and images, in very much the same way.

Well, they do not. We as teachers have to understand that. That point leads me into the topic of this section: the exploration of learning disabilities as a possible factor in a student's failure to achieve academically. Clearly this is something I need to learn much more about. It has not been part of my training at all. I try to say enough here to get us both started in studying this issue.

I first confronted the term learning disabilities about 7 years ago when I was working with what are labeled "troubled students." These young people were confronting serious difficulties in their lives: in school (suspensions, vandalism, disruption), at home (serious conflicts with parents, brothers, and sisters), and in the community (often involving contact with the legal system). At that time I was studying juvenile delinquency and came across a monograph that cited research evidence demonstrating that up to 80% of juvenile delinquents have learning disabilities. (I was astounded by this statistic, and still am.) My understanding is that the term learning disabilities refers to something defective in the way the young person processes information from the world. It has to do with brain functioning: there is a neurological, physiological basis for the problem. It is not that the individual has low ability. Nor is it a function of low motivation (though low motivation could be a consequence of it), social-cultural disadvantage, or inadequate schooling. Everyone does not work with the world just as you or I do. They are not looking out from the same place inside them that we are. So that is the basic idea of learning disabilities, an internal processing problem. We have all heard of dyslexia, where letters get turned around and reading is very difficult. (Some well-known dyslexics: Nelson Rockefeller, the former governor and vice-president; and Bruce Jenner, the Olympic decathlon champion and television personality.)

A book I am reading currently that has been useful is *Learning Disabilities: Understanding Concepts, Characteristics, and Issues* by Cherry Houck.[24] Much of what I know came from this book. Houck defines the problem as being what she terms a "psychological process disorder." Something is not right about the way the person takes in, transforms, and manipulates information. Of course, these processes are internal to the individual; we cannot see them "misfiring." But we can surmise from observed behavior that these disorders exist. So the disorder is covert rather than overt.

Houck listed five information processes of special importance:

1. *Attention*. This is the ability to focus selectively on appropriate factors in the environment (a page of a book, etc.) for the time necessary to process information accurately. Some researchers see, for example—and this gives you a feel of this concept of learning disability—the reticular activity system in the mid-brain as being the location within the neurological system where this dysfunction may occur.
2. *Discrimination*. The localization, identification, and differentiation of features (colors, form, shape, size, etc. and perception of patterns and sequences.
3. *Sensory integration*. The integrating of information received by the various sensory systems (sight, hearing, taste, etc.). Much research here on myelination of the brain, the angular gyrus, and things like that. Look them up.
4. *Memory*. The ability to "sift" and "scan," retrieve information, and so forth.
5. *Cognitive organization, concept formation, and problem solving*. The ability to classify, form generalizations, manipulate ideas in order to solve problems, make sense of things that present an issue.[25]

It is important to know what learning disabilities are not as much as what they are. They are not due to low intelligence. They are not due to sight or hearing impairments or serious motor deficits. They are not due to emotional problems. And they are not due to environmental, cultural, or economic disadvantage. Rule out all that and what do you have? There is something organic, perhaps genetically based, physiological, that gets in the way of a student's effectively taking in, storing, transforming, retrieving, and/or making use of information. And needless to say, if you have a problem somewhere in all that you are likely to have some problems in school—because dealing with information is the "name of the game" academically. The processing problem shows up a reading problem, or in writing, or in listening or oral expression, or in doing math, or in any one of a host of areas.

And that is just the academic part of it. Imagine what years of academic failure can do to someone's confidence and sense of identity. He or she has probably been called dumb or lazy, or both—and to some extent he or she has accepted that as a true observation. I don't think most teachers, at least fairly successful in school ourselves, can really relate to the reality of this: to see yourself as being "low ability" in a school culture that praises ability. And how difficult it is for us to understand the level of self-disdain that can come out of being seen, and seeing yourself, as unmotivated and a slacker in a setting that makes a such big deal of diligence and effort. Beyond all that, to go to a school every day, year after year, and fail! How many of us would try to work at a job for 12 or 13 years—the period of elementary and secondary schooling—that we could not do. We would want to leave. And if we felt compelled to stay, how many of us could emerge from it personally unscarred by the experience? I know I could not.

I remember a talk I had with a high school student whom the school defined as having a learning disability. This rather rough, formidable looking young man of 17 started telling me what it had been like for him to go to school. He told me how every year he tried his hardest—he referred back to the fifth grade and on up for illustration—and year after year he failed. He was silent for a few seconds and just looked at me. And then tears rolled down his cheeks. I admit tears rolled down mine too. We just sat there with each other for a time. I really did not know what to say or do. But as I think back on it now, for a few minutes I experienced what it was like for some of our school failures. If nothing else, I understand a bit better how some of the macho posturing and put-downs of schools and teachers and the failure to get involved as enthusiastically in school as we would like them to are ways for these students to cope with the world of school and maintain some measure of dignity. If my hopes had been dashed as often as some of these young people—after all, 6 years ago a 15-year-old, quite mature looking now, was 9 years old—I know I would be pretty skeptical, fearful, and hostile. At a time in adolescence when I was trying to put an identity together that makes sense and is acceptable, I know I would see myself as defective and flawed. And none of that would be good for me at all.[26]

My conclusion is that learning disabilities do exist. If nothing else, my understanding that human beings vary on any dimension you can name makes me believe that they exist. The problem for you and me is to discern whether they exist in a particular student. After all, we cannot see learning disabilities; they have to be inferred. How can we be sure that what we are calling a learning disability is not just a skill that has not been learned yet? After all, Indian gurus spend a lifetime in meditation developing their ability to concentrate, so we cannot assume that some 15-year-old who lives on soft drinks and music videos has a learning disability if he cannot concentrate. Letteri's and Feuerstein's work, among others assumes that cognitive skills are learnable. And since a human being is always in interaction with a physical, social, and cultural world, how can we be sure that environment is not the prime factor in the problem we see? I remember the adolescents in jail I worked with, victims of sexual abuse and violence at home, full of caffeine, sugar and nicotine, whose eyes darted and hands trembled as they tried to read. It is beyond me to say whether a learning disability was to any degree involved; and if it were, to what extent it was the cause of their problems or the result of other factors. All I can do is share my dilemma with you and hope both of us can find others more expert than we who can give us some direction.

It is beyond my knowledge to say just how much of a factor learning disabilities are in school failure. My assumption is they do play a significant role. Perhaps if nothing else, the idea of learning disabilities can make us pause when we are in the midst of assuming that the student would be fine if he would only try harder. (Trying is not what is between me and dunking a basketball at this moment.) We need to measure to what degree we help a learning disabled student accommodate for this limitation by taking alternative routes to achieve his or her goals (my basketball analogy, I could compensate for my lack of jumping ability by learning to shoot from long-range), finding ways to avoid problem situations (I could quit spending my energy trying to dunk basketballs), or remedying this problem (I could buy a step ladder or work with weights to increase my jumping ability). In reading through Houck's many examples, it appears the answer is sometimes accommodation, sometimes transcendence—and that leaves us with the judgment to make of when to do one over the other. These are issues that we need to study carefully with the help of professionals in the field of learning disabilities.

There is one thing I am quite certain about, however. The people who ought to be studying learning disabilities are those who experience the problem, the learning disabled students themselves. They need to confront their own problem. They need to understand the nature of their difficulty, how it has affected their academic performance and the way others have treated them, and the way they have come to see themselves and their own possibilities. They need to, with our informed help, devise a plan to get over or around or through—whatever the right metaphor—the issue they confront. It is they, with our support, who must confront the issue of whether they have a learning disability. In this regard I am struck by Barry Schneider's research with learning disabled students which shows that most students have very little insight into the nature of their own disability. Sadly, they tended to attribute their learning problems to their own lack of effort, and few sought or received an explanation for their handicap.[27] Perhaps students and teachers can set up a class and study the issue together. That might be a good solution.

SOCIAL AND CULTURAL FACTORS

If we are going to understand why students succeed or fail in school we must analyze the social and cultural context in which these students live. By social and cultural context I mean such factors as the home life, income level, racial and ethnic background, and social class status. The generalization I support in these next pages is that this context, this world of the student, significantly influences his or her educational aspirations, school-going capability and style, and level of achievement. The school is both part of this world and responds to what it perceives in the student and the social–cultural setting in which it must do its work. And as well as being shaped by the school and the other social–cultural elements, the student shapes his environment, even if this is not done with critical awareness and intention. Thus the student, the cultural-social setting, and the school are in dynamic interrelation, each affecting and being affected by the others. Let us spend some time exploring these reciprocal relationships.

First I am going to supply some definitions. What exactly are we trying to understand here? All along, the emphasis has been on academic achievement and what accounts for it among students, and that continues to be the case in this discussion. In particular, in this section I want to explore the effect of several interrelated and overlapping phenomena on achievement. First, there is the effect of *culture*. I defined this term briefly in chapter 1, but to reiterate, by culture I mean the way of life of a people, including fundamental ideas about what is so, values concerning what is preferable or worthy or right, and customs and styles. As I said earlier, Americans do have enough cultural similarity to allow us to to refer to American values and an American way of life. But at the same time we are a culturally pluralistic nation made up of the descendents of immigrants from diverse cultures. And there are economic, political, religious, geographic, and other distinctions among us. So in this sense we can speak of a number of contrasting cultures—subcultures—as well as a general American culture. As Americans we are alike and different at the same time. To understand us is to see that.

There is also the term *social*, or *societal* or *society*. When I use those terms I am referring to the way we arrange or organize ourselves. I am talking about the institutions we set up, the rules we establish, the roles or slots we devise for people to fill and the way we allocate power, status, and wealth. For example, there are families and work institutions, governing bodies and their processes, the media, and economic arrangements (with the resulting social class distinctions based on income, occupation, housing and life style, and other factors). And there are schools, contrivances made up of buildings, formal purposes, rules, roles, and operations. The school, then, is a social institution itself, charged with accomplishing a large piece of the educational task necessary to maintain and further the culture and society.

Of course, culture and society are not completely separate from one another. Societal arrangements are grounded in cultural beliefs and values. They are a means for making possible or extending cultural patterns. Then too, social entities have an impact on the culture from which they grow. For example, the medium of television, a societal phenomenon, not only reflects American culture(s), it shapes American culture. It affects what we do—watch television for one thing— and what and whom we think are important, and how to go about solving problems. Even more important—I hope this is not confusing things—culture and society are so intertwined that whatever one you are talking about, society or culture, is often just a matter of perspective. To illustrate this point, social class can be seen as a position in an economic, occupational, or status hierarchy—a societal phenomenon. It can, as well, be viewed as a culture, or as containing a culture, or a means for manifesting a culture. This is also true of the television example cited earlier. From one perspective it can be viewed as a complex of functions and formal relationships, i.e., a social institution. Or it can be seen as a culture. Television *is* a culture. It embodies values, customs, fundamental assumptions about what is true, and all the rest. In any case, the two concepts, society and culture, although they differ in emphasis, are inseparable, overlapping, and interactive.

In this section, we should also be concerned with *race* (Americans come in colors) and *ethnicity* (and we come in hyphens, Italian-Americans, for example). Where you fit in those categories can make a difference in how you are treated in America. In addition, there are the ideas of *sex* and *gender*. The distinction between these two terms for me is that sex refers to the biological or physiological differences between boys and girls, men and women; gender refers to all the social and cultural distinctions and meanings that are derived from sex differences. Consequently, gender would be the prime focus in this section.

I do not equally emphasize all of these factors in this section. Instead I reflect on a prime interest of mine: the relationship of social class background and academic achievement. Particularly I want to focus on the potential effect of growing up in a lower socioeconomic circumstance on a child's educational and occupational aspirations, school-going capability, and school success. In your own study you may decide to focus elsewhere, but this is my particular concern here. A book I have found particularly useful in the study of the impact of social class on achievement is Christopher Hurn's *The Limits and Possibilities of Schooling*.[28] I draw much of what I say below from this book and I recommend it to you.

What can we say about social and cultural factors and school achievement? We can say that these factors do influence a student's work in school for good or for bad. And we can say that if we are going to make it better for students we had best understand the manner in which these factors influence students and schools. It is not enough to examine only the theories of curriculum, instruction, learning, development, or school organization. Social and cultural realities have to be factored in as well.

Simply, we need to look hard at the environment in which students live. We do not have to be hard-core behaviorists (believing that external conditions determine behavior and internal states) to realize that the environment affects the minds and actions of students—and, it should be added, educators as well. All of us are to some extent products of this world. Consider these conclusions drawn from research evidence:

> The basic facts are straightforward: Social class or socioeconomic status is clearly associated with educational success, both in terms of persistence in school, or what is usually called *educational attainment*, and in terms of grades and test scores, or *educational achievement*. A student's race or ethnicity also affects school suc-

cess. Black and Hispanic students are less often successful in school than white students, and Jewish and Oriental-American students are more likely to be successful than the majority. And while there are obviously many exceptions to these generalizations— black students, for example, who score higher on tests of mathematical skills than Japanese-American students—it is noteworthy that most of these differences seem to be cumulative over time. Lower class and disadvantaged students begin their school careers with measurable but not huge differences in skills compared with middle class students, but by the age of seventeen or eighteen, these differences are consistently larger than they were at age five or six. At the age of high school graduation, the advantage of high-status over low-status students in continuing some form of higher education is about two to one; and three or four years later, high-status students often enjoy a four to one advantage in college graduation over low-status students.[29]

Hurn pointed out that every study has shown that students from low-status backgrounds do less well on cognitive (intellectual) achievement. He also noted a relationship between social class, grades, and track assignments: Low-status students tend to get poorer grades and are less frequently represented in the academic or college-bound track. He cited research showing that the home environment, even more than the school, explains educational success. Hurn concluded: "There is little question that disadvantaged children enter school without a number of the intellectual skills and aptitudes that most advantaged children possess." Not only do these students lack some of the wherewithal to achieve success in school, they lack the *desire* to succeed. Hurn pointed to research revealing that students from high-status origins tend to have higher aspirations for educational achievement and to have friends with similarly high aspirations.[30]

Notice that Hurn did not use *caused* to describe the link between social-cultural factors and school success. Instead he uses terms such as *associated* and *relationship* and *explains*. Or he just described things as occurring, without designating the nature of the connection between the two. That is because research in the social sciences and education is not at the point where it can say where causation lies. All that is possible now is to infer a relationship between two phenomena. That is, when one happens the other happens; which is not to say one causes the other. To illustrate what I mean, could it be that the relationship one sees between social class background and test scores in school exists not because social class causes certain scores, but because both are caused by a third factor, say intelligence? Or, alternatively, might the precipitant of low test scores not be social class but rather the distinctive way schools respond to low-status children? Another possibility, it may be a matter of multiple causation, where a number of elements must all be present—social class, certain school characteristics, a particular student personality profile, and more—to create the relationship between class and achievement? And then again, what exactly is a cause? What does it mean for one thing to cause another?

Whatever the case, we are able to predict school attendance and success, for groups of students, from knowing such things as social class, ethnicity, and race. Looking back to chapter 1, notice I said *groups* of students. These research findings are only statistical generalizations, tendencies. We can never predict for certain about a particular student. We cannot say, for instance, "He's from a low income background so he won't do well in school." He or she may just turn out to be the most ambitious, self-directed, capable, and achieving student in the school. We can point to so many wonderful and inspiring examples of kids from the wrong part of town who do great things academically. But nevertheless these generalizations are important because they reveal patterns in American life. Though a student from a disadvantaged background will not necessarily be impeded by forces and events within his world, he probably will have obstacles to overcome when he enters school that can be attributed in some way to the environment in which he lives. We do need to look closely at this; it is important. I invite you to study the Hurn book as a beginning.

What Is Going On?

Why do these relationships that show up time and again in the research exist? The experts do not agree, but I list several theories I find intriguing. To begin with, some years ago Oscar Lewis wrote about what he called a "culture of poverty." Lewis saw this culture as characterized by the belief that individuals cannot control their environment. Instead, fate or luck determines the course of a person's life. He also noted low control over aggressive impulses, a present as opposed to future orientation, and low levels of aspiration for educational and occupational achievement.[31] It is interesting to contrast this perspective on the world with the children in the Woodard study that began this book. For whatever reason, those achieving students did not buy into the notion that they could not control their own destiny. Referring back to Lewis' ideas, it is easy to see how school can be a problem for a student who does not feel what he or she does makes much of a difference (it's all luck, who you know). It is certainly no asset to be aggressive and impulsive in a school culture that values decorum and self-control. And there are going to be major problems if one does not do work with an eye to the future reward, because school—well, most things worth doing—can be pretty tedious from moment to moment. Last, if one does not aspire very high, it is hard for the school and its teachers to carry him or her along in spite of this posture. So if Lewis is right, there is a serious clash between the school and the culture of poverty that we need to address.

This general orientation is supported by some studies of parenting done around the time Lewis published his work. These studies showed that middle class parents were more active than low-status parents in helping their children plan the steps to achieve a task, and communicating each of the steps in the process. They were also more promotive of active, initiating behaviors among their children; put greater stress on self-control, shaping the environment through one's own efforts, and controlling aggressive impulses; more supportive of exploration and curiosity; and provided greater encouragement to adopt high educational aspirations.[32]

You can draw your own conclusions from this material, but as I see it, if these studies accurately describe what is going on, students coming out of low-status situations probably do need a fair amount of order and structure in school. At the same time this does not mean that students need a fare of movies and worksheets and a gross of carefully sequenced learning tasks. Rather, they need to be taught to do what the high status kids have learned from their world: go after it. If they do need to be under tight control, it should be in the initial stages as a way to get things going academically by providing an early taste of success. What should characterize their schooling, however, are experiences and lessons which teach them how to shape their world rather than only respond to it or "do their job." Success in American life is a result of reaching out, creating, and figuring out how things work. Due to the circumstances of their lives, it appears that some young people more than others need to learn how to take action in their lives.

Response to Cultural and Social Factors

In contrast, other theorists place less emphasis on the social and cultural factors themselves and instead stress the school's *response* to these factors. In short, they see the school reacting in very negative ways to socially disadvantaged students.[33] As these writers see it, schools take one look at these children and expect less of them. If that is true, it presents a major problem. For if we have learned anything in education it is that you get what you expect from a student. If students receive the message, "I don't think you'll do much," they buy it, internalize it, and accept it. And, indeed, they fulfill the prophecy the school has made.

To continue, this perspective contends that schools conclude that if you are poor and scruffy, you cannot think or speak very well and are not likely to go anyplace in your life. What school professionals do is run a small-scale factory in which you do a lot of busywork. They talk at you (not with you), group you by ability down with the dummies and away from models of ambitious and achieving students, give you worse grades and less encouragement than advantaged kids, and track you into general and vocational programs that, however well intentioned, sort you into, at best, so-so slots in the American social arrangement. So instead of schools being a vehicle for people to become all they can become, they are training grounds for accommodating to your status in the world—just about where you are right now; or, perhaps a bit more accurately, at the top of where "your kind" fits and belongs, but not above that. According to these writers, instead of "get up and go," schools for the have-nots stress "sit down and do what you are told."

I think it is fair to say that those who hold this view do not necessarily affirm that school people consciously plot or intend to keep the disadvantaged where they are. In fact, they may well be dedicated to the welfare of their students. Rather, it is a matter of basically good people, themselves a product of their experience, doing what they think best and see as possible. So the argument is not necessarily based upon some notion that evil, or even incompetent, people are running our schools. It is a lack of wisdom and perspective among school personnel, coupled with the social machinery of modern schooling that takes on a life and a direction of its own, that results in an education that sorts low-status people into "their place," near the bottom. (Though at the same time I know some theorists in this camp do not see it as benign and impersonal as this.) However it happens, these theorists see the reality of the operation of America's schools as antithetical to the truly meritorious society of our rhetoric, a society in which your inherent worth, not where you came from, determines what you can become in your life.

Impact on Academic Capabilities

Still other theorists and researchers concern themselves primarily with understanding the impact of these social and cultural phenomena on students' school-going capabilities in more detailed ways. What functional (ability to succeed in school) differences among students are the outcome of their experiences in their home, community, and school? What can or cannot they do in school as a consequence of living in their world? An example of work reflective of this orientation is that reported by Basil Bernstein in England.[34] Bernstein describes middle- and lower class children as differing in what he calls "communication codes." Middle-class children learn to use language in a way that speech and writing is freed from a specific context and is thus understandable to someone who did not share the experience. In other words, middle class children learn to "paint a picture" so that someone can "see," and understand quite fully, what is being described. This is a very useful skill for making yourself understood, making a point, and looking impressive in school. In contrast, for lower class children meanings are left implicit and the context is not spelled out. It is sort of "you had to have been there" speech characterized by private or understood (to the speaker) connotations and little sense of the overall setting or the significance of the message. As I see it, this is a good way to get labeled "nonverbal" or "not too sharp" by the school. In addition, this is not the best linguistic style to bring to the wordy school culture if you want to achieve academic success. Bernstein concludes that the school should teach students to use language in what he terms the *universalistic* mode, a skill vital to both school and, increasingly, occupational success. High status and high reward occupations increasingly require the ability to process information and use language in sophisticated ways. My worry is that the school will spend so much time accommodating for what it considers to be the students' "natural" ways, that it will not provide the necessary challenge and opportunity to students to develop their ability to use language well. I can think of no more empowering skill than to master the subtleties of the English language.

But to learn to use language takes practice. I have followed individual students through their entire school day, observing them in all their classes. It was notable how little they spoke (a few clipped phrases) and wrote (some short, fill-in-the-blank and single sentence replies). In some instances, *classes* spoke a lot—but if you watch an individual student, he or she does not say much. Ironically, students do not talk or write—or read, for that matter—during the 6 or so hours they spend in school each day; mostly they listen to teachers. Schools need to promote serious, extended, expressive speaking and writing, especially among the socially disadvantaged; every day from the first day on through to graduation.

Personally, I find worth in each of these theories and perspectives just described. It is important that we keep in mind and integrate a number of contrasting orientations into our understanding of the issue of underachievement, shifting them as needed from concern for social and cultural forces, to the operations of schools, to teaching practices, or to analyses of student capability. We have to adopt multiple perspectives in order to more fully comprehend the problem of less-than-optimum academic achievement. That certainly does not mean we have to buy into everything we hear. We must still decide whether some theory or another has any validity. It does mean that we should not turn away from an insight because it happens to be outside some particular frame of reference.

My Human Being-in-the-World Concept

Allow me to add one more frame of reference to your repertoire. I have a human being-in-the-world concept that is an organizer I use to study issues of the sort we are considering in this book. Refer to Figure 4.1 and let me explain. I will describe each of the components, put them together, and then provide an example of how this perspective can be used.

First there is the human being. At any moment in time any particular human being is a physical entity, a biochemical organism representative of a particular stage in the evolutionary process, with a unique genetic inheritance, and in possession of a certain state of physical health and well-being. This human being is of a particular age and is living through a particular developmental stage in his or her life and has a particular personal history. Inside him are memories, ideas, goals, images, feelings, sensations, drives, impulses, and a living consciousness—all the elements listed in chapter 2. Outside this human being is his world: physical (his home, possessions, buildings, climate); biological, (food and vegetation); social (family, friends, teachers, political and economic arrangements, the media); and cultural (values, assumptions, ways). This being and his

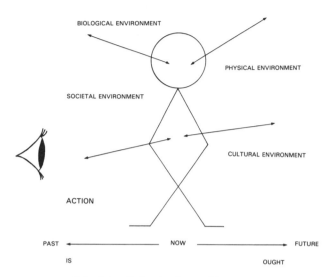

FIG. 4.1. Being-in-the-world concept.

world are at every moment in interaction, with each having an effect on the other. The individual acts and reacts to the world; the world acts and reacts to him. They form a dynamic system. To understand the human being is to grasp this systemic reality. And not only is this exchange with its mutuality of effect occurring now, it has occurred then, over the life history of the human being. And it is going to continue to occur in the future as well. The picture that must be held in mind is this dynamic interaction between an organism and his world over time.

There is one more element to note: you and me, the observers of all of this (the "eye" over on the left). We are looking on, investigating, studying, trying to make sense of what we see. We have our own history and internal workings. We have our own goals, biases, strengths, and limitations. We live in our own world and are to a greater or lesser degree shaped by it. And all of this colors and affects what we observe. So the observer must be put into the picture. Reality is filtered through the observer. For the observer, reality is ultimately what he thinks it is.

What all this means is that to completely understand someone you must comprehend what is inside him and what he does, what is outside him that connects with him, and how the inside and outside affect each other now and have affected each other in the past and likely will affect each other in the future. And that we must never forget that a particular human being, you or I, is watching and making sense of it all. The observer may make every attempt to be objective and unbiased, but the fact of the matter is that the observer-investigator is part of the same world, and affects and is affected by the observed, and filters everything through his subjective, inner being. For the observer, what is out there is what is *perceived* as being out there by this observer. And note the IS and OUGHT distinction indicated at the bottom of the diagram. Since the observer, a valuing being as human beings are, is in the picture, the concern can be both with what *is* and with what *ought to be*. And understand how those two, is and ought, affect one another: what is affects what you think ought to be; and try as you will, what you think ought to be affects what you think is.

Sexism in Schools

The following is an example of how this perspective works in practice: One of the major issues in education over the past decade has been the problem of sexism in schools. Keeping the organism in-the-world concept in mind, to come to grips with this issue as it effects a human being, a number of factors and their interrelationships over time must be taken into account. These include how the culture and society, including families and schools and work institutions, define and decide to treat males and females differently. In addition, there is a need to explore physical, genetic, and biological bases for sex differences. And one must achieve a psychological understanding of the way males and females think, feel, and behave. It also needs to be understood that whoever is looking at all this has a particular personal history, lives in a particular social and cultural environment, has certain political and social philosophies, values, and goals. All that makes a big difference as to what is given attention, what is decided to be true, and what is concluded to be preferable in this or any other issue.

What makes this individual-in-the-world concept useful for me, and this relates to the point I made earlier about being able to adopt multiple perspectives, is that it helps make clear the perspective or focus that one adopts to deal with an issue. To continue this example, on this issue of sexism, most people emphasize one aspect of the total reality at the expense of others. For instance, some researchers and writers see the problem as a social and cultural phenomenon. To them the problem is "out there" in the way the external world treats men and women differently. Others zero in on the physical and biological differences between males and females and draw conclusions predominantly from that, with little reference to social or cultural factors. Others may see gender concerns primarily as an individual, psychological issue, with biological and sociological factors underplayed. Some may have good insight into current reality but they have little or no historical perspective. Some who think they know what is going on are not clear at all about what they think ought to be happening or what they are willing to make happen. Conversely, some know what they are committed to achieve but are not grounded in the reality of what is actually going on. So the challenge to you on the issue of sexism in schools or any other is to note all these factors, including yourself, and decide what is real and preferable. I emphasize both reality and preferability because for us, in our lives, we study something as a way to make something happen, make something exist that did not before. I have never taken to the "learning for learning's sake" idea in education. I want us, certainly within the context of this book, to learn and *do something with it.* Thus I put the word *action* to the left of the figure.

My suggestion is that you keep this being-in-the-world picture in your head and plug things you experience or study into it. No one undertaking a research report or book can cover it all. You must figure out where each piece of the puzzle fits. To illustrate my point, just today I was given a report on the factors affecting the retention of girls in secondary science courses. In the words of the report, the focus was on:

> teaching strategies and teacher attitudes which successfully encourage girls in science. In addition to analyzing instructional techniques, classroom climates, and teacher-student interactions, a selected sample of former and current students received a variety of instruments which assessed attitudinal, cognitive, and socio-cultural variables. Results indicate that teachers who successfully encourage girls in science maintain well-equipped, organized, and perceptually stimulating classrooms, are supported in their teaching activities by parents of their students, are respected by current and former students, use non-sexist language and examples, include information on women scientists, use a variety of instructional strategies, stress creativity and basic skills, and provide career information. Factors which discourage girls in science include high school counselors who do not insist on further courses in science and mathematics; lack of information about science related career opportunities and the prerequisites for them; sex-stereotyped views of science and scientists fostered by textbooks, media, and many adults; lack of development of spatial ability skills; and fewer experiences with science activities and equipment that are stereotyped as masculine.[35]

Given the orientation I have sketched out, I can see what this study does and does not speak to. And I am encouraged to attend to what I am up to in reading it, how who I am colors what I see, what my options are in terms of what to do about this report, and what I think ought to be happening. There is also the matter of what I am actually doing and will do.

Television

This perspective underscores that our studies—this book is an example—are not the evening news. They are not just a series of interesting things to know. They are opportunities to gain insights that are instrumental in living our lives more fully, more ethically, and with more satisfaction. And speaking of the evening news, there is no more important social-cultural phenomenon for educators to study than the effect of television on the school-going capabilities of children and young people. Consider this statistic: A typical American child from kindergarten to high school spends about 11,000 hours in classrooms. At the same time, studies of television viewing habits indicate that during those same years the child watches 15,000 hours of television. And if you add movies, radio, and record listening, the total comes to 20,000 hours with the popular culture—almost double the time spent in school.[36]

The point is, if you want to understand cultural influences on how young people deal with school, it is an enormous omission to overlook the major cultural phenomenon in our time: television. When students are not in school, my best guess of what they are doing is staring at the television. While I do not have hard evidence at hand, my hunch is that socially disadvantaged and less achieving students sit in front of the set more than anybody. Every educator should have good insight into the way television works on students' minds and preferences. And that means going beyond some of the cliches I hear: "Sesame Street is a good show"; "There's too much violence on TV"; and "There are some good things on television but you have to look for them." I recommend some good writing on this subject by Neil Postman. Postman's book *Teaching as a Conserving Activity*, which focuses on the impact of the television medium on schooling, is excellent.[37] A more recent book of his, *Amusing Ourselves to Death*, incisively outlines the influence of the mass media on all of our lives.[38] His book *Disappearance of Childhood* is also quite good.[39]

The major point that Postman—and analysts such as Marshall McCluhan before him—makes in *Teaching as a Conserving Activity* is that to understand this medium you have to look beyond what is *on*, the programs and commercials, to *television itself*.[40] It is this method of transmitting information that we must understand. As McCluhan put it in his famous aphorism, the medium is the message. (Note the two meanings of the word *message* depending on which syllable you stress.) Looking at it in that way, the news is not good. Postman's conclusion is that television, the box itself and not the programming that is usually on it, teaches children a number of things that run counter to doing well in school. Furthermore, Postman uses the word *teach* advisedly, because he believes television embodies a very real curriculum. The TV curriculum, in contrast to the school curriculum, provides immediate gratification. To go to "TV school," you just have to turn it on and let it do its number. You do not have to prepare, anticipate anything, remember anything after it is over, or work up a sweat. TV is not about getting anything created or figured out. It is just about feeling good and staying tuned. In fact, "stay tuned" is *the* ultimate substantive communication of television to the viewer. With television there is no past or future, there is only now. Since TV is only on now, so there can only be now. There is no *was* with TV, only an *is*. There is no now versus then, just on versus off. And ultimately, no matter what is on television, when it comes right down to it, the viewer is always doing the same thing: *watching television*. He is not making or doing; he is sitting there, looking. TV is about pictures, images, and an emotional (affective) response in the viewer. We *like* or *enjoy* TV. School is about words, written and spoken and read, and reasoning. School is about planning (with TV, you do not have to plan other than to know when to show up to turn it on—and then if you are late, the set does not mind). School is about developing a sense of the past and future. It is about organized subject matter. In sum, school is altogether different from TV. The worry is that many kids engage school as if it were just another TV program. One of Postman's great lines, I cannot remember where I read it, is that "Sesame Street" does not teach children to like school; it teaches them to like television.

Postman, especially in *Amusing Ourselves to Death*, contends that we develop our values and frames of reference from television. He notes that a prime value we have absorbed from the tube is a commitment to *entertainment*. We are all in show business, entertaining and being entertained. I am reminded of this point when I hear teachers say a good teacher has to be a good entertainer. How often I have heard that. It is a bromide embedded in the culture of the profession. And how often I have heard students describe school or a particular class as "interesting" or "boring." Or, alternatively, they may say they "like" or "don't like" something about school. When you think about what the students are saying, these are television criteria for judgment. Since you cannot engage television or make it different in any way (the ending of a "M*A*S*H" episode does not depend on what you do), and since its purpose is to hold your attention to the next commercial, all you need to know is whether it is interesting or that you like it.

I observed a secondary English class studying poetry. The teacher was trying to get her students to analyze a poem. One student said it was "interesting." Another said he "didn't like it." The teacher pressed on: "Why do you feel that way?" Several students who replied (grudgingly) said in so many words, "I don't know, I just do."

I may be making too much of this, but I think it is significant that these responses came out of hour upon hour of taking in the popular culture. Perhaps if the students were really insightful about what is going on with them—and cared enough—they would have said something like this: "Look Mrs. Smith, analysis is what you do and you are welcome to it. We don't need it. All we have to know is whether it is yes or no for us. Yes, we'll stay tuned. No, we won't. We're watchers. We watch movies, TV, our parents, you. We like you, we don't like you. We don't need to know any more than whether to turn it on or turn it off. That's what we do with this class. If it grabs our attention, fine. If not, we tune out. We don't need to figure out what it means any more than that. All we need to know is whether it's cool. Your poem? We don't like it. We don't like the way we feel when we read it. It's not interesting. OK?"

The question becomes, of course, if school and the popular culture, TV especially, are competing curriculums, what are we to do? In answering that question, Postman is very clear about one thing: Schools should *not* try to emulate TV. Many of us try to make our classes fast-paced, fun, entertaining—a good TV show. Though a few of us can pull it off, most of us will quickly get "cancelled." We just cannot do it as well as NBC, which has a bigger budget and a larger staff. And even if we could, we ought not to. School should be a place where students learn important things they do not learn from TV: thinking and talking in serious ways; participating and creating; deferring rewards; taking responsibility; and using other criteria of judgment than immediate stimulation (for example, usefulness). School should be the place where students connect with the past, where they confront ideas, where they experience the best that human beings have created and done. Schools should be places where young people reflect on their lives and their future and let the stars of the popular culture, whose agents get us so caught up with how they are doing, take care of themselves. School should be where students learn how to take initiative and make decent and needed things happen. School should be a place to learn how to collaborate with others. (TV, no matter how many may be watching, is one-on-one with each individual viewer.) Moreover, school should be a place where students learn to create connectedness and coherence in contrast to the disparate this-then-that world of shows and commercials. In general, school is a place whose purpose is to educate, not entertain.

Needless to say, all this is easier said than done. And perhaps we will never be able to get it done. But that does not mean we ever have to stop working for it. We can be proud of representing an aspect of this society which says openly to students: "This is a place where you can learn to think and work and make something of yourself. It will not always be fun. But if you really take this on it will be satisfying to you and you'll feel good about yourself and you will be able to live a fuller life. We're here and we'll be here and we'll keep doing our best. What will you do?"

Briefly, before making some concluding remarks, I want to recommend a book to you that speaks beautifully to the issues we are considering in this section. It is Richard Rodriguez's autobiography *Hunger of Memory*.[41] Rodriguez grew up in California the son of working class immigrant Mexican parents. He spoke mostly Spanish until he entered school. The book is the story of his education. It is a very revealing and moving book. Do read it. It may be out of print and difficult to obtain through a book store. I expect libraries have it, however.

What Can Be Said in Conclusion?

First, it should be clear that I believe it is very important that we study the effect that the social and cultural context has on academic achievement. For some students this context does place barriers before them that they must overcome if they are to do as well as their inherent ability permits. I believe the school should work to counterbalance or offset negative influences that exist in the student's circumstance. And I use the term *counterbalance* advisedly. Certainly we should meet students where they are and accommodate for their particular styles, capabilities, and preferences. However, a truly freeing, empowering education directs its efforts at helping students transcend their circumstances and not just adjust to them. To suggest just some of what students need to learn: the attitudes and skills of self-determination; confidence; to use language and to think abstractly; self-control; goal setting and planning; to adapt a future orientation; and emotional control.

I hope this book provides you with some direction in getting at these attitudes and skills. Even if it falls short, I have faith that you can come up with ideas and strategies of your own. I have talked about the power that stems from intending to make things happen. In this case it means intending to help students gain the ability to overcome environmentally-imposed limitations in their lives. If we get it in our heads that we want our students to learn, for example, to take greater initiative, we are going to find a way. Perhaps students will pick up the message of our hope for them and help us find a way.

On this last point, the students themselves need to be brought into this study and analysis, as they are the ones with the most at stake. After all, it is the quality of *their* lives we are talking about here. The students should be seeking to acquire a critical understanding of how this society and culture works, and particularly how it has worked on them. (Parenthetically, students will discover that their circumstance, no matter how difficult, contains gifts as well as limitations. Students need to see what is positive in their situations as well as what they need to rise above.) And they, not just we, should be figuring out what to do about what they find out.

Parents should be doing the same. Perhaps we can do more with parent education programs which are designed to help parents support and encourage their children to do well in school. What do I think some parents need to learn? First they need to learn to communicate what might be called a traditional work ethic. They need to get across to their children that they expect them to do their best in school. They need to learn to appreciate and praise their children's work and encourage them to stay with it. They need to set up a good study space for the child at home. And they need to turn that TV set off. What would you add to or subtract from this list?

Ironically, I do not see much in the school curriculum on the study of the social-cultural circumstance. And there is certainly little on the interaction between students and this circumstance. Social studies classes that draw on the disciplines of sociology and psychology come the closest at present, and these are usually elective courses that I suspect are not taken by many of the students who most need them. Do you know of such curricula? Could there be such programs? I remember from my own secondary school days that the curriculum seemed to be about everybody but me. Abe Lincoln's life sure got a lot more attention than mine. I am struck by social researcher Christopher Jenck's finding that traditional reforms have not done much with the link between social class and school achievement. Achievement as he sees it has to do more with student characteristics than school characteristics.[42] If we could get this kind of information to them, I wonder what low-status students would make of it and what they would do about it.

ADOLESCENT DEVELOPMENT

This section considers the developmental circumstance of adolescents and how it might affect their ability to achieve academically. To get at that, I define what I mean by *development*, outline some significant developmental issues teenagers confront, and point to some things schools and teachers can do to be responsive to the developmental needs and issues of adolescence. There are two generalizations that hold all this together: Yes, an unresolved developmental issue can impede academic achievement. And yes, schools should take developmental as well as learning needs into account as they create the school context and decide on curriculum.

I would like to begin with some definitions: What is meant—or at least what do I mean—by *development*? I mean the overall changes in functioning capability and tendency that occur over the full span of life. A synonym I find useful is *growth*. We grow in an number of ways over the course of our lives. Obviously we grow physically. We grow in size; our body chemistry becomes different; brain changes allow us to think in new ways. Furthermore, we grow socially and psychologically, in our sense of who we are and the way we relate to others. I am distinguishing growth and development from learning, though certainly what we learn has an effect on how we develop. But while they overlap, I find it useful to contrast learning, the new ideas and attitudes and skills one picks up, with development, the fundamental changes in who and what we are as an organism.

It helps to take a look at how development occurs in order to get clear on the dynamic involved. Most developmental theorists share a common perspective concerning the process of development. They begin with something very similar to the organism-in-the-world concept described earlier. The manner and rate of development of the individual is a function of the nature of the exchange between an individual and his environment. Three things count: what the human being is like, what the environment (both physical and social) is like, and the way this human being and his environment interact. The developmentalist looks at this exchange at each moment, taking a "snapshot" of it; and over time, as if it were a movie.

From the perspective of development over time, say over 5 or 10 years, or even the whole of life, developmentalists perceive that human beings proceed invariantly through discernable stages. This is true whether the growth referred to is physical, intellectual, moral, or something I center on in a bit, psychosocial. First, there is stage 1, then state 2, then 3, and so forth. So while life is a continuous series of interactions between the human being and his environment with the result being growth or retardation of development, developmentalists tend to carve up the outcome of this interplay into discrete pieces. Also, they tend to link particular stages to a particular chronological age. For example, stage 3, is reached at age 6 or 10 or 22 depending on the type of development being described. Along with the association with a particular chronological age, each stage is associated with a particular facet of development or issue. For example, one stage of physical development may have to do with the onset of puberty. Or, a different area, one stage may have to do primarily with the development of a personal identity while another centers on relationship issues. Stages build upon the ones that have been attained previously, and each is usually defined as being "higher," more evolved, more mature, than the "lower" stages that preceded it. Although the ideal is a life of ever-increasing maturity and capacity, the real story does not always match the ideal. All individuals do not move onward and upward, but instead remain stagnant or grow in negative ways. Why? It can be due to something in the individual or his world, or in the interaction between the two.

Developmentalists argue that we need to look at the nature of the school to see how promotive it is of positive development among students. In this regard, many developmentalists conclude that however effective the school is in bringing about learning, the news is not good developmentally. An example: Those concerned with cognitive development are often critical of the way schools operate. Essentially, cognitive growth means the stages of growth in thinking capability that culminate in an individual's ability to think abstractly. The highest stage involves being able to play with ideas, deal with principles, and make guesses (hypotheses) about how things work. You may know of the work of Swiss psychologist Jean Piaget. His theories are an illustration of a cognitive developmentalist perspective.[43] Theorists in this camp feel that positive cognitive development is a result of an individual's encounter with a diverse environment in which he has to deal with challenge, solve problems, fix things, figure out how things work, and make judgments. Things should not come too easy; it is good that the individual has to "stretch" to make sense of things. It is best when he or she has to deal with cognitive dissonance, confront situations that do not make sense or the ideas of other people who do not see things as he does, and face things that do not square with his preconceptions. The image is one of taking on intellectual obstacles at the limit of one's capability to handle them—more than that and the individual may be overwhelmed and back down. In this view, school should be characterized by an intense encounter of a student with a complex and challenging intellectual and human environment. The result of this encounter is the development of the capability to process the data from one's world in a sophisticated manner. This ability to think elegantly is requisite to the true study of any subject or discipline, and crucial to dealing with the demands of modern life. That is the ideal, but the developmentalists hold that school is typically not like that. Instead of engagement with a complex setting made up of people and ideas and issues to resolve and projects to take on, there is a relatively simple sequenced-for-you arrangement in which students respond to a series of straightforward assigned tasks with, if the teacher has his or her way, success almost guaranteed. Students may learn something in classrooms such as this, but they do not grow cognitively.

A group of educators who are giving particular attention to the developmental needs of children are those concerned with early adolescence, ages 10 to 14 or so. This group advocates the establishment of middle schools comprising, roughly, grades 5 through 8. This middle school movement advocates that these schools be grounded first of all in the developmental reality and the needs of children this age. Those of us who center our work with children other than in these middle years have much to learn from the middle school people. A good book representative of a growing body of literature in this area is *Successful Schools for Young Adolescents* by Joan Lipsitz.[44] Lipsitz provided case studies of four middle schools that she considers to be exemplary. One criterion that she used in judging middle schools is the degree to which their organization, social climate, curriculum, and instructional processes are responsive to the developmental needs of young adolescents. Lipsitz listed seven in her book:

- Competence and achievement.
- Self-exploration and definition.
- Social interaction with peers and adults.
- Physical activity.
- Meaningful participation in school and community.
- Routine, limits, and structure.
- Diversity.[45]

A measure of a good school, then, is that it is—the term the middle school people use—developmentally responsive.

Developmental Concerns

I hope the discussion so far has created a context for the heart of this section. I want to list some key developmental concerns of adolescence, and their implications for achievement and how we operate schools. In doing this, I am especially reliant on the writings of psychologist David Elkind, particularly his book *All Grown Up and No Place to Go*.[46] Elkind centered on three areas of change in adolescents: physical, mental, and psychosocial.

With physical development, Elkind centered on the changes that come with puberty. For girls, there are pronounced height and weight spurts—and the issues that come with them, too tall, too short, too fat, too skinny—breast development, body hair, the onset of menstruation, and new sexual urges. For boys, there are parallel developments and the accompanying worries over how tall they will become, when they will shave, the size of their penis, spontaneous erections, "wet dreams," masturbation, acne, and so forth. Indeed, these are complicated issues to deal with, and it should not surprise us if some of the issues related to physical development impinge on academic achievement. In his book, *A Place Called School*, John Goodlad, a prominent educator, has wondered publicly how we get any work done in schools at all given these and other upheavals of adolescence.[47]

Adolescence can be characterized as a time of worry. Actually, this tendency to worry is made possible by the mental changes students are going through: namely, the newly-acquired capability to think abstractly. Teenagers are moving cognitively into the stage that Piaget calls formal operations. In this stage their thinking is not so bound by the particular and the concrete. They can now think in terms of ideas and the ideal. Young people of this age can look at their world and think in principled ways about what is and what is not possible. In short, they are learning to think; *really* think. And they begin to make use of this new capacity. They start assessing themselves, parents, friends, everything. Even though they might not think well or deeply enough, they do develop opinions. Many issues become salient that were not previously, and all sorts of worries come flooding in on them.

A third area of change during these years, besides the mental and physical, is psychosocial. This is an area I especially want to emphasize. The term itself, psychosocial, points to the dual focus inherent in this aspect of human development. There is both the psychological (inner, personal) and the social (family, friends, school, etc.) and the interplay of the two. I associate the term *psychosocial* with the theories of psychoanalyst Erik Erikson.[48] Erikson identified eight psychosocial stages that extend over the entirety of a human life. Particularly in the early stages, from birth to age 7 or so, Erikson reflects a Freudian perspective. Each stage throughout one's life is characterized by a fundamental issue that is resolved by the individual either favorably or unfavorably. For example, during Erikson's fourth stage, spanning approximately the ages 8 to 11, the issue is personal industry versus inferiority. Basically, what this means is that during this stage of life one either develops the posture of being someone who is masterful, a doer, one who accomplishes what he sets out to do; or of one who is essentially inept, reactive, inefficacious. What is so crucial about all of this is that how this basic mastery-ineffectiveness issue is resolved at, say, age 10—the age when this is a focal concern—can affect one's involvement in the world at 30 or 40 or 50. If you come down on the side of inferiority at 10, it may well carry over to the rest of your life. It is not clear from my study of the developmental theorists whether the unsuccessful resolution of a stage issue during the time of life when it is *the* issue can be undone later on. I am not completely sure the degree to which the positive resolution of developmental issues is contingent on the positive resolution of earlier stages. It may just be that successfully resolving a psychosocial developmental issue depends on having successfully resolved those central at earlier stages. That is, if you, for example, do not trust the world or feel autonomous at 10 (two early issues psychosocially), are you doomed not only to be untrusting and dependent for the rest of your life but also to not getting anything right developmentally for the rest of your days? However it goes, it seems certain that an individual has some hard work ahead if development has not been successfully achieved during the appropriate time.

To illustrate my point, consider a little, admittedly informal and highly unscientific, "research study" I have conducted over the years. I have asked people I consider masterful adults to tell me about their lives during the ages 8 to

11 (during the Erikson stage in which masterfulness is the predominant issue). In every case during these years, I cannot think of an exception, the masterful adults were active, doing, accomplishing and creating things. They were building tree houses, rowing boats, reading (I see that as active), writing little stories—generally taking on the world. In contrast, "unmasterfuls" were letting the world take them on, watching TV, doing what they were told—generally being inactive or reactive. I am familiar with all the possible explanations for my findings, including that there is not the causal link I am implying at all, and that all my data tell me is that active, masterful people at 40 were also that way at 9. But there is enough here, especially when taken with the analyses I have made of developmental theory, that gives me pause. The theory, my experience, and my basic judgment, tell me that if we want to produce people who feel masterful and effective, allowing them to sit in front of the box at home and do the odd numbered problems on page 60 may not be the way to get at it. More specifically, I worry that the lives of socially disadvantaged kids come down too much to responses, doing what they are told at home and school—and not enough to taking initiative, making things happen, collaborating to get things done, and negotiating with the world.

Drawing on Erikson's work, Elkind affirmed that the formation of individual identity is the central developmental issue of adolescence:

> It is generally agreed today, following the original work of the psychoanalyst Erik Erikson, that the primary task of the teenage years is to construct a sense of personal identity. In Erikson's view, the teenager's task is to bring together all of the various and sometimes conflicting facets of self into a working whole that at once provides continuity with the past, and focus and direction for the future. This sense of personal identity includes various roles (son or daughter, student, athlete, musician, artist, and so on), various traits and abilities (quiet, outgoing, timid, generous, high-strung), as well as the teenager's personal tableau of likes and dislikes, political and social attitudes, religious orientation, and much more.[49]

So if we are to believe this—and I do—an important item on the personal agenda of an adolescent is to come to grips with who he or she is and what matters and how to be. It is not suprising that school problems can result for a student who fails to resolve these vital identity issues successfully. And does it not make sense that a student would find any setting, much less school, beside the point that he experiences as paying little or no mind to the life issues pressing down on him?

According to Elkind, and me, that is exactly the fix many young people find themselves in at school. (I am not saying they are aware of this in an explicit, articulate way, though some are. More than likely, it is probably a tacit, experienced sense that things are off somehow, wrong.) What students need are opportunities for discovering and defining who they are. They need social interaction, discussions of values and beliefs, and opportunities to try out various modes of behavior. Students need to be encouraged to figure out what is worth believing, what is significant, what is good and bad, and what is evolved and base.

They need to explore principles, ideals, and models for conducting one's life, and then have a chance to try them on, test them out, see how they fit. They need to talk about themselves and their future. And more specifically they need to work through issues of sexual and work identity, exclusion and belonging, loyalty and betrayal. The positive result of all of this is the construction of an integrated self in contrast to what Elkind called a "patchwork self," an identity in which this belief is tacked together with that habit and this involvement and that personality trait, and nothing quite fits.

Speaking of patchwork, the secondary school curriculum is a patchwork quilt—without the pieces being sewn together. A recent book has used a different metaphor, referring to the "shopping mall" nature of high school. The picture is painted of a large number of "specialty shops" (the number and variety of courses has proliferated over the past decade) that have little to do with one another. The "shopper" (student) picks and chooses largely on the basis of whim or impulse, or is perhaps told (counselors) where to "shop." And with developmental needs as the criterion, none of the stores really have anything the student-shopper needs.

Adolescents need to integrate the often contradictory, at least on the face of it, callings from two sources: outside (parents, peers, the school, media, etc.) and inside (needs, urges, preferences, etc.). Moreover, the student is faced with the challenge of *approving* of the way he is managing these external and internal forces, and actually *liking* the person he is becoming; all the while being *esteemed by others* as well. Elkind explained:

> The major task of psychological stress management is to find ways to balance and coordinate the demands that come from within with those that come from without. This is where a healthy sense of self and identity comes in. An integrated sense of identity, as we have seen, means bringing together into a working whole a set of attitudes, values and habits that can serve both self and society. The attainment of such a sense of identity is accompanied by a feeling of self-esteem, of liking and respecting oneself and being liked and respected by others.[50]

Whatever else the school does right, and it does a lot of things right, it cannot lay claim to being an optimal setting for getting this developmental work done.

If you follow students through their day as I get to do, and keep the developmental agenda in mind, you will be struck by how little it is served. Very infrequently do students debate values, ideals, and principles. Ironically, the subjects that deal most directly with how we ought to conduct our lives—philosophy and ethics—are absent from the school curriculum as separate subjects, and are rarely integrated into the political-and-military-events-centered required history courses. Likewise, our phobia over church-state separation leads us to stay clear of fundamental questions of meaning and purpose that the religions address. Instead of experiencing diverse models of how to live one's life, there is ability grouping and tracking into programs. In my view, apart from any advantages they may have, these practices of grouping and tracking limit the range of a student's contacts and prematurely limit his definition of where he or she fits in the world. Rather than trying on ideas and ways of being to see how they fit, school is much more about getting through, taking this and passing that, being "responsible" (defined as following the rules), and knowing your place (you are in the seventh grade, not the eighth).

And if that is not a good prospect, society is not any better. In fact, Neil Postman went so far as to say that the very life stage itself—childhood—in which to resolve the developmental concerns is disappearing.[51] Children are all prematurely becoming miniature adults. Postman's primary concern, as indicated earlier, is with the mass media. He argued that children on television are little adults, spouting glib cracks written by 35-year-old speech writers as they "educate" their elders more than they learn from them. Though, I note that this may be getting somewhat better with "The Cosby Show," a recent hit, and some movies about teenagers that are not simply exploitive teasers. But the generalization still holds: there is just not much of anyplace for kids to discover who they are. Elkind described teenagers as being "unplaced":

> Perhaps the best word to describe the predicament of today's teenagers is "unplaced". Teenagers are not displaced in the sense of having been put in a position they did not choose to be in (a state sometimes called anomie). Nor are they misplaced in the sense of having been put in the wrong place (a state sometimes called alienation). Rather, they are unplaced in the sense that there is no place for a young person who needs a measured and controlled introduction to adulthood. In a rapidly changing society, when adults are struggling to adapt to a new social order, few adults are genuinely committed to helping teenagers attain healthy adulthood. Young people are thus denied the special recognition and protection that society previously accorded their age group. The special stage belonging to teenagers has been excised from the life cycle, and teenagers have been given a pro forma adulthood, an adulthood with all the responsibilities but few of the prerogatives. Young people today are quite literally all grown up with no place to go.[52]

Well, I would put it that they *look* all grown up. If grown up means they have put together an integrated self, no, most have not grown up at all. I am reminded of a line from *Death of A Salesman*. Willy Loman's son Biff, even at 34, says, "I just can't take hold, mom, I can't take hold of some kind of life." Developmentalists tell us that a failure to move beyond what Erikson calls "identity confusion" in adolescence will cost an individual greatly, and Biff is paying the price. A clear sense of identity is crucial to a satisfying and productive life. More immediately, movement toward an integrated identity supports qualities necessary to school success, such as the adoption of a future orientation and the ability to postpone immediate gratification. All of this is so important.

Implications of Development

What are the implications of this developmental reality for how we run our schools? I list some, and ask you to think hard about this yourself.

A first and obvious implication is that we need to add to our concern for curricular content, teaching strategies, and school organization an equal concern for students' development circumstance. I have alluded to three areas that need to be studied in greater depth: physical, mental, and psychosocial development. Elkind's writings might be a good place to start. Another book I have found useful is *Teens Speak Out* by Jane Ringler.[53] If you are in or near a university there will be professors in developmental psychology who can give you help. Again I suggest you check out the middle school literature. Middle school people, more than any group I know, are talking about creating developmentally responsive schools.

You have heard this next implication in other contexts in this book, and now I bring it up again from a cognitive developmentalist perspective and the message is the same: more debate and discussion, student-initiated inquiry, problem solving, integration, diversity, and collaboration. (This last one, collaboration, forces students to take others into consideration and negotiate things through—"role-taking" as it is called—very healthy developmentally.) There should be more of that and less teacher talk, recitation-of-facts sessions, worksheet-based lessons, sameness and routine, and fragmentation in a student's life in school.

In terms of psychosocial development, it makes sense to me to move in the direction of a streamlined, integrated core of studies instead of a "smorgasbord" of curricular offerings. I consider this in greater depth in chapter 6. It is enough to say here that we should explore moving away from simply accepting the university department-academic discipline distinctions (math, the various sciences, history, English, etc.) and instead find some way to tie these together in ways that better serve our purposes in secondary schools. This may mean more cross-discipline studies and theme- or issue-based courses. We could also devise courses and subjects of our own that draw upon traditional subjects for their content. For example, there could be a course in work that explores how people have defined and lived out who they are through forms of working. A course like this could draw on disciplines such as history (how people have worked in the past), sociology (how we have organized work), psychology (what personal needs are involved), economics (how the financial rewards are determined), and political science (how government and laws affect work).

Perhaps we can find ways to study adolescence directly. This might mean a course in developmental psychology, but more likely it involves finding places where we can integrate material on adolescence into conventional subjects. For example, besides what Teddy Roosevelt was doing in 1900, what were adolescents up to at that time? Or we could pick the literature we use in English classes partly on the basis of whether it speaks to developmental concerns. Biographies look to be especially promising in this regard. I do want to underscore that this is only one basis for determining what to use, and not the major one at that. *The* criterion, as far as I am concerned for choosing anything for students is that it represents the best humans can produce. On that point, in the *Republic of Plato*, Plato wrote (through Socrates) of the importance of exposing children to models and images of the finest ideals, life examples, and creations.[54] In this time of pop mass entertainment, the school can do better than pulp novels. Can we find diverse examples of what we consider to be most humanly superior ways to resolve the issues of identity and relatedness for students to ponder? Let them consider the best we can find.

Also, it seems right to integrate the study of fundamental questions related to life meaning and purpose into the school curriculum. That means more philosophy and more focus on moral issues and theological studies. How have great minds resolved the fundamental issues of the meaning of the individual's life and the relationship of the individual to the larger whole? Of course the challenge is to find ways of translating what is often esoteric, removed material into themes and issues that adolescent students can readily confront.

If you look for them, there are curricula available that deal with adolescence as the content of study. An example are some materials published by the Quest National Center in Columbus, Ohio.[55] The Center has developed a program that deals with many of the domains of adolescent functioning, including identity formation. The program gives students a variety of opportunities to explore adolescent issues and interact with one another. The Center has created a one semester course called Skills for Adolescence, adopted by over 500 school districts. Edwin Gerber reported that the course includes the following units of study:

- Entering the teen years: The challenge ahead.
- Building self-confidence through better communication.
- Learning about emotions: Developing competence in self-assessment and self-discipline.
- Friends: Improving peer relationships.
- Strengthening family relationships.
- Developing critical thinking skills for decision making.
- Setting goals for healthy living.
- Summing up: Developing one's potential.[56]

This may be good preparation, especially in the junior high years, for what is ahead. It sounds as useful to me as world geography or a study of the explorers.

To continue, I am struck how seldom in history classes that I hear any consideration of the ideas people held. Instead, there is much concern for what people *did* (or anyway, what middle-age white males in politics and the military did). But there is very little intellectual history, I guess it can be called, and very little about the ideas people held that gave direction to their actions. And one can observe schools for a long time without hearing concern for what is right, proper, or just in human conduct. At a time when adolescents are developing cognitively to the point where they can, and do, think about what is right and preferable and ideal, there is predominant concern for what is true in fact, happened, and works; a developmental mismatch.

Perhaps we can find more chances for students to act out their ideals or test out some idea of what they are like. I worry that these opportunities are too narrowly channeled into a limited range of athletic, musical, and dramatic opportunities. Community and school service seems to provide rich possibilities in this regard.

But all of that is formal. Much of worth that happens in school is informal, not part of the standard curriculum, not an aspect of the structured, thought-out way of doing business. There are brief encounters between teacher and student during which the teacher encourages the student to keep exploring who he or she is and to discover how he or she is both different and the same as others. Informal class discussion can become an exploration of what is worth believing or doing or what is right and just. Informally teachers can present models of human beings who have successfully resolved the issue of identity. And just in their posture or manner, teachers, without departing from the curriculum, can convey that they understand what it is like to be 14 or 16, and that they support the students they work with in dealing with the questions that most press them at this age.

I hope the discussion in this section has gotten you to think a bit more deeply about the developmental circumstance in adolescence and how these issues can significantly affect the way a student approaches his schoolwork. At least you might better understand that if your students seem jumpy or distracted, it is not necessarily due to your lesson plan or whether you introduced today's lecture properly.

RELATIONAL ISSUES

By its nature, the human being is a social being, and it is safe to say that, for better or worse, relationships are a factor in our lives for all of our lives. We will have friends, love people, cooperate and do battle, order others about and get ordered about, and are included and excluded by others. We are so inherently social that even when we are isolated or go it alone it is viewed in terms of relatedness. That is, it is an instance of the *absence* of relationship. When you stick to yourself or do something on your own, people usually comment, "Oh, you aren't with others." But the reverse is usually not the case. If you are in some form of relationship, people usually do not usually remark, "Oh, you aren't alone."

While issues of relatedness are crucial to our happiness and well-being throughout our lives, as we all know they are an especially vital concern during adolescence. One factor that brings them to the forefront during these years is the new ability to think about ourselves. Teenagers can now look at themselves as an outside observer. They can conceptuallze about who they are, make assessments about what they see in themselves, and idealize about what they prefer to be. The physical changes, puberty and all, and the greater freedom of movement broaden the possibilities for relationships and all the choices and the experiences, including conflict, that come along with them. The answer to the "who am I" questions of adolescence must naturally involve a strong element of "I am *not* you." That in turn can lead to "and don't you tell me who I am." And it is not far from there to some serious relational conflicts with parents and others. Relationship issues are complex and perplexing in any case, and even more so for a young person very new to the world. My conclusion is that relationship issues will come up for virtually all young people, with some experiencing more serious problems than others. And that unresolved relationship issues can be a factor in impeding academic achievement among students.

This topic of relationships is a large one, a subject that could take up many volumes. What I choose to do here is center on three dimensions of this large concern that I see as having special importance for school achievement. The first is the resolution of conflicts with others. The second is the ability to work cooperatively, competitively, and independently. And the third is the level of justice and morality in one's dealings with others. I hope this provides you with a context from which to study these issues in more detail.

Resolving Conflicts

I do not need to tell you that adolescence can be a time of conflict with others. There are the issues with parents: "I told you to get the car back by 10 o'clock." "What do you have on?" "You are not going there with *those* people." And there are other issues with teachers: It has been striking to me in my dealings with unsuccessful students how often they have an unresolved conflict with a teacher. So often a student's difficulty in class is not so much a matter of being unable to do the work as it is not liking Mr. Jones. Moreover, students often fail to separate relationships from the subject, so not liking Mr. Jones comes to mean not liking the subject. In other words, they do not like history because they do not like Jones. Though not the wisest attitude, it is understandable at a time when relationships are so central to students' concerns.

It is one thing to have a problem and another thing to let the problem persist. And many of these student-teacher problems persist. That is not to say students do not try to deal with them, because they do. However, the *way* they deal with them does not get anything positive accomplished. (I am focusing on student problems with teachers; though I know conflicts with other students can detract from academic achievement as well.) Students may sulk, tune out, or strike out. And though it is understandable that they do, these tactics are not usually effective. By *effective* I mean resulting in the students' academic achievement and personal happiness. And I say understandable because what else can we expect of young people? Who has taught them good ways of resolving conflict? In addition, note that the strategies students employ, if they deserve to be called that, are often not consciously chosen at all. Rather they tend to be unconsidered or habitual ways of responding to conflict.

So yes, we should be looking for ways to help students learn to deal with conflicts that preoccupy them and retard their learning. We do try to help teachers in this regard. It is called training in classroom management. But students rarely receive such training. My style is to deal with issues directly as often as possible. I operate on the assumption that in many cases the way out is through, if you know what I mean. What that means is if a student has a conflict, he or she should learn to resolve it—simple as that. That contrasts with the teacher bearing sole responsibility, or resolving it for the student somehow. Certainly if the teacher experiences a conflict, he or she should attempt to resolve it. And students should do the same. The student is better off learning to resolve conflicts now than doing what many of them do: endure them, wait for them to go away, or assume the teacher or someone else will fix things. For the student to take the issue on and deal with it will be a good experience in taking action rather than reacting. And it just may lead to an improved situation. In any case, the student might as well learn to resolve disputes now because they will persist all through life, and adolescence is as good a time to learn how to manage them as any.

What all that means to me is that we should be teaching conflict resolution strategies to students. Though I want to make it clear that I am not contending that this is *all* we need to do. Surely school professionals must modify their own behavior and alter the school context in the face of disputes. But back to students, if you are going to teach conflict resolution to students, how do you go about it? I will outline below the direction I would take if I were given the task to put together a piece of curriculum in this area. By curriculum I mean material that could be integrated into ongoing classes devoted to other purposes: science, health, social studies, or psychology classes to cite a few examples. Or perhaps it could be offered as a special course or as a workshop for students. And maybe these materials are the ones taught to students who are on in-school suspension, or in any case experiencing a significant conflict at the moment.

The Johnsons' Materials

David and Frank Johnson's writings are a good source of theoretical and practical guidance in the area of school-centered relationship issues. The Johnsons tend to be oriented toward an analysis of group functioning and how conflicts within the group can be resolved such that the group can operate effectively. My focus, in contrast, tends to be more on individuals and how they can resolve their conflicts with specific other people. Thus the contrast between a group (Johnsons') and individual (mine) orientation. Nevertheless I find the Johnsons' material offers much to inform the individual-in-conflict-with-parents/teachers/peers perspective I am taking on here.

The material in the Johnsons' published writings that comes closest to dealing with the issues we are focusing upon is chapter 7, "Conflicts of Interest," in their book *Joining Together*.[57] In this chapter they provide some very promising activities we might use with students. For example, there are self-analysis activities. One asks the students to identify their own conflict resolution approach. Students categorize themselves as turtles (withdrawing), sharks (forcing), foxes (compromising), or owls (confronting).[58] This may sound a little cute, and generally I do have problems with what I consider to be cute classroom activities. Also I am not sure the animal metaphors work very well. In any case, the categories themselves make sense, the animal names can be dropped if desired, and basically you can get the idea of how this kind of technique might work.

The Johnsons define a series of steps in resolving a conflict. They elaborate on each at length and I refer you to their book. But in outline form they are as follows:

1. *Confronting the opposition.* Included in this section is an admonition not to ''hit and run.'' Instead confront only when there is time to jointly define the issue and schedule a session to work it through. Communicate in nonthreatening ways your feelings and perceptions. And comprehend your opponent's views and feelings.

2. *Jointly defining the conflict.* Here the idea is to define the conflict as a mutual problem and not as a win-lose struggle.

3. *Communicating positions and feelings.*

4. *Communicating cooperative intentions.*

5. *Taking the opponent's perspective.* Showing your opponent you understand his feelings and position.

6. *Coordinating motivation to negotiate in good faith.* Increasing your opponent's commitment to work it out by decreasing his costs of doing so and/or upping the payoffs he sees he will obtain.

7. *Reaching an agreement.* The ways each person will act differently in the future, and what will he done if there are slip-ups.[59]

The Johnsons are remarkably thorough in their consideration of these issues. They frequently provide exercises you can use directly or adapt for use with students. One caution about working with their writings, however: I have found their prose difficult to wade through, sort of like one long academic piece for a social psychology journal. But it has been worth the effort for me.

Negotiating a Solution

''Getting nasty. Getting taken. You don't have to choose. There is a better way.'' I quote from a book I have found wonderfully useful in my own life, *Getting to Yes: Negotiating Agreement Without Giving In* by Roger Fisher and William Ury.[60] Fisher teaches negotiation at the Harvard Law School and Ury is Associate Director of the Harvard Negotiation Project. This is all very speculative, but it seems to me their ideas could be the basis for a conflict resolution curriculum for students of adolescent age.

Fisher and Ury provided some very helpful advice that applies to any disagreement or dispute—with a spouse, neighbor, boss, employee, or customer. And as well, related to our interest here, disputes with a parent or teacher, teenage friend, or a group of friends. Among their advice are suggestions on how to focus on interests and not positions when dealing with a conflict. To argue over positions—"it has to be this way"—is inefficient and produces unwise agreements. And very important to our concerns, it endangers the relationship between the two participants. It is not good enough to win this battle if the war will only rage more forcibly later on.

Instead of arguing over positions, Fisher and Ury advocated that the focus be on the interests, both shared and conflicting, that lie behind the positions taken by each side. They included a discussion of the "people" issues that inevitably arise in any dispute (negative perceptions each has of the other, emotions, communication problems). In addition, they defined a most insightful process for inventing and deciding options for mutual gain. I have used this process in my own work and I can endorse its effectiveness. Furthermore, they provided some solid strategies for taking on people who are more powerful, who play dirty tricks, or just will not deal with you. All of this looks immensely useful to students, and particularly to students experiencing conflicts. These insights Fisher and Ury provided sound excellent for a student who just had a blow-out with a teacher. In my view, it is certainly more ethical to do it this way than to use some accommodating tactic that defines responsibility as following the rules or drawing up a contract in which the student assures he or she will never do whatever-it-was again.

Learning to Monitor Our Thoughts. Though Fisher and Ury's work has really caught my eye, there is much good literature in this area to draw upon. For example, Beatrice Schultz and Judith Anderson emphasize learning to turn our attention to the way one thinks during a conflict as key to the acquisition of conflict resolution capability.[61] These writers encourage the development of the ability to monitor and change the way one thinks during a disagreement, especially the replacement of negative perceptions with more positive ones. They also stress the need for the individual to be clear about how his tactics are going to accomplish his goals. Some of what we do, if we would think about it, is just not likely to get us anything we want. In fact, I recently said to a student, "You know, the kinds of things you are doing in that class where you are having trouble with the teacher look to me as if they are going to make him miserable and ready to get back at you if he can, get you a bad grade, result in you learning nothing much, make you look like a trouble-maker to the school, and keep you at least as unhappy as you are now. I'm not saying this is what you are trying to get done, just that's what it looks like to me will come out of what you are doing. What are you doing to get what you want in there?" What I got back, and this is typical, revealed to me that this student was not taking action in any considered way to accomplish goals he clearly understood. More, he was just doing something, acting out of habit or impulse. My point to him was if he wanted the teacher to be nice to him and get a good grade—which is, it turns out, what he wanted—I could not see how skipping the class about twice a week, not responding during discussions, talking when the teacher was talking, and blurting out "bug off" (or some such phrase) when the teacher called on him was the way to get what he wanted. If, on the other hand, the student had really wanted to get back at the teacher, torture and abuse him, he was not doing that as well as he could. Right now the student was more of an annoyance than anything. The lesson is, figure out what you want and go after that.

Another idea: In chapter 3 I mentioned Joel Kirsch's work with "energy training" exercises derived from the marshal art of aikido. In chapter 7 I include portions of an article by Terry Dobson to illustrate a way to deal with student discipline problems. Dobson also draws from his experiences as a student and teacher of aikido. Aikido is, at its core, a way to deal with conflict. It represents a way to blend with the world, in contrast to fighting with it or being its victim, all the while maintaining your integrity and serving your interests. I have recently been speculating on what effect a systematic training program in aikido would have on students who are in conflict with schools and others. A good research study would be to test this idea. Will aikido training result in students being happier and more productive academically, and less of a headache for the school? I think it just might.

Besides this kind of physical training, perhaps there are places in the curriculum where conflict resolution could be studied. For example, Murray Nelson teaches how different cultures resolve conflict as part of a legal education course which is included in the social studies curriculum of a senior high school.[62] Students gain insight and a cross-cultural perspective on the various approaches to resolving conflict, along with the strengths and shortcomings of each.

You can check around to see what published curriculum materials are available in this area of conflict resolution. One source is the book *Creative Conflict Resolution* by William Kreider.[63] If you have trouble finding anything that deals specifically with conflict, perhaps there are elements of programs dealing with general communication that you can adapt to suit your purposes.

Last of course, instruction in resolving conflicts can be done informally as episodes arise. As teachers we can prepare ourselves with a perspective and some insights and advice in anticipation of the need to respond to students or events. Terry Dobson, mentioned earlier, has written a couple of books that should prove valuable. One is *Giving in to Get Your Way* and the other is *Safe and Alive*.[64] You may wish to read them.

Cooperation, Competition, and Individual Initiative

In order to achieve academically students have to be effective in—all three—cooperating, competing, and going it alone as an individual. Some students run into trouble in school because they do not know how to collaborate and get help from others. Some shy away from the competition that is involved in getting good grades and academic recognition. And still others cannot find it within themselves to take the initiative and get work done on their own when the support from others is not there. Students are limited to the degree that they can not operate effectively in all three of these modes, and all three are necessary in schools. I offer a few remarks concerning these three processes.

For some years there has been an movement to teach students the processes of cooperation. The Johnson brothers (mentioned earlier) are particularly prominent spokesmen for this orientation.[65] They and others have developed strategies for getting students to work together rather than competitively or individually to get class assignments completed. For example, the following are some instructions of the sort the Johnsons give to teachers:

The Teacher's Role in Cooperation

1. *Select the group size.* This will vary according to the resources you need in the group, the skills of the students in working in groups, and the needs of the task. Experiment and find out what size works in your situation.
2. *Assign students to groups.* Heterogeneous groups have the potential for the most power. Differences among group members make the group function.
3. *Arrange the classroom.* Chairs and desks should be arranged in small cluster arrangements.
4. *Provide the appropriate materials.* Students can all have the same materials or each group member can have different materials which relate to the task.
5. *Set the task and goal structure.* Make your expectations clear for the finished product and the behaviors you expect students to exhibit.
6. *Monitor the student-student interaction.* Be sure you always monitor. Eavesdrop and then ask questions of the group. Make it clear they are all accountable for their group. On a rotating basis, have one student in each group observe the group and give data on how it worked (use observation forms).
7. *Intervene to solve problems and teach skills.* There will be problems. Stop the students and teach them the skills you see them needing. Turn problems back to the group to solve; act as a consultant.
8. *Evaluate outcomes.* Each student gets the grade his group received. Remember you are evaluating how well they learned the material or accomplished the task and how well they helped each other.[66]

I applaud this work. Students can profit academically, as well as in other ways, from learning the skills of cooperation. I refer you to the chapter notes for how to make contact with the Johnson material. But while I welcome the efforts to make students more cooperative—schools can be a selfish individual hustle—I also have some reservations about the cooperative education movement. A major problem for me, I find that although its advocates pay lip service to employing cooperative learning processes only when *appropriate*, acknowledging room for competition and individual work, what they really wind up doing is leaving the impression, and operating themselves, as if cooperation is inherently *better* than the other two and should be employed in every possible instance. The cooperative education adherents would probably deny what I just said, but I have read their material quite carefully and talked with many teachers, and I say it comes down in the last analysis to a view that puts cooperation at the top of a hierarchy of ways of getting things done.

What I worry about in all this is that competition and individualism are getting set up as straw men to be punched around. Competition is equated with a cut-throat, dog-eat-dog, aggressive, I win-you lose struggle. And individualism implies the worst possible self-serving, "me-first" mentality. Indeed, there is a kind of competition that is limiting, dehumanizing, and destructive. And yes, there is a brand of individualism that leads to abuse of ourselves and others. However, there is competition and individualism that is uplifting and liberating. Just look at the wonderful things that business people, artists, and athletes have produced within a competitive situation, and on their own as individuals. The point is that competition and individualism are not, each of them, a single phenomenon. There are a variety of forms of each, good and bad. (Well, that is true of cooperation as well. There is cooperation that is truly positive and mutually enhancing. And some of the most negative and senseless activities in the history of humankind—need I give you some World War II examples?—have been done with remarkable cooperation.)

Certainly in my own life I have had to learn to be competitive at times, and cooperative and "go it alone-ish" at others, in order to accomplish what needed to be done. My hope for students is that they learn all three modes of relating to others and themselves. My reading of the nature of the American political system and the current economic and social situation is that one needs to be capable in all three. Especially for the kids who are disadvantaged in their lives or who do not do well in school: they had *better* learn all three or they are in trouble. At times, they are going to have to cooperate with other students and their teachers to be successful academically. Furthermore, they are going to have to learn not to back down in the face of competition. Because the reality is, schools are exceedingly competitive, rank order people, and give out a limited number of rewards. In addition, to be good at school there are times when it is just you as an individual. It is either your job alone and it is not appropriate for others to help; or there is not anybody helping, perhaps not even the teacher, and you are left to count on yourself.

So this is a plea that we should not define away the value of competition and individualism in schools by labeling them with the worst possible meanings. Nor should we misread the American, and human, experience to the point that we obscure the value of competition, individual initiative, and achievement in our lives generally. Let us seek to empower students to engage in the best, most evolved, most human, forms of all three modes. In fact, instead of setting these modes off against each other, let us aim to help students *integrate* all three into their value system and in their actions. That is what the best of us do: transcend the apparent dichotomies and contradictions between cooperation, competition, and individualism, and achieve a synthesis of all three processes. In such a person all three things exist concurrently and harmoniously. Is he or she cooperative? Yes. Competitive? Yes. Individualistic? Yes. For that person it is not a matter of either–or: it is an integration of all three. The challenge, therefore, is to help students find decent and productive ways to employ individual, cooperative, and competitive action in their lives.

A Place for Decency and Morality

The word *decent* in that last sentence leads me into the last point I want to make about relationships: as trite as this may sound, the importance of being decent and just to other people. It is never enough to just come out on top in a conflict, cooperate effectively, compete well, or be good at getting things done on your own. There is doing it in a morally justifiable way for a morally justifiable reason. There is being ethical in one's conduct with others. There is being kind and respectful. You can sit in classes for many hours—days—and not hear consideration of the moral issue, the moral dimension of human beings. There is much talk in schools about the facts of a matter. And in the area of conduct, with the recent popularity of the so-called reality based approaches to maintaining order, there is a concern for rules and one's responsibility for following the rules, with no excuses. But that is not necessarily the same thing as doing what is right. The rules, your obligation, the "way things are done here," even "what we've democratically established"—none of that necessarily gets at what is right to do. Tennessee Williams, the playwright, has said that the one unacceptable thing is intentional cruelty. Every institution, including the school, has the obligation of challenging the student with the human responsibility of being decent and just and fair to other human beings. (Including, by the way, to teachers. A lot of student behaviors toward teachers I see as unjust and cruel, despite the reasons offered to justify them.) A number of approaches have been offered to promote decency and morality in school.[67] Though, there is more than curricular content and instructional strategy involved in this concern. There is the need for an ethos or culture of a school which says we are first of all human beings and, no matter what else we are attending to, what we do should first of all be worthy of a human being. That is the fundamental criterion for judging actions in a relationship or anywhere else, that it is worthy of a human being. Whether it is a decent place and contributes to the development of decent people is a fundamental criterion for judging the worth of a school.[68]

PERSONAL/PSYCHOLOGICAL ISSUES

I know this is obvious but students are people. And as people, just like us and the rest of the human race, they do not live trouble-free lives. They, as we, confront personal and psychological problems; and they, as we, at times let them affect their work. Again, I realize I am not telling you anything you do not know. But nevertheless I think it needs to be reiterated, because we sometimes forget that students are not the embodiments of a role—student—and thus a totally predictable element of the teaching-learning process. Of course we know that as people, students have other things going on in their lives besides our class and that they bring a particular mental set and level of mental well-being to the classroom. And we know that this matters; it has an impact on what is accomplished by them and by us. We also realize that we need to recognize that if we are to teach well. But we do have to remind ourselves every once in a while that this is so.

What problems am I talking about when I refer to personal problems? I mean such things as a divorce or abuse (physical, sexual, psychological) in the family. It could be a love relationship going bad, or getting fired from an after-school job, or being threatened by something or somebody (have you ever tried to pay attention in school when you knew you were going to get beaten up at 3:00?). It could mean getting in trouble with the law. Those are the kinds of issues that most of us had to deal with in adolescence, though likely not to the serious extent that some students face. By psychological problems I mean depression, obsessions, neurotic behavior—issues of mental health. I know the line is blurry between personal and psychological problems, but nevertheless I find it useful to distinguish between a psychologically healthy person confronting an unwanted pregnancy and a deeply troubled young person experiencing serious mental health problems.

I share some thoughts I have with you on what this means to our work as teachers. In doing so I hope to give you some things to think about and study.

To begin with, we need to bring a good amount of humility into this business of teaching. Yes, we need high hopes and strong ideals, but we also need humility. The fact is, no matter how good we are at what we do, no matter how appropriate the content or effective the instruction, no matter how good the school, some students simply are not at a place in their lives to learn what we have to teach. It is important to remind ourselves that teaching is an indirect action. By indirect I mean, to use an art metaphor, that as teachers we do not paint the picture ourselves; we get the student to paint it. Since ultimately the student must do the "painting," the schoolwork, we do not have total control over getting it done. All we can do, staying with this metaphor, is provide the canvas, the materials, a good subject to paint, and much encouragement. But if the students are not in a position to paint due to distracting problems in their lives that may detract from their ability or desire to paint, the picture just will not get done.

And yet so often when the painting does not get completed or it is poorly done, we blame ourselves. We are wonderful in the extent to which we take responsibility for the level of student achievement. But at the same time, speaking of mental health, one of the ways to inflict psychological strain on ourselves is to blame ourselves for things we cannot directly control. Teachers can be responsible *to* a learning situation, but we must share the responsibility *for* learning with others: parents, administrators, and especially students. So the point is, the reality of the effect of personal problems on student achievement should be a sobering reminder to teachers who sometimes think they are, or have been led to believe they are, the sole powerful element in the classroom. We can be credible and self-respecting as professionals without that level of, I think this is the right word, hubris.

I say all this because there is an "accountability" movement afoot that wants to make the teacher responsible for the level of student learning. I understand the laudable impulses behind this thrust, but at the same time there are just too many other powerful elements in the circumstance for that to be fair to teachers. It also takes all these other factors off the hook—among them, parents, school boards, administrators, counselors, and students. They are responsible along with teachers, or should be. If we take the teacher accountability route we could wind up focusing all our attention on teacher competence; which is a good thing in itself, but at the same time it fails to give the necessary concern to other vital elements in the educational endeavor. Secondly, simply because experience or research data shows us that something affects academic achievement, it does not mean that we have to or should do something about it. It is very open to debate whether schools can or ought to help students overcome the personal or psychological problems they experience. There are at least two defensible points of view on this question. One states that schools and teachers should stick to doing what they were set up to do and do well: teach the academics. This position holds that the school should not and cannot be a personal counselor, parent, or psychotherapist. For one thing, we have not been given that charge by the society. For another reason, we do not know what we are doing in the personal areas, and we do not have the resources to take those problems on. And to the degree that we get into dealing with personal issues of students it detracts from giving the gift we really have to share, and that is intellectual development and learning. Furthermore, if schools take on the job of straightening out students' lives, not only does it send the message that we can correct them (which is very open to question), but it also indicates that since we will do it, the other elements in the culture and society do not have to. What should be happening, according to this view, is that schools should communicate that it is the job of these other elements—parents, churches, social service agencies, political and economic institutions—to get the kids in shape to learn and that we, the schools, are going to take it from there and teach them. Too much has been laid on the schools already, such as teaching people to drive cars and cook, and we should not tack on still more items to the school agenda just because other institutions and the young people themselves are not doing their job. The more we get into this area, so this argument goes, the more we are in fact part of the problem, because it obscures the need for others to assume the responsibility that is rightfully theirs.

The response to this argument goes something like this: It is nice to talk about limiting the schools' responsibility to teaching the academics. But what if as a matter of fact these other elements of society do not help as you think they should? And what makes you think they can or will do so? Have you looked at the circumstances in some homes? Have you analyzed the churches, the social services system, and the nature of our communities? If the schools do not pay heed to the lives of the children and not just their intellects, who will? The answer is nobody. For many kids the school is the one hope they have. If the school adopts a doctrinaire policy of non-concern for the personal well-being of children, no matter how "right" in some abstract philosophical sense, what results is that some children are abandoned by the only people who could have made a difference in their lives. And, really, why not the schools? Are not schools and teachers closest to the kids, spending all day, day after day, with them? And is it not a fact that in America schools have always been places that were concerned about the whole child and helping him or her to become somebody? School has never been just about the academics; personal growth has always been a responsibility of the schools in the eyes of Americans.[69] Is it not at least the job of schools to acknowledge the personal issues students deal with and provide some leadership and form alliances with other professionals and social institutions to help confront them? Is this not morally and practically more justified than standing back with a "that's not my job" purity, exclusivity, and isolation from the rest of society? And speaking of practicality, the academic agenda is not going to get served unless something is done about the personal and psychological issues that many young people in modern America must confront. No matter which way you look at it, it is not beneficial for schools to deny the prospect of dealing with the lives of the human beings they teach.

Both these perspectives have been articulated these days. What is your response to them? Where do you stand on this issue? Below I outline some thoughts on the issue of the responsibility I feel in regard to students' personal and psychological problems.

Helping Students Solve Problems

First of all, I am a teacher. I am not a psychotherapist, a counselor, or a social worker. I do not have those skills. And even if I did have the skills, most often I do not have the time to do that kind of work. I can teach school. And I think I can teach people how to go to school.

My posture is that I need not feel guilty for not taking on every personal problem of a student that comes my way. I am professionally ill-equipped to handle them; and in fact may well do harm if I try. My attitude is that I expect students, with the help of parents and the rest of society, to get their lives straight enough so that they are ready to work when they come to class. My message to students goes something like this: "I realize that personal issues are going to come up that could affect how you do in school. What I want you to know is that I care very much that you are well and happy and that you are able to do your maximum best in school. I support you in acting in a responsible way to deal with the problems you face. I am not the person who will pull you out of your difficulty. But I will, to the degree I am able, do what I can to help you decide where to go for help.'' I hope as a teacher I have a referral system I can use. At least I need to know what school counselor is assigned to each student. And, in turn, I hope that counselor is linked with some kind of network in which psychotherapeutic and other referrals can be made.

My own view of myself as a teacher—you decide your own view of yourself—is that I am not professionally obligated to give advice or help solve personal problems. I know there are teachers who have proven themselves useful at doing just that and more power to them. However, I do have some reservations about non-professionals providing what amounts to counseling or therapy. It may be fine to do. Though, this kind of assistance from teachers could be unwise advice-giving, or could act to obscure or ''band aid'' issues that call for more systematic attention by other professionals, parents, and the students themselves.

So that is what I do not do. What I do is work to create a climate, a setting, conducive to making students feel encouraged to resolve the issues that confront them. In this regard I have always been impressed with the writings of psychologist Carl Rogers. Rogers pointed out that the qualities in a therapeutic relationship facilitative of positive outcomes for the client also have applicability to education. Rogers wrote widely, but a book that is directed especially at education is *Freedom to Learn in the 80's*.[70] For many years Rogers advocated three qualities in the helper as crucial to empowering other people (empowering them to deal with problems they face, empowering them to learn). I find Rogers' work appealing because that is what I seek to do: empower others to get in charge of their own lives. The three ''facilitative conditions'' Rogers listed are the best way I know to be supportive in a positive way. I describe the three Rogerian qualities in my own words.

Realness

When a student comes to me with a problem I want him or her to feel responded to by Robert Griffin, the unique human being that shares the gift of life with the student, my parents' child, me. Not the impersonal role, teacher; not a facade or cardboard cutout; not the flight attendant who ''welcomes'' you aboard; not the ''receptionist'' who invites you to take a seat without ever seeing you.

Prizing, Acceptance, Trust

When a student comes to me with a personal issue I try to communicate through my words, my bearing, my general manner, that I value him as a human being. I accept him for who he is. And I trust that he can handle this issue successfully.

I believe in his capability and strength. I care that he is happy and well. I am rooting for him. I am on his side.

Empathic Understanding

In times like that I try to let a student know I understand his or her situation. That does not mean that I know all the details. But it does show that "I know how you feel right now."

For a more complete description and a discussion of these three empowering qualities refer to Rogers' book.[71] Based on the brief descriptions so far, note what these qualities are not as well as what they are. They are not about giving advice or taking over responsibility for the problem or its remediation. They are about saying I am here with you, I value and accept and care about you, I know what it's like for you, and I believe you can deal with the situation you face. These conditions are not a technique or a series of steps to carry out. They are a way of being with another person. The essence of this approach lies not in the words that you say as a helper but in what you are. If you are accepting, prizing, caring, empathic, real (authentic), somehow the words and gestures will flow out of that.

From personal experience I know how empowering these qualities can be for someone with a problem. Over a decade ago in La Jolla, California I participated in a program for helping professionals which taught us the Rogerian orientation. Rogers himself spent some time with us. We participants had opportunities to test out Rogers' ideas with each other and with volunteers from the surrounding community. I experienced how powerful these conditions are in a relationship. I say this for a couple of reasons. First of all, there is a lot of cynicism about the Rogerian approach. Many find it an overly nondirective and passive way to help. My response to this criticism is that there is nothing passive at all in offering these qualities to another person. For more on this point I refer you to an essay/review on one of Rogers' books I wrote with a colleague.[72] In addition, as educators we are so trained to take over, fix things, that placing trust in the results of just saying in effect, "I am on your side" is very difficult for us to do.

A last note, I consider these Rogerian conditions to be very beneficial in defining a healthy school environment. We could give students a great gift if we could create an overall school setting in which they are known and cared about in this way. It is certain that we need to do more than create these three Rogerian qualities, but I do not want to underestimate how freeing they can be for those who experience them. Certainly they do not cost much in money to implement. But they do take people with wisdom and care for others to make them a living reality.

Beyond what I have said, I suggest that schools, as some already do, provide— say in health classes—education in mental health and personal problem resolution. Within this, a particularly important issue to help students confront is stress. Adolescence is a time of stress and stress management is a crucial skill to develop.[73] Peer support programs may also prove useful. Another possibility, for a time I worked with an effort to set up what was called a teacher-counselor program in a school. Teachers were taught basic counseling skills and were assigned a group of students to work with one-on-one and in semiweekly meetings. In addition, I am sure if you talk with counselors or mental health professionals you can learn of many promising approaches schools have adopted. Of course you will hear some educators say that all of this is none of our business, that we are in over our head, and that we ought to get to the business of teaching history and math. Others will point out wonderful teachers who are all but mentors, even parents, to students. As I have said, personally I worry about my ability and right to intervene into the personal lives of students. I also worry that trying to do that detracts from what I do best—get people motivated and able to think and learn. But that is just me; you decide what you are going to do. One thing I hope we can agree on, however, is that apart from what we decide to do about it, personal and psychological issues are factors to be considered when making an analysis of student effectiveness.

I want to make one very last point before moving on to something else: There is a wonderful old book I recommend to you. It must be out of print but you can check the library. It is *Teacher and Child* by Dr. Haim Ginott.[74] Until his death a few years ago, Ginott was a therapist. These are his words of advice to teachers.

HEALTH AND NUTRITION

I speak to the issue of health from the perspective of an educator. To me, a healthy student is one who is rested, alert, clear-headed, calm, able to concentrate on the day's work, and just generally ready to get at the work of school. In contrast, an unhealthy student is one who is sick, high, speedy, or sleepy; not ready to get at it. Physicians would have another view of health and disease, but given my purposes as an educator, this is mine. And it is my assumption as an educator, thus its inclusion in this chapter, that some students do less well than we hope and expect because they are not healthy and alert enough to do their best. As laypeople, I think there are a couple of things we can do about this fact, if we can agree that physical health can retard a student from achieving up to his or her potential. First, we can become more aware of the impact of student health on academic performance. If nothing else, it will give us a more realistic view of what is possible. That is, if a student is high, no matter how good our lecture or engaging our teaching activity, it just is not going to get through. And second, we can formalize working relationships with health professionals and parents in order to get direction from them (what to look for, what to do about it) and learn where to refer students who are having physical health problems.

My basic posture toward students on this issue of physical health is the same as it is on the mental issues I considered in the last pages: "I am a teacher. That is what I do. What you [the student] do is show up awake and clear and in the best health possible and be prepared to do your best. I care about your health, but I am not a physician or a nurse. It is your job and your parents' job and the society's job—most of all your job—to get you here healthy. I will not take responsibility for that. I will take responsibility for my own health and make the commitment to you that I will care for my health so that I can participate fully in this class. I expect the same from you. And I will share with you what I consider a fact of life: you cannot do your best work here unless you take care of yourself physically. Understand, if you have a health issue that is something you cannot completely get over, although I will accommodate you in any way I can, it still comes down to your having to work harder than other kids to get things done. I do want you to be healthy and to succeed in school. If you are having a physical problem let me know, and if you would like I will try to help you find assistance from someone who can help."

Beyond that, my basic position is to turn it back on the school and parents and community. I cannot effectively teach someone who is sick, and I am especially impatient with someone who is *making* himself sick. I will not and cannot administer to the health needs of a student. I will do the best I can as a teacher, but I must point out that that is others' job to get that student to class healthy. As I write this, however, I realize I am not talking about some persistent, permanent, chronic health problem such as hearing loss, diabetes, or crippling illness. I am willing to match or go beyond students' effort to transcend and compensate for those kinds of illness. It is more the self-imposed sicknesses—drugs, alcohol, improper nutrition, bad living habits—that turn me into a "hard-liner," if that is what I am. I also realize that I may back off in what might seem to be a "you take him, I won't work with him" stance if I were a new teacher or otherwise in a tenuous position. I am not willing to lose a job arguing about something like this.

Drug and Alcohol Abuse

Some selected comments on health problems: First, of course, there are the major problems of drugs and alcohol abuse among young people. I do not pretend to know any more than you do about this serious problem. Though I will say I find it interesting that we speak of drugs *and* alcohol as if they were two separate categories. Alcohol *is* a drug, and it messes up and kills far more people than all the other drugs combined. But then again, alcohol is the drug of choice of the finer folk, and they get to separate it out as a special category and legalize the stuff. A ballplayer would never be able to come on TV and push cocaine. But there they are, the ex-jocks in full flush-faced color, pushing alcohol on young people for a buck. Have you ever noticed you never see them *drink* it on TV? You can hype the poison but you cannot drink it on the tube. It is a funny world.

I must admit I am not the most unbiased person on this issue. My sister, an elementary school teacher, was killed by a drunk driver a few years ago on her way to school one morning. And I have seen it torture so many people I know.

But apart from that, all I can say is that we need to gain consultation from professionals in the area of substance abuse and learn how to respond to students confronting drug and alcohol problems. Perhaps we can be helped to respond in some curricular way to the issue. I do begin with the belief that education and prevention are a crucial dimension of any effort to combat these problems. We can, as schools do now, set up special programs in substance abuse for students. And we can be helped to find ways to integrate attention to these concerns into regular classes, say in health, science, and social studies. We can also benefit from the knowledge of how to support the work of other professionals who work with these problems.

At this point, however, I need to educate myself on the problem. What are drugs and alcohol about for the people who turn to them? Why does it happen? How does it happen? What does it get them, or protect them from? Are problems in this area learned behavior? A matter of choice? Are individuals genetically predisposed to become addicted to drugs and alcohol? Is the "disease" different in origin in different people? By the way, disease is in quotes in that last sentence because I honestly do not know what the term *disease* means in this context. I hear, for example, alcoholism is often referred to as a disease. I simply do not know what that means. A virus? Bacteria? Does a problem resulting from genetics or body chemistry—if it in fact does, I do not know—warrant the label of disease? I think of a disease as something you catch or get. Or does disease just mean impairment? Do you *have* alcoholism; and if you do, what is it besides the acts of drinking and the physical and personal damage that results? If it is the acts, then it sounds like you do not *get* it, but rather *do* it. In that case, does someone *recover from it*, or simply *quit doing it*? That raises the fundamental issue of whether alcoholism is a matter of *disease* so much as it is a matter of *will*. Which leads me to ask: "Just who is in charge of one's life?"

It is fascinating to me how we look at these addictive problems. Someone has something and I do not know what it is he has. I defer to what the experts in this area can tell me. What I will ultimately have to decide, of course, is what this information leads me leads me to do professionally about these substance abuse issues.

Food Abuse

It has been my experience that we assume it is drugs and alcohol that we are talking about when we refer to substance abuse in schools. I want to add another substance to the list—food. Some students abuse food in ways that affect their general well-being and success in school. Unlike alcohol and drugs, I have done considerable study and work from an educational perspective with this issue of food abuse (another term, eating disorders). I can speak with some authority on this problem, both from my study and from the experiences of working with many individuals, young people and those older, over the past few years. I hope my comments about eating disorders give you an area to think about and study. This is a real "closet" issue in the schools and deserves more attention than we give it.

As with alcohol and drugs, there is a debate over what to call this phenomenon. Depending on the theoretical frame of reference it might be referred to as a disease, a disorder, a syndrome, a compulsion, or simply a problem. Personally, I fall into the eating problem camp, mostly because it is the most open-ended and does not bind me to explanations that I do not understand, such as disease and compulsion. My second choice is eating disorder. So I use either eating problem or eating disorder for the rest of this discussion.

I describe four categories of eating problems.

Anorexia

Some individuals—young and old, we are not only referring to adolescents here—may undereat in ways that make no sense to the rest of us. I mean, say, 300 calories a day, if that. Of course, these individuals become emaciated and the problem becomes very noticeable. The medical profession has observed this phenomenon of persistent undereating and tacked on the formidable label of anorexia nervosa. Psychologist Steven Levenkron lists the following characteristics of this malady:

1. *Phobias* concerning changes in bodily appearance are the illness's most outstanding feature.
2. *Obsessional thinking* about food and liquid intake constrict the mental activities of the anorexic.
3. *Obsessive-compulsive* rituals dominate much of the anorexic's day.
4. *Feelings of inferiority* about intelligence, personality, and appearance are common.
5. *Splitting*, or perceiving decisions and consequences in terms of polarities, is typical. The anorexic never sees choices as moderate, and fear making "mistakes." This results in an inability to make new decisions and leads to extremely rigid, repetitious behavior.
6. *Passive-aggressive behavior* often develops as parents and health professionals try to coerce the anorexic in what becomes a power struggle over eating and nutrition.
7. *Disinterest in sexuality* is often a personality characteristic of the anorexia nervosa syndrome and results from:
   (a) general immaturity and a need to see oneself as a child, to ward off feelings of parental abandonment,
   (b) fear of intimacy, physical or emotional,

    (c) failure of father to romance daughter healthily, to offer affection and compliments,

    (d) In the case of maturity-onset anorexia nervosa, sexual energies are distracted by obsessional fears of weight gain and ritualistic behaviors—over-planning of meals, special ways of cutting foods.

  8. *Delusional thinking develops*, especially with regard to body size and quantities of food ingested.

  9. *Paranoid fears* of criticism from others are often experienced, especially with respect to being seen as "too fat."

10. *Depression* can be observed, particularly in the chronic anorexic.

11. *Anxiety* is alleviated only by weight loss and fasting.

12. *Denial* is used, along with delusional thinking, to keep the anorexic starving, exercising, and away from people as well as the food she needs. Basically, then, she denies her emaciated appearance while continuing to view others who are substantially heavier as thinner than herself.[75]

Levenkron notes that anorexia is primarily found among females, with men and boys rarely confronting the disease (his term). He estimates its incidence as 1 out of every 250 adolescent girls. Depending on whom you read, various explanations are offered for anorexia. Some see it as a product of a personality disorder. Others cite childhood experiences, especially during puberty. You will hear it described as a misguided attempt to feel safe, special, powerful—anorexics can, after all, undereat anybody, and nobody can make them change their ways. And it is viewed in some quarters as a way to take out aggression toward parents and others. Alternatively, in recent years more and more researchers are citing the involvement of physiological factors—brain chemistry especially—rather than psychological factors. Whatever the cause, anorexia is serious business. At times it is a life and death matter, in some instances anorexics literally starve themselves to death unless they are put on intravenous feeding. One positive, if that is the right term, element in this tragic situation is that the problem is readily noticeable and thus at least it is apparent that help is needed. It is hard to miss someone who weighs 83 pounds. Can anorexia get in the way of academic success? If you have ever worked with the listless, disengaged, slightly hostile anorexic you would know that the answer is yes. Indeed, this is a serious matter, one that should be handled by skilled medical and psychiatric professionals.

Bulimia

Bulimia is a far more common problem than anorexia. We may not realize that because bulimia often goes undetected. It does not tend to get the "Pat Boone's daughter" publicity (she was an anorexic and wrote a book about it) that comes the way of anorexia. Bulimia—sometimes called bulimarexia—refers to a persistent pattern of bingeing and purging. By bingeing I mean the frantic, out-of-control intake of huge amounts of food—most often "junk" or "forbidden" food such as donuts and potato chips, food high in calories, fat, and simple carbohydrates. This binge occurs over a relatively brief period, say 45 minutes or so. To give you an idea of what it is like, a binge may begin with a package of cookies and move on to a loaf of bread, a half gallon of ice cream, a basket of fried chicken, and fistfuls of candy and pastries. Needless to say, the binge leaves the individual stuffed and bloated. The bulimic is frantic with guilt and fear of weight gain and possessed of an enormous desire to get rid of the food. Thus the food is purged from the body, usually through vomiting, and sometimes through the use of laxatives or diuretics. Bulimics are also prone to engage in abusive exercise. And they may embark on periods of fasting. Anorexics, by the way, often have bulimic episodes. Every once in a while the pattern of undereating breaks, and the binge begins.

From one perspective bulimics get away with the practice. They keep their weight constant and look pretty normal. But they do pay a great price: guilt; a sense of inadequacy; feeling washed out and fatigued; "squirrelly headedness" (thoughts here, there, and everywhere, unable to stay focused); esophageal irritation; infection of the salivary glands (causing a chipmunk appearance); and, for females, a loss of menstrual periods. Not exactly conducive to doing well in school. At the same time we cannot assume that bulimics will do poorly in school; many plug on despite feeling sick half the time or the preoccupation with food and eating. I think it is best to say that this condition *can* get in the way of achievement, but not that it necessarily will.

Some bingers do not purge. As one would expect, the result is weight gain, perhaps even obesity, if they do not fast or diet effectively enough. A newspaper story reported data from a study that showed 40% of adolescent boys and 34% of adolescent girls report periodic binges.[76] That is not to say these young people necessarily fall within the category of bulimia. Bulimia commonly implies frequent face-stuffing episodes, and purging. That is not to say that a good refined carbohydrate binge alone cannot send one into a negative spin. By the way, the presence or absence of purging is at the heart of a definitional conflict over the use of the terms *bulimia* and *bulimarexia*. Those favoring *bulimarexia* (the minority) contend that strictly speaking the term *bulimia* refers only to the gorging of food. Thus the need for another term, *bulimarexia*, to denote both bingeing and purging. But that is sort of an insider's argument, since conventionally bulimia is used to refer to the binge–purge disorder.

What causes bingeing, or the binge–purge episode? There are virtually as many reasons offered as there are theorists. Some see this problem as a way to deal with—take your pick—guilt, anxiety, boredom, low self-esteem, a "hungry heart," feeling "out of place" in one's life, hopelessness, sexual concerns, or a sense of inadequacy. Although theorists differ over the specific nature of the issue, most agree that the binger is stuffing himself over something that is unresolved in his or her life: some emotion, fear or problem. The eating serves to mask the issue or numb the individual to the point where for a time at least, it is not experienced. That is not to say that the individual himself knows what is going on. Pathological eating can occur without the individual being consciously aware of the issue that he or she is eating over. Or, if sensitive to the issue, that the pattern has been adopted as a way to cope with it.

At the same time, however, as with anorexia, many researchers are turning away from psychological and adjustment problems as explanations and toward the identification of physiological and genetic factors. Some writers, for example, see eating problems, and other addictions such as alcoholism, as arising primarily from flaws in the individual's brain chemistry.[77] Specifically, they point to a deep-seated and pervasive disturbance in the way the body metabolizes carbohydrates. The result is chronic depression and a persistent itch for the substance—sugar, caffeine, alcohol, drugs, whatever. At their core, compulsions are not a matter of moral weakness, due to a mental quirk, or a response to overwhelming personal issues. In this view, the life problems and psychological distress so many theorists see as the cause of the out-of-control eating are actually the *result* of a physiological abnormality. The real problem, then, is the physical dysfunction and the compulsive behavior itself. If you can deal with that, according to this perspective, the so-called underlying issues will begin to be manageable and fade away.

Again, whatever the cause, bingeing with or without purging, though particularly with purging, is a serious problem. Bulimia is especially a problem for adolescents, as its onset is often in early adolescence, perhaps beginning as a means of losing weight. I advised a graduate student who did a doctoral study on problem eating. Her review of the literature showed bulimia in between 2.2 to 7.7% of adolescent girls.[78] That means that in a typical high school of, say, 500 girls, up to 40 are bulimic—a significant number. Contrary to common belief, bulimia is not just a middle class phenomenon. Dr. Sue Bailey, medical director of the eating disorders unit of the Washington, DC Hospital Center, is quoted as saying that as high as 12% of teenage girls suffer some form of eating disorder, and that this problem crosses socioeconomic class lines and includes the children of blue collar and professional parents.[79] As with anorexia, bulimia is considered primarily a female problem. Estimates are that about 5% of bulimics are male. However, because this is a highly secretive condition for those who have it, percentages are difficult to pin down. Bulimics have two major fears: gaining weight and having their problem discovered. Consequently, reliable statistics are hard to locate.

If you want to read further, two good books on the subject are *Bulimarexia* by Marlene Boskind-White and her husband William, and *Bulimia* by Janice Cauwels.[80] Chapter 4 of the Whites' book focuses on adolescents. There are also many useful writings on bulimia in periodical literature.

Compulsive Overeaters

Another group are the compulsive overeaters. These are people who are hung up about food. They think about it day and night, organize their lives around it, and are frequently out-of-control with it. (It should be noted that with the exception of anorexics, eating problems do not involve "nuttiness" around food at all times. There are periods during the day when eating behavior is normal. Though usually the preoccupation with food in one's thoughts—How am I doing,? What am I going to do?—never ceases.) The compulsive overeaters simply chomp away for hours on end. The result of course is obesity. Or perhaps a yo-yoing of 30 pounds up and down. Incidentally, you may hear the term compulsive overeater used in another way. The self-help organization, Overeaters Anonymous, based on the same principles as Alcoholics Anonymous, uses compulsive overeater as a generic term to refer to anybody with an eating problem.

The point is that if you are thinking about one thing, you are not thinking about something else. If a student is obsessive about food, he or she may well not be attending to school as much as necessary. At the same time, I am not saying problem eaters are necessarily bad students. Some are as compulsive around academic success as they are around food. Some see school success as a compensation for their feelings of guilt and inadequacy. Feeling shaky and vulnerable in the world, problem eaters may be committed to do well in school to protect their safety and position. And of course some can deal with school work for itself and get about the process of learning the same as anyone else. However in my experience, the person with a real food issue wants out of everything, including school. They do not usually leave. They just want out, and either do things in half measure without realizing it, or rig it so that they are kind of pushed out while at the same time they hold on and want to stay in. In fact, holding on may be a good metaphor to describe the lives of people with eating disorders. They do not live as much as they hold on.

Mis-Eaters

Mis-eaters are people who, to put it bluntly, do not know what they are doing around food. Or if they know what they are doing, keep doing dumb things anyway. They break nature's rules, eating the wrong things, perhaps in the wrong amounts, probably for the wrong reasons (to deal with stress, for example). They wind up feeling bad, looking bad (puffy, dim-eyed), fat and generally all-around miserable. And this can affect their schoolwork. Though here again, that is not to say it will affect it. This eating pattern may, for example, lead to academic overcompensation as the student tries to overcome his or her self-disdain at looking like Porky Pig at the very time boy–girl relationships are becoming such a major issue. It is enough to say that some students, anyway, are so dopey and hyper (at the same time) from junk food, or so depressed or distracted by their eating habits, that their work in school is affected.

What Can We Do?

A good first step is to become aware of the problem. In that regard, I hope this book has helped. Here is another area in which we may work collaboratively with health care professionals to conduct sessions on eating disorders for school professionals, parents, and students. These are serious problems that can significantly affect a student's happiness and success in school. These issues are the business of health care professionals. The ideal is a system in which schools can support students to become informed about the issue and can encourage those with the problem to get professional help. Ultimately it is the students' business to analyze themselves and make a decision of whether or not to do anything. We can provide a setting which promotes this action.

Proper Diet

So far I have talked only about what goes wrong with eating. We also need to consider the opposite side—nutritional health and its consequences. I feel that there is no better way for a student to provide the foundation for academic achievement than to eat well. To me that means plenty of fresh fruits and vegetables, whole grains, poultry and fish. We should all stay away from excessive calories and fats, which means easing back on dairy products. We should stop ingesting caffeine, sugar, alcohol and drugs.[81] Keeping in mind, I am saying this tentatively. I am not a nutritionist, and I am not certain what teenagers need nutritionally. I know adults are being advised to cut down on fats and to increase fiber, but is that good advice for a growing young person? And what about the need for calcium? Anyway, I defer to the professionals in this area. I do feel confident, however, in saying that teenagers should get off junk food, caffeine, nicotine, alcohol and other dope. We in education need to consider how to get the reality and the choice before students in health and other classes. There is the need for schools to decide whether or not to counterbalance the media as it tells young people that "Coke is It" (98% sugar is what "it" is), that a candy bar is a perfect pick-me-up, and that alcohol is an ideal way to reward yourself at the end of a hard-working day.

Personal Change Process

A wonderful book on the subject of eating disorders is *Binge Eating* by Gloria Arenson.[82] It may be out of print. Check libraries, or perhaps you can contact Gloria by writing her through her publisher. What is particularly useful is Gloria's understanding of a personal change process that provides a way out for people living with eating problems. As teachers and students we can learn much from her analyses, not only about how to deal with eating disorders but how to bring about changes in other areas of our lives. When you think about it, confronting an eating problem parallels other issues we face, including academic problems.

We have a problem, we know it, and we want to change. But we do not change, we just spin our wheels. What is that about? Why do we fail to keep our agreements with ourselves to be different in ways that we know will make us happier? Very often that is the problem that underachieving students must face. They are not happy with their progress in school and vow to do better—but wind up staying in the same old place, unhappy and unappreciated by themselves and the others around them. From that perspective, an eating disorder, or being a problem student, is a gift. It is the opportunity to learn how to get in charge of your life and make yourself different. It is an opportunity, to stop coping, get out of the rut, and change the "story" of your life. It is a wonderful opportunity when you think of it that way.

I refer you to Arenson's book, if you can obtain it, for the details. Basically, she advocates a four-level plan. Level 1 involves what might be called behavior management processes. If you have studied the ideas of B. F. Skinner and his followers you know what I am getting at: defining clear, quantifiable objectives, and identifying measurable behaviors as a means of achieving them; setting up monitoring systems to record progress; and establishing payoffs to one's self to reward success. Levels 2 and 3 deal with understanding and altering feelings and thoughts in such a way that you are more likely to change. And the fourth level includes an exploration of your hopes and potential. These themes of self-directed behavioral change and the study of the "inner curriculum" of feelings, thoughts, and images are recurrent in this book.

The Arenson material reminds us that, in education, we have not really focused intensely enough on the personal change process. Our insights into subject content, curriculum development, instruction, and classroom management do not really get at how a student can be helped to make himself or herself different. Without that we are left with beseeching, scolding, and hoping. We have much to learn from those outside the field of education in this area. The promotion of personal change is just another form of teaching and learning. It is teaching yourself or another how to be *different*, not just how to learn this or that. For students it is learning the skills of coming at life, in this case school life, in fundamentally new and more satisfying ways.

An example of something you might explore in this area of personal change is a book by Peter Miller and Ray Hodgson, *Self-Watching: Addictions, Habits, Compulsions*.[83] They talk about cigarette smoking and the like in this book. Viewing poor academic work as a bad habit, a student may find this material useful in getting direction on how to take on his "habit" of doing inadequately in school. Miller and Hodgson outline some processes for overcoming bad habits that I think apply to our work as educators. For example, consider these two ideas, with some comments of mine tacked on:

Analyze the Habit. Become aware of what you are doing and the various circumstances that provoke your usual behavior. [There are usually situational cues or "triggers" that set you off on the wrong actions. One needs to identify them and learn to deal with them.]

Develop Self-Management Strategies. 1) Identify new ways to deal with these situations. 2) Do some advance planning and mental play-acting to rehearse these new behaviors. 3) Rearrange your environment. [In terms of schooling this could mean setting up a study area at home or sitting in a different place in class to avoid distractions.] 4) Reward yourself for good behavior. [Do not wait for teacher rewards.] 5) Readjust how you talk to yourself. [Do not say "I'm just too dumb to get anything done." Instead say, "If I plan it right, I can succeed."] 6) Practice restraint. [A lot of bad studenting has to do with succumbing to temptation—"Hey, forget tomorrow's test, you want to go to a party?"] 7) To build up to being able to gain control of that moment of temptation, practice in small ways staying with your goals. [Practice being on time. Make your bed. Keep small commitments like washing the car because you said you would, even though you do not feel like it right now.] 8) Focus on success, not failure.

Notice how similar these processes are to those outlined during the discussion of sport in chapter 3. Also notice how personal change does not just apply to students. It applies to us, too. We need to learn to get out of ruts in our own lives. I have often thought that personal change processes would be a good way to teach prospective and inservice teachers. Research has shown that teachers often agree with some new approach they learn about in a course or workshop or elsewhere. They want to use it. But they just never implement the new idea. They master the teaching strategy, but they do not have self mastery. So often in our lives it is not a matter of being able to figure out what to do or being able to do it. Instead, it is that we know what to do, we just do not do it. We ought to look at the personal change process far more than we do. Both for our students' sake and our own.

Let us close on a hope. The hope is that students, and their teachers, do not just come at their work free from disease, but physically healthy. There is a big difference. Even those of us who are considered healthy are only free from the commonly accepted definition of disease. Our standard of health is way too low. I am no zoologist, but based on looking, I cannot think of an adult animal in nature that looks as bad as we do. As far as I know, no other animal stuffs as much junk into itself as the human animal. No adult animal in nature looks as bad without clothes on as the adult human. I am serious: if humans, like animals, went around without clothes, it would by and large be a bad aesthetic scene. The average mid-life lion in Africa—at least if I can believe TV—looks OK. If you put the average mid-life human, even a "healthy" one, out there, he looks awful. We are being "saved" by the fashion industry.

My point is that if so many of us look that bad on the outside, why do we think it is any better on the inside? Modern living is tough enough without trying to conduct it from a physical foundation based on bad nutrition and hygiene, inadequate exercise, lack of proper sleep, and general physical neglect. The challenge is for all of us, students and ourselves, to treat our bodies as if we loved ourselves. If we did that, we would eat in ways that were a true gift to ourselves. Surely we would not pour seven to nine spoonfuls of sugar (the amount in a soft drink) into anyone we loved, even if he or she liked the taste. We would "play by the rules"—and we know them—that would result in our being alert, energetic, attractive to ourselves and others. We would stop the self-torture no matter how attractive the short run pleasure (the comfort that comes with eating cake like mom use to make). We would give ourselves the gift of health instead of depending on the medical profession to bail us out. I do not know what more to say except that we need to consider health as much as we do illness. We need to establish an ideal of health to shoot for, and then have fun trying to make it a reality.

CONCLUSION

I have sketched out a number of areas that I consider to affect studenting capability. Look back over them. Tie them together with the material in chapter 3 (generic goal attainment capability, etc.) and see what kind of overall picture begins to form. These two chapters were selective, things I care about. What would you add to what I have considered? And last, think through what all this, any of this, means to you. What stood out for you? What is the particular significance of this chapter for you? What do you need to know more about? What does it imply for what you do professionally?

I move on in the next chapter to the other side of the coin—teaching. What is good teaching for students who are not achieving to their potential?

5 An Exploration of Teaching

This chapter turns the coin over, from a concern with studenting, as I am calling it, to a focus on teaching. The point I have been making is that we need to give attention to all of the elements that comprise the teaching-learning circumstance. Obviously, how teachers teach is crucial to determining the nature and quality of learning and growth outcomes for students. In these pages I outline some ideas regarding the teaching of underachieving secondary age students. In addition to learning what I think, you have studied, or are going to study, instructional methodologies in classes and other contexts, and I hope these ideas give you a frame of reference from which to assess and incorporate these other teaching ideas you encounter. The last section of the chapter applies the perspective established thus far in the book to a critique of a couple of examples of the instructional technology movement currently in vogue, especially as it applies to these less-successful-than-they-could-be students. Two things should come from that. First, we can find one way to look at this technological approach to instruction. And second, I provide an example of how general values and concepts can be used to make sense of aspects of our work.

TEACH FOR WHAT?

First, let me sketch a picture of what I hope we as teachers can create for these students. Talking about teaching only makes sense if we are clear about what we are trying to get done. No method or strategy can be called good or bad unless it is considered in light of the purposes that it accomplishes. Unfortunately, in education we tend to place our value on means to ends, with less attention on the ends themselves. For example, if I see a lecture I do not know whether it was a good lecture until I am informed about what the teacher's goals are for that particular day, week, or month. That is, the lecture may be dynamic, exciting, informed, and so on, but it still may not be getting the teacher where he said he wants to go, or ought to go. The same with a discussion: teachers and students may be working enthusiastically, but the discussion may still not be contributing to the attainment of the expressed or tacit purposes of the teacher or school. Yet I have seen a teacher applauded for a lecture without reference to either the education goals or the actual results of the activity. It may have been a "great lecture," but what did the students learn from it?

Anyway, the hope for these students is to create an achievement-oriented context for them. That is, a school situation where, supported by others and by a rich context, the student is setting manageable and appropriate goals (remember Johnson?). Through these efforts the student can surpass his or her present standards and levels of academic achievement. It is important that the *student* is setting goals; he or she "owns" them psychologically (even though they may also be the goals of the teacher). These goals are not so easy that they do not "stretch" the student, but at the same time they are not so difficult that they amount to a set-up for failure. In an achievement-oriented classroom the student clearly sees the connection between effort and outcomes: work hard and you get results. An achievement classroom counters the notion that you can get something without working for it, that it is all a matter of luck or fate, being in the right place at the right time, or beyond your grasp (too dumb, cards stacked against me, etc.). Do the work, achieve the outcome, see the link between effort and results—that is the persepective we should encourage.

This achievement-oriented classroom contrasts with what psychologist Martin Covington has described as the failure-avoiding classroom.[1] In this kind of classroom, students are essentially "covering their behind," not pursuing academic success. Students experience the classroom as a place where their sense of self-worth is threatened. As they see it, if they put in a great deal of effort and still do not accomplish much, they feel shamed, and their low ability and incapability are revealed. Furthermore, they cannot afford to sit back and do nothing because they will be reprimanded by teachers and their parents. They will feel some guilt because they have bought into the cultural/school value that says you should not just "sleep in the mid-day sun." What this boils down to is that for the students the classroom is a context in which they are just trying not to get hurt. Rather than going for something positive, they try to avoid something negative happening to them—being revealed as an incompetent, looking lazy, being ridiculed, and so forth.

What do they do to deal with the situation and maintain their self-value? They may make up excuses for their lack of success: "I don't care about this class." "This is bo-ring!" "The dog ate my assignment." They may even rig failure, let you know they did not put much into it, and then leave the impression that they could have done the work if they had wanted to. All of which we may unintentionally reinforce by raving about their potential as a way to get them motivated. In that case, from the students' side they did not have to work too hard, avoided being revealed as low ability, and received praise for all that they could have accomplished. But the student did not learn how to go to work and accomplish something. He or she remained ignorant of whatever might have been learned by doing the assignment with the maximum degree of effort. Of course this is not to say that failure-avoidance is all that is going on in classrooms. Indeed, as we have explored in this book, there is much else happening. What this analysis does for us, however, is draw an important distinction between a class where a student is making an attempt to get things accomplished rather than trying to save face or avoid getting hurt.

The achievement-oriented classroom is characterized by student use of the kind of achievement skills described by Eric Johnson (chapter 3), Covington (strategic learning, chapter 4), the sport people (chapter 3), and other theorists I have alluded to along the way. In this type of setting, students view the class as a problem-solving event. They, the students, analyze the learning situation, develop challenging but realistic goals, devise and implement a plan of action, monitor and evaluate their progress, and make adjustments in their work as needed. Their standards for judging their own work are essentially internal ones. They assess themselves on the basis of their own prior levels of attainment and on the basis of what they consider to be excellent (not perfect) in themselves. This perspective among students contrasts with a predominant concern to compare themselves with some norm or competitively against other students. Though at the same time, I do not want to rule out the usefulness of those other criteria of self-assessment. The reality is that there are norms and there is competition, and it does not make sense for a student to ignore these realities. Still the major focus for a student should be on expanding his own limits.

A last point, to me an achievement-oriented class is a place where students are learning important, crucial things. They are not learning just this or that. They are learning what it will take to empower them to live as productive and fulfilling a life as their inherent capability will allow. As I see it, that includes learning what it takes to be acquainted with and connected to the human heritage we all share, and the conditions in which they are going to have to forge their lives. It is an education that makes it possible for them, if they work hard, to learn to transcend the limitations in their world and become the finest version of what is most natural to themselves. And it is education that encourages and makes it possible for students to give and receive to their utmost as human beings. Yes, those are high hopes. But our children are worth our very highest hopes.

SOME TEACHING STRATEGIES

What are some things that teachers can do to more a class in this direction? I will list a few. You add some of your own.

Make Students the Agents

I know this is a point I have made in various ways before, but it bears reiteration: *School ought to be about what students do, not what teachers do.* My experience, and this is asserted in report after report on American schooling, is that school tends to be about what teachers do. If you are in a contest to make the best guess at what is happening in any secondary classroom at any moment, here is my advice on how to win the bet: Just say that there is an earnest adult standing in front of a group of young people—chalk in hand, book in hand, paper in hand, it varies—and that adult is talking. I am not saying it is uninformed or useless talk by the teacher; just that that is what is going on: teacher talk. The teacher talks for a while, then he or she asks students something. The students respond briefly, and that triggers a brief "lecturette" from the teacher with the intent of correcting or extending the student responses. Then there is another question, another lecturette, and so it goes. Then maybe something like, "For the rest of the class read pages so and so [answer questions 1 to 5, do problems 1 through 10] for tomorrow." The bell finally rings and the students are gone in a flash.

That sounds rather deadly, and in truth it is much of the time. In fact, I think I understand the concept of relativity after sitting in on a lot of classes. Two minutes is not always 2 minutes. That is, the last 2 minutes waiting for the bell to ring, between 8:48 and 8:50 a.m., is only matched in endlessness by a dreadfully slow rendition of the National Anthem before a ballgame. As you can tell, I am more than a bit fed up with the lectures, question-and-answer recitation sessions (not a real exploration of anything, just a retrieval of facts and opinion sharing), and those 15-question worksheets. Maybe it is just the classrooms I happened to have observed. And believe me I do not mean just to point the finger at others. I do my share of this kind of teaching. It is tough to think of anything else to do, the students often do not seem to care one way or the other, and it always seems like the right thing to do at the time. But it does make school predictable and flat. Despite all that, however, the point is not how good or bad it is but who is doing the doing and who is responding to the doing. I am saying it is the teacher who is the doer or the active one. And that the doing can get very engaging for the teacher, because like all human beings he connects to what he does. All human beings are inherently doers. We are most ourselves when we are creating, solving, fixing, and figuring out in order to get to some goal that has meaning to us. We learn and grow best when we take on the world, try to make sense of it, and make it different.

A shorthand way to put it, in schools students need to become more causal and less reactive, more like what teachers are now. The students need to become agents who take action to make themselves better. That is not to say that they cannot learn by receiving from others, through a lecture, or presentation—they can. But as I see it, this reception occurs best in the process of students going for something. When you think about it, this has been the message all the way through, from the sport psychology material, Nielson, the Lipson research, and on through. Schools ought to be a place where students make it happen. In terms of this book, schooling ought to focus more on studenting than on teaching. What it comes down to is that the core of teaching is thinking up good work for students to do, rather than getting your lecture together.

Coach Them

I do want it understood, however, that because I emphasize student-as-agent I am not arguing for a passive, noninvolved, benign role for the teacher. Not at all. What I am calling for is a different, though still very positive, responsibility. There is a good discussion of what I am talking about in Theodore Sizer's book—as good as anything I have read in recent years—*Horace's Compromise*.[2] Sizer uses a metaphor to describe the teacher's role that I relate to quite well—and that is *coaching*. I know Sizer is using the coaching notion as a way to get at the skill training aspect of our work, but I think it has broader applicability. When I think of coaching I think of the kind of coaching that goes on in sport. Good coaches define what the game is about at its best, amd make it clear that it is the player who plays the game. Note the first part of that last sentence. It is important that teachers put some ideals in front of students about what it looks like when a class *really* works and when a student *really* goes to school. Sometimes we are so busy conducting our lessons that we do not lay those values out there so that they can become guides and criteria for assessment of student actions. The coach's job is to do what is necessary to help the athlete excel to the maximum of his or her potential. I remember a comment from Steve Boros in the tape Joel Kirsch and I put together. He said that good coaches help players learn to coach themselves. We should teach students to teach themselves. Coaches teach the skills of goal setting, self-analysis, self-correction, and teamwork. So should we. The coach challenges the player to produce his best. It is the player's job to produce something and he either does or does not. And if he does not, the coach does not let the athlete off the hook by getting across somehow: "Oh, you aren't responsible. I guess I just didn't coach you right." We can do the same kind of things.

When you think about it, good coaches turn things around from the way they usually are in school. Instead of coaching (teaching) while the players watch and judge (in teaching, "This class is boring"), the athletes play while the coach watches and judges. In football the coach sometimes watches from a tower. I am not advocating anything like that, but it does emphasize who the doers are in sport. Instead of saying "I'm going to coach so well you are going to be motivated an interested," the coach challenges the athlete to find motivation and drive within himself. The coach also points out when it is not there, does not take on all the blame. Certainly coaches do not always succeed in producing self-starters. But everything I know tells me they are increasing their odds in the way they approach the issue.

Plan a Different Way

One implication of centering schooling on what students do is that it changes the way we think about planning our curriculum. When putting together lesson plans, most teachers whether they do it formally or not, are guided by the following questions:

1. What do I want students to learn?
2. How can I teach them that?
3. How can I evaluate them?
4. How can I organize the class in order to get this accomplished?

This is the classic model of curriculum planning. I associate it with an orientation passed down by educational theorist Ralph Tyler years ago.[3] Basically it asks us to figure out what we want to get done; do it; evaluate it to see whether we got there; and set up the class, schedules and so forth, so that it can happen.

On the face of it, this all sounds unimpeachable. It is consistent with the way we have been taught to think in other contexts. I have heard little analysis or criticism of this way of going about our business. But if you look over the steps and reflect on the discussion just passed it is clear what issue I take with this model. Look at who is doing and who is reacting in this. True, students can become causal agents within this planning format, but I think there are better ways to go at it.

Here is my proposal. Instead of resolving the four questions in the aforementioned model, work through these five:

1. In what direction do I want students to learn and grow; what challenges do I want them to confront?
2. Why are these outcomes the most important for students to achieve?
3. What do students have to do to attain these purposes; and what insights, skills, and attitudes do they need to have in order to do this work?
4. What factors in the setting and actions by me and others will best support students in doing their work?
5. How can students show me that they have gotten significant things accomplished?

Put a bookmark here and keep referring back as I go through each of these questions and explain my thinking.

Notice that step 1 considers more than learning (the inclusion of the terms *grow* and *challenges*). Including growth underscores that the schools ought to be attending to students' developmental (growth) needs as well as their learning needs. In chapter 4, I made this point in the context of an exploration of the developmental circumstance of adolescence. Certainly we want students to learn. But also important are intellectual or cognitive growth (which I see centering on the ability to think abstractly about one's self and the world), psychosocial de-

velopment (the creation of an integrated personal identity), and physical development (managing all the stresses of physical maturity in a positive way and
enhancing the physical dimension of one's being). As I have indicated I can imagine situations—well, I think I observe them now—in which students learn some
things but they do not develop very much. They may be put in a tightly structured learning circumstance in which they are taught some fact or generalization
from history or how to do some math process, but still not grow. A major premise
of this book is that the promotion of developmental maturity is a key to empowering
students to live effectively in their world.

I also included the term *challenges* in this first question to remind me that
there are times where I know what work I want students to take on, but I am
not sure how this engagement by a student is going to turn out. I am not exactly
certain what he or she is going to learn. I know that what I am calling challenges
can be framed within a standard learning goals format, but the inclusion of the
term emphasizes that there are instances when what I want fundamentally is for
a student to take on a challenge and see what he can produce. An example that
comes to mind is for a student to identify a contemporary American fiction writer
and convince me and others in the class that he or she is a superb writer. Also,
probably as an addition to this project, the student can convince me and others
that a particular well-regarded writer is not up to his or her reputation. Or, another
example, perhaps a student, or group of students, could devise a way to improve
their level of academic achievement in school.

But whatever the goals, it is not only important that the teacher is clear about
purposes but that the students are as well. The students should be every bit as
aware of the aims and the hopes of the class as the teacher. Good teachers, however
they do it, help students become purposeful. It can be as simple as teachers devoting
class sessions to working through what positive things that students can get done
through their work together in the next week or month. However it is done, it
is crucial that *students* be able to picture and articulate those positive outcomes,
not just the teacher. So often students go to class and have little idea what is happening. All they know is the topic (and sometimes not even that) and that the
teacher is going to do something or another, even if they do not know exactly what.

Question 2 deals with rationale. As an educator, I not only need to be clear
on my goals, I must also clarify for myself and others the justification for those
goals. Why those goals and not some others? Without an articulate rationale we
are technicians and not professionals. Professional teachers have a clear understanding of *why* they are teaching what and as they do. They have rigorously
reflected on the nature of society, school, and students. They know themselves
thoroughly, and their work as educators is consistent with the significance of their
life as they experience it and with their sense of purpose. Moreover, their curriculum is in line with what they, after serious study, consider to be ethical and
necessary work. They select their goals with a clear awareness and sense of responsibility for the consequences of their work with students. In other words, they

choose goals. The goals are supported by a justification grounded in the teachers' most deeply felt insights, values, and commitments.

One implication of teachers developing a sound rationale for what they teach is that it will not only make it explicit why they are teaching what they are, but also what they are *not* teaching. The value of what we are doing can only be fully determined if we consider it in light of what other things we could be doing. It is not enough for some goal to be a good, useful aim for students to pursue. Given the finite amount of time available, it should be *the best of all possible goals*. The way we normally approach curriculum planning does not usually resolve the question, "What other things can we do?" We have to remember that no matter what we are doing, we are not doing every other possible thing. This may sound obvious, but we really do not consider alternatives as much as we should.

To point out an illustration, I worked on a project which revised the eighth grade geography curriculum in a junior high school, a course in the social studies program in the school. We wrestled with what goals ought to direct the geography course, what texts and teaching activities to use, how to evaluate students, and so forth. What we did not deal with was the reason for teaching geography in the eight grade. What else could it be if it were not geography? Is this *the* best content for 13-year-olds? Really, it had *better* be the number one, absolutely most important, positively most needed, subject to study at 13. If it is not, teach the subject that is. But we did not get into those issues because we never posed the question of why we were doing what we were doing, which would have then led to whatever else we could or should be doing with students. Just knowing where you want to go (goals or objectives) does not deal with why you want to go there or where else you might go. If you teach about the Civil War, you are not teaching about the contemporary family (though I understand we can draw comparisons between the family in those times and now). To summarize, too often we focus on goals and objectives without equal concern for the rationale that gives them justification, and we need to be aware of what we are not doing as much as what we are doing.

Question 3 points out that we should focus on what they do to learn rather than what I do to teach. This encourages me to look at the process from their, the students', perspective. What do students need to read, write, create, figure out, resolve, present, experience; what projects do they have to take on, with whom, and where? What do they have to do to accomplish the desired outcomes? They are the agents. Question 3 also emphasizes that students are going to have to have the capabilities necessary to getting their work done. The issue here is not what skills the teacher needs to possess, but rather what the students have to be able to do.

Question 4 underscores that the teacher has a positive role, that of supporting student work. As a teacher I may need to help students learn what earlier was described as strategic learning skills in order for them to be able to frame goals and identify issues, challenges and areas of study. Perhaps I need to help them find books and films, lecture to them, lead discussions, or set up panels and reports. These are the same kinds of things I normally do, but in these instances they are done within the context of supporting students' actions. Note too, I think about how I *and* others can help, not just what I can do. The help does not have to come just from me. There are librarians, knowledgeable students, parents, other teachers, people in the community, and experts in the particular area of study who can be called upon to help as well. This encourages a break from a teacher-and-students exclusivity that characterizes the way we work. And last, notice the emphasis on the importance of creating a rich context for students. By "factors in the setting" I mean such things as scheduling arrangements, school organization and climate, learning materials, and the classroom physical arrangement. Teaching is more than a series of teacher-up-in-front instructional strategies.

Question 5 turns around the way we usually evaluate things. Instead of my testing them to see if they have achieved the goals of the class, students have the job of showing me how far they have come. A natural outgrowth of the focus-on-student-action approach is to make it their responsibility to demonstrate that they have used their opportunity well. Sizer uses the term *exhibition of mastery* to describe the process of student display of their progress. I am very excited about his concept, though I do have some problems with the use of the term mastery in describing what Sizer wants. First, what he is talking about can get mixed up with the mastery learning approach associated with theorist Benjamin Bloom an others. This strategy requires that teachers determine precisely what is to be learned by students and then repeatedly test until it is shown the students have learned it. I am sure Sizer would find that mechanistic, more or less a series of hoops for students to jump through. A deadly process if student initiative, inquiry, and creativity are valued outcomes. Also, use of the mastery label can imply that there is some absolute standard of mastery, a ceiling of attainment that has been predetermined. What Sizer, and I, want is a situation in which there is no ceiling, no clear upper limit. The issue for evaluation is not "Did you learn it?" but rather "Where are your limits right now?" Psychologically there is a subtle but crucial difference between those two questions. In most human affairs there is no simple, defined standard so that once you reach it you just move to the next thing. You proceed on from what you are doing, but with most things that matter in life you have to live with the knowledge that with greater effort or the development of greater skill, you could have done better than you did. What happens in life is that you create to a certain level of quality, and you are proud of it if it is excellent. At the same time, however, you know it could have been better. And awareness of that makes you conscious of the current limits of your motivation, capability, and level of achievement. It is vitally important that schools be places where students understand and test their limits, not just pass the requirements.

Review these five steps and try an example. Think of something you teach or contemplate teaching—a week or a month's worth. Using the planning process I outlined, jot down notes on how you would answer each of the five questions. Now think through if you went at it differently than you would if you had used the first model.

Encourage, Support, Acknowledge, Appreciate, Praise

Given this orientation to planning and teaching, crucial skills for a teacher are the capability of providing *encouragement* and *support* to students. Encouragement is a natural outgrowth of an achievement-oriented classroom. Encouragement carries the implication that someone else is doing something self-chosen. (And again, to me self-chosen does not necessarily mean students thought up the goal or activity. It may have come from the teacher. But they have *affirmed* it and made it their own.) In effect, encouragement says "keep it going." Support is getting across "I'm with you," "I'll help," and "I'm on your side." It is saying in ways that students catch, "I'll do what I can to provide you with what you need to get your job done." And then you do it. Praise, on the other hand, carries the connotation, to me at least, of a reward for doing what I want you to do. Clearly, praise has its place, but I think it important to play a bit with the distinction between encouragement, support, and praise. They are different, and I am looking for ways to be encouraging and supporting. Just the fact that I can be encouraging is a sign to me that I must be doing something right, that students are moving out and testing their frontiers. (At the same time, however, I also want to give *direction* and *advice* and provide *structure* to students. I do not mean to imply I think we should create a vacuum, let students come up with some work to do, and, whatever this work, cheerlead them on. Teaching is a creative interplay of a number of contrasting processes, which includes a teacher giving direction to where things go from a position of greater experience and wisdom.)

What exactly does a teacher encourage and support? It is clear from what I have said that these processes are used to prompt students to exceed their own prior limits. That is a major focus: to attend to a student rising above his past standards. That is what I am encouraging and supporting. And that is also what I am *acknowledging* and *appreciating*, two more crucial skills for a teacher within this perspective. To acknowledge is to communicate to a student that I see what you are doing. I notice you. You matter. To appreciate is to say how I feel about what you are doing: "I value what you are doing." "I see that work as worthwhile." "I really admire your paper." Appreciation can come down to a "thank you for that" from a teacher to a student. And yes, I do want to *praise*. "That's fine work," "Good for you," "That was the right [correct or morally justified] thing to do." What all this comes down to is that I want to get good

at letting students know that I am aware of what they do and that it matters greatly to me. And too, this underscores a basic point from behavioral psychology:
attend to what you want and reinforce it and you are likely to get more of it.
Focus on rewarding what you want instead of punishing what you do not want
and the class will probably go better.

Take a moment and reflect on these processes: encouragement, support, praise,
acknowledgment, and appreciation. How are they different? Where do they overlap? How do they relate to other valuable teaching strategies?

Neither a Floor Nor a Ceiling —
Do Your Best

Another basic idea, *establish neither a floor nor a ceiling to achievement.* Here
I disagree with Covington. Recall his analysis of failure avoidance motivations
among students. Since school is a threatening place to be for them, he advocates
that a teacher make public to students a set of minimum achievement standards
that every student is likely to meet. As Covington sees it, if this is done students
do not have to worry so much about failure. A "floor" is established, and thus
students can be sure of their footing. This sounds reasonable enough. But I worry the minimums will become maximums. It is like saying to a potential buyer,
"The least I will take for this car is $3,000." There are few things I am abso-
lutely sure of, but in this case I will guarantee that the *most* you will get for that
car is $3,000. Another illustration, from education this time, there was a "mini-
mum competency" movement in many states a few years ago, including the one
in which I live, which still has an effect on how schools operate. The result was
to clearly define what a student minimally should know and be able to do in basic
skill areas such as reading, writing, and math. The idea was that possession of
these fundamental abilities is the least that should be expected of students and
our schools, and that no student should be allowed to get through school without
them. Graduation, then, becomes contingent on passing tests which measure competence in these basic abilities. This basic competence thrust sounds impeacha-
ble on the face of it. The knowledge and skills that are on the list are simple,
and who can argue that it is too much to expect of our schools to at a minimum
assure that students can handle the basics.

In my view, the problem arises because human nature was not taken into account in setting up this system. What I see happening is that what was meant
to be a minimal expectation (a floor) has become *the* expectation for some students (acquire these skills and pass these tests and you get by). Likewise, all the
discussion of minimums led to a kind of "minimums mentality": What is the
least we can expect of young people? As a practical matter it is difficult to send
out qualified or multiple messages in any context, including school. By that I
mean it is tough to say, "Do at least this, but in fact I want you to do much more
than this." What tends to be heard, as in the car buying example, is that "bottom

figure.'' Students say to themselves, "So that is what I have to do to get through."
I really believe this is how many students, especially the "lower" ones, come
to view the situation. All the talk about basic skill acquisition and minimums by
teachers starts to affect the way they see school and themselves. They start to
think minimally.

As you can tell from reading what I have written so far, I think we should
talk maximums and not minimums. In fact, psychologically, the best way to get
minimums is to communicate an expectation of maximums: to talk and think max-
imally. To do that is to remove any notion of a "ceiling." By ceiling I mean
the precise definition of maximal achievement. The message should be: "I believe in you and expect a lot from you as a student. Let us see how good you
can be." I assume nobody that really counted told the young Picasso, "This is
how good a painting can get. Get this good, do it this way, and that is it." Instead of this "ceiling," there was a message, from his father I understand, himself a fine painter, "Go as far as you can and show me."

I worry that some of the less advantaged and unsuccessful students live with
floors and ceilings that are similar. There is the message that they had better get
so much done or they will not complete the class or graduate (the floor). And
at the same time, the message to them is that this is about all that they are likely
to get done (the ceiling). I prefer a simple "do your best" perspective which
creates a limit-testing challenge and taps into the inherent human tendency to see
what we are made of. One element in our society that is aware of that fact about
people is the military. They have done quite nicely recruiting young people, many
of whom have not been markedly successful in their lives, by promising them
a chance to "be all you can be."

That still leaves a potential problem of the class becoming threatening, a setting for a failure avoidance posture among students. I agree this is an issue, but
I believe we can get at the problem without a lot of talk about minimums. For
one thing, teachers must make it clear to students that we believe in students'
capability and are willing to be supportive. And especially early on, we can contrive assignments that have the highest likelihood of giving students some success experiences, and that will help to boost their confidence and motivation. We
should also teach students how to use their own internal standards and level of
prior performance as criteria for judging themselves, instead of being preoccupied
with comparing themselves with other students or some absolute standard. So
we do need to accommodate a students' past history of failure or, another way
to put it, less-than-optimal level of school success. But still, I think the basic message ought to be, "Do your very best." Referring back to the discussion of this
culture in chapter 1, excellence, not minimally acceptable competence, is a deeply ingrained aspect of this culture. It is a cultural value that needs to be reflected
in the schooling of all of our children.

Make Them Think

Another central teaching skill is the ability to get students to think. All along I have affirmed that the ability to think clearly is the most crucial skill a student can acquire. Before I was talking about it as a fundamentally important school-going capability. But it is also a vital "life-going" ability. There is a lot of talk these days in education about "survival skills." This usually refers to such abilities as being able to maintain an accurate checkbook balance, fill out a job application form, read a newspaper, or repair a broken appliance. My reading of survival needs in modern America shows that these skills are undoubtedly valuable, but they cannot stand up in importance to the ability to use the brain. Educators need to keep inviting students to learn to use their minds, even if they seem predisposed not to. If we in the schools do not get students to think, for many young people there is no one else who will. An employer, for example, is more likely to give them a dead-end job with little money or prestige, or no job at all, than try to teach them to make decisions or process information.

The question is: How do you go about getting students to think? For a variety of cultural, social, and personal reasons some students do not think very well. The "upside" of this situation is that I believe human beings are natural thinkers. We are genetically predisposed to think. It has been passed down through the evolutionary process. Our ancestors way, way back, in the caves, were the ones who could figure out how to get what they needed and avoid getting eaten up, because they were certainly not the biggest and fastest creatures around. Our environments sometimes dampen that tendency to think; but it is there as a predilection, even if it needs refinement and development. Thus we are not fighting an impossible battle trying to get kids to think, no matter how resistant they may seem.

There is much good literature on the teaching of thinking. One good source is *Developing Minds: A Resource Book for Teaching Thinking* edited by Arthur Costa.[4] Do look into this literature. What I can do here is share is the way I go about teaching thinking. I believe it is a fairly simple, manageable system. In contrast, I have found that some of the strategies offered for teaching students to think are quite involved and difficult to implement amid the hustle and bustle of the ongoing work in schools. Anyway, I have put together a manageable model. See what you think about the ideas.

Top Three of Bloom Plus Personal Meaning

In planning curriculum with an eye to promoting thinking I make use of Bloom's Taxonomy, as it is called, plus one additional thinking category. This "taxonomy—plus one" orientation gives me direction in devising student assignments, discussion topics, and so forth, that promote critical thought. The system says to me: "Here is what thinking is about. Now your creative task it to, one way

or another, get students to do this.'' To explain, Bloom has developed a categorization scheme which describes ways of thinking, ranking them from least to most
sophisticated.[5] Perhaps you know of it. If anything in educational theory has gotten through to the masses it is Bloom's Taxonomy.

I work with the top three levels of Bloom's rankings, which are—from lowest
to highest—analysis, synthesis, and evaluation. I do not bother viewing these hierarchically, however. I deal with them as if they are equally valuable processes
for students to undertake. The following definitions (to these "top three" I add
one more category) may depart from Bloom somewhat, but in my words this
is the sense I make out of each of these processes:

Analysis. This has to do with figuring out something on your own, i.e., you
cannot be just repeating what you read or heard. It is seeing how something
works. You discern what is connected to what. You get at why something
is happening. You break it down and the result is, "Oh, this is what's going
on."

Synthesis. If analysis is taking things apart to see what makes them tick, synthesis is putting things together. And again, this is on your own. Synthesis
is solving a problem, making something whole out of a bunch of pieces nobody told you how to put together, or creating or devising something.

Evaluation. This is deciding on your own, and in an informed way, whether
something is preferable; whether it has merit or worth; or whether it is morally right, just, or fair.

Personal Meaning. This is reflection on the personal significance, consequence, or implication of some object of concern. Whatever we are talking
about or studying, what does it mean to me?

Operationally, in my work thinking comprises these four categories. The
challenge becomes one of devising work for students to do (step 2 of the planning format) that will involve them in analyzing, synthesizing, evaluating, or deriv-
ing personal meaning. Perhaps I should, but I do not make it a point to get students
involved in all four processes over a particular span of time. I am content with
making sure students are engaged with one of these four at any point. Frankly,
I cannot always tell which category students are in, whether they are analyzing
or synthesizing, and so forth. But I can feel when the students are "in the ball-
park," employing these four taken as a whole, versus being "out in the parking
lot," if you know what I mean. All involve students who engage in content which
is *problematic*: something does not make sense or go together; and through thinking
about it the students get it straight or clear for themselves.

An example: Let's say I am teaching about America's involvement in World
War II. Using these categories what might I ask students to do? I might present
them a description of Franklin Delano Roosevelt's actions toward the Japanese
and ask students to figure out his policies and motivations (analysis). Or assign

them to devise a better way to have fought the war in Europe (synthesis). Or to assess the actions of Truman at the Potsdam Conference (evaluation). Or to decide what difference World War II having occurred as it did makes to them (personal meaning). Resolving these issues can take the form of written or oral reports, group assignments, they can be classroom discussion topics, panel topics, questions to orient students when watching a film, and so forth.

Try an example of your own. Think of something you teach or are going to teach. Now think of two examples of good work for students to do that will involve the use of each of these four categories of thinking: analysis, synthesis, evaluation, and personal meaning. See if you can get comfortable with the four. Apart from all that, it is enough for me if you simply get a feel for the distinction between thinking as I have operationalized it and a fact recall or recitation process ("When did the Korean War start?").

Get Students to Use Lanaguage

It is empowering to learn to use the English language. It is crucial for life in our society that people know how to use words and sentences to describe things in their internal and external world that give them explicit meaning; to gain insight from written and spoken language; and to communicate through language with facility. And I am speaking of the *English* language here. In my view there is a standard form of the English language that, whatever else you can do, you had better learn to use well if you want to live effectively in this country. This is to say that it ought to be a primary goal to develop the capacity of every student to employ language excellently. We should use every chance we get to have students use language: reading it, writing it, and speaking it. I do not mean just listening to it, which students get to do a lot, especially the group we are talking about in this book.

There is some good literature in this area of language arts education. English professors of methods of instruction are a good source of references. A good place to start reading is the Carnegie Report on Secondary Education in America, which declares that language should be the first curricular priority in the secondary school.[6] This is a big, complicated issue that requires intense study. What I can do here is throw out a few suggestions for your consideration.

One thing we could do to help students learn to use language is, to put it bluntly, shut up. Teachers talk, talk, talk all the time. And if we are talking, students are not talking, simple as that. One way to check on yourself in this regard is to audiotape one of your lessons in which you want students to talk. On the basis of the tape, simply run a check of the percentage of time you talk and the percentage of time students talk. If you run true to the norm established by the research, it is 75% you, 25% all students combined. This is not good. If anything, it should be the reverse. But whatever the outcome, keep taping and work at getting their percentage up and yours down. It saddens me that many of the students who most need to learn how to be heard in the world do not get the chance in school. They are considered unable or unwilling to express themselves. So the teacher, who most always has one more thing to say in any case, talks on, shows the movies, monitors silent reading (which in itself is not a bad idea), and passes out the worksheets.

Getting students to communicate their thoughts and exchange with one another can be extremely difficult with some students. We may not be able to get some students to do it. But that does not mean we have to stop trying. We can show them how to do it and continue to invite them to participate in serious talk. The school year may run out—and the year following. But we still cannot stop trying whatever we think is necessary to get students to say what is true for them.

One suggestion in this regard, I have a "ask three times and you shall receive" rule I go by when trying to get a response out of students. My notion is that if you ask anybody anything, by the third invitation they are willing to tell you. Test it out for yourself. Also, I am not above rigging verbal participation. I have had success by telling a nonparticipating student privately: "Tomorrow, I'm going to ask who was right on the slavery issue, Lincoln or Douglas. What I want is for you to raise your hand and answer it, OK? So get ready tonight." I have never had a turndown on that invitation. And then the next day, after the student response, I flash him a little knowing eye contact as he walks out the door to communicate, "Hey, I caught what you did. Good for you, good for us." The point is I am willing to do anything to get students to talk, and that includes calling on them, assigning oral reports, setting up panel discussions, anything. I do not want students sitting silently in the world, and I tell them that.

The same goes with reading, writing, and listening for students. Instruct them in how to do it. Continue to invite them. Encourage, acknowledge, appreciate, praise, and support them. To a student, the message: "If you cannot do it now, I will do anything I can to support you getting to a place where you can do it. I will not back off on this ever, because there is nothing more important for you than to learn to use language." Again, refer to English methods books for procedures. Or you can use your own common sense as to how to proceed. Most important, get it into your head that these kids, even the reluctant ones, are going to learn to use our language well.

Whatever They Study
Should Be Crucial Material

Some educators tend to set off content against process. By content I mean *what* is being studied as opposed to process or *how* it is learned. Content refers to the topics, issues, or subjects that provide the substance of the course. It is what the course deals with, whether it is algebra, geometry, general science, physics, poetry, drama, the Colonial Period, or the contemporary popular culture. At times educators downplay the importance of content. Some school people contend that how a student encounters material, how the student goes about his or her work, is more important educationally than *what* the student studies. And some teachers like to say, "I don't teach subjects, I teach kids." In contrast, some educators say content is the main thing. There is material students need to know and our job is to get it to them, period. Tell it to them, drill it into them. Anything that gets it into their heads.

My response to this is that it is a false issue. We do not have to choose between process, kids, and content. We can value all three equally. In the next chapter I outline what I consider to be the best content for students. I just want to make the point here that I think it makes a self-evident difference whether students are studying the climate of the Yukon or the American economic system. Whatever content students study, we ought to be convinced that there is nothing more compelling of their consideration at this moment. I say this because I sense we give over more time to deciding how we are going to teach it than we do in pondering just what the it ought to be.

Dialogue with Them

Another instructional idea is the process of dialogue. It is a technique that you will not read about in the methods of instruction literature—at least I have not. A *dialogue* is not a discussion in the sense that a teacher throws out a question, fields the replies, and works toward a clarification or resolution. A dialogue, instead, is a "talking with" about serious matters. You tell me what is inside you that counts most about some vital concern—your ideas, hopes, plans, experiences—and I will do the same. I am not leading you. I am not defining myself as being better than you in this exchange, even though I am older and perhaps know more. What is important is that we share what is there for us regarding this important area. What we will aim for is to understand ourselves and each other better, to express ourselves to others, and to be clearer about where things go from here. Dialogue is not centered on the fact that one knows and one does not know, or that one is superior and the other subordinate, as is the case in most teaching situations. Rather, it is a sharing of our most central thoughts and feelings as a human being (in contrast to "school-talk": externalized opinions and ideas that are not really connected to who we are as people).

It seems clear to me that the kind of classroom of my vision would be characterized by dialogue. Dialogue is a natural outgrowth of a class centered on the work of students to exceed their own previous standards. For the teacher, dialogue depends on a willingness to be with—not above—students. It is saying "I'll tell you and you tell me." But do note that I am not saying that teachers are no different from students or on a par with them. Teachers are older and presumably wiser and probably have greater insight. And given their role as teacher, their ideas will undoubtedly have more influence. But beyond those inequalities there is the larger equality of our shared humanity—and that is the grounding for a dialogical exchange.

Deal with Right and Wrong

Moral and ethical concerns are inherent in any area of study and to teach well is to promote student consideration of these concerns. By moral I mean matters of rightness, fairness, goodness, justice, and decency. I have always been somewhat uncertain regarding the difference, if any, between morals and ethics. I have concluded that when the term *ethics* is used, it is usually referring to a code of conduct or to conduct itself (as opposed to moral ideas or principles on which it is based). Not the clearest distinction perhaps, and there is overlap between the two concepts; and the theorists I have read and spoken to are not particularly predisposed to slowing down and defining terms. You may be able to do better than I have here.

As with the other areas we have discussed, educational literature contains some highly sophisticated schemes for dealing with moral and ethical issues. Particularly, you may want to investigate the writings of Harvard cognitive psychologist Lawrence Kohlberg and his followers which deal with the way moral reasoning strategies can be used in your classes.[7] But apart from that, as teachers, we can simply make it a point to identify and raise moral-ethical issues: Was that right? What do you think is fair? Where does justice lie in this instance? And why do you think as you do? Ask those kinds of questions, either in discussion or by building them into assignments. Keep inviting, and then wait for an answer. Get as many students to respond as possible. The ideal is that whatever students say is *informed*. That is, the result of rigorous study of themselves and what others—writers, theorists, other people they encounter in their lives—have to say on the particular issue. When students become clear on their views a teacher can say, ''Tell me one way you can put what you believe into practice,'' and then help them do it.

There is a question about whether teachers should share their own moral views on particular issues with students. In my opinion, if it will not detract from the students' own confrontation with these issues, yes, go ahead. But if it is going to short-circuit this healthy struggle among students to work these matters through for themselves, my view is that teachers should tell students that our highest priority is to encourage independent thinking in them. And then hold back our own views. Teachers can say that when we are assured that students are truly taking on these issues, then, indeed, we look forward to expressing moral views. However, we can always let students know we are committed to, and want them to be committed to, high standards of fairness, generosity, tolerance of others, and respect for ourselves as individuals.

Kindness, Respect, and Decency

Beyond all that has been said, a teacher can bring some basic human qualities to a classroom. There is simple kindness and respect for students. We can be decent people who will never betray students or our responsibility to do what is in their interest. No matter what else happens, whether they learn from us or not, we can give them those things.⌐

So much more could be said. I do hope you pick up teaching ideas elsewhere in this book. Though, with just what has been outlined in this section you should have a picture of what I consider to be good teaching. Of course it must be underscored that I was referring mostly to what teachers *do*. I paid less attention to what teachers *know* and *are*. I think they should know the field well that they are teaching; that goes without saying. I also believe they should bring a strong background in the liberal arts to teaching. And last, I think they should be people of character, individuals worthy of the trust society places in them by putting them with their children. Teachers should work to be the kind of people who not only *point the way* for students but *are the way*, or at least *a* way, to live one's life with dignity in America.

A CRITIQUE OF TECHNOLOGIES OF TEACHING

It is important to spend some time reviewing what can be called a teaching technologies (another term, instructional technologies) approach to working with students. Many consider this orientation to hold special promise for dealing with the students of concern in this book. An example, in his report, the prominent educator John Goodlad conducted a large scale study of schooling in America, and noted that schools are not necessarily ideal places for even the most successful students. Along with other recommendations, Goodlad endorsed mastery learning, an approach to teaching which typifies what I am calling the technological orientation:

> My concerns are magnified, however, on turning to that larger group of students who do not grow up in academically oriented households, or who experience cumulative difficulties with school-based learning, or who are not turned on by academics, or who simply cannot or do not wish to defer employment. The academic program is much less "for them." There is evidence to suggest payoff for these students from intervention programs that comprehensively include a frequent use of motivational devices, alternative approaches to learning, and that whole array of assumptions and techniques subsumed under the concept of mastery learning.[8]

Later in what has become known as the Goodlad Report, Goodlad cited two particular advantages of the mastery learning strategy. Mastery learning has the potential for counteracting the practice of ability grouping which he (and I, more on that elsewhere) finds detrimental to students sorted into the "lower" groups. Also, he considered mastery learning, properly used, to diminish the need for corrective work with students, thus freeing up teachers' and students' time for enrichment activities and elective study.

The theorist I most associate with mastery learning is Benjamin Bloom (of

Bloom's Taxonomy fame, mentioned earlier). I refer to Bloom's ideas in this section, but for an in-depth consideration of the mastery learning approach refer to his writings. Also, a book I have found useful is *Implementing Mastery Learning* by Thomas Guskey.[9] In this section I critique both the ideas associated with Bloom and those of another prominent educational theorist, Madeline Hunter. Hunter's strategies have also been praised for their usefulness with "lower" students. Although Hunter and Bloom are similar in many ways, they are dissimilar as well. What ties the two together in my mind is that both call for the development of a *technology of teaching* (a term I define as we go along). By focusing on these two educators I am not trying so much to make you familiar with their ideas—that is beyond the scope of this book. Rather, my comments on Bloom and Hunter serve to explicate my reactions to the instructional technologies orientation itself; particularly as it applies to the students of our concern here. At the same time, I hope this discussion provides you with an example of how the ideas I outlined in the first part of this chapter, and throughout the book, can be used to make assessments of trends and proposals in the field.

A last point before moving on, note in the last paragraph I said I was going to review ideas *associated* with Bloom and Hunter. What I was getting at there is that to understand the impact of any theorist in education, or in any discipline for that matter, you must speculate on not only what the theorist actually says, but also what people *think* he or she says. A movement centering on a theorist's ideas includes both the ideas themselves and the interpretations (including misinterpretations) of those ideas. In fact, in terms of influence on practice in classrooms, what teachers and other translators of these ideas think they mean, plus the ideas that followers knowingly or unknowingly add of their own, are actually more important than what the theorist really says. Or, I should say, what the theorists really *said*. Because it is not what a theorist is saying now that is getting implemented in schools. Noting the time it takes to have things published and then considering time for diffusion and implementation, once it gets into practice, the theorist is usually working on something else. Thus theory-to-practice always involves a time lag as well as distortion as concepts filter through the interpretations and add-ons of others. This is an especially significant point in Bloom's case, as he is saying some things lately that practitioners, including some of his avid followers, have not caught on to yet.

Neither Bloom nor Hunter are new to education. In fact, both have been working in the field a long time. Bloom is professor emeritus at Northwestern University, and for many years Hunter was involved in the laboratory school at UCLA. As you will see in my sketch of the ideas of each, while they differ in significant ways, they have much in common at the level of fundamental assumptions and values, and this connects them within this technological perspective. Both ground their work in behavioral science with its emphasis on quantitative, empirical research and the objective verification of the effectiveness of any intervention strategy. Both seek to use the investigatory methods of the social sciences to derive scientifically proven principles and theories to guide practice in schools. Both have little faith in what can be called "armchair philosophizing" or personal experience-based conclusions about what is going on in classrooms or will work with students. Instead, their focus is on conducting objective, statistically verifiable tests of reality, and then letting the data speak for themselves.

There is a fundamental optimism in both Bloom and Hunter (and, as I am using these two writers as illustrative, overall among those who adhere to a technological frame of reference). Teaching is *understandable*, not an elusive art that can be appreciated but never fathomed, as some have contended. This understanding comes from the scientific, controlled study of the processes of teaching and learning. Out of this study, just as in other disciplines, are developed tested principles and theories. There is created a science of teaching. Science makes the outcomes of teaching predictable. Science makes good teaching replicable. If these research-verified concepts and procedures are applied in classrooms, learning *will* occur. There are teaching strategies that work! As teachers we do not have to live with the fond hope of being blessed by the universe so that we "have it," the magic something that makes us good teachers. The scientific test can provide practical, results-getting answers for all of us to employ. A corollary to this optimism about the possibility of finding a teaching approach that works is the faith that with the proper teaching all children can and will learn. If we find the right teaching approach, even the most reluctant and heretofore unsuccessful students can be turned around. I think you can see how welcome a message this is in a profession that can get quite pessimistic about its prospects of success.

One reason for the recent popularity of the theories of Bloom and Hunter is their compatibility with the "effective schools" movement. The effective schools movement was particularly prominent in the early years of this decade, though its influence remains in the later 1980s.[10] The effective schools advocates did what their name implies: provided a definition of the characteristics of effective schools. Among these characteristics, at least as generally understood, were such elements as clarity of academic goals, emphasis on basic skills, "direct teaching" (teachers assuming a clear responsibility for taking charge of the learning process; expository, teacher-telling, methods), and frequent monitoring and evaluation of student progress. Both Bloom and Hunter have provided ways for effective schools advocates to create these classroom conditions that they associate with the kind of school they favor.

But beyond their general prominence these days, it is important to discuss Bloom and Hunter, and the technological orientation to teaching they exemplify, because wherever unsuccessful students are being discussed, someone is bound to propose a curricular and instructional strategy that will at least have the feel of this orientation. With that in mind, I sketch out some of Bloom's and Hunter's concepts as a prelude to an analysis of this way of teaching "lower" students.

I must say at the outset, my conclusion is that I do not write off their usefulness entirely; they do have their place. But I do have serious reservations about adapting this kind of teaching as *the* way to go. With that, I now move to a brief sketch of the central ideas I associate with the two theorists.

Bloom's Ideas

Bloom's concerns center primarily on the learning side of the teaching-learning endeavor. His work calls for us to attend to the learnings students demonstratively achieve, more than to the teaching act itself, as is so often the primary focus. However, I do not want to seem to be implying that Bloom sets teaching off against learning and gives all of his time to learning outcomes. He is also deeply concerned with what teachers do to elicit learning among their students. It is only to underscore that the approach associated with Bloom is mastery *learning* and not mastery teaching.

A major responsibility for a teacher within the mastery learning model is to be very clear on the learning objectives for students. The teacher needs to resolve the question of what exactly students are to learn so that everyone concerned knows what is expected, and also to give direction to instructional and evaluative activities. The question that drives this emphasis on specificity of purpose is how, if you do not know where you want students to go, can you decide what to do to get them there or know whether or not they have arrived? There is a tendency within this model to break down large, inclusive aims and goals into small, discrete objectives that are stated behaviorally. By behaviorally, I mean the learning objective is framed in the form of a description of what the student will do, or be able to do, if the learning objective is attained. Learning tasks are made small and manageable to the greatest degree possible; for one reason, in order to maximize the chance that students will be successful with them. What results, usually, is a long series of discrete learning tasks. Each is circumscribed and manageable, so there is a high probability of achievement by students as they proceed objective-by-objective through the list.

Mastery learning replaces the usual final-test-at-the-end arrangement with a series of "formative evaluations." The idea here is to follow each learning step with an evaluation to check to see whether the student has been successful in attaining a particular learning objective. Depending on that formative evaluation (in this model the final test is called a "summative evaluation"), the student either goes on in the learning sequence to complete the next objective or a corrective measure is taken to help the student successfully meet the objective that is giving him trouble. What this comes down to is being very clear on what is to be learned and staying with each objective until the student learns it. Since the objectives and the sequence of learning activities are predetermined, and there is the faith that all children can and will learn, the key variable is time. Some students will get it right off and some will take longer; but they *will* get it. Students do it until they get it right is another way to say it.

Loren Anderson summarized the learning for mastery model as follows:

1. Clearly specified learning objectives.
2. Short, highly valid assessment procedures.
3. Preset mastery performance standards.
4. A sequence of learning units, each comprised of an integral set of facts, contents, principles, and skills.
5. Provision of feedback of learning progress to students.
6. Provision of additional time and help to correct specified problems and misunderstandings of students who are failing to achieve the preset mastery learning standards.[11]

To this list I would add a seventh: teachers are ready to provide enrichment activities for students who quickly accomplish the expected learning objectives. Anderson has written an excellent analysis of Bloom's work in a book edited by Margaret Wang and Herbert Walberg, *Adapting Instruction to Individual Differences*, which you can read if you want to go further into this subject.[12]

Bloom's theories have been widely used in a variety of contexts, from special education to advanced courses in science, and in both elementary and secondary schools. To cite a few examples, Baltimore and several other Maryland cities are using mastery learning to teach mathematics, science, and social studies. In New York City, 46 high schools use this approach. When I worked in Los Angeles several years ago I saw this kind of strategy employed in secondary schools called continuation schools, established for students who had difficulty in regular high schools. Gaining particular attention has been the Chicago school system's investment of 5 years and 8 million dollars to implement a mastery learning reading program for its elementary school students. Up in my area, a number of school districts have joined together in a network to help themselves implement what they term ''outcomes-based'' approaches that lean heavily on the mastery learning perspective for their inspiration. Many other examples could be listed. I am sure you can learn first-hand about mastery learning in a school near you.

To continue your study of Bloom, refer to any of the sources I list in the notes.[13] Notice especially in his later writings—*Developing Talent In Young People* an example—Bloom's emphasis on higher mental processes, the playful exploration of fields of interest, the importance of the home environment, and student interest and commitment as crucial to successful schooling. Concerns such as these are what I was talking about a while back when I said that sometimes followers do not always keep track of the directions the thinking of their leader takes. Instead, followers operate on what the theorist may have said some time ago, or think he said. Or, they may select only certain aspects of what he said; or color what he says so much with their own views that the theory is distorted; or use the theory in a rigid way when it was intended to be but a guide to be used flexibly in practice; or employ the theorist's strategy as an across-the-board method rather than seeing it as one approach among several, useful in certain circumstances and not in others. I am afraid Bloom's advocates have done him in some in all these ways.

Hunter's Ideas

Whereas Bloom's system focuses on the sequencing and monitoring of student learning activities, Hunter's work centers on the act of teaching. She sees the teacher as the vital element in the classroom. To her, the teacher is most fundamentally a decision-maker. With that as Hunter's central premise, she has created a conceptual structure of the areas of teaching to use as a frame of reference and guide by teachers as they make their choices. Hunter sees teaching as an applied science, derived from research findings in the disciplines of psychology, neurology, sociology, and anthropology. Drawing upon data generated from these fields, as well as empirical (observed, statistical) research in education itself, Hunter has defined what she calls the "total teaching act." This total teaching act includes the elements of instruction, human relations, content (subject matter understanding on the part of the teacher), planning, and classroom management. As you will notice, Hunter's concerns go beyond instruction to include other elements of the teacher's responsibility. Though, in my experience it has been her writings on instruction that have drawn the most attention from school people attempting to make use of her ideas.

In her later writings Hunter centered her analysis on three decision contexts directly related to classroom instruction: content, learner behavior, and teacher behavior. These three categories provide a conceptual "scaffolding" for the description, evaluation, and improvement of instruction:

1. *Content*. Are the teacher's decisions about the degree of difficulty and the complexity of content to be learned (cognitive, affective, or psychomotor) appropriate for the learners? If the learner has made the content decision, is it achievable in the foreseeable future, or is that learner's level of aspiration too low or too high? Regardless of who made it, a content decision that is "over the learner's head," because its attainment is highly improbable, or "under the learner's feet," because that learning requires very little effort or has already been attained, constitutes a pedagogical error for which the teacher is responsible. For example, is it appropriate that a particular learner participate in a discussion, or should he or she be learning to guide or summarize the discussion, or be learning to listen without interfering with the discussion?

2. *Learner behavior*. Is what the learner is doing in order to learn appropriate not only to the learning to be achieved but also to that learner? Does observable behavior validate that learning has occurred? For example, if discussion skills are the objective, are ways of successfully acquiring those skills available to the

learner in a mode he or she can assimilate? Is there behavioral validation that simpler skills have been acquired before more complex skills are introduced? Does the learner eventually demonstrate productive participation in a discussion?

3. *Teacher behavior decisions.* What evidence indicates the teacher is using principles of learning to accelerate achievement? Or, is the teacher unaware of or abusing those principles by overuse or omission? For example, is the teacher linking new learning to students' past knowledge and experience to make new learning meaningful and its acquisition enhanced by transfer? Is the teacher testing the meaningfulness of new learning by encouraging students to generate examples from their own lives? Is the teacher regularly reinforcing productive new behavior when it emerges, but changing to an intermittent schedule of reinforcement for productive behavior that is not new? Or is the teacher committing pedagogical errors by persevering with potential reinforcers that are not needed, hammering in meaning when there is evidence it already is present, massing practice for fast learning, but forgetting to distribute that practice for long-term retention?[14]

This should give you a feel for what I am calling a technological approach to teaching. Note the writing style, the language, the attitude toward teaching here. As you might expect this rather scientific tone has been very attractive to many educators in search of greater precision and predictability—and pride—in their professional lives.

Hunter grounds her thinking about instruction on two assumptions. The first is that learning is by its nature incremental. That is, learnings build one upon the other, with basic learnings proceeding and providing the support for later, more complex learnings. The second is that instruction must be guided by research-tested principles and theories that explain the level of student motivation to learn, the rate and amount of learning, retention of learning, and the ability to transfer learning to new situations where it applies. In addition to these foundational assumptions there is another major concern: time. Hunter sees time as a currency of sorts that must be invested wisely to purchase learning. This attention to time has made Hunter extremely attractive to the effective school advocates mentioned earlier, who themselves place great emphasis on the actual time students spent ''on task,'' as they call it.

Hunter asked five questions of the teacher which should give you a good sense of the way she views teaching:

1. Is the instructional process proceeding toward a perceivable objective? She wants teaching that is purposeful.
2. Is the instructional objective at the right level of difficulty for the learners who are investing time? The teacher must see that each learning step is indeed the best one—not too easy or too hard.
3. Is there a constant monitoring of the degree of achievement of the objec-

tive so redundance or acceleration can be built into the instructional process? She uses the metaphor of "dip sticking" to describe a process of checking on learning achievement and pace. The results of this process are the basis for adjusting teaching methods where necessary.

4. In which ways are the time and energy expended by the learner and teacher consonant with principles of efficient and effective learning? There are scientifically validated principles of learning. There is a science of pedagogy. Learn it and adhere to it. [15]

Note the cross-over between Hunter and Bloom. Her first three questions are consistent with Bloom's stress on specificity of learning objectives. In fact, Hunter uses Bloom's taxonomy of intellectual difficulty and complexity as a way to assess the appropriateness of objectives (question 2). Her "dip sticking" in question 3 is similar to formative evaluation in mastery learning. Question 4 and its concern with time parallel's Bloom's. And the base-what-we-do-on-research emphasis in Hunter's question 5 is shared by Bloom.

Hunter is perhaps best known for a basic, all-purpose lesson design she calls the "basic white sauce of teaching." She intends this to be—to stay with the metaphor—a basic recipe creative cooks can use to bake up elaborate culinary delights in the classroom:

1. *Anticipatory set.* Has the teacher developed in the students a mental set that causes them to focus on what will be learned? An anticipatory set may also give some practice in helping students achieve the learning and yield diagnostic data for the teacher. *Example*: "Look at the paragraph on the board. What do you think might be the most important part to remember?"

2. *Objective and purpose.* Not only do students *learn* more effectively when they know what they're supposed to be learning and why that learning is important to them, but teachers *teach* more effectively when they have that same information. Consequently, in words that are meaningful to the students, the teacher often states what will be learned and how it will be useful. *Example*: "Frequently people have difficulty in remembering things that are important to them. Sometimes you feel you have studied hard and yet you don't remember some of the important parts. Today, we're going to learn ways to identify what's important, and then we'll practice ways we can use to remember important things."

3. *Input.* Students must acquire new information about the knowledge, process, or skill they are to achieve. Regardless of whether that information comes from discovery, discussion, reading, listening, observing, or being told, the teacher must have task-analyzed the final objective to identify knowledge and skills that need to be acquired. Only then can the input phase of the lesson be designed so that a successful outcome becomes predictable.

4. *Modeling.* "Seeing" what is meant is an important adjunct to learning.

Usually, it is facilitating for the learners to directly perceive the process or product they are expected to acquire or produce. So that creativity will not be stifled or generalizability impeded, several examples should be a routine part of most (not all) lessons. Demonstrations, live or filmed, of process and products are facilitating rather than restricting to student initiative and creativity.

5. *Checking for understanding.* Before students are expected to do something, it is wise to ascertain that they understand what it is they're supposed to do and that they have the minimum skills required to do so. Sometimes this checking occurs verbally before actual student action. Sometimes it occurs simultaneously with the next element.

6. *Guided practice.* Students practice their new knowledge or skill *under direct teacher supervision.* New learning is like wet cement; it is easily damaged. An error at the beginning of learning can easily "set" so that it is harder to eradicate than had it been apprehended immediately.

7. *Independent practice.* Independent practice is assigned only after the teacher is reasonably sure that students will not make serious errors. After an initial lesson, students frequently are not ready to practice independently, and the teacher has committed a pedagogical error if unsupervised practice is expected.[16]

Many schools and school districts have drawn inspiration from Hunter's work. An example, Newport News, Virginia school district personnel have developed what they call a "lesson line" that provides a basic structure for most lessons that teachers implement.[17] Included, in order, are an explanation by the teacher to provide new content; teacher questions of the students to check for their understanding of what the teacher has presented; responses by the teacher to reinforce and correct student understanding; student activity to practice using the new learning; and teacher response to outcomes of student practice, again to both correct and reinforce student efforts.

I hope this gives you a beginning sense of the Hunter approach to teaching. To go beyond this initial sketch, refer to sources listed in the notes section.[18]

My Reaction

I would like to describe my reactions to Bloom and Hunter and this general orientation to teaching. To keep our terms straight I refer to Bloom's approach as *mastery learning* and Hunter's as *mastery teaching.* Other terms that are used in the literature are outcomes-based instruction (which I associate with Bloom), learning for mastery (Bloom), and effective teaching (Hunter).

First to some positive aspects of these approaches to teaching. And certainly there are some things to like about them. For one thing they force us to be clear about our objectives for students. They do not let us get away with "covering

216 A CRITIQUE OF TECHNOLOGIES OF TEACHING

the chapter'' or "discussing the Civil War" as the purpose for the lesson. Both Bloom and Hunter insist that we state precisely what students are going to get out of a particular lesson: precisely what skills, what understandings, what attitudes, are students going to acquire? This insistence provides a good counterbalance to our tendency in education to focus on means at the expense of ends. That is, we are prone when critiquing ourselves to ask questions such as: "Was this an interesting lesson?" "Did students participate in the discussion?" "Was my lecture well-organized and presented?" Bloom and Hunter force us to turn from how we did to the point of it all: what did students learn?

Also, both Bloom and Hunter insist on an understanding among teachers of what students already know before designing learning and teaching activities for them. So often we proceed ahead without enough concern for students who might lack the requisite prior knowledge or skill to learn what we are teaching them. Or, just as bad, students may already know what we plan to teach them. What they need in that case is to go on to something new.

Another advantage, and this is a major one as I see it, is that mastery learning may be a good way to individualize learning opportunities for students. It especially provides an effective means for students who are behind in basic skills to get the remedial help they need and to remain in mixed ability classes.

Mastery approaches have also been shown to be a good way to provide students with success experiences who may have known very few of them in their school career. These strategies provide a way to break learning down into very small, manageable pieces with achievement exceedingly likely; and then rewarding or reinforcing each student "victory" along the way. These success experiences can prove highly useful in motivating students who are discouraged by their history of unsuccessful attempts to learn. Mastery learning and teaching may be a good way to get heretofore unsuccessful students moving in a positive direction. If they can go some distance in breaking the discouragement cycle, as evidence indicates they can, that is a major contribution to the field. For one thing, research has found that discouragement over school failure is one of the primary reasons for school dropouts.[19] Yes, this is a major contribution.

These strategies provide teachers with a way to organize our work. They demystify teaching. They define the territory or, as my father used to put it, "the lay of the land." To their adherents, teaching is not an unknowable art form that people gain through grace. Teaching is not simply a gift that can only be gloried in when it happens and talked about anecdotally and suggestively in the most general terms. Teachers do not have to spend their professional lives waiting to receive the "gift" of teaching ability and/or rue their misfortune that they are not a, as they say, "born teacher." While both Bloom and Hunter, especially Hunter, acknowledge that there is an element of art to teaching, they nevertheless stress that teaching is a set of identifiable and learnable teaching skills that even those of us who are not educational geniuses can pick up quite readily. You can imagine how encouraging that is for teachers to hear.

Mastery approaches give us clear, readily discernable constructs and theories that describe what teaching is about. They give us an understandable step-by-step process for developing and implementing curriculum, and criteria for judging the effectiveness of our work. They provide a conceptual framework which defines the areas for further study and research. These approaches provide us a link to other teachers who we now can see clearly do what we do. Teaching can be such a lonely profession without others with whom to identify. And all of this leads to teachers feeling more professional and prideful in what they do: "Yes, *this* is what I do as a professional. Yes, I *am* a professional." It is important not to underestimate the value of the pride enhancement and increased sense of professional identity that results for many who employ mastery approaches. This is a real gift to a profession which may internalize much of the disparagement that comes our way.

For many teachers mastery models provide great encouragement because they work! They get results! Students actually learn! It is a wonderful experience to think and feel this after working in a profession characterized by negative reports and "no significant difference" research findings for so long. It is hard to miss the optimism and positive outlook among the instructional technologies advocates. Clearly, they are focused on success and not failure. Clearly, they believe, and see evidence to support their belief, that all students can and will learn. So if you put all these elements together—greater clarity regarding the teaching act, heightened professionalism, optimism and enhanced morale—you can get some sense of why these approaches call up the fervent support they do among many educators.

Some Problems I See With This Orientation

My comments include reference to both the mastery theory and practice. To gain the greatest level of insight into any educational approach or movement we need to understand the dynamic interplay of theory and practice. We cannot look only at the theory, because ultimately, the theory results in practice. So we have to see how the theory directs classroom practices. What actually results from these theoretical formulations? And of course we cannot just ignore theory and look only at practice, as some in education advocate. Because whatever the practice, it is directed by some, tacit at least, theory of what is going on and what is worth doing. Really, we have to engage in vigorous reflection on theory and practice as a single entity, comprehending the reciprocal relationship between these elements within this larger whole. And, even more, we need to understand how this theory–practice complex interacts with other elements in the schooling process: among them, choice of goals and content, employment of other instructional methodologies, organizational and leadership practices, and human relationships. So it is from this theory-practice unit frame of reference that I discuss some features of mastery teaching and learning that give me pause.

I start with a summary statement of my reservations: Mastery approaches, this entire technology of teaching orientation, tend to prop up the very practices that

I have identified as the villains in the education of less successful students. You have heard it before: Too much teacher initiative and not enough student initiative. Teachers talking, giving directions, asking low-level factual questions; students silent or speaking in terse, clipped phrases, or jabbering away with friends in an attempt to entertain themselves. Learning becomes trivialized, as today's lesson is centered on some isolated and unimportant subject that happens to lend itself well to the mastery format. Instead of problems and issues to engage, tasks to complete and check off; and without any allowance for difference in student need and interest, so that everyone learns the same thing. The image I have is one of students, individually and with little emotional investment in the enterprise or sense of its meaningfulness, plugging away dutifully at completing today's objective. There is too little student choice, exploration, or creative challenge. There is too little opportunity for students to collaborate, develop facility with language, and work with ideas. There is not enough chance for students to write or say what they deeply care about. In sum, classrooms are all too teacher dominated, mechanical, and pedestrian for my blood. Whatever gains may result from mastery learning—and, remember the last section, they are significant—too often they are purchased at the expense of pointing us away from what really matters in education, that students learn how to take charge of their own learning and growth and empower themselves to live freely. What compounds these problems for me is that these tightly structured teaching strategies always seem to be especially suited to dealing with uninvolved and drifting students.

If that picture is to any extent accurate, and do check this out for yourself, why is it this case? What is there in the theories themselves, or in the manner in which they are interpreted or put into practice, that results in what I see as an undesirable state of affairs.

First, I hear a message in these mastery approaches telling teachers that they should assume control of the classroom. Teacher, it goes, figure out exactly what students are to learn and make sure they learn it. Just at a time when students have to be the primary causal agent in the classroom, these approaches say to a teacher that he or she, the teacher, is *the* element that makes things go. The students' job is to respond to what the teacher asks them to do. If there are enrichment activities, it is the teacher who will provide them. There is a top-down, "Chief and Indians" quality to these technological models. This is not only true in the teaching practices themselves, but also, in my experience, in the "Chief-like" way supervisors who buy into this approach act when they monitor teachers' work. My experience is admittedly limited in this regard, but the supervision by downtown office types and administrators I have encountered has not exactly been marked by collegiality and the promotion of dialogue, inquiry, and collaboration with teachers. There has been the word to teachers of the sort: "We [downtown, or in the principal's office] know what good teaching is and it is the policy here. If you work here, you do it our way. We will familiarize you with the prescribed model, and then we will observe you to assess the degree to which you can approximate it is your classroom.''

This is not a book on supervision, but I must say a word or two on this subject because this is something that a teacher or future teacher has to live with. Rather than a single best answer to instruction decided by somebody on high—me included—teachers ought to be given information and resources and trusted to do their job as they see fit. This is better than having an administrator, who may well know less than the teacher he or she is supervising, dictate the way to go. It is better to create a context in which teachers can help one another become more effective. Give them time during the week to discuss their work. Give them money for books and journals and consultant help. Encourage, support, acknowledge, and appreciate them. Allow them to be unique. Trust them. As a teacher I am very willing to talk *with* others about my work. But I do resent it when supervisors assume that they know more than I do, and that I should discard the results of my study and experience in education in favor of the revelation they have recently experienced.

Let us now explore the theoretical foundations of the mastery approaches in order to better understand why they work as they do. Since behavioral science provides a central underpinning to both mastery learning and mastery teaching, we need to analyze the nature of the social sciences. We particularly need to look at social science research strategies to see what practical effect they can have on the applied discipline of teaching. Remember, this perspective views teaching as an applied discipline, grounded in tested principles and practices derived from research in the social sciences and educational studies that emulate their research practices.

The major point I want to make is that the social sciences—well, all of science really, the natural sciences as well—tend to be reductionist. By reductionist I mean guided by the fundamental notion that in order to understand a large complex phenomenon, one needs to break it down into its component parts, which are smaller and more easily controlled and readily understood. In short, the large thing is reduced to a number of small things. The assumption is that it may well be too much to tackle understanding the whole thing. But you may be able to understand all the small things one at a time, and then add them up and make sense of the whole thing. This reduce-to-parts process has great value in science. Dealing with pieces of the whole allows for the careful, controlled (avoidance of extraneous influences) study of concrete reality. It allows for conclusions to be drawn from hard, tangible evidence and not simply from conjecture, and in turn these conclusions can be the basis for the development of principles and theories. These principles and theories tell us for certain what part of reality is like and, when integrated with other research-derived insights, begin to paint the "big picture." It is sort of like putting a jigsaw puzzle together piece by piece. That may all seem quite abstract, but consider this quote from Hunter that reflects this way of making sense of the world: "I break it [teaching] into small, meaningful pieces, pull out the key concepts, and check to see whether I know that before I move on."[20]

This reductionist tendency pervades the technological approach to teaching. Large goals and projects for students are broken into smaller segments. These smaller objectives and activities are then sequenced and taught to students. On the surface, that process makes logical sense, but upon close scrutiny the logic breaks down. One problem is that, unlike the scientist, the student does not bring the clear sense of the meaning or purpose to the particular task that elevates it to something more than a rote exercise. As a practical matter students are not, as they should be, engaged in the achievement of some objective from a perspective of, "I am trying to learn how to read and I need to gain control of this skill before I can learn the related and more advanced skills coming up." I am afraid it is more likely that from the student's perspective it is along the lines of, "It is 11:15 a.m. (25 minutes to lunch) and I have to get this worksheet done." The result of this is a system that makes abundant sense to the teacher and probably keeps students busy; but in the end, the work does not add up for students to much more than a collection of partly recalled, discrete understandings and skills.

Over and over in these approaches one sees this predilection to sequence little pieces to be learned one at a time. An extreme example, I read of a training program for teachers to teach them teaching skills consistent with this perspective that were doled out one at a time for 5 years. What is better than a "reductionist approach" is concurrent and dialectical attention to both the whole and the pieces. Human beings need to be able to comprehend what it is "all about" and deal with the matter in a total, holistic way. Humans need to be able to shift attention to a particular aspect of the matter under concern, all the while aware of the relationship of this aspect to other aspects and the overall concern. The human being is a problem solver. So while I am pointing out the need to attend to both wholes and parts, if I had to choose whether to begin with one or the other, I would say start with the whole. Start with the overall problem or project, not with the discrete elements. If human beings, for example, know they are building a house, have a design for it, and know what it will look like when done, then they will be more motivated to take on the job of constructing the kitchen cabinets with care, and in such a way as to complement the rest of the kitchen and the whole of the house. I am hard pressed to think of any examples in nature or the "real world" of work and human activity where we learn this little thing, check it off, and then to on to that little thing. Literally, the way we conduct schools is often, not in any malicious way I concede, antihuman. Despite the apparent success of these kinds of approaches, I believe ultimately they serve to deaden the human spirit. We need to be very careful in applying the methods of science to our work with human beings.

I have been told that there is nothing inherent in the technological strategies that prevents integrated, holistic activities and learnings. That may be true, but we must attend to what actually goes on. I do not see it happening. A major factor driving how things go in is the tendency for theory to become simplified in practice. A theory may be replete with qualifications, contingencies, and a healthy humility. But invariably, theoretical statements about "this *if* that" or "this *and* that" becomes "this is best *every time*," "this and *not that*." An example: The Chicago mastery learning program in reading that received so much national attention has been dropped. It seems, at least as the critics of the program charge, while the students were mastering all the component skills of reading—and getting pretty bored with the whole thing—they never got to read. Bloom himself is quoted by E.R. Shipp as saying, "The children got good in learning those darn things [the hundreds of separate reading skills] but they weren't reading. These skills are not bad skills, but you've got to learn them and use them in reading." The system, Bloom went on, "became almost too mechanical."[21] Children were taught a set of separate skills that were never applied to anything concrete. What happened? I think it is an example of our inability to think in qualified ways or about two things at the same time. In the vernacular, what was supposed to be *part* of the action—learning the subskills—became *all* of the action. What was supposed to be about skills *and* reading became just about skills.

It must be frustrating to theorists to see their work distorted. I could cite example after example of the theory-to-practice distortion. The following are examples from Hunter. She indeed stresses an active teacher instructional role, but she also emphasizes meaningful student participation and a concern for the content of learning as well as how a student is studying. In my experience, only one of these points, the first one, tends to be really heard. Also, I have seen her "white sauce" lesson suggestion that is meant to be but a guide to lesson development turned into a virtually-every-time teaching procedure in which the teacher is invariably expected to lead off with an explanation, follow with the elicitation of student response, and so on through the sequence. My reading of her work indicates she does not have that kind of rigid arrangement in mind at all.

This over-simplification problem has its advantages as well. The fact that the technological approaches are so simple, seemingly at least, is in a large part what makes them so attractive to the busy educational practitioner. They are theories that can be understood in a short time and put into practice. They clearly tell you what to do. They readily allow teachers the satisfaction of creating materials and devising teaching activities that can be shared with others. For supervisors they can appear a godsend. A relatively quick study can familiarize them with an approach that applies "across the board," from elementary math to senior high English. Learning these systems is a way to become an expert fast—certainly faster than reading all the books and journals on math or social studies curriculum and instructional methods. Also attractive to administrators and other supervisors, these systems break up neatly into component parts, making it quite easy to set up training sessions for teachers far into the future, each session dealing with a single element in the model. For a supervisor, that provides a structure for each session, the comfort that comes with predictability, and a way to justify one's role and worth for some years ahead.

For teachers the system is rewarding, at least initially, for reasons that have been mentioned. It puts teachers in charge, makes them feel professional and linked to others, defines their tasks clearly and in manageable terms, and reflects a positive, upbeat attitude toward students and the work of teaching. Also, and this has been particularly true in my experience with Hunter, it is quite nonthreatening for teachers. By and large it tends to reinforce what teachers are already doing. As I have seen it employed, the Hunter instructional skills model does not challenge the content and instructional choices of teachers in any significant way. Rather, it gives them a way to organize their thinking and name what they do. I have heard teacher after teacher say, "I'm OK. I've been doing this all along." This lack of fundamental challenge to the way teachers do their business is another attractive element for supervisors. Supervisors can center their discussions on the more noncontroversial areas of goal clarity and keeping instruction in line with the day's objective, without having to get into sticky arguments over content selection and teaching style. Though at the same time, to the degree that the mastery models lean toward rigid formulas, after an initial "honeymoon" period ("Oh, now we know what teaching is") teachers may get impatient at being dictated to and restricted by the central office. But that problem can get obscured by all the plus features. And it does work. Kids learn. Or at least they learn the objectives that are taught them, whether or not they are what students ought to be learning. Really, everybody wins. Or so it seems.

There is no doubt that mastery systems are fun to play with. You can learn them quickly and then extrapolate from them virtually forever. For practical minded educators who do not want to spend endless hours wrestling with theory and just want to get on with their work, this is extremely appealing. The problem develops when these theories become so captivating and educators get so used to how easy they are to handle, that attention to vital areas of teaching gets shortchanged. There are many crucial areas that demand our rigorous attention if we are to teach well. I have mentioned many of them as we have gone along. They include issues of philosophy and educational purpose, content or subject selection, developmental concerns, and student efficacy. Also, in each field, in math and English and social studies and physical education, there is a body of literature and research that has been developed over the years, and this warrants our study. A preoccupation with classroom skills development arises from the conviction that teachers make *the* difference (another basis of the appeal of these systems to teachers, as we are told that we need not stray too far from our immediate concern, classroom technique, and that we are what counts) and can make us forget that factors beyond teaching matter as well. Among these other factors are school policies, leadership in the school, parent support, and school climate. But instructional technologies can distract us from all that, or spoil us by being such a quick study that we are less willing to pay the price in time and effort to probe deeply these other areas.

An example of what I mean: A graduate student in education in a class of mine last semester spent time studying outcomes-based approaches and Hunter and

Bloom by visiting classrooms and talking to teachers and administrators. Really though, what she wanted to do for the major work of the course, she informed me, was to develop some lessons that would cross the subjects of art, social studies, and language. I provided her with material on integrated curriculum theory and the current trends in the three subjects she wanted to include. But I could see that she was getting caught up in the teaching technologies material. My conclusion is that these systems were just so compelling and fun to consider that they discouraged the attention and hard work that should have gone into the other curriculum construction work she wanted to do. In fact, not only did they discourage this other work, they provided a justification for not doing it—the apparent importance of talking to one more administrator or teacher about mastery approaches.

I also have problems with the insistence on research data as *the* support for educational claims and *the* guide to educational practice. As I pointed out earlier, mastery approaches take their lead from the behavioral sciences that emphasize the discernment of truth through reference to the findings derived from scientific experiments. By this I mean controlled (random samples, control and experimental groups, etc.) studies which arrive at conclusions meeting rigorous standards of valid statistical inference. I think you know the kind of research I mean. The kind of research a scientist would conduct. Quantitative research in contrast to what is called qualitative research such as an anthropologist, or even a good novelist, poet, or essayist, might do by immersing himself or herself in a particular circumstance. In education it is the kind of research published in the *American Educational Research Journal.*

Very often I have heard mastery proponents justify a particular strategy with a reference to what "the research says" about that particular area of concern. By this they mean empirical studies (empirical referring to what is actually "out there" in the world—facts, concrete events, things you can discern with your senses—as opposed to "in there," feelings, values, suppositions, etc.). This "the research says" reference is an epistemological statement. Epistemology has to do with the way we know things and the way we test the truthfulness of what we know. Thus the scientific test as *the* test for truth is the epistemology of the mastery movement. And from one side that is to be applauded. The mastery adherents call for a willingness to move beyond what we think is so or hope to be true or believe should be the case to a scientific investigation of what is really going on. They should be commended for reminding all of us that we must be willing to hold up our theories and practices to objective scrutiny, and for underscoring the value in allowing both theory and practice to grow out of systematic observations of reality. This is a very positive message to a profession, education, that tends to hold on to ideas that *feel* right or *ought to* work, even though events in classrooms do not support the validity of these ideas. In effect, the instructional technologies perspective brings us back to reality: What *is* so? What *does* work? Another advantage, and this relates to educator morale, is that the stress on scientific research makes us feel more professional. When teachers see that their practices have been validated through such research, they view themselves as members of a legitimate research-based, applied discipline, akin to something like the field of medicine.

However, this stress on "the research" has its costs as well. And here we come back to this tendency to make something that should be "part of it"—one option, one element in complementary relationship to other elements—become "all of it." As a matter of fact, epistemologically there are a number of very useful ways beside the empirical test to find out what is so or to support a claim. I list some of these other ways of knowing:

- I can know through my own analysis of events and circumstances, even though this analysis is not part of a scientifically controlled study. I can look and see what is going on, draw some conclusions, talk it over with others, and trust that I have come up with some valuable insights. In other words, I do not have to limit my view of reality in schools to only those findings presented in journals and other research literature. I have eyes and ears and a brain of my own. And not only do I have current reality to observe, through the use of my memory I can review in my mind events that happened some time ago as a means of figuring out what happens and should happen in education.

- Another way I can know is to refer to authority that I trust. There have been very wise and experienced men and women who have gone before me and who are my contemporaries, and I can learn from what they say. In education there have been theorists such as John Dewey, and historians such as Lawrence Cremin and, more recently, Diane Ravitch. In the 1960s and 1970s there were writers like George Dennison, Herbert Kohl, and Jonathan Kozol. There are the theorists in my teaching field, which happens to be secondary social studies, such as Howard Mehlinger and, lesser known but important to me, Miriam Wasserman. Learning from authoritative teachings has always been a valid way to know, whatever the field. Philosophers have learned from Plato, Christians from Christ, and the social activists from Ghandi. None of these figures claimed to derive their wisdom from laboratory experiments and statistical analyses—but that is not to say they knew nothing that was true or worth listening to.

- Also, logic is a way to arrive at truth. I can think about things and see that, yes, this follows that, and if this is so that must also be true. I can figure out in my head why something does or does not work and how to solve a problem. I can employ the wonderful gift we have of a brain that can reason. I can use my critical faculties to decide for myself what must be the case in the world.

- Another way, and this is tougher to talk about, though as far as I am concerned it is very real and very useful, are the intuitive processes. Other terms that may be used are "hunch" or "feeling." I think we all have available to us if we use it valuable understanding that is contained in an inarticulate way, in the form of a literal feel or bodily sensation. In addition, we have images, pictures, or associations in our head that can be translated into explicit insights that can prove useful. We have notions and dreams that we cannot explain that turn out to be accurate guides to reality. If you read the personal writings of scientists as well as their formal published findings, they would reveal how important sensitivity to one's inner, subjective processes are in giving them direction. Often these inner sources are bases for the identification of research problems and hypotheses, and for the solutions to the dilemmas they confront as scientists.[22]

As you might expect, given my integration-of-contrasting-elements perspective, I believe we should value and become proficient in using all of these epistemologies. The ideal is to maintain them in a kind of dynamic interrelationship in which each extends and completes the others and each acts as a check on the others. We need to have them all available as part of our epistemological repertoire. Then, depending on the need, we can choose one or several of these methods to investigate reality. Simply, I do not want to limit myself to one best way to know.

I cannot be sure how Bloom or Hunter would react to what I have just said. My guess is that they would take the position that while they value all of the ways of knowing, they do view them hierarchically, with the scientific test being the ultimate test of truth. If that is their view, I cannot support it. In my mind, education is simply not that close to physics, chemistry, or some other laboratory discipline. To me education is more like politics, a somewhat inexact, human undertaking. And in politics, while I welcome the men and women with the computers, I do not want to write off the value of what Thomas Jefferson had to say.

This discussion is important not just in relation to mastery approaches. For instance, some teachers act as if immediate observation is the only test of truth. "It is not so unless I see it" is their epistemology. That means that books, experts, research, logic, none of that, counts. The only thing that counts is what goes on in my classroom or the one next door. (While I am listing them, there is also the "conventional wisdom" epistemology. In that method, what is true is what "everybody knows," the common sense about the matter. Education, and I am sure every other field, is full of these "truths": "The people you really have to get along with are the secretaries and the custodians"—consistent with prevailing populist sentiment in the profession. And one I spend some time with in chapter 7, "Kids will always test you to see how far they can go.")

I have heard mastery advocates say many times that the research shows such and such to be the case, that's it, no need to discuss it, we can go on to implementing it in practice. Another reason for its popularity, by the way: it's certainly about things. While this is an approach that values research, it does not want to spend a great deal of time pondering it. These are doers, the mastery people, as are teachers generally, and this "we know what is so, let's get to doing it" tendency is very compatible with a results-oriented, pragmatic, and, ironically, somewhat anti-intellectual profession. I notice often, however, the research remains unspecified: What studies? Where? With whom? With exactly what outcomes? No, not much if any of that; rather, just the research shows that such-and-such is the case. The message is that we really do not have to spend time worrying about our own experience, logic, or introspection, or referring to any great minds we may have read. But the point is we need to do just that. Or at least I do. I will not give over my critical judgment to any outside authority, no matter how impressive the scientific, "white coat" style and argument. I am interested. I will take in what is offered. But as a professional I will not allow anyone to ever tell me that he has discovered truth and my job is but to put it into practice. I am afraid I would seem a real problem case if some administrator or curriculum director were to inform me, this is what works and this is how we do it here and we will check you over until you get it right. Yet this is exactly what some teachers are hearing. To teach is not to be on the automobile assembly line doing the bosses' bidding—or at least as it used to be before the workers directly and indirectly indicated they had had enough. Teaching is the work of a professional, and a professional must make decisions based on his own best critical judgment, in reference to his professional colleagues (not just supervisors higher up in the bureaucracy), and with a sense of connection and responsibility to the educators who have gone before and those who will follow in the profession. As for me, my attitude is if some expert has a good idea, great, let me hear it. And then let me respond with my best thinking. Let us dialogue. At least we may be able to enrich the understanding of the other and make each other more effective in his work. At most, we will see that we share a vision for what is worth doing and will decide to work together and support each other in what we do as individuals.

Certainly as a professional I have to place research findings into the larger context of all that I consider important in education. An example, if I hear of research on the effects of some teaching practice on the learning process, I need to say to myself: "Hmmm. They are talking about learning. I wonder what impact this technique has on motivation, student autonomy, development, creativity, and critical thinking." I care about values, moral development, character, self-value and cognitive growth. I wrote about developmental maturity earlier and expressed my belief that the best classrooms were settings that emphasized social exchange, diversity, confronting manageable dissonance, accommodating to ideas that do not square with one's views, debate, dialogue, taking others into account (role-taking), collaboration, self-appropriating rather than receiving knowledge, and making sense of things when faced with complex and problematic circumstances. Now, if someone tells me "the research says" I have to filter that contention through these concerns of mine. And also, I need to square it with what I already know. I have had a persistent problem with mastery approaches because when I run them through this developmental agenda of mine, they just do not measure up. But I know this is not an issue to the mastery people because they do not emphasize development as an educational concern. I do, however.

Even more fundamentally, I need to be sensitive to just what scientific conclusions mean. For example, if a piece of research shows that teaching method X is better than teaching method Y, what is really being said? Is it better in every case, with every student? Better with the vast majority? I need to ask those questions. It could be that method X is better with 55% of the students and Y with 45%. Y worked better with almost half the students. Yet if the sample size is large enough, the laws of statistical inference allow the conclusion that X is a better approach. So if we go only by the research finding it might sound as if X is better, period. There is a real danger of overgeneralization here.

Another example: I attended a seminar on the impact of divorce on children in preparation for writing chapter 3. We in the audience were informed that "the research says" girls are more traumatized by marriage break-ups than boys. That generalization was projected onto a screen and remained there for an hour. No one asked any questions, like what the numbers were for girls versus boys, and so forth. We were running the danger of some undue stereotyping (girls are one way, boys another) and misleading ourselves (if the child is a boy, he is not affected; if a girl, she is). I am struck by our unquestioning faith in science.

Also, when I am told "the research says" I need to be careful that inappropriate extrapolations are not being made. That is, I need to watch out that a teaching strategy that upped reading scores among primary school special education students is not used as "the research says" to justify using the same strategy to teach poetry or science to gifted eleventh graders. (This example is not hypothetical. I have lived through this one.) I need to ask, as do you, what exactly was the nature of the research, how was it conducted, with whom, and where? What are the limits of its applicability? Do you create a talented musician this way? A novelist? A political leader? Were people who have done or are doing significant things with their lives educated that way?

And more important than that, I need to ask if this is actually important. No matter how valid the findings, is it related to what I consider to be truly significant? One of the problems I see with the reliance in education on empirical research results is that they are often firm conclusions about things that I do not care much about. And I do not want to spend too much of my time attending to things I do not consider vital. Time is precious, after all. What is at the core of this problem is the nature of the scientific experiment itself. In order to be able to trust the results obtained from scientific research, researchers must narrow their study in such a way as to define their terms precisely and prevent the effect of extraneous variables. To do that they may wind up dealing with a matter that is of minor importance but one that lends itself well to the controls that must be imposed for the experiment to be valid. Instead of deciding what is important in education and then setting up a test of that, they may unwittingly test what they can and make that important. For example, critical thought, personal empowerment, or facility with language may be too ill-defined and hard to control to put to the scientific test. We can, however, measure a basic skill through a standardized test of achievement. If the only test of an educational practice is what "the research says,'' then attention and attribution of importance is going to tend to get tacked on to whatever comes out of the research. The result thus is a predominant concern for basic skill attainment, and other such things you can easily count, and little or no concern for anything else. And this is precisely what I have seen go on in the technologies movement. Now that focus may be good enough for educators with a different focus from mine. For example, I know many special educators are enamored with mastery approaches because they seem to be good ways to get the necessary life maintenance skills to the children of their professional interest. However, goals and processes appropriate to them are not what I consider appropriate to other children, and I must take that into consideration when making decisions regarding these approaches.

Also, when I listen to advocates of these instructional models I remind myself that I need to factor in my concern for *what* and *why* as well as *how*. Technological orientations tend to focus on the how of education, the means of schooling, the processes through which teaching and learning can be accomplished. Indeed, that is a vital concern. But in addition to the process of schooling there is the *substance* of schooling. What *content* is most important for students to engage? Should they study art or history, Hemingway or Joyce Carol Oates, philosophy or psychology, algebra or general math, business training or drivers education? And the minute you start asking these questions you are brought face-to-face with issues of purpose: Why are students in school? What is the mission of this school? What are my aims as an educator? These are bigger questions than getting clear on the objective of today's lesson, as important as that is, or deciding on a particular teaching technique. Objectives and instructional strategies are only legitimate, only have meaning, to the extent that they grow out of the answers to these fundamental questions. Unless what we do is grounded in our resolutions to these fundamental issues, I consider us technicians and not professionals. And in order to resolve them, each of us has to reflect on matters of philosophy and ethics. We need to engage in social and political analyses. We need to develop insight into the nature of the particular students whom we teach. And we need to take time for serious introspection into ourselves and to search out our own deepest wisdom and most deeply felt sense of the purpose and meaning of our lives. Technologies, instructional models, mastery learning, effective teaching, whatever it is, only make sense in terms of the larger context of what we and students are doing with our time on this earth.

I worry that if we get too caught up with seeing ourselves as applied social scientists, take on too much of a value free, ''just the facts'' orientation, we and the students as well will get caught up in how we are doing and cease to pay enough attention to what we are doing and what it is making of us. I sense that one of the attractions of the technological orientation to educators is that it allows us to focus on technique and stay out of sticky political, social, and personal issues. This is especially appealing for educators who lived through all the schooling debates of the late 1960s and into the 1970s. So much of the literature and movements in those years were grounded in political and social arguments.[23] In many ways it is so much less draining to just talk about scientifically validated techniques without getting into issues of politics or human ideals. The problem with that, though, is that schooling is ultimately about these very concerns, even though we may choose to look away from them. We are, after all, making decisions about what children will do with a good portion of their lives. We are deciding what they need to know and what they should be capable of doing in their lives. There is a wonderful old book on education by George Dennison called *Lives of Children*.[24] This is a classic; do read it if you can find it in the library. Notice Dennison called his book the *lives* of children. It serves as a good reminder to me that this is, after all, what we are dealing with in school, the lives of children—and our own lives. And that is more than a matter of technique.

In terms of content I worry that instructional technologies have built in biases regarding curricular content and purpose that we sometimes fail to reflect upon. I mentioned earlier that a basic skills (in the sense of the conventional three Rs) content bias could be the outcome of this orientation. Since research is most easily conducted in these areas, this then becomes what we refer to because of our "cite empirical research evidence as the way to know" tendency. And that in turn can lead to the uncritical assumption that because this *is* what we talk about and know, this must be what we *should* be focusing upon in schools. Also there is a parallel between a rational, no-nonsense, scientific attitude and what is usually taken to be the rational, no-nonsense way of teaching: sit the kids down and teach them the basics. Consequently these approaches are not as benign and neutral toward matters of educational aims and content as their advocates would have us believe. If we get caught up in matters of technique without an equal concern for purpose and substance, at the very least it may serve to maintain whatever the current state of affairs happens to be. We will be spending our time with systems that often do not seem to challenge us to do more than use them as processes to enable us to do better than we are already trying to do. I am uncomfortable with a "back to basics" or status quo outcome to mastery approaches (and I think it can be one or the other depending on the specific circumstance) since I do not like either outcome very much.

Even more important than not meeting my preferences, I think these strategies are out of rhythm with the times. Ironically, given the mastery label, these approaches are about minimums in a time of maximums. To explain, I need to sketch out the overall "tenor of the times" in education now in contrast to some years ago, say the early 1980s. To get at this I review in greater depth the effective schools and minimum competence movements mentioned earlier that came to prominence in the late 1970s and early 1980s and what can be called the excellence movement of the mid-1980s. The point of this discussion is that schooling practices do not operate in isolation, but rather in relation to a complex interplay of social forces and ideas that provide the context for schooling at any point in time. I reach the conclusion that mastery approaches fit in very well with the early 1980s and are not so well adjusted to the current times.

One of the major tenets of what came to be known as the effective schools movement in the early part of the decade was the school's need to assure minimal competence in basic skill achievement for all children regardless of their social class, income, or family circumstance.[25] One of the characteristics of effective schools, according to research in England and here in this country, was an academic emphasis on basic skills. This is what we were reading and hearing in those days. (And now. I do not mean to imply that this thrust is dead and buried, just that it is less prominent now than it was then.) Basic skills was usually taken to mean the "three Rs," and especially fundamental math and reading skills as measured by standardized tests of achievement. At this time there was the "basic competencies" trend that tended to complement the effective schools support for a basic skills focus. The idea here was to make sure that students were not graduating from our schools without being able to read and write and compute at even the most rudimentary levels. Many states reacted by adopting basic competency requirements to be met by all students before graduation.

I think it is fair to say that this "make sure they get the minimum level of achievement" orientation was the predominant climate during the early 1980s. It was the ideological context from which decisions were made. And do not let anybody tell you that ideas do not matter, in education or politics or any other area of life in America. They do matter. But again, it is important to distinguish between the "feel of it all," the conventionally accepted interpretations of what the movements were advocating, and what they were actually saying. To be sure, both the effective schools and minimum competency people wanted schools to go beyond assuring a "floor" of academic achievement. They wanted *at least* that—and much more. But what was put forth as *a* goal of education was heard as *the* goal. What was meant as "this and more" was interpreted as "this is enough." I have gone through all of this before, but it bears repeating that you get what you seem to expect of people. If you expect everyone to get over minimal obstacles, that is what they will do and no more. In any case, a few years ago there was what I would call a "minimums" mentality. In good part this mentality came out of a feeling that the schools were getting virtually nothing done with many students due to the excesses of humanistic education and a kind of cultural malaise. Assuring a minimum level of achievement seemed better than nothing, which is what it seemed we were getting. Though I offer that minimal is still minimal, and it is not a goal that tends to bring out the best in human beings. It brings out the minimal in human beings. A better way to get minimums is to go for maximums.

You can see how attractive the mastery approaches looked in those days: Children can and will learn. It is a step by step method that will work, even with the most difficult student. It puts responsibility in the hands of the teachers and the schools where it belongs. It is especially amenable to teaching basic subjects.

But then in mid-1983 a report came from a group set up by the Secretary of Education called the National Commission on Excellence in Education. The report was entitled *A Nation at Risk*.[26] It was short, used snappy phrases, and was widely read, at least by journalists and other interpreters; certainly by many more people than is usually the case with these kinds of reports. As far as I know, not since the Conant Report, as it was called, in the 1950s, has anything gotten such reaction. Here again I am not saying people knew exactly what was in it. But they did know it said something about—the catch phrase of the document— "the rising tide of mediocrity" that characterizes the public schools. And they figured it said something about beefing up requirements, getting "hard" subjects like math, science, and computers into the curriculum, lengthening the school year, and just generally tightening up the school's operation. People knew that it was a commission on *excellence*, and they had a sense of what excellence meant.

I invite you to read the document for yourself. It was fascinating for me to read it and see what people were doing with it. On the one hand, liberals were decrying it as a soulless pitch for technological competence in some kind of pathetic race to out-Japan the Japanese. (Actually it called for a well-rounded program of liberal studies.) At that time President Reagan and other conservatives said it was about tougher discipline and prayer in the schools. (I cannot find that in the report at all.) People either tend to see what they most fear or most want in any report or proposal. But that aside, *Nation at Risk* did get the idea through to the American people that we are a nation of excellence, not minimal accomplishment. And it should be noted, this message was addressed to the American people, to the culture directly. Unlike other reports, *Nation at Risk* was directed not at politicians, professional educators, and other context-shapers. This is a point missed by many who have assessed *Nation at Risk*. Most of these kinds of reports call for the government or the professionals to do something or another. This one called for that, but the primary thrust of the report was a call for cultural change. The pitch was for the culture to reaffirm its commitment to excellence in education. And on that score I think the report was fairly successful, though, as always is the case, it had to share time with those saying what they thought it meant or were afraid it meant and those who seized the opportunity to use it as a vehicle to say what they wanted to say.

What the report did, among other things, to use a golf metaphor, is get the greens mowed so that putting was a little easier for a number of books and reports that followed in the next couple of years. I lump these writings together and call them the "excellence movement." I refer to such material as Mortimer Adler's *Paideia Proposal*, and books written or edited by people like Chester Finn and Diane Ravitch.[27] William Bennett, who echoed these views, became Secretary of Education. Generally, the argument was that although schools must promote basic skills, the primary purpose of schooling is to provide an environment for intellectual growth and a program of liberal studies for all students. Although there is always a difference of opinion in education, this excellence or, perhaps a better term, *neo-essentialist* perspective became highly prominent.

This is not the place to go into lengthy analyses of the two orientations, the effective schools and excellence perspectives, but I think you see the basic distinction between the two. I also think you can see that the excellence people are not likely to be the champions of mastery approaches. They are prone to see these strategies as another convoluted scheme coming out of the well-intended but small minds of educationists that only gets in the way of achieving academic excellence. It should be clear from reading this book thus far that I sympathize with much that comes out of the excellence movement. I said early on that at its core, this country has always been about excellence. It has always been about rising above barriers and reaching out for exceptional accomplishment. Parents in our culture, most of them anyway, want their children to be somebody, to do their best, to rise above their present station in life, to become everything their character and talent allow. Certainly I can speak for myself as a parent. I have not sat down with either of my two boys and said, "Son, my dream for you is to be minimally competent." My message to both my children is more of the sort, "The sky's the limit. Let's see what you can do."

From all that I have read, heard, and seen, the instructional technologies do not seem to encourage the realization of my hopes for my own children. Maybe these approaches are good at *individualizing* learning, allowing students to learn predetermined content at their own rate; but I worry that they do not *personalize* learning enough. By personalize I mean that, within the subject being studied and overall goals of a class, students explore their uniqueness by probing areas different from other students, expressing themselves verbally, and through what they create in ways that clarify and distinguish them as one-of-a-kind human beings. It seems to me personalization (I only hear talk of individualization) is extremely important for developing adolescents as they deal with the challenge of self-definition.

A last point, and I think this is the most damning criticism of the mastery technologies is that, however successful they may appear, they are simply—I am groping for a word—unhuman. And that tells me that ultimately they must fall by the wayside as a predominant instructional approach. They may work like a charm for awhile. But in the long run you do not get quality work, or initiative, out of paying people off for diligently doing small tasks one after the other at the bidding of the somebody else. The human being just isn't that way. The human being is a goal setter, puzzle solver, creator of the whole thing, collaborator at times and individualist at times, and show off ("Look what I did"). Human beings want to be in charge of their lives, make policy as well as live by it, create as well as emulate, lead as well as follow. The human being is obviously motivated by external rewards, but give him or her a chance and here come self-expression and limits-testing. To be sure, our nature can be misread because it is obscured by the dampening forces of the culture and society (including dead-end schools and dead-end jobs). No, maybe for a time an unhuman system seems good, but eventually people cool to it when they realize it was not for people in the first place. It just seemed like a good idea at the time.

In sum, I see instructional technologies as tools we ought to know about and use when they are clearly appropriate for getting us where we want to go. But from what I know, I cannot recommend them as *the* predominant mode of instruction for a school. Most of all, though, I hope this discussion has given you some ways to think about not only this teaching orientation but others us well. Do look into mastery approaches on your own and make your own judgment. A good source of reading in addition to the others I have mentioned is chapter 3 in John McNeil's book *Curriculum: A Comprehensive Perspective* called "Technology and the Curriculum."[28]

CONCLUSION

Those are some key ideas I have about teaching. Do these ideas create a perspective on teaching that makes sense? Some challenges to you: Add three major ideas about teaching that you are sure I would agree with and might have written here if I had the necessary space. List three areas where you disagree with my views and state why you think as you do. Also, employing the ideas of this chapter, critique a set of ideas or practices as I have done with mastery approaches. Think about this chapter in terms of the one on studenting that preceded it. Do they go together well? Any incompatibilities? Pick a subject you are teaching or might teach: If you taught it "my way" how would you go at it? If you were to write *your* chapter on teaching, what would you say?

I move from what students do (studenting) and teachers do (teaching) to what they do it about (curriculum). Curriculum is the topic of the next chapter.

6 Curriculum for Underachievers

What should these young people study in school? My first response is to offer that it probably does not matter very much what answer you and I decide to offer. Schools are going to do as they will. And that, likely, is to continue what they have been doing right along. I hold out the distinct possibility that schooling for the less-than-successful students is not going to change fundamentally. Despite all the promising talk, you and I may very well recognize schools 10 years from now. This possibility, that schools will not change a great deal, is one reason for my emphasis on teaching students to go get what they need and not wait to be saved by an improved school environment. The same goes for us as well. Certainly we need to create hopes for schools and work toward realizing them. But we must also learn to take maximum advantage of the positive possibilities within the current reality. And anyway, the current reality, with all its limitations, is from moment to moment all we ever have to deal with in any case. So that is the first point, that the following discussion of curriculum may be, as they say, academic. What underachieving, poor, socially disadvantaged, and developmentally blocked kids encounter in school now may just be what they will continue to encounter. And if that is so, these kids had better learn how to deal with the present circumstance.

I outline some of my preferences regarding the curriculum for could-be-so-much-more students in secondary schools. By curriculum I am referring to the *content* of the students' school experience: the topics, subjects, concepts, issues, problems, and the like, that comprise the substance of the formal academic program. Simply: what students study in school.

The curriculum I prefer and consider possible for the young people we have been talking about in this book is what I hope schools will offer all secondary students: a sound general education. By that I mean a program of studies which has the purpose of educating these adolescents in a general or all-round way (thus the term *general education*).[1] This is in contrast to a specialized technical or job-preparatory curriculum. As I see it, a general education is one that acquaints students with significant ideas, creations, and events from throughout human history. It is one that connects them to their heritage as human beings and Americans. As well, in my view of a good general education, and others may not emphasize this, it brings young people into contact with their uniqueness and potential, and empowers them to proceed toward being who they are within the circumstance in which they will live their lives. The insight, appreciation, and sense of relatedness that grow out of such studies are foundational to students assuming membership in the human community. They gain strength from such a program in becoming decent and productive elements of the world in which they live. They see that they belong. They belong, each of them, in the very best form of the unique individuals that they are. In practical terms, the curriculum in such an education would be a traditional pattern of studies. Included would be math, science, literature, and history—especially history—and philosophy and the arts.

The curriculum would include one more thing that I want to spend some time talking about: physical education. By physical education I do not mean a program that aims to produce middle linebackers, avid spectators, Sunday afternoon golfers, tennis players, or volleyball spikers. Rather, I mean a program that promotes the development of the physical aspect of each student, and the integration of this development with the student's overall growth as a unique human being. Too often, physical education has been set off against the rest of the learning and growth experiences. Physical education has been overly compartmentalized and limited, and this separates academic from physical education, mind from body, curricular from extracurricular, and work from play. (On this point about the extracurricular nature of much of physical education: I have never been able to figure out how something can be *extra*-curricular. To me, something is either part of the school's curriculum or it is not. By having the term *extracurricular*, it allows us to be less articulate about the educational purposes the program serves, keep it isolated from other elements of the school program, deny it to students who need it, and pay teachers less for working in it.)

What I hope for in physical education is a curriculum that aims at counteracting the mind-body dualism I see in this culture. I hope for a program that promotes an understanding of how physical development and expression contributes to other aspects of our being. I hope for a physical education that helps adolescents become alert, healthy, and respectful of their bodies; controlled and harmonious and expressive in the ways they move; capable of concentration and relaxation; and sensitively responsive to the physical dimension of themselves. Physical education of this sort would operate to serve the larger aim of uplifting the total human being, and contribute to the unfolding or evolution of the culture in positive and natural directions.

Reading over this last paragraph I can see how it may sound quite obscure and abstract. But stay with it and work to understand what I am attempting to say. It affirms the importance of physical education at a time when many are downplaying its usefulness in school. It points toward the inclusion of content that does not usually come to mind when we think of physical education, such as dance and mime, martial arts like aikido and tai chi, yoga, meditation, relaxation and concentration techniques, sport psychology, analyses of sport/society/culture interrelationships, biofeedback and autogenic techniques (ways to control internal processes we usually do not consider amenable to control), health maintenance, and nutrition. Some of the areas we do see in today's schools; but major team sports and a kind of Marine Corps notion of "fitness" are still prominent as far as I can judge. In sum, what I am calling for is a physical education grounded in some ideal of physical development. What is your conception of such an ideal?

Notice I put philosophy on the list of subjects. Probably more than any other, philosophy runs counter to the usual notion of what we ought to be offering to the kinds of students we are talking about in this book. Many educators take one look at these kids, or many of them anyway, especially the scruffier looking ones, and decide what they need is a basic skill oriented, "down-to-earth," practical education. Teach these young people how to survive in the *real world*. Train them in such areas as personal finance, applying for a job, business subjects (especially if they are female), and trades (especially if they are male). These are relevant and practical things. And yet here I am talking about philosophy.

Why philosophy? Because philosophy is the subject that gets at that quality that is so special to human beings. That is the part of us that seeks more than survival or pleasure. It is the impulse in us to figure out what it all means. It is the desire to get at the purpose or significance of our lives. It is the urge to rise above our limitations and realize our possibilities. People get at this human quality in different ways. Some describe the development of a "high consciousness," the movement by an individual from a life based on delusion and selfishness to one growing out of wisdom, compassion, and love. Some equate it with the creation or adoption of a religion or life philosophy. Others speak of moral development, social responsibility, or a sense of the sanctity of human life. Still others refer to the ability to experience what is true, beautiful, and good. And some talk about such things as the capability of giving and receiving love, and the necessity of learning to deal with the inevitable suffering and pain in life with courage and dignity.

Admittedly these concerns are difficult to write about without sounding overly idealistic and impractical. Here we are discussing underachieving students and I am going on about awareness of the sanctity of life. And indeed an argument for practical skills can seem so compelling in light of schooling that has been so beside the point for large numbers of students of the sort we are considering in this book. It is true, many students have emerged from years of formal schooling without being able to read or write well enough to function as true adults in our society. And yes, we need to attend to basic literacy and the fact that some students are leaving formal education virtually unemployable. But at the same time, I am arguing for an education that deals with more than getting along—even for those young people whose interest, past record, and life circumstance would seem to encourage a program directed at the most minimal kind of training.

What would be included in a program that focuses on this transcendent dimension of a human being? Well, I have been putting in a pitch for the discipline of philosophy. Philosophy gets right to it: the central concern is the issue of what kind of life is worth living. Philosophy deals with issues of purpose, value, ultimate reality, wisdom, beauty, character, goodness, justice—the fundamental human issues. And should not school be about fundamental things? I say yes. And I also say that what is typically considered basic does not always get at what is fundamental. Basics—reading, writing, computation, those kinds of skills—make sense only when one has gone some distance in working through what I am calling the fundamental human issues. The fundamentals give a *reason* for learning and using the basics. Why learn to read if you or anything else do not matter? You cannot grapple with the fundamentals without the basics. As a practical matter it is very difficult to work with fundamental concerns if you cannot read, write, or think. The conclusion I reach is that we need to give equal and concurrent attention to these ultimate human concerns—what I am calling the fundamentals—and what we typically call the basics.

What else is part of this "higher education"? For one thing, students should study the statements and life examples of exemplary individuals in order to ascertain how these individuals resolved issues of meaning and direction in their lives. I am thinking here of making use of personal writings, biographies, and autobiographies. Also, students can interview individuals in the community as part of their investigation in these areas. Religious concerns would be part of the curriculum, something downplayed currently in most public schools. Of course I do not mean sectarian indoctrination, but rather a study of the issues with which religion deals. The issues of one's place in the universe and destiny are not the sole province of organized religion. Just because a young person is not from a religious family does not mean that issues of a religious nature should be absent from his life. It can be most beneficial for students to study the way various religions and life philosophies have resolved the fundamental human questions within a secular context. Moreover, students can confront issues of social importance and find ways, even in their current station in life, to take action consistent with their views and commitments. In this regard, the proposals contained in the Carnegie Foundation report on secondary education regarding social service as a required unit for graduation are good food for thought.[2]

The arts should also play a central role. The school's art program can provide a counterbalance to the popular culture and mass entertainment that, sadly, provides the "art" that so many young people experience. As I see it, the school should let students in on the fact that there is a world beyond prime time television and the junk Hollywood produces for teenagers. For many students, especially the socially disadvantaged, I do not know where else they are going to get that message. Human beings have written magnificent books and created marvelous music, paintings, sculpture, dance, and theater. We may fail in our efforts to get this message to young people, but nevertheless, I think we have to work to introduce this magnificence to then. And I am not at all relativistic about this. I am willing to affirm that some artist's creations are aesthetically superior and more worthy of human beings than others. Beethoven, Picasso, Martha Graham, Ingmar Bergman, Eugene O'Neill, and Hemingway are great artists and students should know about them. And in our own time it is no gigantic secret who the fine artists are—critics are not that much in disagreement. Our standards as people are not that discrepant and subjective. School does not have to be the place to hear more "all hits" radio. Students need a chance to be invited to experience the finest that human beings have produced. They need the chance, too, to be challenged to produce the finest art of which they are capable, the art that stems from the core of their being.

I can understand how this talk may sound elitist. That is probably because it *is* elitist. I think school should be a place that reflects what *is* elite rather than what is base and common and "relevant." I am indeed critical of a society where dining has become McDonald's. Play has become commercial sport; sit and watch the pros and a multitude of beer and tire commercials. And drama takes the form of slasher movies. Hang in there for next summer's even more tasteless, more exploitive sequel. Yes, I realize that junk probably has always been more prevalent than quality, reaching back to vaudeville and before. And I respect the right of students or anyone else to choose their own preferred form of artistic experience. But true choice involves options. My worry is that for many young people they do not have the chance to choose quality because it is nowhere in their lives. PBS? Maybe I just have not been watching closely enough, but every time I tune in, it seems to be English people talking, insects mating, or "Sesame Street" banging out its little lessons. Experiencing and creating good art should be in every student's program. That is where I stand on this matter. Where are you?

And then there is wisdom. What is our wisdom as a species and as a culture? In all of human history, what are the wisest things that people have thought? Students have a right to ask and get answers to those questions. For that matter, what is your wisdom? A *high* school education concerns itself with that. The academic disciplines from which we take our cue may not need the concept of wisdom. They just have to know what happened and how things are connected. But a secondary education worthy of us is most certainly not just a setting to teach junior versions of college courses. It is about how to live in America and the world. And living means seeking wisdom, not just knowledge. You and I know so many knowledgeable people who, despite their knowledge, just are not very wise. Wisdom is a slippery concept to be sure. But we have a word for it for some reason; it counts for something in our culture. It is worth our time to search with our students for what is wise in science or literature or history or any other area we study.

While all this may sound impractical to some, it just may be that finding out there was, and is, a Mozart, or that there is a meaning to life other than hanging out, will contribute to a student's motivation to learn those things conventionally considered more basic. It could just be that a student, after years of failing to read, might start to succeed in reading when he gets a glimmer of the notion that he is connected to the history of the human endeavor and to the other human beings who share the gift of life with him. He might realize that there is some purpose to life that makes possessing this skill worthwhile.

Also, since I am talking in ideals, ideally school should help students learn how to balance the private and public dimensions of their lives. First of all, there is the need to be an individual. One must learn to find pleasure and satisfaction in one's personal and work life. In addition, there is the need to join with others, serve others and the community, and uphold and extend the American political and cultural tradition. Living well in America involves concurrent attention for both the public and the private. Students need to be challenged to integrate both into a life that is coherent and natural to themselves. The best situation I can think of is when self-exploration, investigations of social and cultural reality, and service to others occur simultaneously in a student's life. This circumstance offers the best chance for students to transcend the apparent contradiction between the private and public dimensions of life. The ideal is for a student to reach a place where commitment and service contribute to individual expression and pleasure; and, conversely, where the manifestation of one's individual uniqueness results in cultural maintenance and transformation. In any case, the issue of achieving a balance between private attachments and public involvement is central to our lives and should be an aspect of the school curriculum. Just how do you who is reading this meet both the demands of being a private person and citizen?

I know all that I have said in the last few pages sounds very much like a pitch for a good liberal education. And while I do not want to get labeled away, I guess it is. As I see it, that is the kind of education that is most empowering for young people. Though that holds as a generalization, there was a great deal more emphasis in these last pages on subjective, personal concerns, self-exploration, and so forth, than I associate with a liberal arts focus. And speaking of focus, my perspective focuses not so much on the academic subjects per se. Rather, it centers on the student who is learning these subjects. Another way to say it, school is not about the curriculum. It is, instead, about the student's encounter with this curriculum and himself. The "and himself" in this last sentence is important to me. There needs to be a balance between self- and other-reference in school. I find myself searching for ways to attend to the needs, hopes, actions, and internal workings of students and at the same time honor the organized knowledge and ways of knowing that comprise the subjects we teach in schools. So while I am basically in a liberal studies camp, there are those qualifications.

There have been a number of writers and reports in recent years that have endorsed what I am calling a "liberal arts orientation." For example, the Carnegie Foundation for the Advancement of Teaching states the fundamental purpose of the high school in these terms: "The high school should help all students learn about themselves, the human heritage, and the interdependent world in which they live through a core curriculum based upon consequential human experiences common to all people."[3] Note the use of the term *core curriculum* in this quote. It refers to having the same curriculum, at least for a good portion of the time, for all students rather than having a number of separate curricula or tracks. For example, one group does not get an academic curriculum while another gets a "practical" curriculum. One group does not study the Federalist Papers while another learns that Ben Franklin flew a kite. The secondary school experience, then, is a common one, shared by all students.

Similar to the Carnegie proposal, John Goodlad's group, mentioned earlier, advocates a revival of a Harvard proposal issued in the 1940s called *General Education in a Free Society*.[4] This proposal urged that schools center curriculum around the "five fingers" of organized human knowledge and experience: mathematics and science, literature and language, society and social studies, the arts, and the vocations. By vocations is meant the study of working as a cultural-social phenomenon and as a means of individual expression. It does not mean training in specific entry-level job skills. High school is not the place you learn to get along at the local factory or how to smile at Wendy's. Rather, there is an investigation of how human beings find good, needed, and personally enhancing work to do. A vocational curriculum supports students' inquiry into the ways individuals and societies have decided what kinds of work are worth doing and who does them, and the significance of all that to the students themselves. Many call for the schools to provide students with job training. I worry that the people who get job training are the people seen to be less promising, and that the job training will serve to put a ceiling on personal aspirations and set people up to do work without growth opportunities. We can take our cues from parents who are consciously raising their children to occupy positions of wealth, security, status, and power in America. They do not put them into a machine shop. They have them in a prep school where they learn how to think, use language, and become familiar with the ideas and insights associated with an educated person. Just maybe these parents know what they are doing.

Another example of this perspective, Diane Ravitch and her colleagues have argued eloquently for humanistic studies (literature, history, philosophy, classics) in secondary schools.[5] Do read her work. She is a powerful and pervasive writer.

There is the question of electives. By electives I mean the classes that a student can choose on the basis of individual interest or need in addition to the subjects he is required to take for graduation. It is appealing to think of students being allowed to select from a number of elective classes. Certainly this process makes sense as a support to the developmental process of self-definition. Students could explore different areas to see if they fit who they are. However, I do not want a situation in which the school curriculum becomes a smorgasbord of discrete special interest courses reminiscent of a community education center. And this is not just a hypothetical problem. Some writers have compared the American high school to a suburban shopping mall.[6] The curriculum (the mall) is comprised of a series of unrelated classes (shops) that are browsed by the students (shoppers) who then take (buy) them on the basis of whim.

This "shopping mall" problem, whether it is real or more a potential issue, does bear close attention. It further supports my endorsement of the idea of a large core of subjects required of every student, say two-thirds to three-fourths of the total program for a student. Also, it points toward the need to create a limited number of elective *clusters* of related courses and the need to allow students to select from among these clusters. To work still more against a hodge-podge curriculum, the clusters could be related to each of the core curriculum areas of math and science, social studies and philosophy, physical education, and literature and the arts. Notice I tied some of these subjects together (math and science, etc.). That is to indicate a way we might integrate departments to increase the likelihood of greater faculty collaboration and integration of curriculum.

I am somewhat torn on the idea of electives. On one side, who can be against choice. And I do resonate with Fred Newmann's arguments for allowance for individual dignity (chapter 1). But I also see the need for schools to be simpler, less segmented and disparate places for students. I come to the conclusion that the way to proceed is toward the implementation of a system which provides for elective study within the core of required subjects, rather than one that offers a large number of separate elective courses. If the work of the school is centered more on student work than teacher work we may be able to make room for individual exploration within the required curriculum. I will have to think more about this, however. It is a tough issue. Anyway, the basic notion is a common core curriculum plus a limited number of elective clusters.

Another idea, and this is very speculative, is to organize the secondary curriculum around the developmental needs of adolescents rather than around academic disciplines. (Practical or not, perhaps this discussion may stretch our thinking about secondary curriculum.) If you reflect on it, you will notice that whenever we set up curricular programs in secondary schools we almost automatically think of drawing course titles and content from academic disciplines that make up university departments: English, math, science, foreign language, and so forth. Indeed that may be the best way to go, but we also need to remember that it does not *have* to be that way. If the purpose of secondary schools is to equip young people to live a fulfilling and productive life and to contribute to the culture in which they live, it does not follow that all a student needs to become motivated is familiarity with selected aspects of the scholarly disciplines. It is not automatically the case that the job of a secondary teacher is to teach his college major to students. It could be that a secondary school curriculum is made up of something other than or more than simplified versions of university courses. We need to reflect on this.

An alternative way to organize a secondary curriculum, in whole or in part, is around the developmental needs of the adolescents themselves. These include the need for people of this age to gain a critical understanding of themselves and their circumstances and to begin to forge an integrated personal identity. They need to learn to relate to one another and to begin to take membership in the human community. They need to resolve issues related to physical maturity and sexuality. They need to find something to believe in, and to express themselves through their art and their work. (Though perhaps art and work should not be seen as separate areas.) They need to develop cognitively so that they can think in sophisticated ways about themselves and their world. It could be that these are the issues that they should study directly rather than the academic disciplines. It could be that these concerns are the best organizers for putting together courses and programs. Academic disciplines could then serve the purposes of these courses where they can do so.

But though this is a way to go, I would bet anything that we will never move in that direction. The traditional subjects are too ingrained in our thinking of how it is supposed to be in school for anything like that to happen. And I am not even ready to say we should go that far in the direction of what can be called a developmentalist curriculum. What we can do, though, is put these two perspectives together, the academic subjects and developmentalist perspectives. Both have merit. Certainly it is of value to adapt what the scholars have found out about the world. At the same time, schools are remiss if they do not support developmental maturity and exploit built-in student interest related to developmental issues. In addition, I would add one more perspective to the mix: a curriculum centered on the cultural, social, and personal realities in the lives of these young people. Too often, a traditional curriculum excludes the life experience of the students themselves. It is just not about them.

With that said, one way to go—and this is the one I prefer and think possible—is to stay with the basic academic disciplines-based curriculum. But from an understanding of the social-cultural and developmental circumstance of students, we should integrate these concerns into the study of these subjects. For example, if the children are poor it makes sense to study the nature and effects of social class and poverty in an historical, sociological, and psychological context. We can find ways of dealing with the "Who am I?" questions in a number of subjects. We can do the kinds of things that promote cognitive development in all of the courses. This approach requires that we develop a sketch of the social-cultural and developmental circumstance among the students we teach. And then find ways, guided by our hopes for student's lives, to incorporate what we know about that circumstance into the classes we teach. A reminder, one group of educators who is getting at this, at least in part, are educators at the middle school level. I mentioned earlier the Joan Lipsitz book *Successful Schools for Young Adolescents* as a good start into a rich body of literature coming out of the middle school movement.[7]

To add even more to it, we should keep in mind the needs of our culture and society both now and in the future, as well as our own commitments as professionals. I hope that does not sound like too overwhelming a set of concerns. How about this as a summary statement? We need a secondary school curriculum centered on a common core of liberal studies, with limited elective clusters related to this core, and all of these studies responsive to the social-cultural and developmental circumstance of students as well as our cultural traditions. And a curriculum that the professionals who teach it believe in deeply because it is consistent with their aims as educators.

One last thing, I want to reiterate that student effectiveness education should be part of the school's curriculum. That is not to say that it must to be a required experience for all students; some may not need it (though I suspect at some level, most all do). It is to say that it should be a formal, planned aspect of the curriculum available to those who need it. Again, this does not mean entire courses have to be given over to student achievement skills. Though as I indicated in a previous chapter, there could be such courses or programs. And there could be courses in achievement, problem solving, life management, or personal change that use school achievement examples to make their points. Again back to a previous chapter, the student effectiveness material could be organized into workshops, summer school programs, and weekend and after-school classes, as well as integrated into regular classes.

Below is the description of a school effectiveness program I designed for a private, religiously affiliated school for which I served as a consultant:

Program of School Achievement

The school achievement curriculum is a formalized program directed at the development among students of a heightened commitment and increased capability to attain academic success. The program aims to increase levels of motivation; develop a generic goal attainment capability; and enhance students' awareness of the factors contributing to school success and failure, along with insight into their own circumstance relative to these factors. Also, the program provides support for each student in his or her work to resolve issues in any of the dimensions of school achievement/underachievement: academic skills; study skills; learning disabilities; emotional or psychological issues; health and nutritional issues; issues of personal identity; life meaning or purpose, and schooling aims; relationship/conflict issues with parents, peers, and school authorities and structures; and social, cultural, and economic circumstances as these factors affect school aspiration and accomplishment. The program includes an integrated, coordinated, and evaluated series of activities, including classes and workshops especially designed to focus on school achievement. These classes and workshops are complemented by the integration of these achievement concerns into ongoing school courses, dormitory activities, and the spiritual aspects of student life. The program depends on the collaboration of school faculty, dormitory staff, and consultant and referral professionals.

So what all this comes down to is the same curriculum for everybody, electives within the subjects rather than in separate subjects, a traditional subject organization, a developmental/personal/social–cultural responsiveness, and a student effectiveness program as part of the curricular offerings. What do you think?

CHARACTER EDUCATION

In the last chapter I illustrated my ideas about teaching through an exploration of instructional technologies as a way to work with underachieving students. I do the same thing in this chapter through a discussion of character education for these kinds of students. I also follow this same format in the next chapter which deals with school context, this time using the topic of classroom discipline. What I hope you get out of each of these analyses is a deeper understanding of my overall point of view regarding the chapter topic, as well as insight into my views on a particular issue which I consider important. So read the following pages with those purposes in mind.

Consider this quote from highly respected sociologist Amatai Etzioni, "Education commissions are looking at what's wrong with our schools from the wrong end. How can a child learn if he or she doesn't have the psychic stamina (character)? The prerequisite for all learning is inner strength and self-discipline."[8] This statement speaks to the issue I wish to explore at some length: What is character and what should the schools do about it? I know character is an ambiguous concept, meaning very different things to different people. But at the same time, despite the lack of agreement about its precise definition, it does provide us with a good organizer or conceptual handle for bringing attention to an issue which I consider to be crucial for the school to consider: Do schools have any obligation to teach specific traditions and personal qualities to students? In short, do they have any business engaging in character education?

Let me offer you some key definitions, at least as I see them, before I move on. First, I draw a distinction between *values* and *morals*. *Values* relate to a person's preference and commitments, ideas about merit or worth, and concepts of goodness, rightness, and fairness. Notice that there are three areas: What is preferable and what am I disposed to do? What is worthwhile or of high quality? What is right? Values also have to do with actions that grow out of these ideas. *Morals* pertain to that third category of values, those dealing with what is good and bad, right and wrong, just and unjust. Thus, moral issues are a subset of value issues. Some but not all value issues are moral issues. Diagrammatically it looks like Figure 6-1.

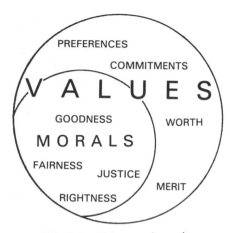

FIG. 6.1. Values and morals.

To illustrate, I may prefer golf as a recreational outlet and I may be really committed to playing the game and furthering the sport. I may play golf every chance I get (do not schedule appointments with me on Wednesday afternoons). That is, I value golf. But with all that, golf is not a moral issue for me. I am not saying that it is right to play golf. I am not contending you are a bad person if you do not play. I am not claiming that golf is morally superior to bowling. I just like it, think it is a great way to spend time, very challenging, and I do encourage you to get some clubs and give it a try. That is all. Similarly, I may decide some movie I saw was a great film. It had a superior script and direction, the cinematography was terrific, and the acting superb. It was just a fine work of art. I value the film. But although I see the film as having worth or merit, and it gets a very positive rating from me, I am not making a moral argument for it. I am not saying the film was morally superior to some other film, just better as an esthetic expression.

Similarly, I might make it clear that I place low value on killing civilians in wartime because it is a wrong thing to do. I am not saying it is ineffective or tactically a bad move. I am not saying it cannot be done well. I am saying it is bad and unacceptable for human beings to do. It is immoral.

A related term to morals is the concept of *ethics*. I defined this briefly earlier, but it is worth repeating in this context. As I see it, ethics are a code of conduct, or actions that grow out of this code. Ethics are grounded in values, particularly in one's principles of morality. Ethics are a kind of cluster or set of integrated, mutually consistent rules of behavior that define just and decent action. An ethical act is one consistent with this formulation. The point to underscore is that not every act stemming from a value is necessarily an ethical act. For example, referring back to the Etzioni quote that began this section, self-discipline may be a cultural value. It may be preferable for a whole host of reasons. And it may be encouraged vigorously. But it is still an issue for debate as to whether it is a moral or ethical concern. Those who push this value may stop short of asserting that one is unjust or bad for being undisciplined. They make take the position that one who lacks self-discipline is just out of step with a cultural tradition that is preferable. Let us say, though, that you systematically overcharge elderly, somewhat senile customers in your store. Most would agree that conduct is unethical on your part. It violates an informal code of business dealings largely agreed upon in this society, and probably goes against a formal code of ethics adopted by your business association. It is unethical to do what you are doing.

Admittedly it is somewhat of a judgment call to decide exactly when a value is or is not a matter of moral concern, exactly what the distinction is between morals and ethics, and just when some behavior in question is an ethical versus nonethical issue. I have never been able to become completely clear on these distinctions in my own work. But these definitions have nevertheless proved very useful to me. Test them out for yourself. They are particularly important when dealing with the topic of character education.

I realize I have not defined the term *character*. There is no simple agreed-upon definition for that term. I try to give you a sense of its meaning(s) as we proceed through this section.

These days there is a strong movement to bring character education into the schools as part of both the formal curriculum and informal operations of the school. To understand this movement, a bit of historical perspective will prove useful. I think it fair to say that in the 1960s and 1970s there was a predominant orthodoxy regarding schools and the teaching of values. I label it a liberal in contrast to a conservative position. If a typical advocate of this orientation were asked to state his position, I think his reply would go something like this: "We want students to think about and form values. And we want to give them a chance to act on their value choices. However, although schools have an obligation to encourage students to reflect on value questions and to teach them processes for how to think about values, schools do not have the right to tell students *what* to value. Students should autonomously decide what to prefer, what to uphold, what is of worth, and what is right. The proper role of the school is to provide for objective, critical analyses of American traditions and contemporary situations and to let students make up their own mind. Our goal is to create a context in which this freedom of open inquiry is possible. Our hope is to produce students and, later, citizens capable of critical thought and insight into matters of value." For an excellent analysis of this perspective, see Diane Ravitch's book *The Troubled Crusade*, which provides a very readable history of education since 1945.[9] Ravitch, an educational historian, makes no pretense of being unbiased in her views, but she writes well and persuasively.

Two approaches typify the classroom strategies growing out of this 60s–70s orthodoxy (and 80s, I do not mean to imply this is an historical relic): values clarification and moral development education. The values clarification movement was spearheaded by such writers as Louis Raths, Sidney Simon, and Howard Kirschenbaum.[10] The emphasis in these strategies was to promote student clarification of their own position on values issues—thus the label for the movement, values clarification. A number of classroom exercises were created which encouraged students to choose and affirm—and, less frequently, act on—values. Values clarification did not concern itself with the distinction between values and morals. Thus one day a class might be devoted to deciding "Twenty Things You Love to Do," the merits of cigarette smoking the next, and the third day take on the issue of when killing is justified, without attending to how these issues were, in any way, different in kind. Since the values clarification theory made no big thing of the distinctions between value and moral issues, teachers were not especially called upon to write moral and ethical issues into their lessons. As a practical matter, weeks and months could go by without focus on those value issues that were of a moral nature.

Another approach used during the 1970s was a process for learning to think about moral issues. The primary theorist associated with this moral development movement was Lawrence Kohlberg.[11] (Well, he still is. Again, I do not want to imply that this thrust is dead, or unused in today's schools. It is just that it was more prominent a few years ago than it is at present.) Kohlberg, who was a Harvard developmental psychologist, concerned himself with the maturity in a students' ability to think about moral issues. He created a theory that maintains that all individuals proceed invariantly through a series of stages characterized by the way they justify moral choices. The stages are distinguished from one another on the basis of the complexity and sophistication of the thought processes applied to resolving moral issues. There are six Kohlbergian moral reasoning stages. (Kohlberg vacillated some, at times going with five, though most of the time holding that there are six.) Stage 1 is the lowest because it is characterized by the least elegant reasoning about moral concerns and, at the opposite end, stage 6 is the highest on the basis of this same criterion.

An example: The moral issue is whether or not it is right to burglarize a drugstore to get some drugs. I might decide it is wrong because, if I did it, I would probably get caught and then I would be in trouble. I would go to jail and get a record and that would mess up my life later on. On the contrary, I might say it is right because I know a person who works there, he will leave the door open, tell me where everything is, and I can get in and out of there in a flash; there is no way I am going to get caught. Kohlberg would call both of these positions stage 1 responses because the basis for deciding the issue was whether or not I could escape blame and punishment. This is a simple kind of law of the jungle, me or you, whatever-I-can-get-without-getting-hurt way of looking at things. Alternatively, I could have decided it was right or wrong to take the drugs on the basis of some universally applicable principle of justice that I use in this and all such instances to decide what is right. In this latter case I see the issue in broader terms. My thinking is abstract and inclusive of the many factors that are involved in this matter, including the consequences for the druggist and my obligation to society and its laws; more than just whether I can score these drugs without running up against the law.

Notice what put me in stage 1 or 6. It is not *what* I thought, the position I took on whether it is right or wrong, but *how* I thought about the moral issue inherent in this situation. (There are stages 2, 3, 4, and 5 as well in Kohlberg's theory, but I am not going to take the space to go into them. You can read about them on your own.) What makes stage 6 better than stage 1 is that it goes beyond avoidance of pain and discomfort to a position that is more abstract and principled.

A typical Kohlbergian moral development strategy is the use of what are called "moral dilemmas." These are brief, hypothetical case studies in which the protagonist faces a moral issue. For example, should Mary turn her best friend who has just shoplifted some clothes in to the store detective? Students take a position: yes, she should; no, she should not. Most important to Kohlberg, students do not just state their positions; they offer the *reasons* for their position. Then they debate the merits of their justification for their choices. As the theory has it, this defense of rationales for a moral stance will result in increased capability and tendency among students to bring more highly developed cognitive (thought) processes to bear on moral issues.

The aim, then, of these moral development strategies is to produce students who can think in highly abstract and sophisticated ways about matters of morality. Again, like values clarification, the emphasis is on how to think and not on what to think or how to behave. The belief is that schools have no business telling students what to believe or how to go about their lives. What the school should do is pose moral issues and promote moral reasoning development. One more thing, the school should provide students with a school context that operates on the basis of concepts of fairness and justice that are more elevated than, as is usually the case in schools, a message to students that "authority makes right" and "your job is to follow the rules."

Keeping this historical context in mind, consider some more contemporary positions and contrast them with these earlier perspectives. The major difference is that now, instead of the promotion of values clarification or moral reasoning development, there is greater emphasis on the schools teaching particular values. However, I do not want to go too far with this distinction. Upon analysis, the 60s–70s approaches had a tacit agenda regarding what, as well as how, to value. They tended to come down on the side of privatism (focus on the personal rather than the public) and relativism (though there are better and worse ways to think about them, there are no right answers in values matters—instead it is relative to a particular situation and a matter of personal choice). They also leaned toward being antielitist, antitradition, and proliberal rather than conservative in their political and social preferences. The generalization is that there is no such thing as being value-free in one's teaching approach, even though educators prided themselves as such in the 1960s and 1970s.

Anyway, an example of more recent thought on this issue of values is this selection from the writings of Theodore Sizer. Sizer advocates that schools direct their efforts to inculcating decency among students:

> Decency in the American tradition (obviously the creation more of our Judeo-Christian than of our republican tradition) comprises fairness, generosity, and tolerance. Everyone should get a fair shake. People who are in trouble or who for whatever reason are weak deserve a special hand; the big guys should not force their way on the little guys. It is difficult to imagine a citizen who would seriously quarrel with any school that tried to stand for these values and to persuade its students to make these values operative parts of their character.[12]

Notice here that he is not talking just about teaching critical thinking, the skills of objective analysis, or any of that. He is talking about the school assuming an advocacy position on a matter of personal character.

Another example, consider a mid-1980s invitation by the Federal government for grant applications. Character education was one of the areas in which it sought proposals. In the words of the invitation, the Secretary of Education "challenged the American people to consider character as an essential aspect of educational excellence." In the *Federal Register*, character was defined as "instilling fundamental qualities of mind and heart that form the basis for sound judgment." More specifically, the Secretary invited applications for projects that contributed to the "fostering of student character development in the Nation's elementary and secondary schools. Applications should propose ways schools and parents can encourage such qualities as thoughtfulness, kindness, honesty, respect for the law, knowing right from wrong, respect for parents and teachers, diligence, self-sacrifice, hard work, fairness, self-discipline, and love of country."[13] Again, a clear indication that in the eyes of the Federal Government schools should be aiming at more than the promotion of clarification of one's view or cognitive development.

A third example is the recent writings of Edward Wynn. To be fair, Wynn has been saying this for years. It seems it is his time to be heard. Wynn's position is that America's public schools should teach what he calls the "great tradition" that Western civilization has passed down to us. He contends that in the United States there has historically been agreement on certain behavioral ends and that the schools have the right to teach them to students. Wynn outlines what he considers to make up this "great tradition":

- *There is a concern for good habits of conduct.* Wynn emphasizes visible courtesy and deference in contrast to moral concepts or rationales.
- *There is a focus on day-to-day moral issues: telling the truth in the face of evident temptation; being polite; and obeying legitimate authority.*
- *There is no single agency in society with the sole responsibility for moral*

education. Here, he is arguing against schools being morally neutral. Get on board, he is saying to schools. Reinforce what is going on in the home and neighborhood.

- *Moral conduct, especially among the young, needs persistent and pervasive reinforcement.* He lists avenues such as literature, proverbs, legends, drama, ritual, folk tales, awards, praise, and criticism.

- *There is an important relationship between the advancement of moral learning and the suppression of wrong conduct.* Punish wrong acts. Develop the concept of "scandal."

- *The tradition is not hostile to the intellectual analysis of moral problems; but nevertheless there is a strong foundation of habit-oriented, mundane moral instruction and practice.*

- *The most important and complex moral values are transmitted through persistent and intimate person-to-person interaction.* An argument against teacher neutrality, emphasized during the last several decades as a way to create conditions in which students can freely weigh matters for themselves. Instead, there is the idea here of the teacher as a moral mentor of sorts.

- *Students are treated as members of vital groups, such as teams, classes, or clubs.* The focus is on the collective, on group life and group loyalty; the group as the referent and socializing agent. This contrasts with the individualistic "Things I Like To Do" 1970s approaches to values.

- *There is a pessimistic opinion about the perfectibility of human beings; and there is pessimism about the feasibility or advantage in breaking with previous socialization patterns.* Because someone believes something does not make it right. Being clear on one's position and capable of sophisticated justifications does not mean a position is warranted. Whatever the stance, it must still be measured against a moral consensus growing out of thousands of years of human history.[14]

As you might expect, Wynn has been criticized for blurring the necessary distinction in a free society between indoctrination and education, for substituting tradition for critical thought, and favoring authority while playing down individual responsibility. Whatever you may think of his views—and Sizer's and others' that could be presented—they have certainly broadened the debate and raised some challenging issues.

Now I would like to share some thoughts I have in a couple of areas within this large issue of the school's role in educating for character. First, I consider it an important task of schools to acquaint students with the culture and traditions of this country and the responsibility they have as citizens of this republic. I agree with these later writers that it is not enough for schools to simply give students the means for getting their thoughts together, as if they were simply cultural shoppers deciding what to consume. Wynn is right: We all inherit a tradition. We are individuals to be sure, but we are also members of a culture, and that culture has a past and a future. Things did not start with our birth and will not end with our death. We need to be responsible to both what has gone before and what will follow.

I made the argument in the initial chapter that schooling must be grounded in the cultural and historical reality in which it functions. In this culture that means helping students meet the challenge of living freely with dignity and supporting the particular political and cultural heritage they inherit. Students must understand that, simultaneously, they are both private and public beings. They are one-of-a-kind human beings and, by the luck of their birth, holders of a tradition and part of a political and social experiment. Surely the job of integrating private and public responsibilities often results in the experience of tensions and contradictory demands. But that is a reality that young people, and all of us, must face. We should work toward a life in which these tensions and contradictions are managed well; or even transcended. Schools should be in the middle of this issue, presenting the reality and helping students work through the individualism/commitment balance issue. I think schooling in the 1970s focused too closely on the side of individualism and privatism, as worthy as these qualities are in and of themselves. There was a predominance of what *I* want, what *I* think, what *I* like, what feels good to *me*. Again, these are legitimate concerns. But these explorations need to be integrated with an equal concern for the values and traditions passed down to us, and it is our responsibility to uphold them and the social institutions that embody them. Simply, it got too one-sided in the last decade. It was too much about me and too much about now. These are both good things, do not get me wrong. It is just that there is more to it than that. Some years ago I wrote an article that goes into this in greater depth called "Worries About Values Clarification" which you may want to read.[15]

I am calling for a greater concern for culture, tradition, and public responsibility. But that of course does not mean that schools should be in the business of socializing students into uncritical loyalty and deference to convention and authority as some character education advocates appear to be advocating.[16] At the core of this society is a commitment to individual freedom and expression. The social contract ideas that so influenced the framers of our government underscore the inherent rights and dignity of the individual. At the heart of the American experience there is a commitment to individual thinking, deciding what is so and what is right, and charting the course of one's own life. In this culture schooling can never be just about the internalization of ideas and values from others. It cannot just be about duties and obligations and the acceptance of "right ways," even as it cannot back away from the search for unimpeachable values (self-discipline? fairness? tolerance? generosity? a commitment to human dignity?). School has to be about the tensions between the dual realities of individual and collective life and their resolution.

What I hope for are schools that help students successfully come to grips with the challenge of living a good life in the context of our culture. By successful I mean the transcendence of apparent contradictions between individual choice, happiness, and fulfillment and allegiances to tradition and community. This means a school that promotes individual expression and fulfillment, personal reflection and critical thought, *and* tradition and service. I would like to think that schools can reflect a commitment to freedom, loyalty, and responsibility—all three— because a life that integrates these values is at the heart of the challenge of life in America. Among the best of us it is not an either-or choice between private concerns for one's self and family versus tradition and cultural and public engagement. The best of us see the potential for the private and public dimensions of our lives to become polarities that complete and enhance the other. It is possible to be individualistic and personally realized when we are at the same time most referenced in the culture, most serving to the society and other human beings, and most connected to the past and future. Schools can hold up the examples of what the best of us do for students to emulate: find a way to be both individual and public beings without sacrificing, at least greatly, one for the other.

Of course there is the challenge of how to put this theory into practice. And admittedly it is a tough job for students to take on successfully. Education has a rich body of literature from which to take guidance. There are materials on the teaching of critical thought.[17] There are the values clarification and moral reasoning strategies mentioned earlier. Throughout this book I have been referring to ways to promote personal freedom. The Wynn material outlined a bit ago provides good direction in identifying the elements of tradition and we should consider it as we plan our curriculum. There is some good writing on how to use the humanities to connect students with our cultural heritage.[18] Also, there are guides to organizing opportunities for students to be of service to others and participate in community life.[19] The cooperative learning material I discussed earlier in this book, although I have some reservations about it, can nevertheless be very useful.[20] One last reference is a wonderful old book that I consider the classic work in education. It is John Dewey's monumental work, *Democracy and Education*, originally published in 1916. I will admit it is tough going. I remember reading it about 10 pages at a time, but it was worth it. The purpose of the book was, in Dewey's words, to "embody an endeavor to detect and state the ideas implied in a democratic society and apply these ideas to the problems of the enterprise of education."[21] That is what I have been attempting to do here. If you want to read a masterful treatment of this issue by arguably the most significant educator of this century, read the Dewey book.

A second reaction, this time to some of the contentions regarding the teaching of certain specific values as put forth in more recent writings on character education:

In a quote some pages back, Sizer called for schools to encourage decency among young people. In the grant invitations the Federal Government came down on the side of schools consciously promoting self-sacrifice, diligence, hard work, self-discipline, and respect for parents and teachers. I know many would see these as lay-ons, imposing our values on young people, inappropriate intrusions into students' lives and all that. I do not. I am fine with the school deliberately teaching such qualities, for one simple reason. I see a connection between these qualities and achievement, in school and in life. To be successful one does need to be diligent and persevering, able to delay gratification, and respectful and decent to others. Many times it takes courage to do what we need to do in the personal and public dimensions of our lives. It most always takes what Plato called temperance and we call self-control. It always takes a willingness to accept the responsibility of making something positive happen in our lives and in our world rather than waiting around and hoping. In other words, in its best sense, achievement takes character. And it especially takes character if you are a young person faced with the job of turning around a history of failure. It takes character to rise above barriers that are a product of your family or economic circumstance. It takes character to overcome a personal problem or skill deficit or to deal with a learning disability. Yes, it takes character. To teach character is to strengthen human beings.

I asserted earlier that we have much to learn from the ways advantaged parents bring up their children. (A book, mentioned in a previous chapter, that has influenced me greatly in this regard is Robert Cole's study of advantaged children, *Privileged Ones*.)[22] 'Here is another area in which we can learn from them. They make sure they instill the qualities of character. They are not hesitant about it because they understand the importance of these qualities if one is to live well. Ironically, however, many children who need this instruction from school because they do not get it at home are not receiving it. Because their teachers, as they put it, ''respect the children and their culture too much'' to impose such values as self-discipline, persistence, and respect for authority. School people who adopt this posture are right if the good at stake is maintenance of cultural differences and social distinctions. But it is a bad policy if the goal is promotion of human dignity. If you ask teachers, and I have, to list what allows them to make the most out of their chance at life, these elements of character are high on their list. The irony comes in when teachers hold back from teaching students the very things that allow us to live fully.

Character is something each of us earns. Students, especially these underachievers, must hear that. It can be modeled. It can be encouraged. It can be inherent in the school culture. And in school a student can read about it and talk about it and get some practice with some aspects of it. Educators can invite students to develop into people of character and acknowledge and appreciate them when they act with character. But ultimately, a young person has to decide if he or she wants to be a person of character. He or she has to go get it. And it is not easy—many of us fail at it. We are bright enough, have the right goals, and acquire the necessary academic skills, but we do not develop character. The truth is that some students do not achieve in school, and probably will not achieve in life, because they lack character. They want to blame their status on society or their parents or teachers; and they are right as far as it goes, they could have had a better shake. But no matter how correct they are about how shortchanged they have been, they are still left with the challenge of becoming a human being with character. Without that, talent and skills and even opportunity are of little value.

So, yes, the schools should teach character. I do not know of any one best strategy to approach this, though perhaps what I have just said is enough for you to go on. Primarily, each of us has to find our own way with the particular students we work with. The reality is, if we aim to develop character, we will succeed sometimes and fail sometimes. In a way I am envious of the optimism of the instructional technology people who just know they have a system that will work with all kids. Not me. I know of no "lead pipe cinch" methods. All we can do is be responsible to the situation and do the best we can to stay consistent with our own way of doing things. Then rest is up to the student. I do hope this has stimulated your thinking regarding a most important area, and particularly for the students of focus in this book. One last suggestion in this regard: I have always profited from the writings of Herbert Walberg. He has a pamphlet out, coedited with Edward Wynn, entitled *Developing Character*.[23] I recommend that you read it.

CONCLUSION

Those are some of my ideas about curriculum. Respond to what I have said: What are your ideas about curriculum? Especially, what have I not considered that needs attention? (For example, I have not gotten into the place a study of technology—computers and all—in the school curriculum.)

The next chapter moves from a focus on teachers and students and on, to the school setting itself as a place for teachers and students to do their work. What is this setting like? What should it be like?

7 The School Context

I now move to a consideration of the school context in which the curriculum is delivered. By context I mean the way we organize courses and programs and assign students to them. Schools schedule classes in a particular way—hour one and two and three—which we conduct daily or in some instances less frequently. These classes operate for a school year of around 36 weeks, or perhaps for a half year. Students sign up for one class over another or get placed in a class or are encouraged to take some class, a pattern of classes, or a certain program. Frequently students are assigned to a particular ability level of a course on the basis of some criterion. Sometimes they enroll or get enrolled in special or alternative schools. Context refers to these kinds of factors. By context I also mean the social climate or "feel" of the school—whether it is a warm and inviting or a cold and distant place, whether it is challenging to faculty and students, or a setting where nothing much seems to be expected of people. As well, context has to do with whether the school is disciplined and orderly, or chaotic. Another contextual concern relates to the institutional, bureaucratic nature of schools. Schools organize into various roles and departments, maintain certain hierarchal arrangements, formal and informal ways of operating and relating, leadership patterns, and power differentiations. The school, then, comes to have an identity and a life of its own. It has stated and tacit purposes and ways of doing things that must be reviewed if we are to understand how schooling works. All this counts for a great deal in determining whether students learn effectively or poorly. The school is not just a neutral arena in which to do the business of teaching and learning. Sometimes in our preoccupation with events in the classroom educators miss the effect of the school setting on our work.

I comment on some contextual factors, as I am calling them, that I consider

255

particularly relevant to the concerns of this book. I hope my remarks encourage you to probe more deeply into the nature and consequences of the institutional arrangements and school culture that influence the environment in which students learn.

THE PHENOMENON OF GROUPING

Remember the "bluebirds" and "robins" reading groups in elementary school? Though I do not remember anybody talking it over with me when I was that age, the idea was to put all the children of the same achievement level together (or was it ability level? interest level? some combination of these and achievement level?) to make it easier to accommodate for their particular learning needs. The same sort of things goes on in secondary schools. We can call it ability grouping. However, there is one major difference: While the "bluebirds" and "robins" stay in the same room, although in separate corners, usually in secondary schools they have their own classroom. To illustrate, the high ability secondary English students tend to be a class together; and similarly, the "middle level" have their own class, as do the "lower" students.

This process of putting like students together, ability grouping being one example, is called homogeneous grouping. Homogeneous grouping contrasts with heterogeneous grouping, which puts students of various abilities, skill levels, and interests together in a class. (Another term for heterogeneous grouping: mixed classes.) One way to operate them, homogeneous or grouped classes can be the same in terms of the content (areas of study) with only differences in readings, assignments, and class activities to suit the styles and capabilities of the group being served. For example, levels 1, 2, 3, and 4 (level one the high ability students) of an American history course might cover by and large the same topics; just do it in different ways. Alternatively, course titles and content can differ from group to group. The better students, for example, may take one English or math course, while less able, achieving, and/or motivated students take another.

Ability grouping (I find myself using ability grouping and homogeneous grouping synonymously) can be quite formal, with courses designated level 1, 2, and 3, or some such labels. The arrangement can also be informal. It is just understood that the "top kids" get put in Jones' third hour English class, or take certain science classes. Criteria for determining ability groups vary as well. Maybe it is decided on the basis of a student's past achievement or interest. Perhaps we decide on the basis of reading scores or some other standardized measure of capability. It could be in reference to a student's record of conduct in classes—the troublemakers go into certain classes—or his or her personality or style characteristics. Or perhaps we employ some mix of these factors that together create an overall sense of who this student is and where he belongs.

I think it fair to say, however, that with all of the sorting done by school personnel, the most important influence on ability grouping is the process of student self-selection. That is, students come to "know who they are" and group themselves in school. They decide they cannot, or do not want to tackle the work in the top level course or enroll in some subject. With the concurrence of parents, counselors, and other students they volunteer to "go where they belong."[1] Of course the question is, where did these students get the idea of who they are? Their notions may be in large part a response to conditioning that results from their cultural and social circumstance, which includes the shaping forces within the school itself. In other words, it might be that students have internalized, taken in as so, what they have directly and indirectly been told about themselves, and are simply acting accordingly. This is why school people need to be very careful and should not just accept a student's self-definition. We have to ask ourselves, and the student, "Where did that idea about what you should be doing come from?"

There is also the process of tracking in schools. In some cases, the way educators use the concept makes tracking synonymous with ability grouping. The way I prefer to use the term *tracking*, however, calls up the image of a railroad track. That is, rather than have tracking bring to mind the steps of a ladder (which is the image I have of ability grouping), there is a picture of several separate sets of railroad tracks going off into the distance without ever interconnecting. One track may be the *academic* track (another term, college preparatory), another the *general* track, another the *vocational* track. A student "rides" on his particular rails, ending up at his particular "station" (learning outcomes, self-conceptions, life goals) at the end. And given how one thing leads to another in life, perhaps he is on his way to a particular station in life. The ultimate in tracking is the establishment of separate schools for groups of students for part or all of their schooling. For instance, some students may attend the regular school in the morning—perhaps in ability grouped classes—and then go to a vocational program in the afternoon. Another possibility, if a student messes up badly enough he may be assigned, or volunteer, for an alternative school or program within the school building itself or in a different location.

The point is that sorting of students starts very early in elementary school, and by the time students get to secondary school, they are grouped in classes with "their own kind." These grouping practices tend to result in quite different forms of education from student to student. One student, even though he attended the same high school as another, may in fact have been taught very different things in very different ways. And this does not even include the differences in the education received by a student in one school versus another. A school in an affluent suburb may go about its business very differently from a school in the heart of a city. The result is an inconsistency of process and content in the secondary education system.

Adherents of grouping practices marshal several arguments in support of these arrangements. Sorting students by ability, past achievement, or skill, or whatever, narrows the range of diversity in a classroom and enables teachers to gear materials, assignments, and content to the students' capabilities, interests, and styles. Moreover, ability grouping allows students to go at their own pace. It avoids a situation where better students have to hold back and wait for the slower ones; and less able students will not get so frustrated as others progress so much faster than they can manage. Tracking also gives students the opportunity to specialize in their own areas of interest or where they are best suited. One thing is certain: School professionals find the rationale for grouping and their own experience with the practice to be compelling, because virtually every school I have been around makes use of grouping to one degree or another.

Despite the support for grouping, however, I have serious reservations about it. As they play out in practice, I think these arrangements may "ghetto-ize" less achieving students. For the "lower" or non-college-bound—whatever the label that we use—too often the result of grouping is a "watered down" curriculum, lower expectations directed at these students, less thinking and problem solving and intellectual challenge, less opportunity for language development, less agentry and more reactivity. In other words, less of the very things I most value. It is widely known that one of the ways human beings learn is by emulating the models around them. It is not a good situation to create a "bottom" class in which there are few, if any, students who are motivated academic achievers for other students to use as examples. So often the lower classes are tightly structured, teacher-directed, and "right answer" oriented. They are characterized by a sameness and predictability that only makes sense if control is the most important goal. The cognitive developmentalists shudder at the thought of such a circumstance. What they see as increasing intellectual capacity among students is not sameness and a series of correct responses; it is diversity, challenge, and a fair amount of cognitive dissonance (ideas that do not fit one's current assumptions). Furthermore, even when the content is supposed to be the same, I find it is often very different from level to level. For example (an extreme but actual case), in a top class of a world history I observed a discussion of the advisability of the United Nations' action establishing the State of Israel. In the lowest section, supposedly the same course, students were filling out a worksheet on Eskimos ("Eskimos live in structures made of snow and ice called _____."). As for tracking, I have made the point that I favor a general education for all students. Tracking too often results in a kind of training for the "nonacademic" kids instead of a freeing education consisting of liberal studies. Tracking might well result in some young people, I am talking here about the less advantaged or those who have not done well, coming to the conclusion, "Oh, this is who I am"—and not shooting for as much out of life as they should. Is it not true that there are many people of 50 years of age who think that the world does not owe them much or that they cannot do much with themselves because they did poorly or took certain courses 30-some years previously? Do not underestimate the societal sorting that results from schooling.

The conclusion is that, for the middle and lower level students, their education often does not stretch them in healthy ways. I wish that proponents of grouping and tracking would scrutinize the costs as well as the advantages of these practices. Consider what some educators say on this matter. John Goodlad wrote:

> Ability grouping and tracking appear not to produce the expected gains in students' achievement. Students of average and especially low achievement tend to do less well when placed in middle or low than in mixed groups. Studies have shown there is lower self-esteem, more school misconduct, higher drop-out rates, and higher delinquency among students in lower tracks. Track placement affects whether or not students plan to go to college and the probability of their acceptance, over and beyond the effects of aptitude and grades. Finally, minority students and those from the lowest socioeconomic groups have been found in disproportionate numbers in classes at the lowest track levels, and children from upper socioeconomic levels have been found to be consistently overrepresented in higher tracks.[2]

This statement should give us pause, no matter how objectively schools look at past achievement in making grouping decisions, and no matter how much the students themselves and their parents cooperate with the process.

Fred Newmann and Thomas Kelly pointed out:

> Research on ability grouping has shown adverse consequences to the academic achievement and self-esteem of slow learners and also that teachers devote less attention and effort to teaching slow learners. Reports on the effects of individualized instruction are mixed, but evidence that slow learners benefit more in heterogeneous classes may suggest support of individualized instruction within heterogeneous classes. Teachers' general preference to work with fast learners suggests the need to allocate special staff resources for slow learners. This can be accomplished through tutoring and special labs which can be offered in conjunction with standard coursework in heterogeneous classes. Often, however, some students have such difficulty, even with special tutoring and lab services, that they may require a more comprehensive alternative program. Such programs can be successful, but they involve two serious dangers. They may sponsor standards of achievement so different from the main program as to deprive students of the chance to master critical skills, and they may be stigmatized as a dumping ground for failures, rather than as a unique support community where the challenge of excellence is taken seriously.[3]

Again, no endorsement of ability grouping, and caution about the establishment of alternative programs and schools.

But if we do not ability group and track what do we do? It is clear from what I have written so far that I would prefer a policy of mixed or heterogeneous classes—everybody in class with everybody. It is clear that I would like to see a situation where, by and large, there is the same curriculum for everybody. But I know there can be real problems with this situation. Or at least there *looks* as if there will be problems with a single curriculum-mixed classes circumstance.

Whatever the case, between real and anticipated problems, most educators seem to be on the side of grouping. I do think that what I have written here about student-as-agent-multi-task classrooms gives us a start toward an alternative to grouping. As long as we center on teaching we will fall back on grouping because, no, we will not find one mode of presentation or one assignment that fits every student. Ability grouping is geared far more to accommodating the teachers' desire to teach in ways to which they are accustomed than it is to meeting students' needs. In particular, ability grouping is as much as anything a result of our inability to individualize and personalize teaching. The best we have come up with is "proceed at your own rate" mastery approaches or "go to the library and work on your own" independent study strategies. For reasons I outlined in a previous chapter, these approaches, though useful at times, do not go far enough in getting what I want out of schools. Unless we learn to accommodate more effectively for differences among students within a mixed class (which is not to say there are not great differences among students even in homogenous classes) we will be left with grouping practices and the negative consequences that come with them.

One promising idea in this regard is what Herbert Walberg and his colleagues are calling "adaptive education." They have reviewed a number of research studies and have concluded that adaptive education brings positive results. They list the following characteristics as comprising adaptive education strategies:

- Instruction is based on the assessed abilities of each student.
- Students work at their own pace.
- Students receive periodic reports of their mastery.
- Students plan and evaluate their own learning.
- Alternative materials and activities are provided.
- Students have a choice of goals and activities.
- Students help one another to achieve individual and group goals.[4]

There are some features to this concept of adaptive education that sets it apart from mastery learning, a process I am not enthusiastic about. Students plan and evaluate their own learning and have some choice of goals, and there is an emphasis on cooperation. Though I do wonder exactly what test results Walberg and his colleagues took to be indicative of the success of what they are calling adaptive education. Does it result in more than just knowing? How about problem solving capability? Higher order thinking skills? (The top three of Bloom and personal meaning that I discussed before.) Creativity? Commitment to further learning? Does it result in the "tail wagging the dog" problem, in which simple "just the facts" content is selected because it fits the instructional mode? Or, short of that, does the adaptive education approach by its nature fail to press teachers to challenge students with material of a more complex sort? Despite all that, I do respect Walberg's work a great deal and find anything he brings up worthy of serious consideration. He and his colleague Margaret Wang have edited a book called *Adapting Instruction to Individual Differences* on adaptive education you may wish to read.[5]

Although it is clear from the discussion just ended that I have a favorable disposition toward mixed classes, it should also be clear that I do not consider them to be problem-free arrangements for the heretofore-less-than-successful students. And it is also not to say that I see no room for grouped classes. Rather, I am arguing against homogeneous grouping as the *predominant* pattern of organization in the school, the *characteristic* way of structuring the academic program. As well, while I am indeed unfriendly to tracking, that does not mean I absolutely rule out the possibility of it being a useful path for some students. Certainly I do not mean to imply that I oppose all curricular experiences tailored to just certain students. Schooling comes down to doing whatever gets us where we want to go, and it is shortsighted to arbitrarily preclude the value of any option.

Allow me to expand on this idea. I worry that we could be setting up some students for failure if we just throw them into classes with everybody else. Due to a number of factors, chief among them those described in chapter 4 of this book, some students may not be ready to succeed in mixed classes. This problem is compounded by the fact that we are living in a time that places great emphasis on increased levels of academic achievement in our schools. The excellence movement, as I have called it, has encouraged all of us—school professionals, parents, students, the culture generally—to set our sights higher than we have in the past. Because it is important to expect the best from schools and our children, this is a healthy trend. However, if we break from differentiated experiences (ability grouping and tracking), and increase the academic expectations for all students (the excellence movement), we might put some students in a difficult situation. That is, even if they are bright enough to take on the new job, they may not, for reasons inside and outside them, be ready to go to school in a new way.

What do we do? My position is to stay with the heightened academic emphasis, push toward a solid core of general studies, and institute mixed classes wherever it is at all possible. It would be so easy to bail out and stay with grouping, watered down courses, and lowered expectations. We need to dig in and keep the curriculum and instructional processes geared to the best program we can provide; and then work even harder to bring students to the point where they can and want to take advantage of a top flight education.

Organizationally, what that may mean for many of the underachieving students is a combination of mixed and grouped experiences. There would be heterogenity as far as the basic academic program is concerned, and a tendency to homogeneity in any elective classes or clusters of classes they take (since I am assuming that students who share interests tend to be somewhat similar). Homogeneity also comes in for students who need a student effectiveness program. This is a program that teaches the skills of academic success. Obviously some students, particularly the current "top" students, do not need such a program, or at least have no pressing need for such a program (though, they may prove invaluable as peer instructors in such a program). But some students do need it. In the next chapter I describe what such a program might consist of. It is enough at this point to set the stage for that by making the generalization that grouping seems particularly promising as a way to support students in developing the desire and ability to do well in mixed classes and a solid program of liberal studies.

The reason I am taking the time to make this point does not have so much to do with school, although there is that, but rather with life outside of school. True, I want the underachievers to learn to live in a mixed world of challenge and diversity in school because I think it will provide them with a better education than a grouped circumstance could provide. Similarly, I want them to learn in school the skills of avoiding some of the "homogenous groups" they may be heading for after school is finished: deadend jobs and run-down neighborhoods; and the sociological group in our culture in which people live out a reactive existence made up of minor pleasures and accomplishments. Yes, the stakes are high for many students. Because what some young people may really be learning in school is not written on the blackboard at all, and that is how to be a level 2 or 3 human being, and fill out life's worksheets as well as the school's.

I would like to make some comments about alternative schools. There are alternative schools and then there are alternative schools. Some of the specialized schools set up in, say, the arts or other specialized interests can prove most valuable. The alternatives I particularly worry about and want to react to here are the alternatives set up for students who just cannot seem to get along in the regular school. Certainly I can imagine a circumstance where it is necessary for students to be placed in an alternative school. But at the same time I do have a distinctly "show me" attitude about alternatives. I am concerned that when it comes right down to it, too often they tend to reflect values and standards in such contrast to the regular school that students do not get a chance to learn what they need. I worry that these schools get stigmatized, even by some of the students who attend them, as dumping grounds for rejects and misfits. I am suspicious that increased self-esteem and staying in school become *the* point of the school. I believe in self-esteem, but more than that I want a school that strives to provide the possibility for students' to learn what is going on and to get closer to a capability to live *freely* in all of the dimensions of the way I use the term. Yes, I believe in working to keep students in school. But I am more concerned about what they become when they are there. While an alternative may be the right way to go, I am highly skeptical of the idea. To be sure, some kids are extremely problematical and some have life situations so damaging that there is really no choice but to remove them from the regular school. But if there is any choice, and for most of the students of reference in this book there is, the onus is on the educators to show exactly what is going to come out of that brand of schooling. And, for me, unless I hear what I want to hear, the answer is no, keep them in the regular classes.

SLOW DOWN, SCALE DOWN, PERSONALIZE, DEMOCRATIZE

Four values summarize my views on what the school context ought to be like. I think schools should *slow down, scale down, personalize*, and *democratize*. These are values I remember reading about some years ago in a book by Theodore Roszak called *Person/Planet*.[6] Roszak argues that these four values should guide changes in American society as a whole. While I think his ideas have great merit in terms of this larger context, I stick to their appropriateness for schools. (By the way, even though the book is not focused on education there is some excellent material on schooling in Roszak's book. Especially see chapter 7, "School: Letting Go, Letting Grow.") I discuss each value in turn. The aim is to establish some standards that we can use to assess and give direction to the way we set up schools.

Slow Down

Students in secondary schools attend as many as seven classes in a day. These classes are about this, that, and the other thing. First hour has little to do with second hour, and second has little to do with the third. Each class bounces from topic to topic, today on one thing and tomorrow on something else. Schools try to cover so much that a student often winds up skimming the surface. There is little of the kind of in-depth exploration that results in *really* knowing rather than only *merely* knowing (and that distinction, subjective as it is, is a real one to me). Certainly we want to acquaint students with a broad education during their adolescent years. But at the same time we need to reverse the bits-and-pieces, speed-along, cover-everything tendency we have allowed ourselves to adopt. We must slow it down.

What does that mean? It probably means fewer topics studied in greater depth. And it probably means the integration of content, that is, organizing around themes or putting subjects together: for example, the theme of the family, or combining science and math or history and literature. It could mean fewer electives in order to streamline and simplify the curriculum. Or it could mean clustering electives into meaningful packages so they are not so disparate and jumbled. It may involve going to blocks of time instead of 45–50 minute periods. And it might mean allowing students to study a few things in depth and then move on to other areas rather than study everything concurrently for the entire school year.

Of course if we are going to slow things down we are going to have to become very clear on just what is important, truly important, for students to engage. Just what *are* the fundamental aims and goals of the school? If we cannot do as much as we are now taking on, what must go? And of that which stays, how do students study in a way that they proceed at a human pace and strengthen themselves, and not just get to where they are able to pass a test. Students are often so busy going to class that they do not study anything. It should be reasonably clear what my priorities are concerning what to keep and what to discard. But in any case, slow it down.

Scale It Down

Most secondary schools look like a junior version of the Ford plant. They are huge, and as far as I am concerned beyond the size that is natural to the human being. People just do not relate to entities that large. They have less chance of being known and attended to within a scale of that magnitude. There is more chance of feeling anonymous and alienated when things get that big. I remember reading some writings by a zoologist who said that in his view, the human being is fundamentally a tribal creature who lives in groupings of 200–300 people. That is the way we lived for millions of years and that is what is natural to us. When it gets bigger, I believe we pay a cost.

Certainly I understand the advantages of size: one large library instead of many which duplicate one another and none with an adequate collection; with the same principle holding true for auditorium, gym, science facilities and the rest. So there is a clear advantage to large size. But maybe schools can be both big and small (the integration-of-opposites idea again). Perhaps they can keep the advantages of largeness but, at the same time, create small scale units for school professionals and students. For example, instead of one large school of say, 2,000 students, divide the school, everybody still in the same building as before, into five smaller schools or "houses" of 400 students each. Teachers, counselors, and other school professionals work with just one school. Staying with the heterogeneity idea, there could be an equal number of students from each grade level and students of all ability levels in each school. This arrangement maintains the advantages that come with size, but also allows for the positive outcomes of smaller units. My assumption is that with smaller groupings it is easier for the members, students and professionals, to feel a sense of belonging and ownership in a psychological sense ("This is my school"). Smaller-scale organization makes things generally more amenable to human control. Particularly, there is a greater chance of people being *known* in such a situation. To me, it is important to work to create settings in which people are known. That is a crucial quality to have present in a school. It is promotive of achievement for students; especially when being known is coupled with being *valued*. So many of our level 2 and 3 students are just not known or cared about as they should he. It is so easy to be virtually anonymous in a secondary school. That is not good. We need to scale them down.

Personalize

I draw a distinction between personalization and individualization in education. There is a lot of favorable talk about *individualizing* in the school—it is one of our "clean" terms as a profession. When you look at how it works in practice, to individualize usually amounts to students learning the same things in the same way as others. What is individual about it is the pace at which they go; though at times there is some difference from student to student in how they achieve the goals that are established for all students. And certainly that is not all bad; though to personalize is a different matter. *Personalization* involves knowing who a student is, his unique essence as a human being, his particular needs and goals, his manner, and his character. It is a process in which both content and process grow out of an understanding of this student as a person. By advocating personalization I do not mean to imply that I am calling for a student-directed approach in which students decide on what they are interested in and proceed, with teacher facilitation, to learn it. As a matter of fact, I am for a prescribed curriculum so that a school establishes areas of study and goals. It is the job of those older and wiser to set out what is needed by young people. But at the same time, I also want personalization within this framework. I know this might sound like a contradictory contention, but I can envision a situation in which there is a healthy and creative tension between adult responsibility for the direction of schooling and the personalization of learning. Apart from all that, if nothing else, I hope this concern for personalizing the school encourages us to affirm that there are people in those buildings. There are not just roles there—students, teachers, counselors, administrators, custodians, and secretaries—there are people. People are sacred, to be respected, known, and treated with care. In a personalized setting people are supported in becoming who they are, not just in getting in accord with "how it is done here." As I see the goal it is to personalize the school for everyone who lives there, adults and young people.

Democratize

By this value I do not mean everybody voting on everything. What I mean is a setting in which everyone feels, and is, powerful and important. No one, whether it is a student or a teacher or anybody else, should be in the position of just doing somebody else's bidding. All should be able to make decisions and take actions that affect their lives. They should be in charge of their lives. That is what America is about. Charles Tesconi and his colleagues get at this when they talk about the importance of teacher efficacy as an important ingredient in a good school:

> unless people possess a sense of efficacy—the power to produce desired effects—it is hopeless to expect them to assume responsibility for improving their own performance. Unless teachers can feel their efforts matter, what would be the sense in

struggling to improve? To the extent that teachers' behavior is externally controlled, that it is circumscribed by others' policies and teacher-proof technologies, we limit not only their power and prerogatives, but their psychological ownership of the effects of their actions.[7]

The same goes for students and administrators and everybody else. Democratize the schools.

Do you have a feel for these four values? Can you see what it might mean for schools to slow down, scale down, personalize, and democratize? What is your assessment of the merit of these values? If you find them worthwhile, think harder about their implications for the ways we operate schools. In any case, like them or not, come up with three more of your own to guide us and share them with other people.

ASSESSING A PROGRAM
FOR MARGINAL STUDENTS

Now I want to make use of the four values I have just outlined, as well as other ideas I have offered along the way, and to assess a proposal for working with students who are not doing well. Gary Wehlage and his colleagues have issued a report in which they describe some school programs in operation that are designed for what they term *marginal* students.[8] By marginal they mean students who have serious difficulty in getting along in the regular school, who are alienated from school, truant a great deal, and likely to drop out. I comment on the Wehlage report. We can accomplish a couple of things with this discussion. First, there are some ideas in the report worthy of consideration. Beyond the initial familiarization that you can get here, I hope my review encourages you to read the report in its entirety. Second, it should help reiterate and summarize some of the key concepts and proposals central to this book. And last, it should provide another example of how these concepts and proposals can be applied in a specific instance to make sense of things. Sometimes we educators, who pride ourselves as being practical people, do not fully appreciate the practical worth of ideas and ideals in giving direction to our work. I hope this discussion illustrates that usefulness.

Wehlage (though the report has multiple authors, to simplify matters I refer to it as if it has a single author) makes his argument within the context of the presentation of six case studies of programs designed for the marginal student. In the course of describing these schools Wehlage sets out his position. Wehlage argues against job skill-oriented programs. Instead he favors the adoption of a developmentalist orientation which he sees more likely to equip students with fundamental qualities and abilities that allow them to deal effectively and powerfully with the complex institutions in our society. Rather than immediately marketable job skills Wehlage wants what he calls "coping skills." Included among these coping skills are self-management capability; control of aggression; the ability to recognize and handle conflicting demands; adaptation to authority; and cognitive skills such as abstract thinking, problem-solving, and frame of reference flexibility. According to Wehlage:

> To view schooling for the marginal student as primarily vocational training and the criterion of success as immediate employability is mistaken. It corrupts the concept of education and emphasizes a narrow, short-run version of training that is a disservice to the marginal student and discriminates against him. What is most likely to occur is a form of social tracking that leads youth into the frustration of a series of entry-level jobs that are neither developmental nor rewarding.[9]

Clearly his view runs counter to the creation of a conformist and docile subgroup of willing workers; a focus that, intentionally or not, is pervasive in the education of so many "middles" and "lowers" as well as "marginals."

Wehlage contends that the promotion of social bonding is a key element that distinguishes a good program for marginal students. He points out that so many of these young people are either passive or nonparticipative in school life. And, of course, in more serious cases they exhibit conflict with institutional expectations and authority. The components of social bonding as he defines it are attachment, commitments, beliefs, and involvement. In contrast to alienation, social bonding is characterized by integration, engagement, and connectedness. One way good schools help students toward social bonding is by supporting the resolution of the conflicting demands of peers and school that pull them this way and that.

Wehlage's view is that programs centering on remedial courses in basic skills, job training, and work experience—a common focus in alternative programs for marginal students—do not take us where we should be going. What does? I draw the following generalizations about successful schools for these kinds of students from his report:

- Small size creates the likelihood of more intimate personal relations. This is necessary to counteract the perceptions by students that school is an impersonal, uncaring, and even hostile environment.

- A climate characterized by individual autonomy allows school professionals to create the conditions for learning and growth they see best, and it heightens their motivation and sense of ownership of the schooling endeavor. In other words, do not lay on from the central office one best way to teach. Give professionals room to make judgments.

- Small size and autonomy not only empower teachers to make the vital decisions about students and curriculum, they promote the development of teachers' face-to-face relationship with their colleagues and students. Such relationships result in more uniform, less arbitrary, generally fairer, and more human behavior by teachers toward both students and other professionals.

- The teacher culture in a good school is characterized by optimism about student success; a sense of professional accountability; an extended role for teachers (going beyond teaching their subject and a concern for academic needs to the communication of a caring for students and attention to personal, social, and psychological needs); high expectations regarding student conduct; high but variable academic achievement expectations (variable in that the exact same performance is not expected of every student); and a high level of collegiality among professionals. By this last characteristic, collegiality, it is meant that professionals do not feel they are in it alone. They have colleagues, other professionals who support them and stand ready to collaborate with them.

• The student culture is characterized by what can be called a "positive peer culture," one that emphasizes civil treatment of all persons and a cooperative effort in learning and solving problems. Students ask for help. They actively support program goals. There is a family atmosphere in the school.

• Curriculum and instruction is individualized. Students in the same class may be working on different content and toward different objectives, depending on their ability and needs. (I would call this personalized; but that may be splitting hairs.) There is much cooperative learning. Students work together and help one another. The curriculum tends to be problematic. Students confront genuine problems with no clear answer available (in contrast to the tasks that we euphemistically call problems).

• There are heavy amounts of experiential education. That is, students take on activities such as community and school service, career internships, political and social action, community-based study, and outdoor adventure activities. What is particularly important in all this is that they are able to test themselves in new roles and ways to being. Experiential education is more than working the counter at Sears to make a few dollars. It is being in a situation that is challenging, problematic, and where one can develop greater potency and self-awareness as a human being.[10]

To comment, as you might expect I see much to like about Wehlage's report. I appreciate his transcendent rather than accommodative educational perspective. I also like the way he is grounded in the needs of students. I agree that it misses the point to look simply at the academic disciplines and try to figure out how to get them across to young people. And saying that, of course, is not to denigrate the value of academic subjects. It is but to affirm that we also have to ascertain what students need in order to function effectively in society, and then see how the disciplines do and do not serve those needs. I also approve of the concerns that he reflects in his descriptions of successful programs: things such as being sensitive to the developmental needs of students and responsive to the conflicting demands they confront; and helping them to control impulses, interrelate with others, think clearly, and solve problems. Clearly these are matters about which I care as well. I admire his description of direct expenence opportunities (service projects, etc.) that were expansive rather than limiting for students. And last, looking over his case studies, these schools do reflect the values I listed earlier: they are scaled down, personalized, and people—well, teachers anyway—feel in control of their fate. It was tougher to see from the report whether these schools are slowed down in the way I spoke of it, but my hunch is that they are moving in that direction.

Now to some reservations. When Wehlage goes into a discussion of alternative programs, no matter how glowing his review it surfaces all those worries I discussed earlier about alternative programs. I get apprehensive whenever students are separated off from what educators call the "mainstream" of the school. And ironically, the more successful these programs are, the more separate the participating students remain from other students their age. Being successful might seem to provide a good argument for keeping these students right where they are, in this successful program, rather than indicate that they are ready to reintegrate into the larger school population.

Furthermore, I wish I would hear more emphasis on what students learn in contrast to how they learn it. Amid all the talk about individualized instruction, student-teacher relationships, experiential opportunities, and sense of ownership, I wanted to hear more about exactly what students are studying. You may remember from the discussion of curriculum, that I think content is as important as process, and that there are fundamental, consequential, ideas and events and people that students ought to know about. This liberal studies perspective pervades my thinking. I think educational philosophers would call my point of view an essentialist position. In any case, I find it disconcerting, even though understandable, how educators talk about more difficult students and often dwell on the way things get done at the expense of an equal concern with what gets done. And though he was far better than most in this regard, I did see some of this tendency in Wehlage.

Though, notwithstanding my reservations, I am very favorably disposed to the directions Wehlage advocates. What he wants does seem to be geared toward empowering students not just getting them to tow the line. I very much respect his attention to the well-being of teachers and the other school people as well as students. Schools ought to be good places for everybody who attends or works there. Frankly, school can often be a rather dispiriting and stagnating place for the adults who work there. But it does not have to be.

DISCIPLINING STUDENTS

I can think of no more crucial contextual issue than how to create an orderly environment in which to do our work. In any survey of teachers' concerns, discipline is at or near the top of the list. Simply, as teachers we need to have enough peace and quiet to get on with our job. That is not always easy to manage, and it is particularly an issue when teaching unsuccessful students. I take considerable space to outline what I have learned through my experience and study about achieving reasonable discipline in the classroom. As with all that I say, see if these points fit together into a meaningful whole. And do engage these ideas critically: assess their validity, extend them, change them, add some of your own, and think through what all this means to what you believe and do with students.

What do I mean by discipline problems? I probably do not have to tell you what I mean. But just so we agree on what we are referring to here, I mean just the basic everyday common notion of discipline problems: talking when the teacher is talking, fooling around, sparring with the teacher and giving him or her a hard time; generally anything that gets in the way of what is supposed to be going on; teachers teaching and students studenting. Good discipline, or just discipline, is a classroom or school where there are not a lot of those kinds of problems.

You also hear the term *classroom management* used in this regard. To me, classroom management is a larger, more inclusive concept than discipline. It includes discipline but goes beyond the maintenance of order. Classroom management refers to the things that must be done to set the stage for productive work, such as interpersonal relationships, a proper climate or tone; and getting the physical set-up right (chairs in the right place, etc.). My remarks, however, are directed at the issue of discipline.

A first point, we need to be aware that discipline problems are often a reaction to bad teaching; or teaching that students perceive to be bad, anyway. In that sense a discipline problem is a gift. It may be a signal to start improving our instruction. Perhaps we need to establish more of an academic emphasis in class, which research shows to be related to good discipline. Students are often not the most direct people. Creating trouble may be a way to react to what they see as professional inadequacy or their discomfort with some aspect of the class, and to get across the message that something should be done to remedy the situation. To suppress the discipline problem could also be to suppress an opportunity to improve our work. But to find the opportunity in all this we must be willing to open up ourselves to criticism. That means asking the question, how are they viewing the class? If their actions could speak, what would they be saying? That is not easy to do because our egos get involved and we can feel threatened and attacked. But if we can just convince ourselves that we really are competent and worthwhile people and do not give these 14-year-olds the power to define our worth, we might be able to look at the situation more objectively and less defensively. Though I am the first to admit that is not a simple thing to do. The understandable thing to do is to get right to the business of putting these little people in their place.

A warning: Do not trust conventional wisdom about discipline. Actually, I go farther than that and say do not trust conventional wisdom in education, period— but I stick to discipline here. By conventional wisdom I mean those ideas, precepts,

practices, that we just *know* are true. They are so obviously valid that there is
no need to examine them carefully, debate them, consciously test them out, or
any of that. Of course I know that education is not alone in operating on the basis
of conventional wisdom. I remember all the things I knew for certain in the army
that I now realize I had not thought about much at all; and which as a matter
of fact were not so at all (or, more accurately, were not *quite* so, or were only
partially so). And from talking to people in other professions, I hear that what
"everybody knows" can reign supreme in other lines of work as well. This preva-
lence of unexamined common knowledge might have something to do with the
human tendency to want certainty. I have always thought, for example, that fast
food restaurants make a mistake by advertising that the customers can choose
what to put on their hamburgers. One of the attractions of fast food for people,
especially adolescents, who are deluged by ambiguity in their lives, is that here
is one place where uniformity and predictability prevail. My bet is that it is no
great favor for customers to have to deal with the fact that sometimes there are
pickles and sometimes there are not. But then again, maybe certainty is not so
much the issue as is choice and control. It could be that the ability to hold the
mustard *is* experienced as a big deal, because it is about the only time in a day
some of us get to choose anything and be in charge of how things go. But anyway, an example of conventional wisdom from the area of discipline: Very early
in your teaching career you are likely to be—or if you are now in the field, probably already have been—told that kids will "test you." You are informed with
assurance that students are going to see how much they can get away with in
the class. Be on your toes, because they are going to check out the limits. There
is no doubt about it.

Have you heard that pitch? If you have, and you agree with it, it can have
very important consequences. Because the way you think about something provides the meaning of that situation for you. It becomes the framework for making sense of that experience. It becomes your guide to action. With this example,
if you go with the "test the limits" thesis, if you assume that is what is going
on, a number of things are likely to follow. First, if that is what the situation
is about as you define it, you are probably going to do what it takes to make
sure students get the word that you are not going to tolerate their games. They
are not going to push you around or get away with anything. You are likely to
come on pretty firmly—the word adversarial might apply. You will set down rules
and consequences for breaking them. And generally you will try to come off as
nobody's fool. You are likely to be take on a strategy of being tough in the early
days and weeks and then, when you have met the test and have shown them who
is boss, ease up later on. In fact, there is an aphorism in education that describes
this tack: "Don't smile till Christmas" (or in, some versions, till Thanksgiving).
The idea is, assuming the school year starts in September, you can afford to loosen
the reins and lighten up—"smile"—about the time Santa comes.

What has happened is that the "test" notion has become your fundamental assumption to organize and give meaning to that situation. Another word for such an assumption or concept is *paradigm*. A paradigm is a way of holding in your mind, understanding, "all of it," the totality of a situation. A paradigm is larger than this idea or that idea; it is the overall perspective on the whole business. It is a judgment call as to where the term *paradigm* fits—but it seems to me that the "they'll test you" organizer is so central that it warrants that label.

But without concern for whether such a grand, high-sounding term as paradigm fits in this instance, let us explore what happens when you take on any idea to explain what is really going on. A first point, part of what is really going on is this idea in your head. The idea itself is a crucial aspect of the situation. Reality includes both what's "out there" and how we perceive what's "out there." There is always an observer of external phenomena, and the observor's perceptions can never be divorced from the situation. There is no such thing as a "pure perception" of the world. We are always involved in putting words to reality and giving it meaning. So at any point what is "out there" is a relationship between the observed and the observer. To illustrate the point, what may be a discipline problem to you, may, to somebody else, be an example of adolescents working through a developmental issue of personal autonomy. Also, back to Assagioli, your ideas about reality are not only part of the overall reality of the situation, they tend to *shape* the physical circumstance and events in the external world. Ideas about what is going on or will go on actually go some distance in creating what is thought to exist. In other words, if it is not so, your believing it is so tends to make it so. All this is but to underscore that you, with your history, goals, needs, conceptions, and the rest, are looking at things and deciding what they mean. You count for a lot in this process and need to understand yourself as well as attend to the world if you are going to get a better sense of what is going on. Reality is an interplay of what's out there and inside our heads. Actually we never directly experience anything but electrical firings on the inside of our heads. That is not to say that there is nothing out there, or that our perceptions are totally arbitrary or inaccurate. It is to say that it is an illusion to think we purely and objectively connect to external reality. Our reality is internal, therefore ultimately subjective.

Back to the "they will test you" notion (paradigm?): Your assumption, and the posture and actions consistent with it—generally adversarial—will operate to create a circumstance that conforms to your preconception. For one thing, you will begin to interpret events in light of the preconceptions. Some kid asks to go to the bathroom and you think, here they go, pushing the limits. Another kid leans over to tell somebody about a record he brought, and watch out, they are testing me! Two others cough and it is a harrassment conspiracy. And beyond that, it is just human nature to mirror or reciprocate what someone is doing. If I am a student and the teacher is all about "tests," I figure that is the way of life around here and I guess I must be the tester. So I start testing, why not? It is not like I am some skilled anthropologist or something and can decipher everything that is going on. I am like the rest of us, just doing what seems to be in the wind without analyzing the whole thing. Which of course in turn reinforces the teacher's idea that, yes, that is what is going on here, the big test. (Do see that I am using the "test" notion to illustrate an important meaning-making and reality-creating process. I could have used other examples.)

Put another way, as a teacher you get what you expect. If educational research has documented anything, it is that teacher expectations have a significant impact on outcomes, whether academic or behavioral. Expect students to be pushers of limits and, sure as anything, that is what you will get. Looking at it from one side, you are proven right. You thought they would mess around and they did. (By the way, that is one of the ways conventional wisdom perpetuates itself.) But from another side, although you got to be correct, you still did not get what you really wanted. You did not get to work in an orderly, cooperative, and productive class setting. But back to the major point, which is that ideas about the world are not neutral, that they do not just explain or fail to explain external reality: Since you and I are in the world and since our ideas affect how we are in the world, and since they are the reality for us, in a very real way ideas create the world. Or at least our world. What it comes down to is that we need to be very careful about what we think about things because that is what they will become. Another way to put it, one way to change something is to change the way you think about it.

Another thing to note about fundamental ideas, or paradigms, is that they "eat up," take over totally, the phenomena they explain. To expand on this, let us assume some explanatory notion is valid or useful in *some* instances, with *some* students, under *certain* circumstances, *contingent* on this or that happening. What can happen is that this notion overpowers, as it were, the situation and washes away these qualifications and exceptions. This is another example of the "all or nothing" tendency in the way we think as human beings. In the example we are using here, the circumstance is seen as one of kids testing the teacher, period. This does not mean some of the time, some of the kids, if something happens, or maybe. Kids *will* test you—and that is it, so you must deal with it. With that as a pervasive mind set, every event consistent with this thesis becomes evidence to support the notion; while others that do not fit are ignored or misinterpreted. So the assumption that only one thing is going on keeps us from seeing anything else. And even more than that, the favorite idea tends to block out alternative ideas or explanations that might be equal or better answers to the situation. Paradigms are not good coexisters or collaborators—they want to be it all. Our preconceptions about something tend to discourage and detract from a search to find out what is actually happening in a class or with a student. It is as if the assumption had a life of its own and said: "You don't need to look for yourself. I'll tell you what is out there."

But we do not have to give in to pushy ideas. One implication of this discussion is that ideas about things are somewhat arbitrary. We can, and do, change our ideas about what is going on from time to time, whether it is about politics, art, or anything else. And if they can be chosen, why not choose those that best fit our needs and goals. Since, in this case, our ideas about discipline go some distance in defining and shaping reality, we might as well look at the consequences of holding them for ourselves and students. For me, the "they'll test you" perspective, for reasons that should be clear from the discussion so far, has not gotten me what I want. It is true that by eliminating the tests I am sure are present or imminent, I can create a quiet, managed situation. I mean, I can beat back the test if I marshal my forces. Students stay in their seats, do not talk out of turn, and the noise level is at a point where I can be heard. And hear me, that is not all bad. The problem is that I want more than the absence of chaos. The truth is I want students to support me and cooperate with me. I would like them to smile and say hello to me and have a look on their face that says, "I respect you and this class and I am glad to be here." That is what I really want and I have decided I might as well shoot for that.

I have heard teachers say something of the sort, "I don't care if they like me. I just want them to be quiet and get to work and learn something." And that is fine—if it is true. Talking to these teachers, however, leads me to conclude that, like me, they want more than that. They want students to respect them and the class. They want students to show appreciation for their teaching. They want students to actively support their teaching and not merely acquiesce to it. And if that is what they really want, I think they are going to have problems with the "I don't care if they like me, I just want order" orientation. So many of our usual approaches to discipline, while they keep students in line, do not produce the kind of affirmation and cooperation that most of us actually want. In fact, what they may well result in is a controlled environment and a group of rather flat and somehow unavailable students. Months of living with that can get old.

My advice is to decide what you really want in a class regarding discipline. Or better, what you want regarding classroom management, which includes the level of order, the overall feel or climate of the class, and relationships. Can you close your eyes and picture what your class would be like if it were the way you want it? (Do that now.) What words describe what you want? I think you should choose to go for that. Know clearly what you want and intend to create it. You may not get all of that this month or this year, or ever perhaps. But it does not hurt to work for it. And my guess is that you will get a large amount of what you want (the world tends to conform to the pictures we hold in our head). One of the things that keeps us from aiming for what we really want, or defining it in the first place, is that we get so hung up about the possibility of failure. If we never try for it at least we will never fail, is how it goes. If we do not make it to our goals, so what? The earth keeps spinning on its axis. We will not die. We can just assess what went wrong, learn from the experience, and go at it again. That is what good mountain climbers do. They do not waste time torturing themselves if they do not reach the top. They do not feel that they have to quit or that they did not have the right to climb that mountain in the first place. Instead they assess their goals and analyze their strategies and then, most likely, start back up the mountain. The unsuccessful climb was not perceived as a failure. It was just seen as an action on the way to a successful climb, or perhaps the choice to do something else. But in any case, it is all in how you look at it. Failure does not exist in nature, just physical phenomena, people, and events. Failure is an idea of ours. It is all a matter of perception. The inner pain comes out of all of the anguish and negative self-talk we bring to it. And, yes, if we are going to go into that act if things do not work out as we plan, life will be no fun and we will probably stop, metaphorically, climbing mountains altogether and just go watch a movie.

It is important to discuss failure when talking about discipline. Achieving anywhere near 100% of what is ideal is so tough to do. Discipline involves controlling large numbers of itchy adolescents, many of whom have little investment in the class or desire to be controlled. It is likely that we will have to learn to find satisfaction in what most of us would judge as partial success. And that has always been difficult for me to deal with personally.

My contention is that you will probably be a good disciplinarian if you do nothing more than picture clearly what you want and find the words to describe it; and, one more thing, get it firmly in your mind, in your way of being, in your posture, that those good things will happen. Surely it helps to read about theories and strategies for maintaining order in the classroom. But I am convinced that the strongest asset I have going for me is my ability to picture what I want and persistently live from the expectation that this *will* happen.

An example: Several years ago I took over a high school class that had a reputation of being hard to handle. There were 42 students in a "low" section of English. It went well for me. I am convinced that it was not so much that I used the right discipline techniques—though, again, I think they are worth learning. It was due to my posture, my bearing, and my overall manner. There was an expectation I had that got across to students: "I am here to teach, not spar around with silliness." I do not think it was what I said. And I did not go into a lot of rules and consequences for transgressions. Some of that is all right, but if you do it too much, it is like telling students not to put rocks in their ears. They might figure, "Oh that's what this place is about" and go get some pebbles. I did talk a lot about learning and growth and how to accomplish these things. I tried to establish that as the point of our being together.

When I observe classes I think I can spot one where there will be discipline problems after just a few minutes of observing the teacher. Somehow, and we are dealing with subtleties here, the teacher is getting across an invitation, or is it an expectation, that he or she is ready for, or deserves, the "discipline game." And it is a game. I think of the work of the late psychologist Eric Berne, the prime theorist in transactional analysis, and his approach to psychotherapy and personal change.[11] He pointed out that so many of our encounters with others take the form of games, with tacit rules and very real payoffs for both the winners and losers. Losing, by the way, is a payoff for some people. Losing at discipline can get some teachers what they want at a subconscious level: the negation they deep down feel they deserve; freedom from responsibility ("How can somebody be accountable for teaching *those* kids?"); a little excitement. What I try to do is simply withdraw from the discipline game. I will not play. And I know there was a time when I played quite often.

All this leads to my personal alternative to the "adolescents will test you to see how far they can go" idea. I see a "test," but one of different kind, one that makes more sense to me. Viewing it the way I do gets me along better in my work life. My version of the test, if it can be called that, includes two parts. First, I think students are checking me out (well, all teachers) to see whether I am "on top of it." And second, they are sifting out whether I care about them.

Let me explain. I find human beings, including students, to be almost endlessly hopeful. With students, no matter how bad it has been before in school—boring, beside the point, oppressive, whatever—when encountering a new teacher and new class, they have hope that this one will be better than it has been. This class, you, after all the irrelevance and tedium, are going to be good. That is not to say that students are not thinking "Here we go again, more of the same old thing," and somehow nonverbally or directly getting that message across to you. I am suggesting that deep down there is the hope, even in the hard-core reluctants and resisters, that you might be what they are looking for. And what is that? You, the teacher, know what you are doing. You know the material, you know how to teach, you believe in the content and what you are doing, you have things organized, and you show up on time and get to it. In short, you are an efficient, capable professional.

I am not saying that students are completely aware that this is what they are testing out. It is not that they are necessarily articulate about it and could use the words I am using to describe what is going on for them. But nevertheless, that is what I see them doing: testing to see if the teacher is on top of it. This has been my observation, but it is also supported in the literature. In a study of secondary schools in England, Michael Rutter cites research that shows that discipline problems are diminished if the teacher starts on time, values the subject, and is prepared.[12] To me that sounds a great deal like what I am calling "being on top of it."

The second part of the student "test," beyond the "on top of it" check, is whether the teacher cares about them. For the individual student—and remember, for any student the class is a place where I sit next to Mary and Ed and in front of Bill and behind Charlie—it comes down to a two part question: Does the teacher care about us, and does he care about *me*? I am convinced that it is crucial for students to feel cared for, not only for maintaining discipline but also in the promotion of learning. I think the caring from the teacher that matters most to them is directed at them as a student, as one who learns and grows. It is not so much a question of, does he care for me as a person? I have heard students say they wished that the teacher cared about their interests outside of school. I still do not believe they demand a total person-to-person connection with a teacher. It is more, does this teacher care that I am in this class and that I do well as a student?

I recall a lengthy interview with two secondary students who were having trouble in school, both academically and in getting along with teachers. I found their bitterness about teachers favoring other students remarkable. To these two students it was as if they did not count and that the teacher would just as soon they were not there. Though they were not clear on this, I was quite sure that the discipline problems they presented were a way for them to strike back at being disconfirmed. It was not as if these students demanded that teachers concern themselves with every aspect of their lives or be a buddy or pal to them. After talking to them, it became clear that it was more a need for the teacher to validate them by integrating some of their interests—cars was an example they gave—into class assignments and discussions. They wanted to know they counted as students in the eyes of the teacher. They wanted to see that the teacher cared about them.

What if I am right? What if these are very young people preoccupied with trying to figure their lives out, putting a social life together, and trying to find out whether this is a class where maybe they can do better so their mother is not so disappointed in them? What if the "limits testing" game is used more for the substitute teacher than for the regular teacher or a student teacher? What if the fundamental test is to find out if you know what you are doing and are willing to be with this class and to care about them? If that is what is going on, not smiling until Christmas is going in the wrong direction. Doing that, you come off looking a bit worried about your professional ability, more concerned with keeping the peace than teaching, as if you see the students as objects to subdue or as if it were a boxing match and they were faceless opponents. What makes more sense in that situation is to assume a posture and actions that demonstrate that you, the teacher, are committed to being there and to the material, and that the business of the class is to learn and grow. Your effort centers on preparing the lessons, starting on time, and teaching well. The message is, "I know what I'm doing and I believe in what I'm doing." None of this "I don't like the textbook and I wish I could have gotten another teaching assignment, but let's make the best of it" self-protection and whining. I say self-protection because that line is a way to get across: "Hey, don't come at me if nothing happens. Because, after all, the materials don't make it and I didn't want to be here in the first place." Little speeches like that are not the greatest credibility move in the world. Who wants to learn from an adult who cannot get where he wants to be and cannot come by the tools he needs to do a good job? There must be better models to be around. Your effort in the situation I paint also focuses on showing students, through the way you conduct yourself, that you intend to get to know them as learners. And you let them know—*all* of them, not just your favorites—that you support them as learners and that you care whether they achieve. Certainly each of us lives this out in our own way. I think you see my basic point.

Notice that so far I have not emphasized specific methods or techniques. Rather, I have been talking about larger, more inclusive matters such as the way of holding "all of it," the overall meaning ascribed to the classroom situation (or school situation, this discussion relates to discipline at that level as well). In a similar vein, I outline some qualities, general characteristics, in a teacher that I consider useful in maintaining effective control in a classroom. Again, these are not specific techniques. They are best perceived as strategies at a very basic, broad level. Or they can be seen as aspects of who we are as a teacher, what we are like as teachers. Read along and make sense of these next ideas in any way that helps you decide what is useful.

Connection

The idea of connection is much easier to demonstrate than describe as I am forced to do here. One way you can help is to try to experience what I am about to discuss. Connectedness has so much to do with an inner, sensed experience on the part of the teacher at a moment in time. My claim is that being connected to students in the way I describe helps maintain discipline.

The concept of connection has several aspects. A major one, and very crucial in terms of discipline, is to feel—literally feel, a kinesthetic sensation—that at any particular moment you are in contact with the students in your class. You are taking them into your inner flow of experience, into your awareness, into your being, at that moment. You are with them. You, the central consciousness that is most you, the inner buzz of aliveness, what we called the conscious self in a previous chapter, are with them. You, the human being who is alive at this instant; not some aspect of you such as your role (teacher), not your work subpersonality, it is the you that has always existed, from your first memory until now. One way to get at this idea of connection is to contrast it with what it is not. It is not what teachers often do when they are with students. They glance at students in passing, eyes sweeping over them quickly. They objectify them (third hour). They literally talk over their heads. A classic non-school example of what I am talking about is the flight attendant who, with a this-is-a-recording distance, "greets" you aboard an airplane.

To get at what I mean, the next time you are talking to somebody, see them, and be with them. Do not stare, just take them in. There is no confrontation, no attempt to compromise them, no attempt to win their favor or manipulate them. Simply be with them. See what that is like. It will probably be different, because we do not normally do it. Connect. Try connecting with students and see what it is like. It can be sort of scary or disconcerting at first. It can make you feel revealed in a way that might be a bit uncomfortable. Connection is the basis from which I generally try to work with classes, and certainly it is the posture I assume when dealing with discipline problems. A way to practice and better understand what I mean: The next time you are in a restaurant, connect with the waiter or waitress (another of the many people we tend to objectify and distance ourselves from.) See how it contrasts with how you usually deal with individuals who are doing this work. See if it makes any difference in their manner or the service you receive. See what it is like for you. Does it make you feel more or less powerful? Does it give you a greater or lesser sense of well-being? Does it lead you to be more or less on top of the situation?

Of course I am not claiming that we should always be in connection with the people we encounter in our lives. It is but one option from a wide range of possibilities that you can choose on the basis of what you want to accomplish or experience. Indeed it can be to our advantage at times, a necessary self-protection, to opt to be there with people without really being there. And it may just be too draining to be available and connected all the time. What I am saying is that the ability to be connected is a useful skill to have as part of your professional repertoire. Generally, being connected is a power position in this society; it is the manner of the influential person. Glancing away and detaching one's self tends to be associated with lack of concern, low self-assuredness, inadequacy, weakness, or deviousness. Even if they are not always aware of what they are reacting to, people, certainly students, do pick up on your basic manner. I contend that the teacher who is disconnected is somebody who seems more of a prospect to mess over.

I have been speaking of connection mostly in terms of the prevention of discipline problems. It is also useful in the midst of a discipline incident. A student is causing you some grief. Instead of yelling across the room at him or her, it is usually far better to walk across the room, break the physical space that we usually accord people in this society, and connect. Speak softly, confidently, and firmly and let the student know your reaction to what has been going on and your desire for what ought to be going on. Stay in connection until you are ready to leave. That is a more powerful, and to me more self-respecting, position for a teacher to be in than to engage in the "long range bombing" from the front of the room we so often employ to verbally admonish students or deal with disruptions.

I hope I am not distorting or clouding the concept to use it in this regard, but another aspect of connection is connection with the work of teaching itself. The basic idea is that when you teach, *teach*. Connect with the work. Do it completely. There are always a score of reasons not to fully engage our teaching at any point in time. I mean, not *this* class on *this particular* Tuesday afternoon. We are tired, underpaid, these kids are difficult, we just got a call that the roof leaks at home, the administration does not do its job, the ditto never got run off, and so forth. The fact of the matter is we *are* here in this classroom on this Tuesday afternoon with these students. Just going through the motions is not notable for resulting in teacher or student happiness or satisfaction. It has been some time since I have heard someone burst into the teacher's lounge with, "Great class today! Boy am I up! Just went through the motions!" And certainly one way to tame discipline problems is to do the work of teaching fully, with all of yourself. It goes better that way than to, as we used to say in the army, "go by the numbers" (mechanically doing the job with a minimal investment of ourselves). This is not to say that the work is done in what appears to be a "please like me" or "how am I doing, kids?" way. It is a mature, adult-like engagement with a situation. It is saying through one's actions that I want to be here doing this; I want to be here with you. It is part of the caring and on top of it ideas I outlined previously.

Of course, saying it does not make it so. To connect with one's work takes intention and vigilance. And sadly, it often has to be done in spite of students. Though it is self-defeating, students will often, in the way they conduct themselves, push you back from the work of teaching. And in many ways it makes it easier to work if you disconnect from your work. Students and you can then do the minimum and be free of the pressures that can come from being responsible to a situation. You do not have to test your limits and you do not run the danger of being revealed as inadequate to the task. But I just do not find it enjoyable or satisfying that way. I have decided *I* will determine the level of my engagement. I will not give that over to students or anyone else. When I work, I connect with my work. You, the students, do what you do; but although I will not spend a lot of time spelling it out or bother too much with rules and consequences ("Only three absences permitted"), you will get the idea that if you are around me, I expect you to connect with your work.

Level

Leveling is a way to communicate with students. Most of us are familiar with the phrase, "I'll level with you." That is basically what I mean. It is speaking frankly and candidly. When you level, apart from the particular subject of the communication, whether it is about an assignment or some point to be made in a lecture or a request to a student to take his seat, there is another, implicit message. You are saying that you are competent and know what you are talking about. You have something that you want to say and you are informing others what that is. It is spoken in what I call a full voice—your most mature, confident voice. For me, that contrasts with a kind of beseeching adolescent whine that I employ at my worst. And, incidentally, what I say here refers to written as well as verbal communication, though I am emphasizing face-to-face encounters in this discussion.

One way to explain what it is to level is to compare it with alternative ways of presenting oneself to others. Leveling is not blaming, shaming, or embarrassing students. These methods can win the battle at times and get things quiet and manageable. But at the same time it is likely to result in student resentment, antagonism, and the perception that you are an unfair bully. Get that going in a classroom and students well might flatten, withdraw, plot revenge, or live out some other unpleasantness. Leveling most certainly is not fighting with students. Try that and you will get it back thirty-fold, the amount by which they outnumber you. Moreover, leveling is not placating or imploring students. And it is not engaging in self-effacement or self-denigration; that can get you perceived as needy, a victim, or inadequate. Unfair as it might be, the weak get dumped on in schools as well as in the rest of life. Leveling is not babbling on. Coming out of college after listening to the lectures of impressive wordsmiths, we might try to emulate those who have, as my mother used to say, "the gift of the gab," and try to knock over teenagers with a flood of fancy sentences. The problem is that, in fact, in most of this culture speedy, wordy outputs are associated with weakness not strength. So often teachers are up there in front of the class rattling on, figuring we are doing fantastically, and all the while students are either feeling left out or becoming resentful that we are talking over their heads; or getting the idea that we are not very solid in ourselves. And last, leveling is not robot-like, impersonal, this-is-a-recording talk. It is not like the "greeting" you get from the receptionist at some giant corporation.

Instead, leveling is a mature, self-confident human being simply sharing what he thinks and feels and what things mean to him. It is not confrontive. It is not aggressive. It asserts the right to express ones thoughts, feelings, and needs. And it is insistent in a way. It demands that others take heed. Play around with the idea of leveling and see what kind of significance it has to you. Try it out. If you want to read more about this concept, I suggest you consult the writings of psychologist Virginia Satir. My terminology and ideas are somewhat different from hers, but you will see how indebted I am to her work. Especially read her book *Making Contact*.[13]

Being Centered

Being centered as a teacher is not so much a strategy as it is a way of being that is earned through one's overall development as an individual. What does it mean to be *centered*? As with leveling, the term is largely self-descriptive. It is to be in balance as a person and as a professional. A centered person has a harmony to their being, a grace. There is a dignity and a settled quality to them. They belong in the world and are where they belong. In contrast, we all know teachers and others who are off-center. To put it in the vernacular, somehow they are "out of sync." They are in the wrong place. They are, sometimes literally, shaky and wobbly. They are in disequilibrium. To borrow the words of the song, they do not row their boat (their life) "gently down the stream." Rather, they are dragging it upstream across the rocks near the shore. Somehow there is something about such a person that sends out the word, here is somebody you give trouble. It is my belief that centered people get fewer discipline problems.

Of course we cannot hope to ever be totally centered, much less centered at all times. But it is helpful to work toward a state in which characteristically you are centered rather than uncentered, even though you know there are "holes" and at times you are off kilter. So how do we become centered? Each of us has to find our own ways to become balanced as a human being. Certainly achieving centeredness is bigger than attaining professional competence or mastery of technique, though that helps. But more than that, it has to do with the successful resolution of the ultimate questions of meaning and purpose in one's life. It may have something to do with being able to love and receive love in all its forms. It may be supported by meditation, intense introspection, or psychotherapy. Finding and expressing one's artistic impulse might help. Creating a home—in contrast to a place to live—may be part of it. And perhaps attention to one's physical health and nutrition is a way to get at it in part. I could generate other examples, but I think you see what I mean. Becoming centered is not something that is likely to be attained today or this week or this month; or, as I have indicated, in the same way by everybody. What I do want to underscore is that discipline difficulties, and general discord, often mirror a similar unbalance within us as people. An excellent book that deals with this subject is educator Herbert Kohl's autobiography, *Half the House*.[14]

Blend

A fourth fundamental idea is the concept of blend. Blend is a metaphor that gives me direction in resolving conflicts. It is a way of dealing with the inevitable disagreements that we have with students. A problem for me as a teacher was that I had not been around models of taking on disputes that provided me good direction in the classroom. For example, the John Wayne-type, you-or-me shootout approach has not been a winner for me. For one thing, Duke, even on Iwo Jima, did not have to deal with the odds we take on—up to 30 to 1 and more. Plus he did not have to do it all day, every day, just once or twice a reel. And he did not have to work with these people the next day. And besides, life is not the movies. I mean John Wayne is in fact, after all, Marion Morrison. Or as Carole Lombard who was married to Clark Gable put it, "Clark Gable is no Clark Gable."

I draw the concept of blend in large part from some study and training I have done related to the Japanese marshal art of aikido. In Japanese aikido refers to the way of harmony with the spirit of the universe. Aikido is not a technique to fight and defeat an enemy, even though it is astonishingly effective as a means of self-defense. Rather, at its core, it is a means of reconciling with the world, including those who mean you harm. Aikido is not so much a way of doing, though it has developed a series of remarkable strategies, as it is a total way of being. In that sense it is a metaphor for what all of life could be. Aikido is remarkable to see in practice. In a most graceful, flowing, dance-like way the person attacked merges—blends—with the energy of the attacker. He or she joins with the attacker for a time and dissipates the aggression; and often transforms it into something uplifting for both people involved. Through it all, the attacked person maintains his or her integrity and, to use that term again, *centeredness*. All this while using only the degree of force necessary to maintain one's place in the world and without the intent of injuring the other person. George Leonard, himself a practitioner and instructor of this marshal art, includes an excellent account of aikido in his book, *The Ultimate Athlete*.[15]

To begin to illustrate the idea of blend it is useful to establish two other approaches that contrast with it. There may be some exaggeration here to make a point, but bear with me. The first I call the "shoot-out" strategy to resolving conflicts (discipline problems among them). It is the John Wayne tactic mentioned before; or like Gary Cooper in *High Noon*; or Jimmy Stewart in *The Man Who Shot Liberty Valence*. (I have been watching old movies on my VCR and I worry you may not know what I am talking about. But anyway, you will get the point.) In the classroom it is a "me or you, kid" showdown. It is the equivalent of Gary Cooper saying, "Draw!" The teacher says: "I told you to stop looking out that window. Sit down or else." ("This town isn't big enough for the two of us.") The obvious comeback to "Sit down or else" is "Screw you" or some variant of that. ("You're not taking me alive, sheriff.") And then the students (the townspeople peeking out their windows) get to watch you two fight it out.

Let us say you win. The kid sits down. Somehow, at least for me, it is not a victory at all after the first few seconds. In every one of these little battles I feel as if I lost something important, even though I cannot say exactly what it is. (My dignity?) I felt depleted, somehow wrong, cut off from things, diminished by it all. At the very least, it is tough for me to just go on with the class as if nothing has happened. I know I sure am not very proud of myself for coercing a 14-year-old to sit down. There has to be something else to do in life. At times like this I feel like checking the want ads for a Our Own Hardware franchise.

In stark contrast to the "shoot out" is the "victim" discipline strategy. This, as the name implies, involves letting students toss you around and step on you. Why do something like that? Any number of reasons. It could be that you cannot think of anything else to do. Or there is the hope that while they are pushing you around they will see the light and mend their evil ways. Or you maybe think you deserve it because you are an awful teacher (person). It could be, too, coming out of a notion we take on periodically that students are young sages (or saints or martyrs, it varies) and that they must be right, bless them. On this last one, in my view students are just like us, they are right sometimes and wrong sometimes. In any case, the teacher pleads from up near the blackboard, "Please quiet down,'' while the class looks like the mob scene on the field after the home team has won the championship, or the floor of Wall Street during heavy trading, or *The Day of the Locust*. Anyway, the victim approach.

To blend is not to shoot it out, nor is it to be anybody's victim to kick around. Before getting to classroom examples, consider this excerpt from an article by Terry Dobson. Dobson is a holder of a fourth-degree black belt in aikido. He is also the author of an excellent book on conflict resolution, *Giving In to Get Your Way*, and another book that employs the same principles, *Safe and Alive: How Not to Be a Victim*.[16] Dobson describes an incident he encountered on a commuter train in the suburbs of Tokyo:

> At one station the doors opened, and suddenly the quiet afternoon was shattered by a man bellowing at the top of his lungs—yelling violent, obscene, incomprehensible curses. Just as the doors closed the man, still yelling, staggered into our car. He was big, drunk, and dirty. He wore laborer's clothing. His front was stiff with dried vomit. His eyes bugged out a demonic, neon red. His hair was crusted with filth. Screaming, he swung at the first person he saw, a woman holding a baby. The blow glanced off her shoulder, sending her spinning into the laps of an elderly couple. It was miracle that the baby was unharmed.
>
> The couple jumped up and scrambled toward the other end of the car. They were terrified. The laborer aimed a kick at the retreating back of the old lady. "YOU OLD WHORE!" he bellowed, "I'LL KICK YOUR ASS!" He missed; the old woman scuttled to safety. This so enraged the drunk that he grabbed the metal pole in the center of the car and tried to wrench it out of its stanchion. I could see that one of his hands was cut and bleeding. The train lurched ahead, the passengers frozen with fear. I stood up.
>
> "This is it!" I said to myself as I got to my feet. "This slob, this animal, is drunk and mean and violent. People are in danger. If I don't do something fast, somebody will probably get hurt. I'm gonna take his ass to the cleaners."
>
> Seeing me stand up, the drunk, saw a chance to focus his rage. "AHA!" he roared, "A FOREIGNER! YOU NEED A LESSON IN JAPANESE MANNERS!" He punched the metal pole once to give weight to his words.
>
> I held on lightly to the commuter-strap overhead. I gave him a slow look of disgust and dismissal. I gave him every bit of piss-ant nastiness I could summon up. I planned to take this turkey apart, but he had to be the one to move first. And I wanted him mad, because the madder he got, the more certain my victory. I pursed my lips and blew him a sneering insolent kiss. It hit him like a slap in the face. "ALL RIGHT!" he hollered, "YOU'RE GONNA GET A LESSON." He gathered himself for a rush at me. He'd never know what hit him.
>
> A split-second before he moved, someone shouted "HEY!" It was ear-splitting. I remember being struck by the strangely joyous, lilting quality of it—as though you and a friend had been searching diligently for something, and he had suddenly stumbled upon it. "HEY!"
>
> I wheeled to my left, the drunk spun to his right. We both stared down at a little old Japanese. He must have been well into his seventies, this tiny gentleman, sit-

ting there immaculate in his *kimono and hakama*. He took no notice of me, but beamed delightedly at the laborer, as though he had a most important, most welcome secret to share.

"C'mere," the old man said in an easy vernacular, beckoning to the drunk, "C'mere and talk with me." He waved his hand lightly. The big man followed, as if on a string. He planted his feet belligerently in front of the old gentleman and towered threateningly over him. "TALK TO YOU?" he roared above the clacking wheels, "WHY THE HELL SHOULD I TALK TO YOU?" The drunk now had his back to me. If his elbow moved so much as a millimeter, I'd drop him in his socks.

The old man continued to beam at the laborer. There was not a trace of fear or resentment about him. "What'cha been drinkin'?" he asked lightly, his eyes sparkling with interest. "I BEEN DRINKING' SAKE," the laborer bellowed back, "AND IT'S NONE OF YOUR GODDAM BUSINESS !" Flecks of spittle spattered the old man.

"Oh, that's wonderful," the old man said with delight. "Absolutely wonderful! You see, I love sake, too. Every night, me and my wife (she's seventy-six, you know), we warm up a little bottle of sake and take it out into the garden, and we sit on the old wooden bench that my grandfather's first student made for him. We watch the sun go down, and we look to see how our persimmon tree is doing. My great grandfather planted that tree, you know, and we worry about whether it will recover from those ice-storms we had last winter. Persimmons do not do well after ice-storms, although I must say that ours has done rather better than I expected, especially when you consider the poor quality of the soil. Still, it is most gratifying to watch when we take our sake and go out to enjoy the evening—even when it rains!" He looked up at the laborer, eyes twinkling, happy to share his delightful information.

As he struggled to follow the intricacies of the old man's conversation, the drunk's face began to soften. His fists slowly unclenched. "Yeah," he said slowly, "I love persimmons, too... His voice trailed off.

"Yes," said the old man, smiling, "and I'm sure you have a wonderful wife."

"No," replied the laborer, "my wife died." He hung his head. Very gently, swaying with the motion of the train, the big guy began to sob. "I don't got no wife, I don't got no home, I don't got no job, I don't got no money, I don't got nowhere to go. I'm so ashamed of myself." Tears rolled down his cheeks, a spasm of pure despair rippled through his body. Above the baggage rack a four-colored ad trumpeted the virtues of suburban luxury living...

Just then, the train, arrived at my stop. The platform was packed, and the crowd surged into the car as soon as the doors opened. Maneuvering my way out, I heard the old man cluck sympathetically. "My, my," he said, "that is a very difficult predicament indeed. Sit down here and tell me about it"

I turned my head for one last look. The laborer was sprawled like a sack on the seat, his head in the old man's lap. The old man looked down at him all compassion and delight, one hand softly stroking the filthy, matted head.[17]

I will not be so presumptuous as to try to explain this story. Enough to say that there are some lessons to be learned from it. One thing I must say is that it reminded me of all the times I have been a "discipline problem" to others.

To them I was a pain in the rear. But from inside me, what I wanted was to be understood, taken in and included, comforted, and supported. My "acting out," to use the jargon, was not coming out of strength. It was coming out of pain, emptiness, confusion, feelings of inadequacy, and a desire to be attended to. Striking out came out of all of that. Surely the other person would be foolish to play victim and just take it from me. But at the same time he would be missing a fundamental reality and a major opportunity if he did not perceive and respond to the pain, need, and inner turmoil from which my actions emanated. This is not to ignore the times when students need to be clamped down and fast. It is to say that if teachers get off attending to themselves, they might make contact with a lot of "I don't got nowhere to go" inside these students who are giving us such a headache. And when we see that is there, it changes the meaning of it all dramatically.

In any case, when I am in a conflict situation I say to myself, "Blend." I will not give up my integrity. And I will not allow myself to be battered around. I will neither fight you nor give in to you. But I will listen to you. I will join with you and try to see it your way. I will try to make connection with the place inside you that needs and hurts. Instead of fighting you or blocking you, I will try to use the negative energy you are sending my way. I will try to use it to create a situation in which we can come closer instead of farther apart, where we can contribute to one another instead of detract from one another. All of this may sound idealistic and naive. All I can say is that it has been a technique that, when I can get myself to use it, has worked well. All you can do is think about it and test it out for yourself.

One example: I was about to begin teaching a class with a reputation for being tough to handle. I heard especially about Joe (not his real name) who was "hell on wheels." I did not know much more than that about Joe, and I was not exactly sure what I was going to do about him. But I did decide that I was going to blend with this kid. I was not going to be his fool or let him take over the class. (I quickly learned he would from time to time just stand up and walk around or go talk to people. He was also prone to engage in a running commentary on the class: "This stuff we are doing is *real* exciting," and the like.) And I was not going to go hand-to-hand with him either. The details of how it went come out in the next pages to illustrate points on discipline. It is enough to say here that I set out to blend with him, and for me that meant not compromising myself or him. It did mean working toward the goal of merging with his energy and redirecting it in ways that contributed toward making us both successful, him as a student and me as a teacher, and happy in the class. And, within reason, it worked.

Some Tips of the Trade on Discipline

What I have written thus far comprises the foundational ideas I have concerning discipline. Meet the test (get on top of it and care about them) and connect, level, center, and blend. From there I describe a number of "tips of the trade" on discipline. While each of these suggestions stands on its own, do note the relationship of each to the overall perspective I represent. It is important to see how all of these points go together rather than allow them to remain discrete "good things to do." Because what you and I need is a theory, an interrelated set of principles and concepts, that can give us guidance in making decisions in the always-unique experiences of our work lives. Also, a theory provides an entity of sorts—a referent, a structure—to modify and build upon as we generate new insights into the issue of discipline.

Expect What You Want

I have said it before. To a great extent you will get what you expect to get. Expect discipline problems and you are likely to have them. Research has shown that high expectations for students are linked to good behavior.[18] Surely it would be naive to think there is never going to be trouble or to fail to think through what you will do about it if it arises. But do not sit around dwelling on what it is going to be like when trouble occurs. Picture the class in your head, literally imagine it, as you want it to be. Close your eyes and let this well-disciplined class play out in your mind's eye as if it were on a movie screen. What does it look like? What is going on? What are students doing? What are you doing? How do you feel about what is happening? What words describe all that? Tell yourself. Now decide to create the situation. Intend to create it. Do not get worried about failure. If that comes up, let it go. Indeed, you may not get it done. So? You nor I nor anybody else is Superteacher. If students are absolutely set on bringing the class down, they can. Nobody can keep them from their pathetic little victory. No adults should berate themselves for being unable to control boorish and destructive behavior on the part of students. As you can sense, I do and do not want to understand student misconduct. On the one hand, yes, where does it come from, why are they disrupting the class. But on the other, there is a standard of civil behavior in public situations, and everyone is held to that standard, period. Students included. That is an attitude I bring to the classroom. No, I cannot absolutely, every-time prevent discipline problems. But I will not accept it and, no, I will not condone it. Ever. Students can deal with that attitude of mine.

But our inability to control another human being's behavior still does not prevent us from intending to do what we can to create an orderly class. Students are not in charge of our intentions. At some level they may want to think that we should accommodate our goals and expectations to their desires and behavior. But that is one power they do not have unless we give it to them. No, we can run our positive "movie," our hope for how things go, over and over in our head every chance we get. We can believe it. We can rehearse it in our imagination until we indeed *do* expect it. I have talked about the tendency of outside reality to come to square with what is inside you. I am sure there is nothing mysterious about this. In the case of discipline, all this mental rehearsal affects your bearing as you walk in the door. And it provides the basis from which you speak and act in the class. One way or the other, the message gets through that this is a place to get to work and not to spar around and play games.

In any case, I think we should spend far more time than many of us do focusing on what we want, not on what we fear or do not want. As I said, we have to be ready to respond to trouble. But at the same time, focus on the positive. For example, with attendance my message is: ''I want us all here because it can only work if both you and I come to class. So attend class.'' It is that rather than, ''If you miss five days, the penalty is...'' I am not big on listing exact limits, numbers, or consequences for transgression. I know that runs against the grain of what you hear in education. People tell you to be clear with rules and consequences. And some very fine educators say that, so maybe they have a point. But for me, I take my cues from other areas of life: friendships, love relationships, and colleagial relationships at work. Friends, for example, do not say to one another, ''Here are exactly how many times you can be cruel to me, and here is exactly what actions I will take in ascending order of severity of response to each additional offense.'' In fact, there usually is not much said explicitly at all. It is more likely to be something of the sort: ''I expect you to be responsible and civil to me. And frankly I don't know what I'll do if you aren't, though I will do something. I'll decide just what when the time comes. But I don't expect to have to be doing anything, because I don't think it will come to that.'' Essentially that is my posture on attendance, talking out of turn, or anything else: I expect you (students) to do the right thing, period. And I do not add up numbers or think in terms of exceptions.

That may sound impractical to you, but it has worked for me. In a conversation with Edward Johnson, the principal at Kearsarge Regional High School in North Sutton, New Hampshire, I learned that his school operates on a similar principle. Kearsarge focuses on what is expected rather than lists of transgressions and accompanying consequences and punishments. Johnson's view is consistent with the one I have been putting forth, that a focus on the negative ironically tends to result in the negative circumstance it seeks to avoid. This is not to say I am against contingencies for negative behavior. It is just that I do not see as much need as do many others to spend time listing and formalizing them.

Remember, the problem with Joe of a few pages ago? In terms of what I have been discussing here, I made sure I created a clear image in my head of Joe behaving himself in class. I also made sure I let him know I expected him to be a good student: and that I cared whether or not he was a good student, and that I would work to help him become one. So I did not wait until there was a problem to deal with Joe. I led off with these things. I took the initiative.

Acknowledge Others' Power

Another point: Do not pretend you are all powerful in the classroom just because you are the teacher. Because you are *not* all powerful. Students have real power. What is particularly attractive to me about the blend concept is that it acknowledges others' power. It does not assume I can outmuscle others or that others are weak. Instead, it uses—even depends upon—the force of others in order to achieve betterment and reconciliation. Joe had power. I let him know that. I never pretended that he did not. I let him know that I was willing to work with him, and that I needed him to take responsibility for working to be a positive member of the class. Again, the focus was on what to work for, on the positive, and not what to "stop doing or else." I told him I would assume responsibility for working for that better circumstance as well. Not in those words of course—that sounds so stilted. However I said it, that is the idea I got across.

Praise More Than Punish

Praise is more powerful in getting what we want, including good discipline, than punishment. We owe much to the Skinnerians, the followers of psychologist B. F. Skinner—also called behaviorists—for pointing this out. By the way, Skinner's book *Beyond Freedom and Dignity* had a profound impact on me, and I recommend it highly to you.[19] Although I still believe in the possibility of human choice and willful action, this book made me far more sensitive than I had been to the power of circumstance in shaping what we think and do. The behaviorists have marshaled much research evidence to support their claim for the usefulness of what they call "positive reinforcement." Basically the idea of positive reinforcement is that behavior, whether by a pigeon or a human being, tends to be repeated if it is followed by a favorable occurrence. The Skinnerians make the case that to get what you want, you are better off using positive reinforcement when something good happens than punishing what you do not want. Also, positive reinforcement is better at keeping people on the right track (such as acting in a civil fashion) than if they do as they should to avoid something negative happening to them. In the jargon, in this latter instance they are avoiding aversive conditions. This, then, provides a theoretical basis for the argument against the lists of consequences for breaking the rules—which keep students doing what they are supposed to do in order to avoid running into one of these negative consequences. It is not that these aversive stimuli have no affect on behavior, because they do. And it is not to say that punishment and threats should never be used. It is to say that positive reinforcement is our ace in the hole. The Rutter book, mentioned previously, supports this thesis. He cites research demonstrating that high levels of praise and correspondingly few reprimands are linked to good behavior in classrooms. Angry punitive responses directed at students and detention, keeping students after school, are not linked to improved discipline.[20] The practice of detention, incidentally, is another piece of conventional wisdom that does not work. Yet we always come up with some pseudo-logic that obscures us from taking a hard look at the outcomes of the practice. Which in my experience is a pouting, hostile, resentful, or at times defeated, student; a damaged teacher-student relationship; and no better conduct than before. Our solution to this circumstance? We give even more detention. The thinking is that there is nothing wrong with detention; we just have not done enough of it. So the kid gets 2 hours of detention instead of 1 hour, and the resentment and all the rest is even greater. The answer for dealing with that outcome? We enforce even more detention.

To put all this as simply as I can, effective disciplinarians basically attend to what is positive that is going on and pay it off, while bad disciplinarians center their efforts on putting out fires, so to speak. Again, it is so important how you look at things. What this means to me is that one of the major tasks of a teacher, whether regarding discipline or academic work, is to catch a student doing something right and then reinforce it. It is important to remember in all this that reinforcement is not just a tangible reward like money or material things. Attention and acknowledgement can be reinforcing as well. As can praise, recognition, appreciation, increased status, a good grade—well, just think of all the things that are rewarding for you to get for doing a good job. When you think about it, this is the opposite of what we often do with discipline problems. Usually we try to catch students doing something wrong so that we can correct them or punish them in some way. With Joe, I kept an eye on him trying to catch him doing something right. And, really, it was not all that tough to do. Because much of the time, even the students who are giving us the biggest headaches are behaving appropriately. It is just that it gets obscured by their episodes of bad behavior.

Anyway, I would spy Joe doing something right, and without a ceremony I let him know I saw it and appreciated it. I had no script to go by; I just let the words form at the moment. And I did not just wait for good things; I rigged them in the way I mentioned earlier. I would tell him I was going to ask a certain question during the next day's class and that he should get ready because I would call on him. I would ask the question, he would answer, and with a look I am sure others did not see I would let him know I valued what he did. And at times when I had a chance I would say a simple, "Good going, Joe, on that question." In a similar way, I would set him up to do class presentations, help other students, or lead a group. But with any of this, I tried to make sure he was ready to do it successfully and I provided a great deal of coaching beforehand to up the chances that he did it well. What I was trying to do was, in Skinnerian terms, establish the stimulus conditions and reinforcement contingencies for the behavior I wanted Joe to emit. And it worked—I started getting more of what I wanted. In behaviorist terms I guess I was shaping Joe's behavior through rewarding successive approximations of the terminal behavior I set as a goal (the positive picture I had in my head). All I know was that I was happy with Joe; and Joe was learning more and became much happier with himself. Being a discipline problem, we sometimes forget, is not the shortest route to happiness for the student. Joe was smiling more.

So figure out what you want and reward it. For me, I will do things like stop a student going out the door at the end of class and say something like: "Thanks, [and the name]. Your answer to my question on the Philippines really helped me teach the class better today.'' That sounds contrived, I suppose. But teaching, any professional act, is contrived. And anyway, it was not phony. I *did* appreciate it. And it *was* helpful. This kind of thing is part of an overall message that I am trying to get across, that the action in the class is with the students who are contributing to the class and not with those who, for whatever reason, are trying to bring it down. I must say, however, that what I have just said has been the toughest lesson for me to learn. I still sometimes give my energy to negative people rather than let people who support me know that it matters. But I am working on it.

Don't Belittle or Embarrass

Another rule for good discipline, if you want to call it that: Do not embarrass or belittle students in front of others. Well, there is no need for it in any case, but it is especially deadly when done publicly. It may seem obvious and unnecessary to say this. But then again we both know of many instances in which teachers have ridiculed and made fun of students; including, perhaps, us when we were students. I know it happened to me back then. And I know I have never forgotten it, even though I am sure the teacher involved has. Adolescents, just as we all do, have pride and a sense of integrity. Regardless of the reasons, good or bad, they resent it greatly if they are degraded, teased, held up to ridicule, demeaned, or embarrassed.

There are obvious examples that you and I could both cite. But, it is important to be aware of the apparently harmless kidding around that goes on so frequently in school:

''Is John Jones in class?'' comes over the intercom.

Smirking, the teacher banters, ''Depends on what you mean by being in class.'' (Laughter.)

''Would you tell him to come to the office?''

''I'd be *delighted* to.'' (Laughter as John Jones gets up from his seat and makes his way to the door.)

This is a minor incident, perhaps. But not necessarily to John Jones. You just might have a trouble-making, revengeful student on your hands and not know why. Multiplied by a hundred, it can contribute to an uncomfortable climate in the class. Adolescence is a time of enhanced self-consciousness. And it is a time, even though they do not always practice it, of increased concern for fairness. Bullying a student, no matter how tough and formidable we may look as teachers, is just not fair. Standing up there and shaming some young person sitting in a seat is not fair. It is crucial that we be seen as fair and respectful of students. Put-down artists (sublimated hostility?) and classroom explosions directed at students may arrest trouble in the short run. But in the long run there may well be flatness and unresponsiveness among students, or even, outright hostility and resentment.

I am reminded of a student teacher I had when I was a high school social studies teacher. He was constantly sarcastic and ridiculing toward students. I guess it was his attempt to increase his power and formidability and to look "cool." Some students complained to me about it and I spoke to him and tried to stop him. His behavior persisted. One day—about 2 weeks had gone by—I was sitting in the back of the room. The student teacher was going at some student in a harsh way about "getting his tail in gear," when suddenly the student—male, about 6'2"—stood up, strode forward, and decked the teacher with a right to the nose. The teacher was suddenly flat on his back, with blood all over. It was as if frames of film had been deleted. One moment the teacher was standing up. The next "frame," no transition, he was splayed out like a heavyweight champ's tune-up opponent and the student was out the classroom door (and, I found out later, out of the front door of the school). Now in no way am I justifying this student's action. The student teacher did not deserve that. What it does reveal, however, is the frustration and anger that can build up when a teacher uses his position to put a student on negative public display.

A corollary to this point about embarrassment is that one of my personal rules is to handle problems outside of the class period as much as possible. If a look and then a firm, brief, respectful request for what I want does not stop the problem, I talk to the student privately during a class assignment in which students are working on their own or with others, or after class. I would rather put up with the problem until I can meet privately with the student than have a showdown in class in front of other students. This can escalate into a power struggle that depletes my energy, becomes a personal and face-saving war, and makes me look unfair to students. Again, I think that one of the worst things that can happen is to appear to be cruel and, especially, unfair or disrespectful by students.

My position is unequivocal. No matter what is going on, nothing justifies a teacher engaging in a personal attack, yelling, or mockery. The dignity of human beings is a value that transcends any considerations of classroom control. Nothing justifies a violation of human dignity. When I violate this precept, and I do, I owe that student an apology. I am not referring to public apologies, which often tend to be embarrassing and come off as self-serving ("Look at what a big person I am"), attention-getting ("Let's spend the next 15 minutes attending to me apologizing"), or self-denigrating ("I am such a jerk"). So I try to apologize one-on-one, and tell the student I will work to see that I do not do it again. I owe it to the student to analyze the circumstance that resulted in my blow-up, put-down, or whatever it was, and learn from it for the future. At the same time, I try not to torture myself with self-condemnation: "Oh what a loser I am, pushing kids around. I knew I should have gone into selling aluminum siding." I am human. I make mistakes, as humans do. But I can learn from them. And I can forgive myself and get on with life. Students are remarkably forgiving of isolated pettiness if the teacher is basically respectful and fair. Nobody expects us to be godlike and perfect. Except perhaps ourselves.

I want it understood that all I have said about human dignity applies to teachers as well as students. I do not care what evil deeds I have committed as a teacher, that still does not give students the license to diminish my dignity as a human being. And that applies to any teacher—no reason justifies abuse from students. And indeed I see a great deal of just that in classrooms. At times "discipline problem" is a euphemism for intentional cruelty by a student toward a teacher, unacceptable in any human relationship, any time or any place. Understandable, I suppose, but never acceptable.

A month or so ago, I was observing a teacher in a high school. His class that hour was not exactly dazzling, but I thought he was doing a respectable job. Especially respectable in light of what six students were doing. They were really mocking everything he said, twisting everything into a joke, and just generally doing their best to humiliate him. It was a very long hour.

At the end of the class, one of the more vocal students turned to me and asked, "You working with him?"

"Yes, I am," I replied.

He said, "I mean, he's awful, don't you think?"

I looked at the student, was silent a second, and then said: "To tell you the truth I wasn't paying attention so much to the teacher as I was to you. Who are *you*? What did *you* do this hour to make it better for anybody? From where I was sitting I saw someone trying to teach you something, and that looked a lot better than what I saw you doing. Why don't you talk about yourself and not the teacher? What were you doing this hour that you are proud of?"

There was a moment of hushed silence. I guess I had not said what he thought I would say. And I had not asked a rhetorical question; I wanted an answer. But the student only said something about the teacher being a "joke." He and I spoke briefly about the incident and then he and the five students with him walked out the door.

The point I am trying to make should be an obvious one. Students can be wonderfully generous and caring at times, and insensitive and destructive at others. Some of the labels we use—"discipline problem," "acting out," even the label "student" itself—tend to obscure the fact that students are first of all human beings. As human beings they are responsible for measuring up to a standard of respect and generosity toward other human beings. Some of these other human beings happen to work as teachers. No institution-shaped roles and relationships should obscure that human beings are involved or that human dignity is involved. We have to see how these labels (teenager, sophomore, teacher, principal) can make objects of people and diminish the level of responsibility not to use and not to abuse other people.

In our own way, we have to get this point through to students. In the classroom incident just described I am certain that these students did not see their behavior as being directed at a human being. It was directed at a *teacher*. Teachers are fair game, especially if they are the least bit vulnerable or inadequate. From the look of these students I am sure they would not have treated this teacher as they did in a restaurant or in someone's living room. No, it is the classroom setting that triggers and seems to justify this behavior. It is in classrooms that students will read a magazine while the teacher is talking, not other places. Teachers in classrooms have a kind of unreality akin to that of a television image. The television newscaster does not notice if you read a newspaper in front of him or stare at the ceiling, so why should the teacher? Somehow we need to get it through to a student that you just said/did that to *me*. This relates to the connection idea discussed earlier. Without breaking away from the job at hand, which is to promote learning and growth, we have to let students know that despite the fact that we are in school, and that we have labels for each other and what we do, and it is all very formalized, it still comes down to fundamental issues of kindness and gentility. No system of schooling or approach to discipline should obscure that reality. The challenge is for teachers to model this perspective and show students that these human criteria for judging treatment of other people apply to their lives as well. The vast majority of us, teachers and students, are good people. We cannot let school be a place where we openly belittle other human beings. I think discipline is easier under these conditions.

Students Shape Events

Students have to be brought to understand that they do more than react to events; they shape them. The students in that incident, laughing and talking and making fun of the teacher, had an effect on what went on that day. They affected the teacher, the other students, and the level of accomplishment. This is so obvious, but I am convinced that the students who were acting it up in back of the class had no idea how much they created as well as reacted to events during the hour. It should be no surprise if that were the case. In this culture, adolescence is so much a time of watching and judging—rather than participating—that students often fail to realize that what they do counts. They watch television, like it or do not like it, find it interesting or boring, turn it on and off—but they do not alter what happens on the screen. Similarly, they watch and judge their parents, politicians, and business people—and tune them out or mock them if the verdict is negative. To the teenager, with few exceptions, the world runs as it runs and about the best one can do is have an opinion about it. This perspective on their place in things carries over to school and is confirmed by the way schools typically operate. From the students' point of view, "The class and the teacher are as they are. All I can do is like it or not, adapt to it, cope with it, react to it. But there is nothing I can do to shape or alter what is going on. Therefore, what I do does not matter and I have no responsibility to or for this circumstance. All I can do is somehow get the word to the adults in the school that I do not like what is going on and hope they will do something." I remember now how I asked those students who were jumping all over the teacher, "Did you ever think of helping him out? Why didn't you support him so the class would go better? It looks to me as if you checked him out, didn't like what you saw, and then just hung your review of his work out on the line for people to see.'' They said a few words to the effect, ''It wouldn't do any good.'' *They* could not improve their lot in that classroom, at least not in any direct way—that was their assumption.

I do not have any set way of doing it, but I make it a point to somehow let students know that how well the class goes has to do with what they do as well as what I do. I get it across that I want more from them than a ''movie review'' of my teaching. I expect them to participate, which is more than watching and reacting. It is sharing responsibility for making things go well. Of course I do not expect this message alone to lead them to say, ''Oh, I get it'' and immediately turn around their behavior. But this message, and the bearing and attitude from which it emanates, along with all the other things I discuss in this section on discipline, can have a positive effect. Especially if we are patient and do not insist on overnight success. A key to any of this is that it should not come off as preaching. Instead, it is simply a statement of what is so for you or me as a teacher, and what we—I will use the term—*insist* upon.

Even though I think as teachers we can be very powerful in shaping the reality in which we live, I also know that we may not always be able to have it the way we want it. There are just too many factors that operate to produce a particular classroom circumstance. But one thing we can always do at least: We can ask for what we want. I have sometimes said, ''If I'm not doing very well up here or you're bored, whatever, please don't torture me or put me down. Help me out.'' That may be enough to say; students may not need a lecture on exactly what to do. But again it could be that it will be useful to add specifics—''Here's what I mean by helping me, and yourself, out. . . .'' Students have not had much experience supporting teachers and may need some help in figuring out just what it takes. And of course, that puts it back on us: What exactly *do* we want from students? What do you want precisely? In any case, I hope we can start to chip away at the adults-and-sly-kids school game that we so often play in classrooms.

No ''Have To''s

A rule I follow is that I do not *have to* do anything. I will *decide* to do what I deem appropriate at any moment in time. To explain, there is a piece of conventional wisdom in this area of discipline that says you have to be consistent. You have to follow through on things. If you say you are going to do something; you must do it. For example, if you tell a student that if he does this bad thing one more time, whatever it is, you will call his parents and then he does it one more time, you have to call his parents. You said you would and now you must follow through in order to be consistent. If you do not, you will look like a pushover, and kids will know that they do not have to take anything you say seriously.

Now consistency, following through, and keeping your word sound laudable, there is no doubt about that. They are "clean" sounding terms. (There was a comic years ago named Shelley Berman who said that things broke down into "cleans" and "dirties." The "cleans" are those things with a favorable meaning or loading; and "dirties" the opposite.) The challenge, clearly, is to look beyond the words used to describe something and see what is actually going on. The problem with this "you must follow through" principle is that it takes choice away from you. You no longer have the freedom to decide on a course of action based upon experience or insight. You have given over your behavior to the past— the "if you do it one more time I will . . ." announcement. The current situation and what you understand about it, and your freedom to choose what to do, count for nothing. And they should always count for something. Why give up your freedom to do what is best? Why do something that will have negative consequences? For example, you see now that calling the parents would not be the best move. By the way, sales people use prior commitment as a way to sell us things we do not need. They get us to say we will do something in the future. Then they hold us to it, even though it is clear to us that it is not in our best interests to follow through. But most of us will buy the product anyway because we ascribe to the cultural values of consistency and keeping commitments.

For myself, I will not give over my freedom and my responsibility to choose what is most effective or most appropriate. With the "call your parents" example, I *may* choose to remain consistent with my earlier statement that I would call. Or, I may choose to rethink it and not call. If I want, I can relay to a student that upon further reflection I see it was a bad idea in the first place, or that the current circumstances make it inappropriate to take that particular action at this time. Yes, I may seem to be a vacillating creature, and I do have to consider this when making the choice of what to do. But I can explain my reasoning and try to make it clear that my current choice is based on insight and comes out of compassion, strength, and sound professional judgment. If I can establish that, instead of appearing to be someone who does not follow through, I will be seen as flexible, caring, and sensitive (3 "cleans"). What if, to state the extreme case, you see that some commitment you have made in the past is a bad idea? Why should you follow through on this stance? Consistency is not the only value in the world; there are others, including fairness and effectiveness. I hope you see that I am not discounting consistency as a value. Consistency is one criterion to use to assess the advisability of an action, and I may decide to put it at the top of the list. Though, consistency has not proven to be of especial instrumental worth in serving my goals of promoting learning and growth among students or carrying out my work in ways that result in pride and satisfaction for me. What I am saying is that I will "own" my behavior—meaning take responsibility for it—at each instant. There is nothing I have to do because "you have to do it." I will not give over my professional judgment to any such notion.

An example: The class is beginning and a student is standing by the window. The teacher says, "The class is starting, Ted. Would you sit down."

"I don't feel like it."

Hushed silence. Everybody knows what you have to do. The kid called you. You have to make him sit down. Your credibility is on the line. Right? My answer is that it depends on how you look at it. As far as I am concerned you can do anything you want to do in that instance. You can have a showdown. The problem with that, however, is you might wind up in a shouting match, with name-calling back and forth, emotional trauma on both sides, and a damaged relationship. You could have a real war on your hands, because for the student it is a matter of pride and would be forcing him to back down in front of his friends. It could even get physical. In other words, what you *have* to do might not be the best idea in the world. Or it might be a great idea, just the time for it; I do not want to seem to be saying that I preclude any tactic out of hand. What I am saying is that whatever we do should be chosen from options with a clear sense of what it will get us, and not on the basis of some "rule to live by." We may indeed find it useful to develop guidelines, rules of a sort, but they must be held lightly and not obscure our need to think things through for ourselves. And of course that applies to anything I offer you in this book.

On this standing-at-the-window business, I have replied to the "I don't feel like it" with a simple, respectful, "I'm starting the class and I'd prefer it if you'd sit in your seat." Then I just left the student standing there while I started teaching the class. I did not approve of what he was doing; he stood at the window with the burden, however slight, of my lack of favor. But I did not accuse him. I did acknowledge his power. And I did choose not to continue the exchange. And most of all, I did not define it as *the* test of my viability as a teacher, whether I could force this 15-year-old into a desk. Somehow there are other, more significant, tests of adult worth.

The following is another example. I remember one time when three 17-year-olds were looking out the window. I went over to them and said, "I'm going to start the class now. It'd help me out if you sat down." After about 5 minutes they did. One thing that helped me was that I did not assume that they were testing me—or, the point just made, that this was *the* challenge of my professional life. As a matter of fact, the briefest of investigation revealed that they were watching a girls' gym class play basketball. Everything does not have to do with me as a teacher. They were not trying to test me to see how far they could go. They were catching a look at some girls, not an unheard of activity among male adolescents. And no, I did not assume that I had, or had to have, the power to make them sit down *right now*. It took 5 minutes. The world does not stand ready to do my bidding. If you can make things happen right now or every time you are better than I am. If some student does not want to sit down it can be difficult if not impossible to get him to sit down.

With the three students, I made it a point not to challenge their integrity. I did not want to structure the situation such that to sit down would be to lose face. Also, I did not want to look like a bully or a petty bureaucratic type caught up with authority and control for its own sake, or as if a threat to my ego was the prime issue. The issue as I tried to define it, was what to do to get our work done in the class. So in 5 minutes they sat down. And if they had not? I would have dealt with that when it came up. What I want to have available to me if that were to occur is as varied and complete a repertoire of responses as possible, and then the ability to choose the one that is most likely to achieve my purposes. I do not want to be caught having only one or two things I can do, an inflexibility of response. An analogy, back in the Eisenhower presidential years we had something called a "massive retaliation" strategy. The idea was that we had nuclear weapons and if anybody crossed us in the least way we would drop the big one. (The equivalent in education may be sending the student to the office.) The problem was that it was so inflexible—nuking or nothing. Countries soon figured out we were not going to push the button upon every little transgression. They could do almost anything as long as they stayed beneath our true threshold of massive retaliation.

One thing to remember, one option in this or any other situation is to do nothing. That in itself runs up against a piece of conventional wisdom that we must always do something. In the army we used to have the slogan, "Do something even if it's wrong." We lived by that, including the last part; we were wrong a lot. Though we were comforted and praised ourselves for having done something. A better rule to live by would have been: "Do whatever is right to do." I can choose to ignore the situation or take no action. I can ignore it until the end of the week or the month, or for the entire school year. Again, I am not saying that it is best to do nothing, but it is an option. There is one particular time when I tell myself not to act, to do nothing. That is when I get all emotional and flustered. I send a message to myself to do nothing until I calm down and become more clearheaded. At least doing nothing does not result in actions that I wish I could take back, or which might get me in a bigger fix than if I had done nothing at all. A great deal of the name-calling, put-downs, threats, and harsh and punitive actions come in the heat of battle and would have been better off unsaid and undone. Life is not a video tape you can erase. Once you tell some kid he gets on your nerves and you're sick of him, it has been said. What if someone right now said that to you? It would be tough for you to just go on as if it had not happened, wouldn't it?

On this matter of consistency, although I know in many instances consistency is a useful and positive quality to have, in this area of discipline I have found that not talking about how consistent I am going to be is better for me. Even more important, a lack of consistency actually increases my power. Consistency is a contextual virtue. It requires that you define what consistency looks like and where and when it gets displayed so that you know it when you see it. You do not know, for example, from just looking at me if I am being consistent or not. You need to look at my history and define some terms first. The problem with setting out all that context is that, in the course of doing it, I also get across to students that I at least hold out the possibility that trouble is going to occur. If I am going on about the misbehavior and make it clear that I am going to be consistent, this implies that it has happened before, or that I think it might happen, or that this is the kind of place in which it is understandable that it will happen. This in itself can operate to bring about discipline problems. Most people give a situation its due without thinking about it all that much. They act one way in a doctor's office and another way in school. If a doctor went into a big speech about what he would do if you stole his magazines, missed appointments, or joked around when he was treating you, that might redefine the possibilities in his office. The same with classrooms.

Also, if I tell students exactly what I am going to do, they transgress and at least theoretically, they can then weigh the advantages of the little stunt they want to pull against the certain consequences that will follow. They just might decide that the consequences are not all that horrendous and decide to pull their stunt. We need remember, the consequences for misbehavior in school are usually not all that dire. There really is not that much that we can do if students give us problems. On the contrary, if students do not really know what I am going to do, they will have to be prepared for a whole range of possibilities, including the one they would find the most unpleasant to have to live with. I might not be able to think of it, but they know the one that makes problems not worth it. Saying that, however, and whether it diminishes my power or not, they can be certain that if I can help it, no matter what they do I will not be cruel to them, belittle, or embarrass them. That is off limits to me. I try to be consistent about that.

I offer some caution about all of the emphasis in education these days on getting the rules exact and outlining the consequences for breaking them precisely and clearly ahead of time. In the rest of our lives there are not all those rules. In the work place or in relationships it is not that way. In these other situations, there is a general sense of what responsible and decent conduct means and the understanding that this is what you do, period. In classrooms my "rules" are few: attend class, support the work of this class, do your best to learn and grow, and be civil to other people. That is enough, and if there is the need for more details I spell them out.

Tenuousness Helps

While I always try to act respectfully to students and care how they are, I do not unconditionally hang on to a working relationship with them. Another way to put it, there is a tenuousness that characterizes my relationship with them. I do not say I will always be with them. I believe this tenuousness increases my power to carry out my work as a teacher and contributes to both avoiding and dealing with discipline problems. Also, I think this, call it, fragility in their relationships with me is ultimately best for students as well.

To explain, I come back to conventional wisdom in the area of discipline. It is pretty much accepted that a teacher should be able to handle problems in class without kicking students out of class or leaning on counselors and administrators to bail them out. Teachers need to deal with discipline problems. If they cannot get in front of a class and bring students in line, it is indicative that they come up short as a teacher. If you cannot handle things on your own or have to exclude kids from class, it is a black mark against your name, a sign of weakness as a professional. Teachers have to be good disciplinarians, which means being able to manage their own class. Not only do we need to learn our content and how to teach well, we need to know how to shut the door and bring a bunch of adolescents to order. It is this perspective that gives meaning and direction to us in our work in this area.

However, we do have a ritual we go through if the handle-things-in-class system breaks down. We send a student to the vice-principal or someone else designated to deal with these situations, there is a conference, and after a suitable time the student re-enters class. True, schools in some instances have set up special rooms where students serve in-school suspension time or work out plans to deal with the classroom problem. And there are, of course, other approaches we employ. But, the "report to Mr. Smith in the office" is still a common approach. But I do not want to get into this in any detail. What I want to underscore here is the aspect of the school culture which says that the teacher must learn how to work with each of the students in his class, and that a breakdown in the teacher-student relationship is indicative of a teacher not properly performing his job.

As I see it, this "hang on to them at any cost" value gets us into some hot water as disciplinarians. It weakens our ability to control classes. We can learn a great deal from other relationships in our lives. Ultimately what holds us together, one of the main things anyway, is that if we push things in a negative direction far enough the relationship will dissolve. Take, for example, a friendship or love relationship. If you break the agreement, explicit or understood, between the two of you, someday you might call the person and he might say, "I wish you well, but it is over between you and me." This other person does not assume he has to hold on to you in just *any* case. And he does not fight with you or put you down or "send you to the office" in a predictable way that you know will perpetuate the relationship. He does not want you to be punished or unhappy. He simply says goodbye. When you think about it, that tenuousness in the relationship is powerful in keeping both people attentive to their behavior and the anticipated consequences of their actions, because the very continuance of the relationship is at stake. Similarly, in professional relations this time, one reason why kids do not as frequently give a doctor a discipline problem is that the doctor is likely to say quietly, "I can't diagnose or treat you this way. Excuse me, I must see another patient."

The obvious retort to the personal relationship and doctor-patient examples is: "Yes, it makes sense there, but that's not what teaching is about. A lot of these kids would be delighted if the relationship broke down and they could get away from teachers." That sounds so true, but is it? Do kids want to get away from teachers? I think we overestimate how much they do. For one thing, they need us. Most kids want to stay in school and get a diploma, dropout statistics notwithstanding. And they need to get through our courses to graduate. One thing we have sold very well is the value of staying in school. Yes, they need us. And, yes, they want to stay near their friends in school. School is a good place to hang out. And many of them, despite some problems, want to be with teachers. Especially if we have been fair, care about them, and are on top of our work. Perhaps more than we realize, it can be very powerful to say to a student, "I cannot teach under these circumstances. You will have to leave."

The student says, 'What, you want me to go to the office?"

And you say, "I don't know where you go. I know I don't want you punished. I'm just saying I am not going on with it this way. All I know is you cannot stay."

The student says something like, "So what do I do?"

"Whatever you want to do. You are just not staying here as it is. I'm a teacher and I can't teach you when you . . . [being specific about his actions that get in the way of the work that needs to be done]."

The few times I have done this I let counselors and administrators know ahead of time what might happen. In every case the student has gone to a counselor and after a couple of days comes back and says, "I'd like to get back in. What am I supposed to do?" And I tell him. And I ask him what he needs from me and how I need to change to make it go better between us. Then he has to look at me and tell me what he is going to be like in my class. If it is acceptable to me and I believe the student, I ask him or her to come on back in. Though it has never happened, I could see the possibility of the student transferring into another class where he would be happier. And meanwhile I'm not having to put up with wrestling with him every day.

I try not to make all this a personal or moral issue. It is not that I have anything against the student personally. And it is not that he or she is wrong and I am right. It is simply that I cannot get my teaching done this way. Also, I'm not angry about anything. One of the reasons we get mad comes out of the assumption that we have to hang on to the relationship. Anger often stems from frustration due to a sense of powerlessness—you feel all you can do is live with it. But if I do not have to hang in there, I do not need to get mad; I can just quietly say "no more." The doctor did not get mad in the example I described earlier. He did not need to because he could just go on to serve those who both need and appreciate his services.

Another example: I was having some serious trouble with a student. I told her counselor that I had had it and that before I would take her back, I needed a commitment so I could believe that she was ready to get to work. In the weeks previous to this I had told the student what I needed. In her case, I needed her to raise her hand before she spoke, to stay in her seat, and to turn in her work on time. I did not get it from her. So I said that was it for me, I was not going to waste more time. She asked what she was to do. I said that it was up to her but that I suggested she go to her counselor and take it from there. After a couple of days the counselor asked me to sit down with her and the student and see what we could work out. I explained that I was not put out about anything and that I was open to changing what I do if that would help, but that I still had to hear a commitment from the student that she would generally support the work of the class and do the three things I required (raise her hand, etc.). In a couple days, I got the commitment. I thanked the student (and, later, the counselor) and went on from there.

Do hear me, I am not saying this is *the* way to handle these problems. Every choice of strategy has to fit both you and the situation. Do not substitute one "must" for another. And certainly do not do anything that gets you in big trouble. We make a living at teaching. All I hope to have done here is stretch our thinking a bit about the possibilities in the teacher-student relationship. And I hope I have communicated my feelings that I am a teacher and just do not, if I can at all help it, get caught up in these struggles. That attitude alone helps me avoid them. Discipline, like any human exchange, demands reciprocity. Both must play the game. My position is I do not play. And also I do not have to take on discipline problems alone (as the culture of teaching indicates I must in order to prove my mettle as a teacher). I will let the world know that it is everybody's job to maintain discipline, including administrators, counselors, and parents. And I will lean on anybody's help I can get. I will not take it on alone if I can help it.

Create a Professional Relationship

What I am trying to approximate with all of this is a professional relationship between the student and me. At the heart of any professional relationship is a circumstance in which it is clear what each of the participants—professional and client or patient—can expect from the other in the relationship. The two people, then choose to be in the relationship. The way schools work, teachers rarely have such a choice. A computer or some other impersonal process places students with us. We and students have not shared hopes or made agreements with one another. Instead, it is the first day of school and here we are. If you think about it, that is a pretty comfortable situation for students. He or she can have the attitude of: "Hey look, I didn't ask to be here. I got sent here. So I don't owe you anything. It's your job to make this interesting. So you're on. Go ahead, do your number. I'll let you know if I like it." A few, especially in the lower groups, may even think it is their job to screw around until the teacher can somehow turn things around.

What I am saying is that we have set up the most difficult circumstance I can think of in which to create good discipline: the virtual absence of public, shared commitments; little or no tenuousness in the relationship; grouped classes in which there may be no positive role models of how to behave; too many lists of negative sanctions and not enough work to establish positive cultural values in the school regarding comportment; and so forth. And truth be told, those contextual factors may be bigger than you and I can take on. As teachers we may just have to learn to handle the situation as it is. But certainly we should give these school environment issues our best thinking. One area especially: Isn't there a way for students and teachers to choose one another and form "contracts" with one another? Students, even very young students, should have to tell teachers what they, the students, are like and what the teacher can expect of them. And the teacher should be able to say, "Yes, I will work with you." Certainly where there are multiple classes—say four or five classes of junior year American history—students and teachers could "find each other." The stipulation could be made that no class could be over 25 or 30 students, whatever the number, so that class sizes do not get out of balance. But within that, there could be some kind of system—even if it is more in appearance than in fact—in which teachers and students form what I am calling a professional relationship.

Mixed Classes Are Better

Another argument for mixed classes: By setting up grouped classes we are creating little enclaves of trouble-makers who take cues from one another. My experience has been that it is a lot tougher to make things difficult for the teacher if most of the other students are trying to get somewhere. They see some student fooling around as getting in their way. Seriously, if you asked me to be a consultant and wanted my advice on how to set up the worst possible discipline situation and to make teachers as powerless as possible, I would tell you that you cannot improve on what you have: grouped classes with students who are allowed to just show up the first day of class without ever explaining what we can expect.

Make Contact

One strategy that has worked for me is what I call, for lack of a better term, or creativity, the "10-minute interview." Simply, I sit down one-on-one with a student for 10 minutes. I try to establish that it is the two of us as people talking and not two roles having an exchange (though at the same time I am a teacher and he is a student, if that makes sense). I ask him to tell me what he will be like in the class. What I try to get from him is a commitment to be civil and do the work of the class. I find this useful because after this exchange it turns out to be tougher for the student to abuse *me* the teacher rather than *a* teacher. And, if he gets out of line I can look at *him* and speak to *him* and not *a student*. Also, I can respond to him on the basis of the commitment he made to me and the class: He broke it. I can give him the look my mother used to give me that would straighten me out in a hurry. It was a mixture of disappointment and incredulity: "You are doing what?!" Anyway, on the basis of the 10-minute talk it is much more you and me. You, the student, cannot hide beneath the cover of anonymity or embed yourself in the institutional role. I know it's you in there. That gives me a bit more power in dealing with you, and every little bit helps.

Lighten Up

Another piece of advice: lighten up. Maintaining discipline is a task to be taken seriously. But do not take it too seriously. Follow? We have a right to work for an orderly classroom. We have every right to be serious about creating a positive, supportive, and pleasant place to do our work. At the same time, though, there is the nuclear arms race, starvation in the world, and death (not to mention taxes)—which at least equal the problem of too much talking in the back of the room. When it comes right down to it, the problem is just some 16-year-old acting silly. I know one of the things I try to do at night when I run the "video tapes" of some encounter with a student (this includes college students) over and over in my head is to remind myself that it is one, and only one, of the issues in my life. By the way, these incidents never get resolved by dwelling on them. They only seem to loom bigger and more compelling than they already are. We need to learn to stop the compulsive ruminating on discipline issues. The ideal is to give the problem some fixed amount of time, figure out something to do about it, and then drop it. Do not work it around in your head. If a thought or image related to the discipline problem pops into your head, just do not work with it. Let it go back to where it came from. Let it drift away. Or replace it with something more positive. To the same degree that the problem churns you up, systematically relax. For example, for a minute or two attend to your breath in and out, saying silently to yourself "re" on the in-breath and "lax" on the out-breath.

In addition, we should just laugh. This is such a need for me; I am so serious about everything. I remember an imagery experience I had once. I was lying on my couch with my eyes closed, just letting my mind go. A small bird popped into my consciousness. I asked the bird what he had to tell me. And the little imaginary bird said, "Cheer up." That was about 5 years ago and I have never forgotten it. One of the things I did during my teaching assignment in Los Angeles was something I called "comedy tape therapy." I had to drive about 20 minutes to get to school each day. On the way I played audio cassettes of comics doing their act, George Carlin, Robin Williams, and people like that. Listening to the tapes lightened me up and helped me to see the humor in things I was usually so deadly sober and intense about. Interestingly, I also found they provided a philosophy of sorts that gave me a good counterbalance to getting overly wrapped up with some adolescent's smart remarks in the second hour. Life, they said, is so short—cherish it, have fun, play. They had the same message as the little bird: Cheer up, Robert.

Do Some Reading

There are many good writers on this subject of discipline. One is Fred Jones. You may wish to read his material listed in the notes.[21] And there is Rudolf Dreikurs, whose ideas are derived from Adlerian psychology.[22] Another is William Glasser.[23] Glasser stresses that the teacher establish two things with students. The first is that to be happy and successful, the student is going to have to behave responsibly in the classroom situation. And second, that the teacher cares about the student. I add a third. That is the message, "I like you." The singer Wayne Newton has said, "If you like other people they will like you." That is truer than many cynics and "realists" would have us believe. In this society as it is, although it counts so much to experience being cared about or loved, sometimes it can be even more touching to know that you are liked. What a gift it is for a teacher to be able to sift through all the negativity and say, "I like you" to some kid that rarely, if ever, hears it.

CONCLUSION

So that is the context I would like to see implemented for learning and growth in the school. This was a wide ranging chapter, as it is a wide ranging concern. If you were asked to summarize what I have said in four or five verbal paragraphs, what would you say? Of all of this, what are three or four ideas that connect to you, that you think you can use? And again, what are three or four ideas not here that you can add?

The next chapter does not break new ground as much as it tries to pull together some of the material I have already covered. It is devoted to defining what I am calling a student achievement construct. It presents in kind of snapshot form, a picture of student achievement from the student's perspective. It says, this is what comprises student achievement, this is how the pieces go together, and this is what a student has to be able to do or have resolved in order to achieve in school. After doing that, I sketch out a few ways that the construct can be used to organize some promising work directed at improving academic achievement levels of students. But before you being reading the next chapter, why not think about those questions yourself. What would you write if you were to write the next chapter?

8 A Student Achievement Construct

The past three chapters have been about the school, its curricular and instructional practices, and the environment it creates for teachers and students. In this chapter I want to return to a basic theme of the book, that of focusing on the student to ascertain what it takes for him or her to be successful in school. In terms used earlier, it is an attempt to identify the elements of good studenting as opposed to good teaching. The goal in these pages is to pull together what I have written about student effectiveness and create a "picture" of interrelated concepts we can hold in our heads to organize our thinking and efforts with students to help them be more capable and successful in school. This picture, comprises what I am calling a "student achievement construct." By *construct* I mean a theoretical idea that describes the factors, and their interrelationships, that comprise or explain student effectiveness (and, its opposite, ineffectiveness). I present a diagram and then spend some pages explaining its components.

See if this provides you with a kind of intellectual scaffolding that gives you both a sense of the shape of the "building" (student achievement capability) and a structure that you can build upon by adding what you already know and what you learn to it in the future. What I hope results from this discussion for both of us is an overall view of what student efficacy involves. One advantage of this clarity regarding the whole is that it will allow us to see the relationship between what we care about and do and the totality of the concern. Also, it will give us direction in setting up collaborations and divisions of labor in working to improve academic achievement, commitment, and capability among students. After describing the construct I spend some time outlining some uses for it that I consider promising.

306

AN ILLUSTRATION OF THE CONSTRUCT

Look over the following figure and get an initial idea of what is there. Note the terms, and from earlier discussions try to recall basically what they mean. Also, get a sense of the spatial relationship of these terms to one another. You may want to put a paper clip on this page or insert a bookmark, because you will need to refer back to this page. I assume you have read the earlier chapters as I discuss the various components. Review earlier chapters to refresh yourself on any of these factors if you feel the need.

These, then, are the factors that I suggest we think about as we work to understand and improve a student's academic achievement capability. I comment on each element of the construct. As you read this, critically analyze and evaluate what I have put together. Add your own ideas to improve on what is here. For example, I have not dealt with sensory handicaps such as sight or hearing problems. You may be able to think of other things that are not here that ought to be.

Personal Self

Let us begin with the personal self. I described the personal self as made up of the conscious self, the very core of our being, and the will or willfulness, the fundamental capacity to be volitional. Remember I considered the idea of a fundamental wisdom as a third aspect of the personal self. But for now, think of it as a personal self made up of awareness and will.

The terms surrounding the personal self refer to what is present within us every moment. Included are thoughts, images, intuitions, emotions, memories, urges, and bodily sensations. Of course, just because there are different names for things does not mean they actually exist in the way the words or labels imply they do. And because there are separate labels does not mean they are in fact separate in nature. But at least I put those terms up there to give us a start at looking at what actually goes on inside the student. For example, what is a thought? Is it separate from an image? Are images an aspect of a thought in some cases? All cases? Can you have a thought without innerly spoken words? How do thoughts affect achievement? What is the difference between a bodily sensation and an emotion? We can feel our left index finger. How does that feeling differ from an emotion (sadness, for example), also often called a feeling. Is an emotion— anger, fear—partly a physically felt, kinesthetic, sensation and partly a thought? How do feelings affect achievement?

Notice I have included intuition. Frankly, I do not know what it is, or if it is. Is intuition a thought like every other? Or is it something of a different order? Many insist that it exists and say we should be promoting intuition as an important aspect of creativity. Whatever the case, I have included it here so that we can think about it. It could be that effective students are able to tap their intuitive processes. Or, conversely, it might be that good students do *not* do so, because

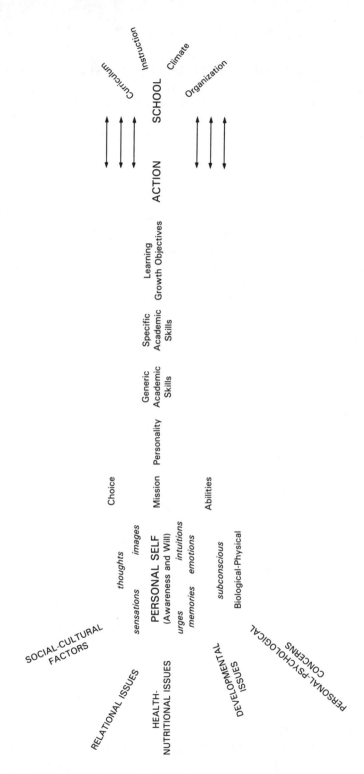

FIG. 8.1. School achievement construct.

they know it gets them off on a tangent, makes them different, and is antithetical to the linear, sequential, rational thinking that is at the heart of what the school requires.

I hope you find this exploration of our inner workings as fascinating as I do. What *is* going on in there and how does it affect our success and happiness? (Well, for that matter, what is happiness? An emotion? A judgment? What?) As self-consumed as most of us are, we have very little understanding of how the inside of us works. Quick, where is your spleen and what does it do? Back to the factors—thoughts, intuitions, and so forth—it is important to remember that the way we put words to things counts for a great deal. To illustrate, we may come to believe a thought or intuition, just because we have a word for it, is an *it* and exists in the same way as a house exists; when, really, it may be the label we tack on to a *process* when the seamless mind–body totality occurs in a certain way. This then gets us into the difference, if any, between things and processes; and ultimately, to the nature of reality itself.

The point of all this is that, so often, we talk in terms of words and logical relationships among words and we do not look concretely, existentially (if I am not misusing this word), experientially, at what we are talking about. For example, what is a hope? A sentence in our head? A bodily feeling? An emotion? An image? All of the above? Some of the above? Is a hope the same thing, whatever it is, every time? Yes, the inside of us is fascinating to explore. Though, as long as everything is going well, there is no big reason to explore any of it. It is when things are not working—like when you are flunking in school or you want to chart a new direction in your life—that it is helpful to learn to pay attention to these inner processes and learn to use them and change them in order to get what you want.

But leaving that aside, the important point to reiterate is that all of these internal elements are changeable. (Yes, including memories.) That is important because I see such crucial concerns as self-concept, self-esteem, self-acceptance, and the like, as being made up of these elements. Our self-concept, for example, is primarily made up of thoughts we have about ourselves, with some images, emotions, and memories mixed in. Well, undoubtedly everything is mixed in, as human beings are all of a piece. While it helps to select out things in order to focus on them, we must remember that, in reality, the human being is a *system* of interwoven elements in which each effects all of the others, not a set of discrete and isolated parts. Back to the main point, since self-concept is made up of changeable elements, self-concept is itself changeable by, for one thing, learning to think differently about oneself. In fact, the only constant in this entire construct is the conscious self. Everything else can be modified and improved. This is a positive thought.

Subconscious

I have put the subconscious in the figure just below these factors that are more readily available to us. (The position below has no particular significance.) Again, I do not know what the subconscious is, or if it is, though I am fairly certain that all that is going on with us is not available to our awareness and rational mind. Of course, apart from whether we are anything more than a bundle of electrical firings some of which we choose to call the subconscious, is the question of whether or not it is useful as a concept. What is a more accurate and useful way to look at it? Is it better to speak of a *sub*conscious or a *pre*conscious, the latter implying that its contents are more available to be tapped (however that occurs). Anyway, we speak of our subconscious all the time. Where is it? What is it? Is it our head? All through our body? Is it a process or a metaphor rather than a thing?

Biology

I add another reality, the biological basis for our existence. We are, each of us, a physical, biochemical organism. We are the product of millions of years of evolution. We inherit our appearance and our genetic composition from our ancestors. We are literally comprised of physical matter. (Or at least it seems. Physics tells us we operate with a Newtonian cause-and-effect, either-or, building blocks concept of reality that does not square with the relativistic Einstein-and-beyond world that is really there.[1]) Our brain has neural connections and weighs so much and can do just so much. We can think in ways that an ape cannot, and that has to do with our biology. Some of our limits are the result of being the species we are and the son or daughter of our parents. Perhaps more than we know, our predilections and preferences are passed on to us at birth. I have not dealt with this way of looking at human beings very much at all in this book. That should not be taken to mean I do not recognize that these matters count. We are physical, mortal, animals. So much of what we need, want, and do is shaped by that fact. We should not forget that. The challenge is to see how much of what we are is a factor of our nature, our nurture, and our choices as willful entities—and how the three factors interact to produce the beings that we are. Some good reading in this area is in the areas of zoology and sociobiology.[2] Sociobiology is particularly useful to study, as this discipline looks at the biological influences on our social conduct.

Because the biological-physical is set up as a category certainly it should not be taken to mean that I think it stands off separate from the others. It reflects a *perspective* we can choose to adopt when it is useful to our purposes. What I am saying in including it is that we *should* be able to adopt this perspective. (I mentioned earlier that sensory problems were not on the diagram. They could be included here, within the physical-biological.)

Choice

Moving to the right (it could be left, or up or down; it was an arbitrary decision on my part) there is *choice*. By choice I mean the individual's potential to choose a goal and course of action that is not simply a predictable response to external and internal forces. The human being can choose. The human being is not bound in its hopes or in its behavior by stimulus conditions and reinforcement contingencies. We are not simply shaped by our worlds. To my mind, a choice is different from a selection, pick, or decision—we have many such terms in our language. A choice is made from the center, the conscious self, from a wide range of alternatives, and with a clear understanding of the consequences of choosing each of the alternatives. These are rigorous criteria I know. Most of our decisions and activities (I save the word action in contrast to activities for considered behaviors stemming from true choices) are on the basis of whim, response, or impulse, and not choice as I have defined it.

What is so unique to human beings is our ability to choose. Some contend that our capacity for choice is our essence as a being. If that is true to any significant degree, if choice is fundamental to our nature, and if schooling does not teach us to realize our potential to choose, it is keeping us from discovering what is central to making us human. If we are to be fully human, choice is a possibility that must be nurtured into a reality. Schooling must do more than just help us respond effectively to tasks and obligations. The inclusion of choice here emphasizes that one way for a student to improve his achievement in school is to choose to do so. A student's choice to do better may be more powerful than improved teaching or any other environmental improvement in increasing the level of achievement.

The important thing is that choice-making is something *students* do, not us. One person cannot choose for another. All we can do is invite and encourage students to choose, in this case, to be better academically. For students to choose to be better in school means they have assumed a different posture in the class. They are not waiting for the class to get good, reacting, judging, any of that. They have chosen to do well. They *intend* to do well. As I described earlier, an aspect of choice is a responsibility—felt? thought?—that "I take responsibility for getting it done." You can decide whether intention must be present for it to be a true choice. Without intention perhaps it is only a true preference. The power to intend improvement to occur, which is always within a student's control, when invoked provides an enormous aid to increasing school achievement. Simply, if a student is to do well in school it helps greatly if he chooses to do well. We must ask a student, "Do you choose to do better or do you not?" How often do educators pose that question to students? And then, if the students say no or equivocate, let them know they should not be surprised if they do not succeed in school.

This power to choose, though it is an aspect of being human, can lie dormant (as can, and do, so many of our possibilities). Students must learn they need to work to make it more than just another unrealized potential. Human beings are very malleable creatures, and just because something is inherent in our nature it does not mean it will be realized. Given society as it is, always holding out a next thing to do, an individual can go his whole life and never truly choose anything. Think of your own day today. You really do not have to choose anything. There are a series of places to go and things to do which are set out before you. String these days together and you have a life. It is not a chosen life, but it is a life.

The concept of choice underscores that it is the students who either are or are not learning and growing. It is they who reap the consequences of what they do with their lives. As teachers we can get caught up with the effects of, say, a student's low achievement on ourselves and fail to remember that. All of this raises the issue of how a student can be helped to realize that he can choose for school to be different from the way it is. If he activates the capability to choose, it can unleash an enormous power and sense of direction that he did no know he had. Yes, the concern for choice raises a most crucial educational agenda: how to encourage a student to explore and try out this aspect of his being. What is education for choice?

Mission

The term *mission* (just below choice) raises the issue of the central meaning or purpose to this young person's life—and not only as a student but as a human being. Apart from the choices we make, do we have a mission—due to our inherent nature, the order of things, God, or something else—that is a part of our being and that directs our destiny? Or, another possibility, do our choices add up, form a pattern, so that we can say we have created a mission? Or is mission simply a concept that has little relation to anything that exists or goes on in human affairs, and thus has little usefulness to us in education? You will hear it both ways, that it matters and that it does not. Assagioli's work pointed toward an inherent mission or path for each human being. From this perspective, one of the tasks of an individual is to align his choices and actions with that mission. If that is true, one of the criteria for assessing choices becomes whether this choice is one that furthers the realization of one's purpose as a human being. Within this view, the job of the school, then, is to refrain from twisting and molding a student into some shape that seems desirable without regard for what is special and unique about this person. It is not enough to just teach the curriculum— whatever it is. Attention must be paid, by the student as well as the teacher, to the special niche this human being is meant to occupy in the nature of things.

Education within a concept of inherent mission helps a person be who he or she is. The contention many make—I am one of them—is that with all the shaping of society and culture, including the school curriculum, people too often become something and somebody, but not themselves. They may be successful in life in terms of accomplishments, rewards, and pleasures, but they are still "off line" in their lives. And no matter how well their lives seem to be going, there is a sense within them that something is fundamentally wrong. There is a gnawing "dis-ease" that accompanies them to the grave. If that is so, a major challenge for a student, and for those who educate him, is self-discovery. He must find his unique gift or purpose and then develop the motivation to manifest it in the world.

In contrast to this view, most of the sport psychology material seemed to deal with mission as a matter of choice. Mission was equated with the overall direction or purpose we choose, which then gives direction to particular goals and actions. Although I do not want to detract from the possibility that sport people also believe that to some degree one *discovers* as much as (more than?) *chooses* one's mission. In any case, the responsibility of a teacher or coach within this perspective is to help an athlete-student adopt an overall mission. The assumption is that a student or athlete with a mission that he or she understands is likely to be more motivated and achieving than otherwise.

Of course there are religious and other perspectives on mission as well. However you view it, including mission in this construct raises teleological issues. Teleology is a philosophical term referring to inherent purpose or destiny. The teleological perspective moves us from a preoccupation with, "How do I teach them?" to "What is the purpose of the lives of these young people whom I teach?" (Well, what is it? Answer that for yourself.) But beyond that, at its simplest level, the inclusion of mission in this construct says that if you want to talk about a student's achievement capability you need to at least consider whether he or she has connected to a mission that enables third hour math class to make sense.

Ability

Moving down the illustration, there is abilities. Simply, what is the student good at doing? As adults, we get to do whatever we are able to do (that is, if we play our cards right). We take on work we can do well and that will be appreciated. We marry someone we can get along with. We belong to this church over that one, shoot skeet rather than play canasta, and read mystery novels rather than biographies. In other words, there is no "required curriculum" in life—you can do what you are especially able to do. You can specialize. I remember some advice that a close friend gave me that has proved to be most valuable. He said, "Find something you can do excellently and do that. Don't spend time trying to do things you aren't good at." What that led me to do was look over my work situation and see how I could manage it so that I could do more of what I was particularly suited to do, and less of those things that were just not in areas in which I am particularly able. School of course is not like that. You have to "do it all," even when your abilities are not equally suited to all the areas in which you must be proficient. As I indicated earlier, I am not saying school should be different from the way it is. I worry about premature specialization, because too often the decision to specialize when you are 16 is a socially conditioned selection, a pick coming out of who people and society have told you you are, not who you really are. So while I favor the idea of allowing for elective study as a support to the process of self-definition, I do favor a broad liberal education for students.

But saying that, there is still the question, "Where are my abilities?" "What am I good at doing?" I phrase it this way because I want to emphasize that this question is one that the person must answer for himself. Teachers, counselors, and parents who deal with us should identify our abilities. But it is crucial that you and I, everybody, look at ourselves and resolve this issue. We must not only ask, "Where are my abilities?" We must also ask, "What abilities can and should I develop?" And then, "What can I do so that I maximize my strengths?" "How can I compensate when doing things that I am not particularly able to do but that I must do?"

I am not trying to make any profound point here. Including abilities in this construct is just to encourage us to look at students' abilities. One last thing, the challenge for both teachers and the students themselves is not only to see the abilities that are obviously there. It is also to see the abilities that are lying there latent, just waiting to be developed. The special teachers and students can go beyond what is to say: "Wow, this is what *could be*. Here is what you are (I am) able to do if you (I) work hard enough."

Personality

As discussed earlier, *personality* is a concept describing the characteristic ways of behaving that make up our "act." Actually, that should be act*s* plural because we have a number of different personalities in the various situations and roles in which we find ourselves. An adolescent, for example, may have one personality at school—call it the school personality—and another on the afternoon job, and still another with his friends. So many times parents will tell us when we inform them about their child's manner in school, "But Mary Lou isn't like that." The parents are both right and wrong. Mary Lou indeed is *not* like that—with them. But she *is* like that in school. What I am referring to in this construct is the school personality. It is the "act" that is played out in school that is the concern here. And of course we can break the school personality down farther into the math class personality versus the English class personality, and so on.

The words we use to describe personality are of this sort: confident, responsible, outgoing, self-reliant, diligent, funny, distractible, prideful, or respectful. Students operate through this school personality when they go to school. This characteristic style, this personality, has a significant impact on how well they do academically. We have to take personality—or more accurately, the school subpersonality—into consideration to understand student achievement capability. My contention is that too often we think that personality is something fixed or immutable. We see personality as something we have; or that it is who we are. Another, and better way, as far as I am concerned, is to see personality as something we do. Then if, say, we want to accomplish more academically, we come up with a better "act" to do. The good news is that we can get that done if we work at it. At the very least we can work very hard at putting together the best package of traits for attaining school success. So many students have a school personality that is perfect if they want to be unproductive and kicked around, but counterproductive if school success is its measure.

I think it is useful to distinguish between who I am (the conscious self) and my characteristic ways of presenting myself to the world (personality). But I am left with other issues. To begin with, I do not mean to say I know to what degree personality is grounded in one's biological, inherited, make-up. So many parents will tell you they could tell the personality of their child when the child was in the crib. And I have read research data to support the notion of a natural personality. That would indicate that personality is not totally arbitrary. This makes sense because we are, after all, biological creatures with a unique genetic inheritance. So, if we can inherit eye color or height, why couldn't we inherit something like temperament. Life is so complicated. Whatever you look at, whatever it is, it also is not. Perhaps personality is like that. Personality is changeable. At the same time it is inherent and natural and cannot (or is it should not?) be changed. The question for me is, where are the limits? What can be changed and what cannot (should not) be? What is my nature? What is the cost to me of changing in ways that are against my nature? But then again, there is my self-interest. Even if it is against my nature—say, to be out-going or to participate in large groups—should I change anyway if it means getting better grades in school? Do I have a basic personality that is constant but modifiable? And if my personality is inherent, isn't it true that there are still a variety of ways to manifest it? At least I hope these comments raise some crucial questions about just how much we can change what we call personality. I think we can all agree there is a relationship between personality and success in life. It is not just how able you are; your style matters too. And as far as I am concerned that applies to school as much as any other area in life. In that light, personality has a place in the student achievement construct. If the concern is with teaching, you may not have to concern yourself with student personality. But when the focus is on the student, yes, personality is a factor to be taken into account.

Social-Cultural and Personal Influences

Let us move to the left side of the diagram. There are each of the influences on academic achievement that I outlined in chapter 4. Social-cultural influences include class, race, ethnicity, gender, and family circumstance. The health issues I discussed were physical illness and the compulsive/addictive problems of drug, alcohol, and food abuse. Relational concerns included conflicts with parents, peers, and school authorities; and the processes of cooperation, competition, and individual initiative. The developmental discussions centered on the physical, mental, and psychosocial changes during adolescence. By emotional-psychological problems I mean the kinds of personal difficulties that in their more severe manifestation draw a student to need counseling or psychotherapy. These five categories provide us with a frame of reference from which we can analyze the impact—both positively and negatively—of some areas that affect academic performance in significant ways. These analyses can provide some direction in improving the academic achievement potential and outcomes for students.

Generic Academic Skills

By generic I mean cross-subject capabilities, the basic "tools of the trade" necessary for academic success. You may decide to see it differently, but in this category I center on the student's ability to think clearly, a skill I made much of in chapter 4. To me, the ability to think is an overridingly important academic skill area for a student to master. As you recall, I discussed the ability to think from several perspectives. One was what can be called an overall or generic goal attainment capability. Part of it has to do with a student's ability to set goals, plan, monitor, regulate, and evaluate his own behavior. Simply, it is the ability to think a job through. There is also the ability of critical reflection. This has to do with the student's ability to analyze himself, his circumstance at home and in school, his internal world of thoughts and feelings, his health, developmental needs, overall mission or purpose, personality, and so forth. It is the ability to look carefully and objectively at oneself and make use of this information in the school context. I also talked about the ability to process information cognitively or intellectually (remember Feurstein's and Letteri's work). And there were the discussions of learning disabilities and learning skills. Some of the work of individuals considered earlier that fit in here are Johnson's achievement strategies, Covington's ideas about strategic learning, Neilson's self-management activities, and the concepts of sport psychologists Charles Garfield and Terry Orlick. Others were considered as well, but this gives you a sense of where I place them in terms of student achievement capability. Again, what all of them have in common is the ability to think and explore oneself and get results. In addition, there are crucial personal attributes that fit in here—self-discipline, concentration, diligence, among them—the character traits I considered in chapter 6.

Specific Academic Skills

These fundamental academic skills just mentioned, while crucial, are clearly not enough. A student still has to be able to apply them in specific classroom situations. All learning—well, all life—is contextual. A student must be able to function in particular settings with particular course objectives and content. In order to apply the generic academic skills and deal with the requirements of the typical secondary school, the student is going to have to possess what I am calling specific academic skills (to the right on the diagram). The skills I think of in this regard—please add to this list—are reading, writing, speaking, listening, computing, estimating, calculating (math people, is that a fair way to refer to fundamental math skills?), and seeing. On this last one, seeing, it seems to me that this is a crucial skill, but not one that is talked about very much. To achieve in school or in life it helps to do more than just look, or glance. It involves the ability to *see* with care. So many young people I work with kind of take it in—but they do *see*. If listening or speaking are crucial skills, even the most perfunctory analysis of this society and schooling indicates that seeing is as well. Anyway, to achieve in school a student needs to be able to do those things well. Also, there are the skills of cooperating, competing effectively, and taking individual action. My point was that students need to know how to cooperate, compete, and go it alone—all three.

I suppose this list of skills in the last paragraph could simply be called basic skills. But I use *specific* academic skills as a term because I want to get away from the notion that academic skills are just the three Rs. I am also afraid that using the term *basic* skills would imply that they were *the* academic skills and that the skills listed under what I am calling generic academic skills would get left out, and so would all the self-related and other concerns that I have talked about. Those are basic too—that has been a major theme in this book.

I have not discussed these specific academic skills very much in this book. That is not because I do not think they are important—indeed they are—but rather because I do not have the professional expertise to go into how students acquire them. Even more fundamentally, I cannot identify them with any assuredness. I leave that to language arts and math people, and others who work in these areas. I have made an attempt at identifying them and putting them into a larger context (the student achievement construct). I hope this provides some direction for professionals who work to strengthen students in these areas. It should make clear, at least from my perspective, what else needs to be taken into account when working with a student to help him get caught up in reading. If things do not go too well in the reading improvement program, it may point to other things that could be getting in the way: social-cultural, developmental, health, personality, or goal attainment skill issues, and so on. The point is we might be doing a good thing with the reading instruction, but other things need to be done as well in order for the student to profit from the training in reading and actually start to do better in school. In other words, I hope this construct gives us a more total, integrated way at looking at the issue of remediating students' academic deficiencies.

Learning and Growth Objectives and Action

Although it is important to possess what I am calling generic and specific academic skills, or any of these insights and capacities for that matter, it is not enough. They must be applied in specific, concrete situations. In other words, a student must be able to take effective *action* at any particular time. All of these concerns discussed so far have to be put into practice to get specific things accomplished in school. My work and discussions with Professor Letteri and others has emphasized that the ability to make use of insights and skills is not necessarily acquired by learning them in a general way. You have to be able to apply them. To use a sport analogy, a player may have worked on his baseball swing so that it is smooth and quick. But he still has to apply this new capability against *this* pitcher, throwing *this* assortment of pitches, under *these* playing conditions, within a certain set of objectives (time to go for the long ball with the team behind). All of what has been discussed so far comes down to the question, "Can he or she do it?" "Can a student put these capabilities into practice?" Thus the inclusion of the terms to the right of academic skills: learning and growth objectives, and action.

The first term, learning and growth objectives, gets at whether the student at any moment, this week, today, at this moment—not just in general—knows what he is trying to get done. Does he have clarity on his learning objectives? Right now, does he know in what direction he needs to grow? And does that objective make sense in terms of who he is and what the school is about? And it all comes down to whether students can take effective action to bring all of this academic ability to bear in a coordinated way in order to achieve these learning and growth objectives. Can he or she take the exigencies of the immediate classroom circumstances into account and get things done? Can the student apply what he or she knows, and can he or she do it right here and right now? Academic achievement is about more than capability and potential—it is about effective action. This raises simple, existential, questions: What action is the student taking right now? What is he getting done? A focus on teaching asks this about teachers. The student achievement construct asks it about students.

We are not finished yet, but let me review a bit. So far, what we have gone over is what the student brings to the school experience. Referring to the diagram, the student brings to the classroom who he or she is (the conscious self); a particular level of willfulness; and a particular conglomeration of things in his awareness (thoughts, images, memories, etc.) and not in his awareness (a submerged, subconscious reality). The student enters the classroom as a physical-biological entity, with a particular inheritance, state of health, and state of functioning. The student has (or has not) made certain choices about his education, has (or does not have) a mission or purpose regarding his schooling, and has a particular school subpersonality. He or she has generic and specific academic skills of a certain sort and at a certain level of proficiency. He or she has (or does not have) learning and growth objectives of a particular kind, and a particular level of capability to take action and to bring all of this capability to bear on the realization of those objectives. All of this is influenced by factors related to social-cultural, health, relational, developmental, and emotional-psychological phenomena. From the student's side, then, that is what is there, or at least those elements are what I consider significant enough to include. Does that make sense?

I am saying that is what walks into the classroom door. From the student's side, that is what affects the level of his or her commitment and capability. That is not to say that any of us, or schools generally, will choose to be concerned with all of that; but it is my beginning approximation of what "all of that" includes.

Exchange with the School

Student achievement does not just have to do with the student. The school counts, too: its curriculum, instructional practices, climate, and organization. To understand why a student does or does not achieve in school the nature of the environment in which the student works must be considered. Drawing on the earlier idea of the individual-in-the-world way of looking at human beings, we can see schooling as an *exchange* between a student and a school setting. The human being is never an isolated entity. He is always related to his environment. What the student is like counts; but what the school is like counts as well. And, most important, the nature of the interplay between the student and school setting counts. The arrows indicate that, at each moment, there is interaction between this student, bringing what he or she does to the situation, and the school.

I have been attempting to balance our tendency to think that *only* what the school does matters. But I do not want to fall into the opposite trap and seem to imply that the nature of the student is the only thing that makes a difference. One point of view, that the school is everything, can lead to school and teaching improvements, leaving the student out of it; the other, that the student is everything, can lead to student improvement efforts that leave the school as it is. Although there has been a student improvement focus here, I do not want to downplay the importance of the nature and quality of the school environment. Thus the inclusion of the school on the right. Chapters 5, 6, and 7 discussed instruction, curriculum, climate, and school organization as crucial concerns. I refer you to those chapters.

I have now sketched each of the elements in the construct. Now look at the diagram again, all of it. Does it make sense? Does it paint a picture of school achievement from the perspective of an individual student? Work with it a bit.

Now, give it life. Imagine everything on that diagram in interaction with everything else, affecting and being affected by everything else. Even imagine the conscious self being affected by the other elements. I have put forth that it is constant, that it is changeless, that there is always the same "me" in there. And I have said it always, this core self, has the power to be willful, to become the "captain of the ship." And that perhaps—I do not know—each of us has a set, ordained purpose to live out as a human being. But, even with that, the everything-in-dynamic-relationship perspective still holds. Even if something does not change, or cannot be changed by other factors, it can still be *hidden* or *obscured* by other factors. Life in our society can make you forget, or keep you from ever attending to, who you are and what your life means. Families can obscure that. Schools can. Being sick can. Thoughts and memories bouncing around in your head can. All these factors, every one of them, can. Just because we are human beings does not mean we are going to live like a human being.

So that is the student achievement construct. What I am saying is that if things are going well academically for a student, it is because these factors are right; and if something is off it is due to something being off in one or more of these factors. Since all the elements in this construct are "of a piece," interconnected, it is hard to imagine just one thing being wrong. If one thing is not right, it will knock other things off kilter. Conversely, if we and students improve in one area it may result in positive changes in others.

Although we will likely choose to focus on one or two elements at any particular time, it helps to keep the "big picture" in mind. For example, I may want to look at the difference social disadvantage has on academic achievement. Of course I can simply correlate social disadvantage and achievement measures and find a relationship. But unless I can change the social circumstance, I may be stuck. What am I going to do about the student's level of achievement? The construct points to some areas that I can assess and perhaps modify if it proves necessary: areas such as cognitive processing skills, academic self-concept, use of language, goal attainment skills, collaborative abilities, and so forth. Too, if I focus on one area I am reminded of what else exists. That gives me some direction in deciding what else I need to do or with whom I need to coordinate my efforts.

A last point before talking in more detail about the uses of this construct: I hope this is just a beginning and that you improve on this effort I have made. With the construct, take elements off, put others on, and change things around. In fact, a good question for you to answer right now is: "What is the best improvement you can offer to make this a better construct, to make it a better "map" of student achievement? What change would you make to improve what is here?"

STUDENT ACHIEVEMENT CONSTRUCT USES

Now that the construct is defined, how can we make use of it? I have already alluded to some uses, and I know you can think of some, but to reiterate and formalize it a bit I list some ways this construct may be helpful. As I proceed through this list of possibilities, see what other uses are triggered in your mind.

First, as I have said, the construct provides a perspective or frame of reference for the study of achievement and underachievement. It gives us some categories to attend to (conscious self, social-cultural influences, choice, personality, general and specific academic skills, etc.). It also gives us a sense of the "big picture," and provides an indication of the totality of factors involved, as well as their relationship to one another. One additional advantage is that it provides a way to decide on a focus for your own work. You can look over the diagram of the construct and decide what you think needs attention the most; or what you can best do, given your situation and abilities. Whatever you do, you will also be clear on what you are *not* doing. And you will be able to see how what others are doing in this general area complement your own efforts. For example, you might decide to concentrate on self-awareness among students. That could be because you think it is the key to turning underachievers around, or because self-awareness is an understudied area and work is needed there. Perhaps it is because you are particularly trained to deal with self-awareness, or good at dealing with it, or most able to get at it in your current situation. Or it could be an area you need to know more about. A last possibility of course is that self-awareness may be a particular student's difficulty; and if you work with the student in this area there is a good chance that you can be helpful.

The construct is also potentially valuable as a diagnostic instrument. We can look at a student in terms of the construct and decide where he needs the most help. Is it a developmental issue? Is it a problem in what I called goal attainment capability? Does he or she need to get clearer on immediate objectives? Is it a school curriculum or organizational issue? Is it a reading problem?

Moreover, the construct gives us a way to bring teams of professionals together to serve the needs of students. First, it indicates whom to have on the team. If you look over the construct you can see a place for psychologists, social service professionals, medical people, academic skill remediation professionals, special educators, and parents, as well as teachers, counselors, school administrators, and the student himself. Perhaps a number of these individuals could form a diagnostic team, each looking at the student from his own professional perspective— but, again, knowing how their skills fit into the overall concern.

Another possibility, the construct may prove to be a guide to curriculum development. We can design lessons geared to assist students in developing ability in areas within the construct where they need help and use it as a way to boost the level of their academic achievement. We can do this in a formal way, or use it as a frame of reference to direct less formal exchanges. For instance, last year I held a series of informal 2 hour sessions with a group of students who were having trouble in school. I found this construct to be useful to me as a guide in responding to them during discussions and deciding where to take things. Also, still within an informal mode, the construct can provide us with some ideas and goals that can be the basis of an overall posture or intention we assume with students. This can result in changes in our behavior as teachers and increased student performance without it being formally written into a curriculum or otherwise calculated in advance. As teachers we just hold it, as it were, as a goal we want to achieve. Remember the Assagioli material which discussed how what we hold in our awareness tends to happen. That concept applies here. For example, you may decide that students in your class will become strategic learners. If you can picture it in your mind, describe it in words, and believe it will occur, somehow it will begin to happen. That is not to say that it is not a good idea to carefully plan how to get the task done. Do that certainly. It is only to underscore that the ideas in our head are manifested in reality (including the negative ones). Be careful about what you dream; because dreams *do* come true.

Beyond the possibility of informal and supplementary work in this area, there is the possibility of formal or direct instruction in the skills of student achievement. I am very impressed with the success of people we have considered—Johnson, Covington, Lipson, among them—in teaching school-going skills directly to students. In these cases, school achievement capability itself was the content of the curriculum. To illustrate how this might work, I made a proposal to a school where I worked as a consultant to set up a separate class devoted to increasing achievement commitment and capability for those students who need it. For these students there would be a two strand program: an academic strand of 5 hours a day made up of social studies, English, physical education, science, and the rest of the academic subjects; and a school achievement strand in which for 1 hour a day these students would study how to do well in the academic strand. Many students need both strands. Also, as I mentioned earlier, this kind of two-strand approach may help some students adapt more effectively to mixed classes, and in this sense provide an alternative to grouped classes. In other words, instead of developing a curriculum and organizational arrangement to adjust to student abilities by grouping them for instruction, we teach students how to adjust to the most diverse and challenging environment the school can offer.

Along this line, a promising piece of research would go as follows: Select a group of students who seem generally capable enough, but whose school record, interests, or style, whatever the criteria used, have led the school to assign them to a lower ability grouped section or to a less intellectually challenging course. For these students, put them in the top academic classes. And at the same time enroll them in a special school achievement class. See how it goes. Perhaps these students can learn to accommodate to the best we can provide. We may learn they can come up to us instead of our going down to meet them.

Furthermore, I have been working with a secondary school to set up a program of Student Effectiveness Education. The concept is to identify a group of 16 capable but underachieving students. These students will attend a week-long program of school achievement education just before school begins in the fall. Sessions will be for full days. The faculty will be a teacher or counselor from the school and me.

Four achieving students from the school will enroll in the program. These students will participate in dual roles as learners and instructors. They will study achievement skills along with the other students. In addition, they will give presentations on what they can do to be effective in school and provide peer support to the other students. During the fall these four achieving students will continue to give support to other students, each working with four underachieving students. The achieving students will work closely with faculty as members of the instructional team and will attend a 2 day training session to prepare them for this work. They will receive service credit from the school for their efforts. For the achieving students, there should be several positive outcomes in the program. They will likely learn some valuable insights and skills related to achievement to enhance those they already possess. In addition, they should increase their capability to engage in mature collaboration through working with the other faculty. Hopefully, these students will enhance their ability to help others through their work with the underachieving students.

The summer program will be followed by twice-a-week sessions during the school year led by the school professional and the four achieving students, with consultation help from me. One way to organize this is to assign these students a common study period, though those details need to be worked out. And, as indicated, the peer teams will operate, made up of an achieving student and four underachieving students. They could meet before or after school, during lunch, or during the common study period.

A key feature of this program is to be positive in approach. It is important to make it clear to the underachieving students that the school sees their potential, believes in them, and wants to provide them with some help to do better and be happier in school. I strongly believe students should volunteer for a program such as this and not be coerced or assigned. It *is* a positive thing to be able to do this, it is not punishment. Students *do*, most of them, want to be more successful in school. Significant numbers will want to be part of this if they see the possibility of it improving as students; they will not have to be forced to participate. They know it is more fun to do well than not do well. They know it is more satisfying to have your parents proud of you and appreciate you then to be disappointed and disapproving. Not all students feel this way; some say they are fine doing less well than they can, and just want to be left alone. But many underachieving students, perhaps more than many of us think, would work to be better if they knew how or thought that it would make a difference.

There is a very important argument for insisting in volunteers: just the act of volunteering itself is a big step for a student on the way to greater school success. It is taking a stand. It is saying, yes, I am willing to work on doing better in school. Yes, I am willing to look at it. That alone is a great help. And apart from how good the program's activities are, just naming the issue (increasing one's capability as a student and increasing the level of academic achievement), giving time to it, and setting a goal helps. It helps if the school says, "We believe in you and expect you to do better and we will help you." Students stepping forward and schools formally acknowledging these goals and these students may be just about enough of a program right there. Most of us remember studying the "Hawthorne effect" in psychology classes. The idea is that improvement can come from just being the center of attention. Certainly we can work to make the program activities the best we can create. But at the same time we should not underestimate the impact of these psychological factors.

What areas do I suggest we focus upon in such a program as this? Of course it depends a great degree on the particular students you are working with, but I can make some general suggestions.

I would use the student achievement construct as my frame of reference. In the early stages of student effective education I would aim to assist a student to, as they say, be on their own case. It is not enough that we the educators attend to their issues. They have to become informed and take responsibility for helping themselves become a better student. In other words, they have to become part of their own "case-load." They need to get to a place where they can make a decision of whether or not they want to do better in school. The key need for them is to see that it is possible to be more successful, and they need to know how to understand their issues and how to begin to move forward to resolve them.

To get at that in the beginning it makes sense to concentrate on five areas:

- Students need to become aware that they are a conscious self, possessed of a will, and able to make choices and changes in their lives.
- Students need to learn the student achievement construct itself to understand the overall scope of student effectiveness.
- Students need to gain a critical understanding of their own situation in terms of the construct. What is going on for them? Where are they strong? Where do they need improvement?
- Students need to begin to develop goal attainment capability (goal setting, planning, self-monitoring, etc.).
- Students need to choose to take responsibility for becoming better students.

With this start, students can begin to focus on improving those areas that are particularly retarding their school success, whether it be some character trait, a health issue, self-management skills, self-defeating ways they think, writing skills, and so forth. To do that, a student is going to have to learn to ask for and accept help from the school. And the school and community, from their side, must be prepared to give the help students need. For example, if a student sees that he has a problem with alcohol that is getting in the way, somewhere in his world there has to be people and programs waiting to respond. Again, it is the idea of an exchange: a student taking responsibility for improving himself; and an environment that is supportive of that. The construct indicates the areas in which the school-community-family-friends world of the student must be equipped to respond. But it must be underscored that the key to all of this is that the individual student *chooses* to do better. We have to press him or her on that issue.

IN CONCLUSION

I hope students learn from such a program even more than just *school* effectiveness. Just as reading people talk of metacognition, I think there is a metaskill that transcends becoming more powerful and effective as a student: the skill of getting in charge of your life. That is what I hope is a by-product of learning to be a better student. I hope students come to see school effectiveness as an example of a larger process. That is the process of assessing what is going on anywhere in your life, figuring out what you want, and then taking responsibility for using every available resource to make things better for yourself and others. It contrasts with waiting around for the world to serve you or fix you. It is not hoping and wishing and complaining and blaming. It is taking control of how you are.

One of the things I am certain students will learn in this process of taking charge of their school lives is that it does not so much involve learning new things, though there is that dimension. Rather, it is more a matter of discovering what you had all along and have just not used. Paul's second letter to Timothy in the New Testament says it well:

> For God did not give
> us a spirit of timidity
> but a spirit of power
> and love and self control
> > 2 Timothy 1.7

Human beings are born with—it is part of their nature—to be powerful, self-controlled, and loving of themselves and others. It affirms that when you strip away all the social conditioning, this is what we are. This is at our core. Student effectiveness education, then, is in large part letting students see what they already are. It is helping them discover their essence, and then giving them a way to become more effective at living out that essence in their lives.

As far as specific activities that get at this, I think you have to decide that for yourself. You have to look at what it is you are committed to do and what you are capable of doing. You need to take into account the needs, possibilities, and limitations of your own situation. I hope I have given you enough guidelines and examples to give you a start. For you it may be research, writing, starting a program, or helping one or two students you know, or maybe something else. All that discussion about self and will and choice and mission applies to you and me. I have written these words; you must decide what you are uniquely best able to do and most called to do in your circumstance.

Whatever we do, let us do it with a twinkle in our eye. It could be that you and I and the students we work with have only one chance at this life. So let's *do* it, whatever it is. Let's take it seriously and enjoy it and give a wink to those whose hearts, like ours, are beating and not yet stopped. Let's experience the adventure and glory of being alive as much as we can while there is time.

Be well.

Notes

CHAPTER 1: INTRODUCTION

1. I cannot trace the newspaper article (perhaps it is an editorial). The headline was, "The Family Is the Key." The article: Hochstein, Rollie, "10 Ways to Help Your Child Succeed," *Woman's Day*, June 28, 1977, pp. 54, 56, 124–125. Teachers I have worked with have found the ten suggestions in the Hochstein piece very useful. The suggestions include helping the child inventory his assets, family sharing procedures, the value of heroes and heroines, and the use of family scrapbooks and albums.

2. Hochstein, p. 56.

3. For examples of the sort of writings I am referring to, see: Coleman, J. S. et al., *Equality of Educational Opportunity* (Washington, DC: U.S. Government Printing Office, 1966). Also, Jencks, Christopher et al., *Inequality* (New York: Basic Books, 1972).

4. Jencks draws this conclusion in *Inequality*, pp. 255–65. Also, see Coty, C. T., "Making It: Can the Odds Be Evened," interview with Christopher Jencks, *Psychology Today*, Vol. 13: No. 2, 1979, p. 39.

5. Examples of the effective schools literature include: Rutter, Michael, et al., *Fifteen Thousand Hours* (Cambridge, MA: Havard University Press, 1979); and Edmunds, Ronald, "Effective Schools for the Urban Poor," *Educational Leadership*, Vol. 37: No. 1, October, 1979, pp. 15–24.

6. One of the many published articles coming out of that study: Kenkel, W. F., and Gage, B. A., "Life's Predictable Unpredictables and the Career Plans of Youth," *Sociological Spectrum*. Vol. 2: Nos. 3–4, July–Dec, 1982, pp. 307–314. A person to contact about the project is Professor Sara Schoffner, University of North Carolina at Greensboro, Greensboro, NC 27412. For a summary article on this five state project, see: "Career Aspirations of Youth Studies," *Higher Education and National Affairs*, Vol. 34, Number 19, October 14, 1985.

7. A wonderful book that deals with these issues is: Kohl, H., *Basic Skills* (Boston: Little, Brown & Company, 1982). His conclusion is that American schools never have been focused solely on the "three R's." Schools have always been engaged in cultural transmission and personal development.

8. I have written in some detail about American character and tradition with the help of a colleague in a lengthy book review. The book is, Bellah, R. et al., *Habits of the Heart: Individualism and Commitment in American Life* (Berkeley: University of California Press, 1985). Our essay/review:

Nash, R., and Griffin, Robert, "Balancing the Private and the Public," *Harvard Educational Review*. Vol. 56: No. 2, May, 1986, pp. 171–182.

9. A key reading source from which I derive my conclusions is: Wood, Gordon, *The Creation of the American Republic, 1776–1787* (New York: W.W. Norton & Company, 1969).

10. Neil Postman's writings about an "ascent of man" curriculum for schools gets at some of these matters. See: Postman, N. "Engaging Students in the Great Conversation" *Phi Delta Kappan*, Vol. 65: No. 5., January, 1984, pp. 310–316.

11. See Macdonald, J., "Value Bases and Issues for Curriculum," in Molnar, Alex; and Zahorik, John, eds., *Curriculum Theory* (Alexandria, VA: Association for Supervision and Curriculum Development, 1977), pp. 10–21. And Newmann, F., and Kelly, T., *Human Dignity and Excellence in Education: Guidelines For Curriculum policy*, Final Report to the National Institute of Education, 1983. Available through the ERIC system.

12. Macdonald, p. 21.

13. Newmann and Kelly, pp. 2–6.

14. Buddhist thought has a concept of "right livelihood" that is similar to work as I am describing it in this section. Read Theodore Roszak's chapter called "Work: The Right to Right Livelihood" (pp. 205–40) in his book *Person/Planet* (Garden City, NY: Anchor Press/Doubleday, 1978). Roszak draws on Eastern thought in this chapter. Also, I am reminded of the French philosopher Simone Weil's writings. For one year she took a repetitive, difficult job in a factory. She intended while she worked there to organize the workers, raise consciousness among them, uplift them, and all that. As it turns out, what she found was that about all she could manage was to get through the workday and then recover from its deadening, depleting effect for tomorrow.

15. Mirgan, T., "New Federal Study Links 'Protestant Ethic' to Academic Success," *Education Week*, March 19, 1986, p. 10.

16. "Teacher Subculture Central to Schools, Students," *Wisconsin Center for Educational Research News*, Winter, 1985, p. 1.

CHAPTER 2: THE NATURE OF UNDERACHIEVEMENT

1. Krause, J., and Krause, Helen, "Toward a Multimodal Theory of Academic Underachievement," *Educational Psychologist*, Vol. 16: No. 3, 1981, pp. 151–164.

2. Dowdall, C., and Colangelo, N., "Underachieving Gifted Students: Review and Implications," *Gifted Child Quarterly*, Vol. 26: No. 4, Fall 1982, 179–184.

3. McCall, R., "Underachievers: What to Do When They Can But They Won't," *Learning*, November/December, 1985, pp. 62–66.

4. Dowdall and Colangelo, p. 180.

5. McCall, pp. 62–63.

6. To pursue this farther, see: Gardner, H., *Frames of Mind: The Theory of Multiple Intelligences* (New York: Basic Books, 1983).

7. McCall, p. 64.

8. Krauses, p. 158.

9. Ibid.

10. Dowdall and Colangelo, p. 181

11. See Krauses, pp. 153–160.

12. For a good example of materials designed for use by teachers to deal with self-image concerns, see Canfield, Jack; and Wells, H., *100 Ways to Enhance Self-Concept in the Classroom* (Englewood Cliffs, NJ: Prentice-Hall, Inc., 1976).

13. Krauses, p. 160.

14. McCall, p. 66.

CHAPTER 3: A PERSPECTIVE ON ACHIEVEMENT

1. Assagioli, Roberto, *Psychosynthesis* (New York: The Viking Press, 1971); and Assagioli, Roberto, *The Act of Will* (Baltimore: Penguin Books, 1974).

2. Brown, Molly, *The Unfolding Self* (Los Angeles: Psychosynthesis Press, 1983); and Ferrucci, Piero, *What We May Be* (Los Angeles: J.P. Tarcher, Inc., 1982).

3. Assagioli, *The Act of Will*, pp. 46.

4. Ibid., pp. 4–6, 9, 38.

5. Ibid., p. 6.

6. Ibid., p. 10.

7. Ibid., p. 90.

8. For a discussion of the moral responsibility of the artist, see: Gardner, John, *On Moral Fiction* (New York: Basic Books, 1978).

9. For an impassioned plea for greater attention in schools to the moral dimension of political and social issues, see Kozol, J., *The Night is Dark and I Am Far From Home* (Boston: Houghton Mifflin Company, 1975).

10. Assagioli, *The Act of Will*, p. 135.

11. Coles, R., *Privileged Ones: The Well-off and the Rich in America* (Boston: Little, Brown and Company, 1977).

12. To read further about character education in the schools, refer to the theme issue, "The Schools' Role in Developing Character," in the journal *Educational Leadership*, Vol. 43: No. 4, December, 1985/January, 1986.

13. Assagioli, *The Act of Will*, pp. 101–03, 154–155.

14. Cornfield, Francis, translator, *The Republic of Plato* (New York: Oxford University Press, 1980), p. 140.

15. Assagioli, *The Act of Will*, p. 11.

16. Brown, p. 26.

17. Ibid., p. 13.

18. Ibid., p. 12.

19. Kohl, Herbert, *Half the House* (New York: E.P. Dulton, Inc., 1974), p. 37.

20. Bukowski, C., "3:16 and One Half...," copyright *Unmuzzled Ox*, Autumn, 1972, which appears in Field, Edward, *A Geography of Poets* (New York: Bantam Books, 1981), p. 116.

21. For example, see Brown, pp. 111, 116.

22. Roszak, T., *Person/Planet* (Garden City, New York: Anchor Press/Doubleday, 1978), pp. 177–178.

23. Assagioli, *The Act of Will*, p. 51.

24. Moorman, C., and Dishon, D., *Our Classroom* (Englewood Cliffs, NJ: Prentice-Hall, Inc., 1983), pp. 120–124. This book is written for elementary school people, but I find it most valuable for secondary as well. It comes as close as any education book I know to reflecting the orientation I adopt in this book.

25. For some good material on the "inner curriculum," see Moorman and Dishon, chapter ten, which begins on p. 151.

26. Burns, D., *Feeling Good* (New York: New American Library, 1980), pp. 40–41. A clever but unfortunate title, as it makes it sound to be a lightweight self-help book. On the contrary, it is a superb, scholarly volume.

27. Gaylean, Beverly, "Meditating with Children: Some Things Learned," *Association for Humanistic Psychology Newsletter*, August–September 1980, pp. 16–17.

28. Assagioli, *The Act of Will*, p. 52.

29. For information on obtaining the tape for showing, write: Media Library, Pomeroy Hall, 489 Main Street, University of Vermont, Burlington, VT 05405. There is a rental charge.

30. Garfield, C., *Peak Performance* (New York: Warner Books, Inc., 1984). Orlick, T., *In Pursuit of Excellence* (Champaign, IL: Human Kinetics Publishers, Inc., 1980).

31. See: Garfield, pp. 33–60; Orlick, pp. 31–45.

32. Garfield, pp. 64–68.

33. Ibid., p. 26.

34. Orlick, p. 21.

35. Ibid., pp. 118–120.

36. Canfield, J., "The Inner Classroom," in Harris, Anastas, ed., *Holistic Education: Education for Living* (Del Mar, CA: Mandala Holistic Education 1981), p. 30.

37. Garfield, p. 127; Orlick, p. 89.

38. Orlick, pp. 62–70.

39. Ibid., pp. 240–245.

40. For an analysis of aikido and its relation to everyday living, see Leonard, George, *The Ultimate Athlete* (New York: The Viking Press, 1975), especially chapter three, pp. 47–59.

41. Joel Kirsch has compiled a manual of energy training exercises. To inquire about purchasing a copy, you can write him at 109 Ryan Avenue, Mill Valley, CA 94941.

42. Brant, Ron, "Balancing Act," *San Francisco Sunday Examiner and Chronicle*, August 12, 1984, p. 24.

43. Oh, S., and Falkner, D., *Sadaharu Oh: A Zen Way of Baseball* (New York: Vintage Books, 1984).

44. Nielson, L., *How to Motivate Adolescents* (Englewood Cliffs, New Jersey: Prentice-Hall, Inc.,1982).

45. Nielson, L., "Teaching Adolescents Self-Management," *Clearing House*, Vol. 57: No. 5, October, 1983, pp. 76–81.

46. Yates, Richard, *The Easter Parade* (New York: Delacorte Press, 1976).

47. The best book I know on affirmations in a dieting book, no less: Ray, S., *The Only Diet There Is* (Millbrae, CA: Celestial Arts, 1981).

48. Nielson, "Teaching Adolescents Self-Management," p. 80.

49. Johnson, E., *Raising Children to Achieve* (New York: Walker and Company, 1984). Also, another book, this one about adult achievement: Griessman, B. E., *The Achievement Factors* (New York: Dodd, Mead, and Company, 1987).

50. Johnson, E., and McClelland, D., *Learning to Achieve* (Glenview, IL: Scott, Foresman and Company, 1984).

51. Johnson, pp. 5–6.

52. Ibid., p. 8.

53. Ibid., p. 16.

54. Ibid., p. 9. Also, see: de Charms, R., *Enhancing Motivation* (New York: Irvington Publishers, 1976).

55. Johnson, p. 9.

56. Ibid., p. 10.

57. Postman, N., *Teaching as a Conserving Activity* (New York: Delacorte Press, 1979). Postman, N., *Amusing Ourselves to Death* (New York: Viking Penguin, Inc., 1985).

58. Johnson, p. 12.

59. Neitsche, F., *Genealogy of Morals* (New York: Boni and Liveright, 1918).

60. Johnson, pp. 24–27.

61. Johnson and McClelland, p. 107.

62. Bloom, Benjamin, ed., *Developing Talent in Young People* (New York: Ballantine Books, 1985).

63. Bloom, pp. 507–549.

64. Glasser, W., *Control Theory* (New York: Harper and Row, Publishers, Perennial Library Edition, 1985).

65. For a discussion of the power of expectations, read a book that has become an education classic: Rosenthal, R., *Pygmalian in the Classroom* (New York: Holt, Rinehart, and Winston, 1968).

CHAPTER 4: AN EXPLORATION OF STUDENTING

1. Temple, C., and Gillet, J. W., *Language Arts: Learning Processes and Teaching Practices* (Boston: Little-Brown, 1984).

2. See, for example, Paris, S., Lipson, M., and Wixson, K., "Becoming a Strategic Learner," *Contemporary Educational Psychology*, Vol. 8: pp. 293–316, 1983.

3. Paris, S., Cross, D., and Lipson, M., "Informed Strategies for Learning," *Journal of Educational Psychology*, Vol. 76: No. 6, 1984, p. 1241.

4. For details see Paris, C., and Lipson, M.

5. See, Brown, A., Compione, J., and Day, J., "Learning to Learn: On Training Students to Learn from Texts," *Educational Researcher,* Vol. 10: February, 1981, pp. 14–21.

6. Ibid., p. 320.

7. See, Covington, M., "Motivated Cognitions," chapter in Paris, S. G.; Olson, G.; and Stevenson, H., eds, *Learning and Motivation in the Classroom* (Hillsdale, NJ; Erlbaum Publishers, Lawrence Erlbaum Publishers, 1983).

8. See the theme issue "Thinking Skills in the Curriculum," in *Educational Leadership*, Vol. 42: No. 1, September, 1984.

9. Sternberg, R., "Can We Teach Intelligence," *Educational Leadership*, Vol. 42: No. 1, September, 1984, pp. 38–48.

10. Sternberg, p. 41.

11. For more information on Feurstein's work, see Feurstein, Rewan, *Instrumental Enrichment for Cognitive Modifiability* (Baltimore: University Park Press, 1980).

12. Sternberg, p. 42.

13. Lipman has written a book you may wish to obtain: Lipman, M; Sharp, A. M.; and Oscanyan, F. S., *Philosophy in the Classroom,* 2nd ed. (Philadelphia: Temple University Press, 1980).

14. See, Letteri, C., "Teaching Students How to Learn," *Theory Into Practice,* Vol. 24: No. 2, Spring 1985, pp. 112–22.

15. For further study of Professor Letteri's work refer to his chapter in Laguis, M., ed., *Cognitive Science and Education Practice* (Washington, DC: Educational Resources and Information Center, 1984).

16. See, Gall, M., "Synthesis of Research on Teachers' Questioning," *Educational Leadership*, Vol. 41: No. 5, November, 1984, p. 42.

17. I referred you to the September, 1984 theme issue of *Educational Leadership* devoted to the development of thinking skills. Also, there is the November, 1984 issue of that same journal, a theme issue entitled "When Teachers Tackle Thinking Skills" (*Educational Leadership*, Vol. 42: No. 3). In that November issue you will read about critical thinking, creative thinking, dialectical thinking, and lateral thinking. And, another one, "Frameworks for Teaching Thinking," theme issue, *Educational Leadership*, Vol. 43: No. 8, May, 1986. Very much worth studying; but what it all comes down to is the challenge to teach students to think, and make the work we give them require them to use these thinking skills.

18. The *Harvard-Milton Study Skills Program* is published by the National Association of Secondary School Principals, Reston, VA 22091. For an overview of the approach, see Marshak, D., and Burkle, C., "Learning to Study," *Principal*, Vol. 61: No. 2, November, 1981, pp. 38–40.

19. *Harvard-Milton Study Skills Program*, Level Two, p. 27.

20. Their address: Boston College, Chestnut Hill, Massachusetts 02167.

21. From Heiman, M., "Learning to Learn," *Educational Leadership*, Vol. 43: No. 1, September 1985, p. 21.

22. Ibid., p. 23.

23. Ibid., p. 24.

24. Houck, Cherry, *Learning Disabilities* (Englewood Cliffs, NJ: Prentice-Hall Publishers, 1984).

25. Ibid., pp. 11–13.

26. A good article that presents a teacher's account of working with learning disabled students:

O'Conner, T., "Adolescent Development and the Learning Disabled Teenager," *English Journal*, Vol. 73: December, 1984, pp. 33–35.

27. Schneider, B., "LD as They See It: Perceptions of Adolescents in a Special Residential School," *Journal of Learning Disabilities*, Vol. 17: No. 9, November, 1984, pp. 533–536.

28. Hurn, C., *The Limits and Possibilities of Schooling* (Boston: Allyn and Bacon, Inc., 1985).

29. Ibid., pp. 140–141.

30. Ibid., see pp. 60, 127, and 142.

31. See Lewis, O., "The Culture of Poverty," *Scientific American*, Vol. 215: October 1966, pp. 19–25.

32. Cited in Hurn, p. 194.

33. For example, see Bowles, S., and Gintes, H., *Schooling in Capitalist America* (New York: Basic Books, 1976).

34. Bernstein, B., ed., *Class Codes and Controls* (London: Routledge and Kegan Paul, 1976).

35. Kahle, J. B., *Factors Affecting the Retention of Girls in Science Courses and Careers: Case Studies of Selected Secondary Schools* (Washington, DC: National Science Foundation, 1983).

36. These statistics are from Postman, Neil, *Teaching as a Conserving Activity* (New York: Delacorte Press, 1979), p. 50. Also see, Brody, J., "Guidelines for Parents on Children's TV Viewing," *New York Times,* Section C, p. 8, January 21, 1987. This article supports the Postman statistics.

37. Ibid., entire book.

38. Postman, N., *Amusing Ourselves to Death* (New York: Viking Penguin, Inc., 1985).

39. Postman, N., *Disappearance of Childhood* (New York: A Laurel Book, 1982).

40. For a discussion of the contrasts between school and television, see Postman, *Teaching as a Conservative Activity*, Chapter Three.

41. Rodriguez, R., *Hunger of Memory* (Boston: David Godine, Publisher, 1981).

42. Quoted in Hurn, pp. 145–147.

43. A Piaget source is: Bybee, R., *Piaget for Educators*, 2nd ed. (Columbus, OH: Charles Merrill, 1982).

44. Lipsitz, J., *Successful Schools for Young Adolescents* (New Brunswick, NJ: Transaction Books, 1984).

45. Ibid., p. 10.

46. Elkind, D., *All Grown Up and No Place to Go* (Reading, MA: Addison-Wesley Publishing Company, 1984).

47. Goodlad, J., *A Place Called School* (New York: McGraw-Hill Book Company, 1984), pp. 78–79.

48. For more on Erikson, see his books *Childhood and Society* (New York: W.W. Norton and Company, 1950); and *Identity: Youth and Crisis* (New York: W.W. Norton and Company, 1968). Also, review how he makes use of his theories to analyze the lives of historical figures: For example, see: Erikson, E., *Gandhi's Truth* (New York: Norton, 1969); and Erikson, E., *Young Man Luther* (New York: Norton, 1958).

49. Elkind, p. 8.

50. Ibid., pp. 164–165.

51. For details see Postman, *The Disappearance of Childhood*.

52. Elkind, p. 5.

53. Rinzler, J., *Teens Speak Out* (New York: Donald I. Fine, Inc., 1985).

54. Cornford, Francis, translator, *The Republic of Plato* (New York: Oxford University Press, 1980).

55. For more information on this program, see: Gerber, E., "Skills for Adolescence: A New Program for Young Teenagers," *Phi Delta Kappan*, Vol. 1: No. 6, February, 1986, pp. 436–439.

56. Ibid., p. 438.

57. Johnson, D., and Johnson, F., *Joining Together: Group Theory and Group Skills* (Englewood Cliffs, NJ: Prentice-Hall, 1982), pp. 279–333. Also see, Johnson, D., Johnson, R., and Holubec, E., *Circles of Learning: Cooperation in the Classroom* (Minneapolis: Interaction Book Company, 1986).

58. Ibid., pp. 283–285.

59. Ibid., pp. 300–306.

60. Fisher, R,, and Ury, W., *Getting to Yes: Negotiating Agreement Without Giving In* (Boston: Houghton Mifflin Company, 1981).

61. Shula, B., and Anderson, J., "Training in the Management of Conflict: A Communication Theory Perspective," *Small Group Behavior,* Vol. 15: No. 3, August 1984, pp. 333–348.

62. Nelson, M., "Teaching About Conflict Resolution," *Social Studies Journal,* Vol. 15: No. 3, August, 1984, pp. 58–65.

63. Kreider, W., *Creative Conflict Resolution: More Than 200 Activities for Keeping Peace in the Classroom* (Glenview, IL: Scott Foresman, 1984).

64. Dobson, T., and Miller, V., *Giving In To Get Your Way: The Attack-tics System for Winning Your Everyday Battles* (New York: Delacorte Press, 1978). This book is out of print, but you may be able to get it at a library. If they do not have it, check out the possibility of an inter-library loan. Also, see Dobson, T., *Safe and Alive: How to Protect Yourself, Your Family, and Your Property Against Violence* (Los Angeles: J.P. Tarcher, 1981).

65. Their classic book is Johnson, D., and Johnson, F., *Learning Together and Alone* (Englewood Cliffs, NJ, Prentice-Hall, 1975).

66. I am sorry but I do not have a reference on this one. I got it at a workshop in 1986 and it was only labeled as having been taken from the Johnsons' material.

67. For example, see the work of Lawrence Kohlberg. A book of his: Kohlberg, L., *The Psychology of Moral Development* (San Francisco: Harper and Row, 1984). Also, refer to articles by him or drawing on his work under the heading of moral development in periodical indexes.

68. For a very provocative book on the moral and ethical dimensions of schooling, see Kozol, J., *The Night is Dark and I am Far From Home* (Boston: Houghton Mifflin Company, 1975).

69. Goodlad, J., *A Place Called School* (New York: McGraw-Hill Book Company, 1984) supports this point. Especially see Chapter Two, pp. 33–60.

70. Rogers, C., *Freedom to Learn in the 80's* (Columbus, OH: Charles E. Merrill Publishing Company, 1983).

71. Ibid., especially pp. 121–126.

72. Nash, R., and Griffin, R., "Carl Rogers: Still a Teacher for Our Times," *Teachers College Record,* Vol. 72: No. 2, December, 1977, pp. 279–290.

73. See Elkind, especially pp. 210–216. Also, Crowder, W., "Teaching About Stress," *Clearing House,* Vol. 57: September, 1983, pp. 36–38.

74. Ginott, H., *Teacher and Child: A Book for Parents and Teachers* (New York: Avon Books, 1972).

75. Levenkron, S., *Treating and Overcoming Anorexia Nervosa* (New York: Scribners, 1982), pp. 2–3.

76. Rothschild, B., "12 Percent of Teen Girls Report Eating Disorders," *USA Today,* November 8, 1985, p. 1.

77. See, for example: Phelps, J., and Nourse, A., *The Hidden Addiction* (Boston: Little, Brown and Company), 1986.

78. Gross, J., *Weight Modification and Eating Disorders in Boys and Girls,* University of Vermont, unpublished doctoral thesis, 1985, p. 11.

79. Rothschild, p. 1.

80. Boskind-White, M., and White, W., *Bulimarexia: The Binge-Purge Cycle* (New York: W.W. Norton and Company, 1983). Also, see: Cauwels, J., *Bulimia: The Binge-Purge Compulsion* (New York: Doubleday, 1983); and Roth, G., *Feeding the Hungry Heart* (New York: New American Library, 1982).

81. A good book on nutrition: Brody, J., *Jane Brody's Good Food Book: Living the High Carbohydrate Way* (New York: Norton, 1985).

82. Arenson, G., *Binge Eating: How to Stop It Forever* (New York: Rawson Associates, 1984).

83. Miller, P., and Hodgson, R., *Self-Watching: Addictions, Habits and Compulsions* (New York: Facts on File, 1983).

CHAPTER 5: AN EXPLORATION OF TEACHING

1. For a discussion of the failure-avoiding classroom, see Covington, M., and Orlick, C., "Ability and Effort Evaluation Among Failure-Avoiding and Failure-Accepting Students," *Journal of Educational Psychology*, Vol. 77: No. 4, 1985, pp. 446–459. Also, refer to Covington's excellent book with Richard Beery, *Self-Worth and School Learning* (New York: Holt, Rinehart, and Winston, 1976).

2. For Sizer's discussion of coaching, see Sizer, T., *Horace's Compromise* (Boston: Houghton Mifflin, 1985), pp. 99–108.

3. Tyler, R., *Basic Principles of Curriculum and Instruction* (Chicago: University of Chicago Press, 1949).

4. Costa, A., *Developing Minds: A Resource Book for Teaching Thinking* (Alexandria, VA: Association for Supervision and Curriculum Development, 1985). A good book to review: Beyer, B., *Practical Strategies for the Teaching of Thinking* (Needham Heights, MA: Allyn and Bacon, 1987).

5. See, for example, Bloom, B., *All Our Children Learning* (New York: McGraw-Hill, 1980).

6. To read further on the Carnegie report, see Boyer, E., *High School* (New York: Harper and Row, Publishers, 1983), especially chapters four, five and six.

7. Kohlberg, L., "Moral Stages and Moralization," in Lickona, T., *Moral Development and Behavior* (New York: Holt, Rinehart, and Winston, 1976), pp. 31–53.

8. Goodlad, J., *A Place Called School* (New York: McGraw-Hill Book Company, 1984), pp. 90–91.

9. Guskey, T., *Implementing Mastery Learning* (Belmont, CA: Wadsworth Publishing Company, 1985).

10. See, for example, Edmunds, R., "Making Schools Effective," *Social Policy*, September/October 1981, pp. 56–59.

11. Anderson, L., "A Retrospective and Prospective View of Bloom's 'Learning for Mastery,'" in Wang, Margaret; and Walberg, Herbert, eds., *Adapting Instruction to Individual Differences* (Berkeley, CA: McCutchan Publishing Corporation, 1985), p. 257.

12. Ibid., pp. 254–268.

13. Some books: Bloom, B., *Human Characteristics and School Learning* (New York: McGraw-Hill, 1976); Bloom, B., ed., *Developing Talent in Young People* (New York: Ballantine Books, 1985); Bloom, B., *All Our Children Learning* (New York: McGraw-Hill, 1981). Also, see the article: Abrams, J., "Making Outcomes-Based Education work," *Educational Leadership*, Vol. 43: No. 1, September 1985, pp. 30–32. An article I found especially useful by Bloom is: Bloom, B., "The Search for Methods of Group Instruction as Effective as One-to-One Tutoring," *Educational Leadership*, Vol. 41: No. 8, May 1984, pp. 4–17.

14. Hunter, M., "Knowing, Teaching, and Supervising," in Hosford, P., ed., *Using What We Know About Teaching* (Alexandria, VA: Association for Supervision and Curriculum Development, 1984), pp. 174–175.

15. I drew this from a paper, unpublished as far as I can tell, by Hunter entitled "Appraising the Instructional Process."

16. Hunter, M., "Knowing, Teaching, and Supervising," pp. 175–176.

17. For a description of the Hunter-based Newport News program, see: Evans, P., "Improving Instruction Through PET," *Educational Leadership*, Vol. 40: No. 1, October 1982, pp. 44–45.

18. Some good sources include: Hunter, M., *Mastery Teaching*, published by TIP Publications, P.O. Box 514, El Segundo, CA 90245. Ask for a list of Hunter's other TIP publications. She has written, among others, books on motivation, reinforcement, and learning retention. Another good book is, Cummings, C., *Teaching Makes a Difference*. Cummings' book is based on Hunter's instructional skills model and can be obtained from *Teaching*, 33 8th Avenue South, Edmonds, WA, 98020.

19. From a presentation by Dale Mann at *Excellence for All: Northeast Regional Conference on Education*, Stowe, Vermont, August 5, 1985. Also see his article, Mann, D., "Action on Dropouts," *Educational Leadership*, Vol. 43: No. 1, September 1985, pp. 16–17.

20. I apologize on this one. I cannot document the source. My notes say I took it from her writings in the 1984 ASCD Yearbook, "Knowing, Teaching, and Supervising," but I cannot find it there. I am certain that it is an accurate quote, however, so I have decided to keep it in. A couple of other sources I can recommend that get at this point, although I cannot find the exact quote in them either, are: Hunter, M., "What's Wrong With Madeline Hunter?" *Educational Leadership*, Vol. 42: No. 5, February 1985, pp. 57–60; and Brandt, R., "On Teaching and Supervision: A Conversation with Madeline Hunter," *Educational Leadership*, Vol. 42: No. 5, February 1985, pp. 61–66.

21. Shipp, E. R., "New Theory on Reading Goes Awry," *New York Times*, section 3, p. 2, October 8, 1985.

22. For a fine discussion of the subjectivity involved even in science, see Polanyi, M., *Personal Knowledge* (Chicago: University of Chicago Press, 1958).

23. It was very philosophical and political in the 1960's and 70's. A few volumes to illustrate: Neill, A. S., *Summerhill: A Radical Approach to Child Rearing* (New York: Hart Publishing Company, 1960); and Kozol, Jonathan, *Death at an Early Age: The Destruction of the Hearts and Minds of the Negro Children in the Boston Public Schools* (Boston: Houghton Mifflin, 1967). Another Kozol book is a good illustration: Kozol, Jonathan, *Free Schools* (Boston: Houghton Mifflin, 1972). Also, Dennison, G., *The Lives of Children* (New York: Random House, 1969). A couple of radical writers: Illich, I., *Deschooling Society* (New York: Harper and Row, 1971); and Friere, Paulo, *Pedagogy of the Oppressed*, (New York: Herder and Herder, 1970).

24. Dennison.

25. See, for example, the theme issue "School Effectiveness, Teacher Effectiveness," in *Educational Leadership*, Vol. 37: No. 1, October 1979. A book that has an effective schools "feel" is Lightfoot, S., *The Good High School* (New York: Basic Books, Inc., 1983).

26. National Commission on Excellence, *A Nation at Risk: The Imperative for Education Reform* (Washington, DC: U.S. Government Printing Office, 1983).

27. Adler, Mortimer, *The Paideia Proposal: An Education Manifesto* (New York: Macmillan, 1982); and Finn, C., Ravitch, D., and Fancher, R., *Against Mediocrity: The Humanities in America's High Schools* (New York: Holmes and Meier, 1984).

28. McNeil, J., *Curriculum: A Comprehensive Perspective* (Boston: Little, Brown and Company, 1977).

CHAPTER 6: CURRICULUM FOR UNDERACHIEVERS

1. For a discussion of general education, see Roberts, A., and Cawelti, G., *Redefining General Education in the American High School* (Alexandria, VA: Association for Supervision and Curriculum Development, 1984).

2. Boyer, E., *High School* (New York: Harper and Row, Publishers, 1984), pp. 202–215.

3. Ibid., p. 67.

4. Goodlad, J., *A Place Called School* (New York: McGraw-Hill Book Company, 1984), p. 286.

5. Ravitch, D., *The Troubled Crusade* (New York: Basic Books, 1983). Also, Finn, C., Ravitch, D., and Fancher, R., eds., *Against Mediocrity: The Humanities in American's High Schools* (New York: Holmes and Meier Publishers, 1984).

6. Powell, A., Farrar, E., and Cohen, D., *The Shopping Mall High School* (Boston: Houghton Mifflin, 1985).

7. Lipsitz, J., *Successful Schools for Young Adolescents* (New Brunswick, NJ: Transaction Books, 1984).

8. *Character Education Today*, newsletter published by the American Institute for Character Education, San Antonio, TX: Spring 1985, p. 7.

9. Ravtich, D., *The Troubled Crusade*.

10. Raths, L., Hamin, M., and Simon, S., *Values and Teaching*, 2nd ed. (Columbus, OH: Mer-

rill, 1978). See also, Simon, S., Howe, L., and Kirschenbaum, H., *Values Clarification* (New York: Hart Publishing Company, 1972).

11. A good early Kohlberg source: Kohlberg, L., "A Cognitive-Developmental Approach to Moral Education," *The Humanist*, Vol. 32: November–December, 1972, pp. 13–16.

12. Sizer, T., *Horace's Compromise* (Boston: Houghton Mifflin, 1985), p. 21.

13. *Federal Register*, Vol. 50: No. 112, June 11, 1985, p. 83.

14. Wynn, E., "The Great Tradition in Education: Transmitting Moral Values," *Educational Leadership*, Vol. 43: No. 4, December 1985/January 1986, pp. 4–9.

15. Griffin, R., "Worries About Values Clarification," *Peabody Journal of Education*, Vol. 53: No. 3, 1976, pp. 194–200.

16. For an example of what makes me somewhat uncomfortable at times in this regard, review the materials of the American Institute for Character Education.

17. A good example, Orlick, D., et al., *Teaching Strategies* (Lexington, Massachusetts: D.C. Heath and Company, 1985).

18. See, for example, Finn et al.

19. See Boyer, pp. 202–218.

20. Johnson, D., and Johnson, F., *Joining Together*, 2nd ed. (Englewood Cliffs, NJ: Prentice-Hall Inc., 1982).

21. Dewey, J., *Democracy and Education* (New York: The Free Press, 1966 (original publication, 1916) preface, p. iii.

22. Coles, R., *Privileged Ones: The Well-off and the Rich in America* (Boston: Little Brown and Company, 1977).

23. Walberg, Herbert; and Wynn, Edward, eds., *Developing Character* (Posen, Illinois: ARL Publications, 1985).

CHAPTER 7: THE SCHOOL CONTEXT

1. There is support for this self-selection hypothesis. See, for example, Powell, A., "Being Unspecial in the Shopping Mall High School," *Phi Delta Kappan*, Vol 67: No. 4, December 1985, pp. 255–261.

2. Goodlad, J., *A Place Called School* (New York: McGraw-Hill Book Company, 1984), p. 152.

3. Newmann, F., and Kelly, T., *Human Dignity and Excellence in Education*, Final report to the National Institute of Education, 1983, pp. 33–34.

4. Waxman, H., Wang, M., Anderson, K., and Walberg, H., "Synthesis on the Effects of Adaptive Education," *Educational Leadership*, Vol. 43: No. 1, p. 28.

5. See, Wang, M., and Walberg, H., eds., *Adapting Instruction to Individual Differences* (Berkeley, CA: McCutchan Publishing Company, 1985).

6. Roszak, T., *Person/Planet* (Garden City, NY, 1978). The chapter on schooling, "School: Letting Go, Letting Grow," begins on page 177.

7. Raywid, M. A., Tesconi, C., and Warren, D., *Pride and Promise: Schools of Excellence for All the People* (Wesbury, NY: American Educational Studies Association, 1985), p. 15.

8. Wehlage, G. et al., *Effective Programs for the Marginal High School Student: A Report to the Wisconsin Governor's Employment and Training Office*, (Washington, DC: National Institute of Education, 1982). Available through the ERIC system.

9. Ibid., p. 9.

10. Ibid., pp. 171–194.

11. Berne, E., *Games People Play* (New York: Ballantine Books, 1973).

12. Rutter, M. et al., *Fifteen Thousand Hours: Secondary Schools and Their Effects on Children* (Cambridge, MA: Harvard University Press, 1979), pp. 106–118.

13. Satir, V., *Making Contact* (Millbrae, California: Celestial Arts, 1976).

14. Kohl, H., *Half the House* (New York: E.P. Dutton and Company, Inc., 1974).

15. Leonard, G., *The Ultimate Athlete* (New York: The Viking Press, 1975).

16. Dobson, T., and Miller, V., *Giving In to Get Your Way* (New York: Delacorte Press, 1978); and Dobson, T., *Safe and Alive* (Los Angeles: J.P. Tarcher, 1981).

17. Dobson, T., "A Soft Answer," in *Lomi School Bulletin* (Mill Valley, CA: Lomi School, 1980). It appeared in slightly different form in *Reader's Digest*, Vol. 119: December 1981, pp. 187–188.

18. Rutter et al., p. 110.

19. Skinner, B. F., *Beyond Freedom and Dignity* (New York: Knopf, 1971).

20. Rutter et al., pp. 123–126.

21. Jones, F., "Gentle Art of Classroom Discipline," *National Elementary Principal*, Vol. 58, June, 1979, pp. 26–32.

22. See Dreikurs, R., *Maintaining Sanity in the Classroom* (New York: Harper and Row, 1971).

23. For a fine article on his perspective on discipline, see Glasser, W., "A New Look at Discipline," *Learning Magazine*, December, 1974, pp. 611–614.

CHAPTER 8: A STUDENT ACHIEVEMENT CONSTRUCT

1. For a book that explores this point, see Capra, F., *The Turning Point: Science, Society, and the Rising Culture* (New York: Simon and Schuster, 1982).

2. Two books I have found informative in this regard: Morris, D., *Naked Ape* (New York: McGraw-Hill, 1967); and Wilson, E., *Sociobiology*, (Cambridge, MA: Harvard University Press, 1981).

Index